HEALTH AND SAFETY NEEDS OF OLDER WORKERS

Committee on the Health
and Safety Needs of Older Workers

David H. Wegman and James P. McGee, *Editors*

Board on Behavioral, Cognitive, and Sensory Sciences
Division of Behavioral and Social Sciences and Education

NATIONAL RESEARCH COUNCIL *AND*
INSTITUTE OF MEDICINE
OF THE NATIONAL ACADEMIES

THE NATIONAL ACADEMIES PRESS
Washington, D.C.
www.nap.edu

THE NATIONAL ACADEMIES PRESS   500 Fifth Street, NW   Washington, DC 20001

NOTICE: The project that is the subject of this report was approved by the Governing Board of the National Research Council, whose members are drawn from the councils of the National Academy of Sciences, the National Academy of Engineering, and the Institute of Medicine. The members of the committee responsible for the report were chosen for their special competences and with regard for appropriate balance.

This study was supported by Contract No. 200-1999-00023 between the National Academy of Sciences and the National Institutes of Health. Any opinions, findings, conclusions, or recommendations expressed in this publication are those of the author(s) and do not necessarily reflect the views of the organizations or agencies that provided support for the project.

Library of Congress Cataloging-in-Publication Data

Health and safety needs of older workers / Committee on the Health and Safety Needs of Older Workers ; David H. Wegman and James P. McGee, editors.
    p. ; cm.
Includes bibliographical references and index.
ISBN 0-309-09111-X (hardcover)
    1. Aged—Employment—Health aspects—United States. 2. Age and employment—United States. 3. Industrial hygiene—United States.
    [DNLM: 1. Occupational Diseases—prevention & control—United States. 2. Age Factors—United States. 3. Occupational Health—United States. WA 440 H4346 2004] I. Wegman, David H. II. McGee, J. (James), 1950- III. National Research Council (U.S.). Committee on the Health and Safety Needs of Older Workers. IV. Institute of Medicine (U.S.)
    RC963.6.A43H435 2004
    363.11′00973—dc22
                                        2004007008

Additional copies of this report are available from National Academies Press, 500 Fifth Street, NW, Lockbox 285, Washington, DC 20055; (800) 624-6242 or (202) 334-3313 (in the Washington metropolitan area); Internet, http://www.nap.edu.

Printed in the United States of America.

Suggested citation: National Research Council and the Institute of Medicine. (2004). *Health and Safety Needs of Older Workers*. Committee on the Health and Safety Needs of Older Workers. D.H. Wegman and J.P. McGee, editors. Division of Behavioral and Social Sciences and Education. Washington, DC: The National Academies Press.

THE NATIONAL ACADEMIES
Advisers to the Nation on Science, Engineering, and Medicine

The **National Academy of Sciences** is a private, nonprofit, self-perpetuating society of distinguished scholars engaged in scientific and engineering research, dedicated to the furtherance of science and technology and to their use for the general welfare. Upon the authority of the charter granted to it by the Congress in 1863, the Academy has a mandate that requires it to advise the federal government on scientific and technical matters. Dr. Bruce M. Alberts is president of the National Academy of Sciences.

The **National Academy of Engineering** was established in 1964, under the charter of the National Academy of Sciences, as a parallel organization of outstanding engineers. It is autonomous in its administration and in the selection of its members, sharing with the National Academy of Sciences the responsibility for advising the federal government. The National Academy of Engineering also sponsors engineering programs aimed at meeting national needs, encourages education and research, and recognizes the superior achievements of engineers. Dr. Wm. A. Wulf is president of the National Academy of Engineering.

The **Institute of Medicine** was established in 1970 by the National Academy of Sciences to secure the services of eminent members of appropriate professions in the examination of policy matters pertaining to the health of the public. The Institute acts under the responsibility given to the National Academy of Sciences by its congressional charter to be an adviser to the federal government and, upon its own initiative, to identify issues of medical care, research, and education. Dr. Harvey V. Fineberg is president of the Institute of Medicine.

The **National Research Council** was organized by the National Academy of Sciences in 1916 to associate the broad community of science and technology with the Academy's purposes of furthering knowledge and advising the federal government. Functioning in accordance with general policies determined by the Academy, the Council has become the principal operating agency of both the National Academy of Sciences and the National Academy of Engineering in providing services to the government, the public, and the scientific and engineering communities. The Council is administered jointly by both Academies and the Institute of Medicine. Dr. Bruce M. Alberts and Dr. Wm. A. Wulf are chair and vice chair, respectively, of the National Research Council.

www.national-academies.org

Contents

---

*Appendix A and B are not printed in this volume but are available online. Go to http://www.nap.edu and search for *Health and Safety Needs of Older Workers.*

Preface

Age to me means nothing. I can't get old; I'm working. I was old when I was twenty-one and out of work. As long as you're working, you stay young.

George Burns (1896–1996)

In the past decade there has been a great deal of attention directed to the impact of population aging on all of our futures. Much of this attention has been devoted to such issues as the consequences of an aging population to our economy, the viability of the Social Security pension system, and long-term care issues related to survival well after retirement. There has been much less attention directed to the older worker and the interaction between work and the aging process.

The aging of the workforce raises several issues, among them concern about the age-related impact of work on health. Some of these issues are unique to older adults, and some apply to all age groups. Regardless, public health and medical scientists will need to answer the following questions to improve understanding of the impact of work and aging:

- How does aging affect health and working capacity?
- How does working affect aging and the rate of aging?
- In what ways are aging workers more susceptible to occupational diseases than younger workers?
- Does working exacerbate the development of age-related diseases?
- Can changes due to aging be decelerated or reversed?

As understanding in these areas improves, there will be second-order questions in need of answers in order to select, prioritize, and guide interventions:

- How does work need to be remodeled to suit aging workers?
- What remediable work factors cause health deterioration and thus hasten aging?
- What social support is needed for aging workers to maintain working capacity?

Despite the importance of these questions, the answers are incomplete, and the knowledge base is limited. In fact there is no commonly agreed-on definition of "older" worker. Research efforts in the United States tend to focus on those 55 and older with particular attention to the work factors that predict early or disability retirement. In Europe the age group of interest has been somewhat broader, with studies frequently directed at workers age 45 or older. The choice of a starting age for attention should be selected as "young" enough that intervention efforts can be expected to make a difference during the working life.

Recognizing the importance of the health and safety needs of older workers, the U.S. Department of Health and Human Services' Centers for Disease Control and Prevention, the National Institute on Aging, and the Archstone Foundation requested that the National Research Council and the Institute of Medicine convene a committee to consider relevant areas of science and policy. The Committee on the Health and Safety Needs of Older Workers was charged to (1) define and understand the size, composition, and other dimensions of the older adult workforce over the next 20 to 30 years, including the changing nature of work and its implications for workers over the age of 50; (2) identify the range of policy and research issues that should be addressed over the coming decade regarding the health and safety of older workers, including the effects, if any, of inappropriate working conditions on working capacities and occupational injuries and the effects of longer working lifetimes on health; and (3) identify relationships between retirement patterns and these characteristics of the older adult workforce and of their jobs. This report presents the committee's findings, conclusions, and recommendations.

In addition, the Environmental Protection Agency (EPA) requested that the committee conduct a workshop on differential effects of environmental hazards on older persons. The workshop, held December 5–6, 2002, brought together numerous experts with the goal of contributing to the formulation of a research and practice agenda that will help guide the EPA's new initiative in susceptibility of older workers to environmental hazards.

Many individuals supported the work of the committee in various ways. The committee is grateful for the continuing support of the representatives of the organizations sponsoring this effort: in particular, Mary Ellen Kullman Courtright, at the Archstone Foundation; James Grosch, at the Centers for Disease Control and Prevention's National Institute of Occupational Safety and Health; Rosemary Sokas, currently at the University of Illinois at Chicago and formerly at the National Institute of Occupational Safety and Health; Richard Suzman, at the National Institute on Aging; and Kathleen Sykes, at the Environmental Protection Agency.

Several individuals have made contributions to the committee's thinking and have provided very useful information that contributed to the formulation of our report. Janet Holtzblatt, at the U.S. Department of the Treasury, provided summary data on the relationship between age and Earned Income Tax Credit filing. John Ruser, at the Bureau of Labor Statistics, provided and pointed the way to important data on occupational health. David Williams, at the University of Michigan, contributed data and narrative on the topic of the health of minority elderly.

This report has been reviewed in draft form by individuals chosen for their diverse perspectives and technical expertise, in accordance with procedures approved by the National Research Council's Report Review Committee. The purpose of this independent review is to provide candid and critical comments that will assist the institution in making its published report as sound as possible and to ensure that the report meets institutional standards for objectivity, evidence, and responsiveness to the study charge. The review comments and draft manuscript remain confidential to protect the integrity of the deliberative process. We wish to thank the following individuals for their review of this report: Jeremiah A. Barondess, New York Academy of Medicine; Leslie I. Boden, School of Public Health, Boston University; Stefan Gravenstein (with Paul Aravich, Madeline Dunstan, and Maximilliane Szinovacz), Glennan Center for Geriatrics and Gerontology, Department of Medicine, Eastern Virginia Medical School; Franklin E. Mirer, Health and Safety Department, International Union, United Auto Workers, Detroit; Gary Rischitelli, Center for Research on Occupational and Environmental Toxicology, Oregon Health and Science University; Eve Spangler, Sociology Department, Boston College; and Stephen R. Zoloth, Bouve College of Health Sciences, Northeastern University.

Although the reviewers listed above have provided many constructive comments and suggestions, they were not asked to endorse the conclusions or recommendations nor did they see the final draft of the report before its release. The review of this report was overseen by Mark R. Cullen, Yale University School of Medicine. Appointed by the National Research Council, he was responsible for making certain that an independent examination of this report was carried out in accordance with institutional procedures and that all review comments were carefully considered. Responsibility for the final content of this report rests entirely with the authoring committee and the institution.

This report is the collective product of the entire committee, and each member took an active role in drafting sections of chapters, leading discussions, and reading and commenting on successive drafts. Each member of the committee has contributed to the formulation of the committee's conclusions and recommendations, which reflect the consensus of the committee. We commend their tireless and diligent efforts, which have resulted in, we believe, a successful response to the very challenging charge presented to them.

Staff at the National Research Council and the Institute of Medicine made important contributions to our work in many ways. We thank Andrew Pope and Frederick Manning of the staff of the Institute of Medicine, for their work in designing and launching the study. We express our appreciation to Christine Hartel, director of the Center for Studies of Behavior and Development, for her valuable insight, guidance, and support. We offer major thanks to Jessica Gonzalez Martinez, the committee's project assistant, who was indispensable in organizing meetings, arranging travel, compiling agenda materials, conducting extensive outreach with the interested community, copyediting and formatting the report, and managing the exchange of documentation among the committee members. We wish also to thank Christine Covington Chen, Deborah Johnson, Wendy Keenan, and Allison Shoup for their skillful support during the workshop. We are indebted to Laura Schenone, who improved the report by the application of her editing skills, and to the team of Christine McShane, Eugenia Grohman, and Kirsten Sampson Snyder, who artfully shepherded the report through all of its phases of editing and review.

David H. Wegman, *Chair*
James P. McGee, *Study Director*
Committee on the Health and Safety Needs of Older Workers

HEALTH
AND
SAFETY
NEEDS
OF
OLDER
WORKERS

Executive Summary

Mirroring a worldwide phenomenon in industrialized nations, the United States is experiencing a demographic change known as population aging, brought about by a combination of lengthening life expectancy, declining fertility, and the progression through life of an unusually large "baby boom" generation. As part of the overall population aging, the nation's workforce is aging, and the population of older workers—defined as those age 45 and over—is projected to include an increasing number of women and ethnic minorities.

Currently, there are in the United States 93 million people age 45 and over, representing 44 percent of the civilian, noninstitutionalized population over the age of 15. By the year 2050, it is projected there will be 170 million people 45 or older, representing 53 percent of the population. Since the life expectancy of women exceeds that of men and the number of women exceeds the number of men at all age groups, the percentage of the population who are women age 45 and older is expected to grow faster than that of men. Furthermore, the number of ethnic minorities is increasing at a faster rate than the white population at all ages. By 2050, ethnic minorities are projected to represent approximately 40 percent of those over 45.

Even though the elderly population today is on average healthier, better educated, and wealthier than the elderly population of previous generations, there are two major reasons for focusing on the health and safety needs of older workers. First, to maximize benefits to the economy and investment capital, it is important to know which older workers can be expected to work productively, what kinds of tasks they are best suited for, and if their productivity can be increased through cost-effective accommodations and support programs in the workplace and community. Second, policy makers want to know how to maximize older workers' opportunities for making employment-related choices that promote health, safety, and life satisfaction in their later years. To date, concern among policy makers about the aging of the population has tended to focus on the adequacy of Medicare and Social Security trust funds, mechanisms for retirement savings, and the need for long-term care. Far less attention has been paid to the health and safety needs of older American workers.

CHARACTERISTICS OF OLDER WORKERS

Older workers differ from their younger counterparts in a variety of physical/biological, psychological/mental, and social dimensions. In some cases these reflect normative changes of aging (for example, presbyopia), while in others they represent age-dependent increases in the likelihood of developing various abnormal conditions, such as coronary artery disease. These age-related differences, whether normative or pathologic, may cause disadvantages to older workers because their work performance is diminished relative to younger workers or because their susceptibility to environmental hazards is increased. In other cases, however, changes associated with age (e.g., increased experience) may actually enhance capabilities and performance at work.

Age-related changes that are most likely important to job exposures and job experience among older workers occur in the following organ systems: skeletal muscle, bone, vision, hearing, pulmonary function, skin, metabolism, and immunity. More generally, the slope of age-related changes in organs or systems declines at a greater rate with increasing age. However, cognitive and adaptive skills that come with experience and extensive training are relevant to meeting job challenges and changes. Furthermore, most occupations (except, for example, some public safety occupations) usually do not require performance at full individual capacity. Workplace or other exposures may cause decrements in function from full capacity without affecting work performance or function at usual levels.

The health, function, and survivorship of each older worker cohort will depend in part on exposures and events that occurred earlier in life in addition to environmental (including work) exposures concurrent with aging. Most general physiological and biological functions in older persons tend to have greater variation than in younger persons (there are exceptions in the realm of cognitive variables), and so performance relying on those functions often does not correlate very well with chronological age. Age-related changes may be accompanied by the presence of comorbidity. There has not, however, been much research on the effects of workplace exposures on health in the presence of controlled clinical conditions or their treatments.

The limited efforts to study the relation between age and job performance have been inconclusive, possibly due to the varying balance between cognitive declines and the benefits of age- or job-related experience. These efforts could be enhanced by accelerated development of the O*NET (Occupational Information Network) database, a replacement for the *Dictionary of Occupational Titles* that describes in detail the knowledge, skills, and abilities required to perform jobs; this would facilitate matching of the capabilities and limitations of older workers to the knowledge, skills, and abilities required by jobs. The O*NET is described on the U.S. Department of Labor website at www.doleta.gov/programs/onet.

In addition to the emphasis on physical, chemical, and biomechanical workplace hazards, there has been increasing recognition of the work-related mental health and psychosocial and organizational issues among older workers. This recognition may be due in part to a shift in the United States and most industrialized countries from a manufacturing to a service economy, where interpersonal issues are more apparent. In many respects older workers appear to have higher levels of emotional stability than young adults. It is likely that among older persons, workers are less likely than nonworkers to have serious or severe mental illness or disorder because of the debilitating nature of these conditions. Yet, certain workplace situations may have disparate effects on older workers' mental health, such as ageism, increasing physical and cognitive demands, and pressure to retire.

Mental health problems with job implications include the consequences of work-related stress, clinical depression, and a variety of other psychological problems such as burnout, alcohol, and other substance abuse, unexplained physical symptoms, and chronic fatigue as well as the secondary consequences of these conditions, such as longer absences associated with injuries. Older workers may bring to the workplace mental health problems that have long histories and origins outside of the job setting. Common or severe mental conditions such as depression may cause stress, conflict, poor productivity and, potentially, threats to individual safety and health related to the conditions or their treatments. There is evidence that work-related stress impairs worker satisfaction and productivity and may contribute to long-term physical diseases and conditions, as well as increase the costs of absenteeism and low productivity. Work-related stressful experiences, including injuries, can contribute to depression, and enduring structural factors in some institutions lead to various psychological problems.

The prevalence of problem drinking and alcoholism among older workers is not known, but the consequences of alcohol abuse are known to be more serious among the elderly. The problem with alcohol and drug abuse at work may increase as the baby boomer cohort grows older, because this cohort had higher rates of substance use, including alcohol, than previous generations. Another underevaluated area is problems associated with medication abuse among older workers.

THE SOCIAL AND ECONOMIC CONTEXT OF WORK FOR OLDER PERSONS

The health and safety needs of older workers reflect not only their individual life course histories, but also factors related to socioeconomic status, gender, race, ethnicity, and recent changes in the labor market and in the nature of work. In exploring how social factors might produce health disparities in the context of an aging workforce, older workers should not be regarded as a uniform population; within the population of older workers, there are disparities related to social class, race/ethnicity, and gender, and this has implications for how best to conduct research and develop policy for protecting older workers' health.

The nature of work may play a part in generating social inequalities in health, since one's job is the principal determinant of general standard of living, important in shaping self-identity and personal growth, and an important criterion of social stratification. Many minority older workers have been exposed to deficits in education and health care, to poverty, and to discrimination; many of these challenges persist into old age and shape the opportunities and outcomes for minority elders.

Gender is also an important social determinant of the work experiences of and related health outcomes for older workers. Gender influences social roles, the types of jobs people hold, the resulting work-related exposures, the patterns of work over the life course, consequent income differentials, and projected retirement experiences. During the second half of the 20th century, there was a decline in the labor force participation rate of older men and a rise in the labor force participation rate of women. The downward trend in labor force participation rates of men aged 62 and over ended in the mid-1980s when participation rates leveled off. The reasons for this substantial change in the labor force participation rate trends of men and women since the mid-1980s are not fully understood but may include structural changes in the social security system, the banning of mandatory retirement rules, and the shift from defined-benefit to defined-contribution retirement plans.

Within the overall pattern of labor force participation there are significant differences in employment survival rates across people with different socioeconomic characteristics and who work in different industries and occupations. There are significant differences in job demands, injury risks, and toxic exposures. Job characteristics that may differentially affect the health of older workers can also affect their retirement decisions.

There have been significant changes in the labor market and in the nature of work to which older workers must respond. During the past century, the median income of Americans increased substantially, many aspects of their working conditions improved, and their life span increased. However, income growth has been uneven across the income distribution, and while the health and safety conditions of workers in some occupations and industries have improved, others have not. There is limited evidence on how these trends are affecting the health and safety of older workers. There is also concern over how well the illness or disorder and injury data that we currently collect measure these trends.

In the mid-20th century, about a third of the American workforce was employed in manufacturing. Today, not much more than a tenth are so employed; about 80 percent are now working in the service sector. The high-growth occupations are concentrated in either low-wage service sector jobs or occupations that require advanced training and pay high wages. The skill distribution of the future workforce is likely to increase somewhat faster at the high and low ends than in the middle.

For most of the past century average weekly hours worked decreased gradually, but during the last 25 years weekly hours have increased slightly for men and more steeply for women, reflecting women's increased partici- pation in the workforce. There also has been a recent increase in the num- ber of those 55 and older who work more than 48 hours per week. A better understanding of the age-specific effects of working hours over weekly and annual intervals will require better information on trends in patterns of working hours according to age, gender, race, and socioeconomic status. The health effects of new organizational approaches such as lean produc- tion, total quality management, new team concepts, cellular or modular manufacturing, reengineering, high-performance work organizations, and patient-focused care are largely unknown for workers of any age, but some studies suggest increased health and safety risks. The extent to which and mechanisms whereby socioeconomic and demographic variables relate to the employment and retirement patterns of older workers and to their health is an area in need of targeted research.

EFFECTS OF WORK ON OLDER WORKERS

The total cost of occupational illness or disorder and injury in the United States for 1992 has been estimated at $132.8 billion, approximately 2.5 percent of the gross domestic product; the estimates have not been stratified by age. The number of workplace injuries, illnesses or disorders, and fatalities has been declining over the years but remains unacceptably high. The Bureau of Labor Statistics (BLS) reported that a total of 5.2 million workplace injuries and illnesses or disorders were reported in private industry during 2001—the lowest rate since BLS began reporting in 1973. Recent years have seen approximately 6,000 fatalities from workplace injuries annually, a number that has been declining steadily for more than 40 years. However, in contrast to younger workers, the number of lost workday cases among older workers has been slowly rising since 1992; workers aged 45 and older accounted for 30 percent of lost workday cases reported by BLS for 2000. Evidence also indicates that, compared with younger workers, older workers experience relatively low overall frequency of work-related injury and illness or disorder but relatively high rates of workplace fatality and high injury severity. The increased prevalence of impairments among older workers, as opposed to younger workers, and the growth of our older workforce will increase the number of workers who bring impairments to the job with them and who will, therefore, be at increased risk for occupational injuries.

High-risk jobs for older workers are jobs that present exposure to relatively common work risks. According to data from 1988 (the most recent available on exposures at work), the most prevalent exposures are biomechanical risk factors. Workers between the ages of 45 and 64 experienced lower exposure prevalence than younger workers, although about one-quarter of those in the older age group reported a substantial amount of bending or twisting of hands or wrists, and one-fifth of older male workers reported repeated bending and twisting or reaching. There is a substantial need for research on the physiological, pathological, and functional effects of common and potentially harmful worksite exposures—physiochemical, biological, biomechanical, and psychosocial—on older workers.

Industries that appear to represent higher risk for biomechanical and other hazardous exposures are manufacturing, transportation, medical services, mining, utilities, agriculture, and forestry/fishing/trapping—most of which are projected to experience at least moderate growth in employment. Almost half of the 333,800 reports of occupational illnesses or disorders and 65 percent of the repeated trauma cases occurred in manufacturing industries. Among those occupations identified as older worker intensive, the following appear to represent higher risk for biomechanical exposures and, in some cases, additional hazardous exposures: administrative support; production/craft/repair; transportation and material moving; farming/forestry/fishing; private household services; protective services; and services-other, most of which are also projected to experience moderate to high growth in employment.

Some changes in work organization also may have adverse health effects (e.g., musculoskeletal disorders and cardiovascular disease) on the workforce. These changes include certain types of organizational restructuring, downsizing, outsourcing, job insecurity, nonstandard work arrangements, and stressful job characteristics. Job flexibility and job control appear also as important factors associated with health outcomes, the best studied of which is cardiovascular disease.

In recent years workers over age 50 have reported in health surveys that their jobs contain many physical and emotional challenges and stresses, but most reported that they enjoyed going to work. Older workers were healthier and functioning at a higher level than their nonworking counterparts, but a majority reported at least one chronic illness or disorder, suggesting that some of these conditions do not substantially interfere with job functions, though they may point to a higher risk of future illness or disorder and disability. About one-sixth of workers reported that their health status was fair or poor, possibly leading to risk of job loss and progression of illness or disorder.

Assessing the causes and extent of work-related injuries and illnesses or disorders and comparing health and safety risks across industries and occupations, for older versus younger workers of varying demographic characteristics and job histories, is hampered by limitations in existing data collection systems. Available data on occupational injuries and illnesses or disorders from BLS and workers' compensation systems reflect substantial underreporting, particularly with respect to occupational illness or disorder. Explanations for the poor assessment of occupational illness or disorder burden include: inadequate recognition of work-related long-term latent illnesses or disorders; inadequate training and awareness of medical providers; and a variety of disincentives to reporting workplace problems. Data from 1988 are the most recently available that permit some estimate of the distribution of work exposures. Additionally, little is known about the age distribution of work-related musculoskeletal disorders despite the fact that these are the most commonly reported work-related disorders.

PUBLIC POLICIES AND PRACTICES RELATED TO THE OLDER WORKFORCE AND SAFE WORK

Public policy interventions affect the ability of older workers to continue to work safely and to exit from the workforce. Laws that govern these abilities include occupational safety and health protections, antidiscrimination laws, and mandated interventions that regulate or encourage leaves of absence and accommodations at work. There are also nonwage benefits that affect workers' decisions regarding when and how to exit the labor market.

Certain elements of relevant public policy are simple to articulate. For example: age-based discrimination against workers over 40 is illegal; all workers who participate in the Social Security system have some guaranteed health insurance and disability and retirement income protections, at least after specified periods of participation in covered employment. Beyond this, there are few special legal protections for aging workers. In general, employment policies must be age neutral, so employers are required to treat older workers in the same manner as they treat otherwise equivalent younger workers.

The key question is whether the laws that mandate intervention in employment provide adequate protection to workers as they age so that they can continue to work safely or have the necessary economic security to exit the workforce at the appropriate time. The answer to these questions is not the same for all workers in all industries. There has been little study of the effectiveness of these mandated interventions in relation to older workers' health and safety needs.

Employment regulation is a patchwork. Independent contractors and self-employed workers are excluded from almost all protective employment laws and collective bargaining agreements. Also excluded are people who do not report their wages. Most protective statutes exclude small employers. Private benefits may be available only to full-time permanent employees. Tension between federal and state regulation further complicates the terrain. In key areas of interest to aging workers (e.g., compensation programs for occupational injuries and illnesses or disorders) the legal rules may vary depending upon the state in which the worker lives and works.

Unlike most other industrialized countries, the United States does not provide universal health insurance to its citizens. In 1995, 72 percent of American workers between 18 and 64 had health insurance coverage under an employer-based plan, either through their own employer or through the employer of another family member; 18 percent of American workers were left totally uninsured. Close to one-third of workers over 55 do not have health insurance provided by their employers. As chronic health conditions increase with age, the lack of health insurance and the accompanying barriers to access to health care may significantly impact the ability of these workers to remain in the workforce.

INTERVENTIONS FOR OLDER WORKERS

The premise of many interventions is that it is preferable to change the working environment to accommodate the needs of workers than to attempt only to adapt the workers themselves through administrative or training interventions. In principle, hazards should be addressed as close to the source as possible. Therefore, job design, including redesign and reengineering to improve the accommodations for older workers, deserves the highest level of attention. There are existing design approaches to accommodate a variety of age-related changes, such as declines in vision, hearing, and physical strength and capacity, as well as approaches that address work-related musculoskeletal disorders that are anticipated to be an important problem for aging workers. There also is evidence for the effectiveness of a limited number of interventions to address cardiovascular disease by improving work organization and job design, and by reducing job stressors. Many effective interventions also involve changing the social climate in the workplace (e.g., empowering workers), training for better work practices (e.g., ergonomic interventions to improve body posture for bending and lifting), improving physical fitness with exercise, and substituting machine work for human exertion. Training is another potent intervention and seems particularly relevant for older workers, as they are likely to be the most distant from their initial professional and job training. Access to training, however, is often too limited.

Health promotion efforts now have received the greatest attention in workplaces within large organizations; smaller organizations have typically paid far less attention to health promotion efforts. Although many of these efforts focus on preventing common diseases that are not uniquely caused by work, mitigating hazardous aspects of the work environment is an important example of health promotion. Attention to general health promotion programs is as relevant for older as for younger workers and may result in greater decrements in preventable disease rates per unit of resource expenditure for older workers, in part because chronic disease rates are higher at older ages. General health promotion programs directed at workers appear to be more effective when tied to environmental controls in the workplace.

Accommodations for workers with impairments and return-to-work programs are important interventions for older workers, who are more likely to bring impairments into the workplace and to be out of work longer than their younger colleagues after an injury at work. Modified work programs have been clearly shown to facilitate the return to work of workers with temporary or permanent impairments.

Factors known to result in shortening the duration of disability consistently include medical and vocational rehabilitation interventions, organizational-level employer factors, and employer- and insurer-based disability prevention and disability management interventions. However, several challenges must be overcome before researchers can establish which interventions are most effective. Multidisciplinary teams are needed to address the social/behavioral, biomedical, and analytic issues in the research. Researchers need to agree on the best outcome variables to use in return-to-work studies, and the methodological quality of research needs to be improved. For example, survival models can be used to improve efficiency, and hierarchical models can be used to assess risk factors from several levels, ranging from the individual to the societal.

Although most employee assistance programs (EAPs) have not emphasized employee needs related to aging, they have strong potential as a support for older workers in relation to occupational health and safety concerns. EAPs can assist workers challenged by the need to provide elder-care support, plan for retirement or outplacement, and address substance abuse and emotional distress.

Many of the existing intervention programs have at least some demonstrated efficacy, but nearly all have been incompletely evaluated. There are enormous research opportunities to develop new programs and modify existing ones. With changing work organizations and processes, a dynamic economic climate, and a demographically diverse workforce, intervention research should be a high priority. This research should include cost-benefit analysis and identification of the components that make interventions effective (their "active ingredients").

CONCLUSIONS AND RECOMMENDATIONS

Chapter 9 of this report summarizes conclusions and presents detailed recommendations pertaining to three major themes that emerge from examination of the health and safety needs of older workers:

(1) Conducting informative research requires improved databases and data systems necessary to track the health and safety needs of older workers and the programs that address them.

• New longitudinal datasets should be developed that contain detailed information on workers' employment histories and the specific demands of their jobs, as well as objective information on the health and safety risks to workers in the job.

• Ongoing longitudinal surveys (for example, the Health and Retirement Study and the Panel Study of Income Dynamics) should either increase the information they gather on health and safety risk factors of the workplace or develop periodic modules to do so.

• The National Institute for Occupational Safety and Health (NIOSH) should collaborate with the Bureau of Labor Statistics in conducting a comprehensive review and evaluation of occupational injury and illness or disorder reporting systems, examining the extent of, and trends in, underreporting and underascertainment.

• NIOSH should develop a database that characterizes types and levels of exposures associated with work; exposures considered should include chemical, physical, biomechanical, and psychosocial factors.

• The BLS should initiate reporting of workplace injury and illness or disorder rates according to demographic characteristics (for age, gender, and ethnicity at a minimum).

• The National Center for Health Statistics (NCHS) and NIOSH should develop a survey supplement on work risk factors and occupational disorders for periodic inclusion in the National Health Interview Surveys.

• The NCHS and NIOSH should collaborate in an effort to identify, using the National Health and Nutrition Examination Survey, subpopulations of older workers where chemical exposure is likely to be an important work risk factor and to develop a list of chemicals to be included in surveys of such populations in the future.

• NIOSH and the Department of Labor (DOL) should collaborate and be funded to develop a survey instrument and periodically conduct surveys to describe the prevalence of and trends in job characteristics and other workplace risk factors in a manner similar to the Quality of Employment Surveys.

• Enhanced efforts should be devoted to achieving a comprehensive, interactive O*NET database as quickly as possible.

(2) Research is needed to provide better understanding of the factors that relate to the health and safety needs of older workers.

• Substantial research should be conducted on the physiological, pathological, and functional effects of common and potentially harmful worksite exposures—physiochemical, biological, biomechanical, and psychosocial—on older workers.

• A research program should be conducted to provide systematic and substantial understanding of the effects of potentially harmful workplace exposures on individual and population outcomes among older workers with existing chronic conditions.

• Targeted research should be undertaken to identify the extent to which, and mechanisms whereby, socioeconomic and demographic variables are related to health and safety risks of older workers; the degree to which these variables predict employment in hazardous occupations and industries; and how they may be associated with retirement decisions and barriers.

(3) Research is needed to identify and clarify the aspects of policies, programs, and intervention techniques and strategies that are effective and that are not effective in addressing the health and safety needs of older workers.

• Evaluation research should be conducted to determine the degree to which public policies intended to enable workers to remain at work safely and productively have met these objectives specifically with regard to older workers.

• For promising job design, training, and workplace accommodation interventions, research should be conducted to determine the prevalence, effectiveness, and associated costs of intervention.

• Research should be conducted to assess the effectiveness, benefits, and costs of worksite health promotion programs and techniques tailored to older workers.

• Research should be undertaken to assess the full (direct and indirect) costs of older workers' occupational injuries and illnesses or disorders to individuals, family, and society.

Requisite funding for these efforts should be provided.

1

Introduction

Mirroring a worldwide phenomenon in industrialized nations, the United States is experiencing a change in its demographic structure known as *population aging*, brought about by a combination of lengthening life expectancy, decline in fertility, and the progression through life of an unusually large "baby boom" generation (National Research Council, 2001; Redburn, 1998; Moody, 2002). The speed of the demographic transformation is dramatic. In recent decades the U.S. population over age 65 has been growing twice as fast as the rest of the population. By 2030 about one in every five Americans will be over 65, as contrasted with about one in eight at present. By 2030, the median age of the U.S. population is projected to reach 42 years old, as compared to 35 years old in 2000.

The rapid expansion in older adults' proportion of the U.S. population is expected to bring about a concomitant aging of the nation's workforce. Many hard-to-predict factors, such as changes in the state of the U.S. economy and relevant social policies, will influence the course of this development over the next few decades. However, even though the older population today is on average healthier, better educated, and wealthier than that older population of previous generations, serious challenges await them, and the rest of the nation, as their numbers grow. In particular, social adjustments may be needed to ensure that employment is safe and healthy for those who continue to work in their older years. This need is especially urgent for subsets of the working population whose resources and conditions of employment have not kept pace with the nation's general improvements.

Policy makers and the public have expressed concern about the adequacy of Medicare and Social Security trust funds, mechanisms for retirement savings, and the need for long-term care. Far less attention has been paid to the health and safety needs of older Americans.

THE CHARGE TO THE COMMITTEE

At the request of the Centers for Disease Control and Prevention's National Institute for Occupational Safety and Health, the National Institute for Aging, the Archstone Foundation, and the Environmental Protection Agency, the Division of Behavioral and Social Sciences and Education of the National Research Council organized a study of the health and safety needs of older workers. The study was directed to:

(1) define and understand the size, composition, and other dimensions of the older adult workforce over the next 20–30 years, including the changing nature of work and its implications for workers over the age of 50;

(2) identify the range of policy and research issues that should be addressed over the coming decade regarding the health and safety of older workers, including the effects, if any, of inappropriate working conditions on working capacities and occupational injuries and the effects of longer working lifetimes on health; and

(3) identify relationships between retirement patterns and these characteristics of the older adult workforce and of their jobs.

THE NEED FOR RESEARCH

We need more information about the factors that influence work decisions at older ages; interactions between work and the aging process; ethnicity; socioeconomic status; gender-related differences in work and retirement patterns, and effective ways to adapt the workplace to meet the needs of an aging workforce. We also need a clearer understanding of what social policies would best support the safe and productive employment of an older workforce, and what research is most needed to guide policy decisions. Too many commonly held beliefs concerning the capabilities of older workers are either incorrect or based on inadequate data. For example, it is popularly believed that older workers are less productive, more rigid in their thinking, and less worth the investment for training in new skills than their younger counterparts in the workplace. Since inaccurate ideas create major consequences for hiring, retaining, managing, and rewarding older workers, it is important to provide the factual basis for such conclusions and to identify gaps in our knowledge that need to be filled.

Other common beliefs about aging workers are better grounded in evidence. For example, in many occupations, older workers as a category are in fact more likely than their younger coworkers to have chronic illnesses or disorders that involve medical costs and health insurance claims; to command higher pay because of their longer work experience; and to need some level of accommodation in their working conditions in order to work safely. These characteristics pose substantial challenges for the older workers themselves, their employers, and the nation. At present, they create economic incentives for employers to prefer younger workers, particularly during periods when labor is not in short supply. There may be ways of changing these incentives by distributing the costs of health care and illness or disorder differently through reform of social policies.

This report presents a picture of what is currently known about the health and safety needs of older workers and what areas still require research. The purpose is to encourage information-based thinking on how best to craft social policies that guarantee older workers a meaningful share of the nation's work opportunities and implement the government's legal obligation under the Occupational Safety and Health Act of 1970 to "assure safe and healthful working conditions for working men and women."

THE AGING WORKFORCE: A MOVING TARGET

Interpreting the individual and social implications of an aging workforce unavoidably requires that we look at our starting assumptions about aging, health, work, and retirement—no simple matter since the meaning of these concepts depends on their context.

Various U.S. laws and public policies offer specific ages after which a worker is considered "older." For example, workers are legally protected against age discrimination after age 40, and the category "age 55 and older" is used in many analyses carried out by the U.S. Bureau of Labor Statistics. But chronological-age thresholds are arbitrary, and they can create artificial boundaries that lead to categorical discrimination (Regan, 1981). Policy makers should be aware that older workers' individual capacities can differ greatly from the average characteristics of their age category. In a sense, all workers are aging workers. As Chapter 5 discusses, both positive and negative age-related physical and cognitive changes occur throughout the life span. Workers' earlier training and adaptations to age-related changes follow them into their older years, influencing later capacities for better or worse. Moreover, some hazardous exposures experienced on the job early in life can cast a long shadow, manifesting as long-latency diseases many decades later as the exposed workers grow older. The adverse health effects of cumulative exposures over many years may become apparent only later in life, perhaps interacting with age-related physical changes or chronic illnesses or disorders. Thus, the health of older workers is closely connected to their occupational experiences as younger workers.

In addition, the definition of health among older workers shifts as improvements are made in available medical strategies for managing and adapting to the chronic illnesses or disorders that become more frequent with age. Depending on the older worker's access to health care, the same set of health conditions—e.g., diabetes or heart disease—can represent either a major barrier to employment or a manageable health situation. Similarly, the concept of disability has been changing over the last decades. Here, we follow the model put forth in the National Academies' Institute of Medicine report, *Enabling America* (Brandt and Pope, 1997): that disability is not just a result of the functional impairments that workers bring to the workplace, but is also a reflection of the supports available in their physical and social environment, both on and off the job. Workers of any age can remain productively employed despite health problems if the workplace offers compensating accommodations such as elevators, lifting aids, increased lighting, more frequent work breaks, and an accepting management climate. The ability to work safely and productively can also be influenced by community support, such as access to mass transportation that eliminates the need for driving to work, or affordable services and amenities that lessen nonwork time demands, allowing more opportunity for health-promoting activities such as exercise, rest, and medical monitoring. Chapter 8 examines some of these accommodations, on and off the job, as a strategy for meeting the health and safety needs of older workers.

The concept of work is also growing more complex. The "work" often connotes a well-defined, full-time job in a setting where the workers enjoy a variety of employer-provided benefits and are effectively protected by existing fair labor standards and occupational health and safety regulations. While many workplaces do fit this description, a quite different and much more precarious kind of employment also exists, particularly in some small firms and in industries where existing regulations are poorly enforced or for which there are important gaps in legal coverage. Moreover, it is becoming increasingly common for workers to be employed on a contingent basis in short-term contracts and other temporary, nonstandard work commitments less likely to provide supports and legal protections (Barker and Christensen, 1998; Capelli et al., 1997; Houseman and Nakamura, 2001; Wong and Picot, 2001).

Certain subgroups are particularly likely to lack occupational health and safety protections, such as undocumented workers employed in sweatshops, restaurants, and as domestic servants (GAO, 1988; Hondagneu-Sotelo, 2001). Reliable information about such workers is scarce and hard to obtain. However, they age along with their counterparts who are better positioned in the workforce, and their health and safety needs as older workers should not be ignored simply because they are underrepresented in currently available data sources.

We find another ambiguity in the question of how to regard productive activities that share characteristics with paid employment but fall outside the traditional definition of work. For example, individuals who are self-employed in small businesses or on farms are not covered by a number of worker protections, such as unemployment insurance and workers' compensation benefits. Yet, as these self-employed workers age they will have some of the same health and safety needs as older workers who are hired as paid employees. Similarly, the unpaid caregiving and labor provided at home within families (typically by women) have not historically been recognized as work, even though the same activities are regarded as work when performed by employees of commercial services (Robinson, 1999). As discussed in Chapter 4, the fact that many women workers have added an unrecognized second shift to their paid employment throughout their lives has important implications for their income security, health, and ability to engage in paid employment in their older years.

Conceptions of retirement are changing. Traditional portrayals of working life have emphasized a standardized, normative pattern of three distinct life stages, through which members of an age cohort progress sequentially at roughly the same time: (1) a childhood education period that can be seen as preparation for work; (2) adulthood, involving a working career that may include some job changes but centers around one primary long-term job; and (3) retirement, a period of leisure without paid employment (Cain, 1964; Kohli, 1986; Best, 1980). While more a product of conventional wisdom than careful research, this simplistic three-stage model of working life has shaped many aspects of public policy (Myles, 1989; Myles and Street, 1995). For example, it is the foundation for age-related eligibility criteria for receiving pension benefits. This model also influences public perceptions as well, reinforcing the sense that a particular chronological age such as 65 is the appropriate point at which all workers should expect to retire (Marshall, 1995).

Research on transitions in and out of the paid workforce suggests that this normative model of retirement fits workers' actual experience rather poorly. Instead of crisp exits from the workforce at a particular typical age, many workers make blurred exits that can occur at any chronological age (Mutchler et al., 1997). Marshall and Clarke (1998) suggest that the familiar three-stage life course model needs to be expanded to include some additional transitional periods such as a precareer series of preliminary work experiences; a preretirement period in which the worker prepares to leave the main career job; and a period following exit from the main career job involving bridge jobs in the contingent labor force and possible additional education and training, prior to full retirement from paid employment.

THE LIFE COURSE PERSPECTIVE

To deal with such conceptual complexities, research regarding aging and working life has increasingly made use of a theoretical orientation commonly termed the *life course perspective* (Riley and Riley, 1994; Marshall and Mueller, 2002; Markson and Hollis-Sawyer, 2000). According to this flexible model, while social institutions and public policy structure the life course into stages that most individuals move through, the connection is a loose coupling (Elder and O'Rand, 1995). Individual workers—based on their particular circumstances—can have a much more varied and disorderly life course than that assumed by the traditional three-stage model (Rindfuss, Swicegood, and Rosenfeld, 1987). Instead of marching predictably through uniform life stages, individual members of an age cohort will move in and out of the workforce in a variety of ways at a variety of age points. Their transitions are still socially patterned, but some patterns depart considerably from the normative model. Assessing the available research literature, Marshall and Mueller (2002) note that departures from the normative working life trajectory are particularly common among segments of the population that are not white, middle class, or male.

Rather than concentrating on "the aged" as a chronologically defined category, the life course perspective treats aging as a process that unfolds throughout life, reflecting each individual's social context and cumulative experiences. The orienting principles emphasize the importance of individual biography, specific historical events and social conditions experienced by the individual, the network of relationships an individual has, the timing of specific events in a person's life, and the choices that people make within the opportunities and constraints of history and social circumstances (Riley, 1979; Elder, 1994, 1997; Elder and Johnson, in press).

Figure 1-1 shows a simplified, schematic representation of how a life course perspective informs the understanding of how environmental exposures relate to age-related health changes and clinical outcomes. The abscissa represents increasing age; the ordinate represents the functional status of the body's organs. The three lines sloping downward represent alternative pathways in the function (e.g., physiology and metabolism) of an organ or organ system. This model assumes that there are a variety of environmental and occupational exposures of varying intensity and pathogenicity both early and late in life. The dashed horizontal line represents a threshold below which clinical organ dysfunction (e.g., disease) is apparent. The upper curve represents the optimal scenario for age-related change, in which environmental exposures are minimized and health promotion and disease prevention are maximized. The middle curve represents usual aging, population averages summarizing varied environmental and occupational exposures and preventive applications in the workplace and elsewhere. The

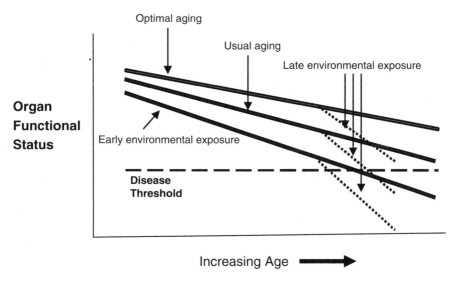

FIGURE 1-1 Schematic view of the impact of early and late environmental exposure on elder health outcomes.

lower curve represents the unfortunate situation where more intensive exposures have occurred and organ function is on a steeper trajectory, thus crossing the disease threshold earlier in life.

The figure also portrays the situation of workers facing unhealthy environmental exposures later in life, such as might occur in older workers. As shown by the dotted lines, these later exposures may lead to accelerated decrements in function for any of the existing aging scenarios. Overall, this model is intended to call attention to several fundamental questions related to older workers: How do early exposures affect the paths of age-related change in organs and in the whole organism, particularly with respect to late life disease and dysfunction? How do occupational exposures later in life alter the trajectories of age-related change with and without a prior history of untoward environmental exposures? Most of these questions, for most occupational exposures, are unanswered and justify an intense research agenda that is a major subject of this volume.

The life course perspective is not without critics. In a review of life course theory, Dannefer and Uhlenberg (1999: 309) identify what they consider three significant intellectual problems in theorizing about the life course: (1) a tendency to equate the significance of social forces with social change, (2) a neglect of intracohort variability, and (3) an unwarranted affirmation of choice as a simple and transparent determinant of the life course. Because of its emphasis on individual behavior and choices, the life course perspective is seen by some as a microlevel theoretical framework with limited value for explaining the macrolevel influences of public policy and social institutions on health and aging (Estes, Gerard, and Clarke, 1984; Estes, 2001).

In this report, the focus is not on intellectual critique or defense of a conceptual orientation per se. We are simply using the life course perspective as a source of ideas that may help in making a useful bridge between individual behavior and public policy. Three themes emerge as particularly important for assessing the health and safety needs of the current generation of older workers:

(1) *Cohort effects* Characteristic attitudes and behaviors can become established among workers in specific age groupings because of historical events they have experienced as a cohort. At the same time, improvements in health and life expectancy contribute to changes in the ways that cohorts view their future working and nonworking lives.

(2) *Linked lives* The attitudes, choices, and behavior of individual workers can be greatly influenced by their social ties with other people, including family members, friends, and coworkers.

(3) *Intracohort diversity* Extreme variation in circumstances can exist within each age cohort, resulting in subgroups of special concern as they enter their older working years. This theme, implicit in life course theory even if not well developed, is highly relevant to the present report.

Cohort Effects

While the life course perspective may shed greater light on actual movements in and out of the paid workforce, the traditional three-stage model of working life remains influential for the present cohort of older workers, many of whom early in life accepted it as normative. The U.S. baby boom generation grew up during the years immediately following World War II, a period when the traditional model's portrayal of predictable, clear-cut transitions from education to career to retirement seemed a realistic description of what a working life should look like. Since then, social circumstances have changed drastically. However, male workers in the baby boom age cohort may still be expecting a permanent exit from paid employment at around age 65. Women workers in the same cohort may consider it normal to add large amounts of unpaid work to their paid employment in the form of caregiving and home labor.

Baby boomers represent a swing generation in an occupational world that may deviate in some respects from their expectations. Indeed, many among the present cohort of aging workers may lack familiarity with varied and complex work-retirement combinations that will become increasingly common, even though these opportunities will seem normal and reasonable to future generations of workers as they age. A number of studies document that workers in the baby boom age cohort are alarmingly uninformed about their actual retirement options and resources (Gustman and Steinmeier, 2001).

Confounding these evolving work and retirement options is the fact that older adults are undergoing cohort changes in health, such as living longer and having less disability. As a consequence, older adults in this cohort may have different expectations regarding both work and retirement options than earlier cohorts. Social policies regarding retirement lag as well (Riley, Foner, and Riley, 1999). As discussed in Chapter 7, some policies and programs that were crafted decades ago are slow in adapting to altered social conditions and still implicitly incorporate the lockstep stages and crisp exit assumptions of the traditional three-stage model of working life. An exception is the Social Security system (the main public retirement program), which now allows people to begin claiming benefits after the age of 62 and allows workers to combine reduced work with receipt of pension. However, some pension systems and tax laws can work against new ways of thinking about paid employment in a worker's later years, such as phased retirement programs (Wiatrowski, 2001). Similarly, the idea that public education should focus primarily on the preemployment years of adolescence and early adulthood fosters a neglect of lifelong education strategies (Harootyan and Feldman, 1990) and tends to encourage business, government, and unions to favor early retirement over retraining of older workers (Schulz, 2000).

Linked Lives

An important theme in the life course perspective is that most aging workers are not isolated individuals making autonomous decisions, but rather persons embedded in a system of social relationships that influences their thinking and actions. Therefore, work-retirement transitions should be treated as products of social interaction and shared decision making within families and personal networks, summed up in the concept of linked lives. For example, retirement decisions in dual-worker families tend to be made jointly, with total family income being a factor in the decision and workers (most commonly women) sometimes deciding to leave the workforce early so as to synchronize their own retirement with that of their spouses (Blau, 1998; Hurd, 1998; Johnson and Favreault, 2001; Weaver, 1994; Henretta, O'Rand, and Chan, 1993). Caregiving roles are intertwined with labor force participation in complex ways, again most commonly for women workers (Moen, Robison, and Dempster-McClain, 1995).

These family choices and their interconnections with social policy are discussed further in Chapter 4.

Decisions about work and retirement in later years may be related to friendship networks inside and outside the workplace; the worker's level of civic engagement with his or her community; and the kinds of amenities and supports available in the older worker's living environment. Older workers with weak community linkages and strong friendship ties at work may find that their psychological well-being and life satisfaction are maximized by staying on the job even with declining health. Others whose community linkages are richer may feel they can increase their psychological well-being and life satisfaction by leaving paid employment and freeing up their time for community-based volunteer work or social activities. More flexible work options would allow older workers to perform these tradeoffs more effectively.

Intracohort Diversity and Disadvantaged Subgroups

The life course perspective implicitly supports increased attention to the extreme diversity among older workers. In addition to identifying modal patterns for the age cohort as a whole, it is important to understand how the experience of particular subgroups of older workers reflects historical events they have experienced, the timing of key events in their personal lives, and the specific contexts in which their lives are lived. It matters a great deal whether their lives have been lived in an economically advantaged situation or a disadvantaged one; whether or not they have faced discrimination; whether they have had good luck or bad luck at key points in life; whether or not they had support from family and friends; and whether or not they were able to avoid conflicts between potentially competing priorities such as caregiving versus paid employment.

Different kinds of social disadvantage can intersect, deepening the effects of factors such as race, class, gender, and age (Dressel, 1988). Moreover, since positive or negative experiences over the life course have a cumulative effect, intracohort variability increases with age. That is, resource and income variations within an age cohort will intensify over time. For example, early completion of college and entry into a favorable occupational role produce ongoing advantages, which can open subsequent opportunities for home ownership and a vested pension (Henretta and Campbell, 1976). This pattern has been termed the "Matthew Effect," reflecting the idea expressed in the Gospel of Saint Matthew that "the rich get richer and the poor get poorer" (Marshall and Mueller, 2002: 23). Warr (1998: 289) points out that intracohort variations in working conditions can also be expected to increase with age, so that "general statements about average exposure to, say, opportunity for control at work . . . may become increasingly inappropriate as the variance in exposure becomes progressively greater."

Therefore, in assessing and addressing the health and safety needs of older workers, it is important to remember that they are not all alike. Those who have been employed intermittently or at low wages for all of their working lives, without medical insurance or pension benefits, are in a different position from those who were more fortunate and who will have different needs. For some, voluntary retirement may not be an option at any age because they need paid employment as a matter of economic necessity. In the absence of other means of economic support, financially insecure workers are likely to work as long as they can, even if the jobs available to them put their health and safety at risk.

Reasons for Attending to the Health and Safety Needs of Older Workers

Why should attention be paid to the health and safety needs of older workers? One reason is that understanding the capabilities, limitations, and needs of older workers can help to address issues of productivity and labor supply. The U.S. Bureau of Labor Statistics projects a serious slowing in the growth of the labor supply in coming years, falling from an average annual rate of 1.1 percent between 1990 and 2000 to an annual rate of 0.7 percent between 2000 and 2025 (GAO, 2001). While some labor needs may be met through immigration, older workers already in the U.S. labor force (especially those with high skill levels) represent an important resource. To maximize benefits to the economy and investment capital, a societal interest exists in retaining older workers in the labor force. From this viewpoint, the highest priority concern is to learn which older workers can be expected to work productively, what kinds of tasks they are best suited for, and how their productivity might be increased through cost-effective accommodations and support programs in the workplace and community.

Another reason for attending to the health and safety needs of older workers is that addressing their capabilities, limitations, and needs can help maximize their opportunities for making work-related choices that promote health, safety, and life satisfaction in their later years. This perspective also encourages attention to workplace and community accommodations and support programs specifically aimed at older workers. It includes broader considerations such as the following:

• adequate and effectively enforced occupational health and safety regulations for workers of all ages, to help them enter their older working years with less pre-existing exposure to occupational hazards;

- policies aimed at providing adequate health insurance coverage for the U.S. population generally, and aging workers specifically;
- dissemination of effective information to workers throughout their working lives to prepare them for the work and retirement decisions they will be making;
- recognition that work/retirement transitions, which occur at many points in working life, could be facilitated by policies that see blurred rather than crisp exits from work, and that these transitions are generally family decisions rather than individual decisions; and
- recognition that the U.S. working population includes some sub-groups that may be poorly protected by existing public policy, are difficult to study, and appear to be underrepresented in available databases.

THE STUDY AND THE REPORT

To fulfill its charge, described above, the study committee gathered information from the relevant scientific literature and community. The committee also heard from the sponsors and invited guests about various data and issues pertinent to older working adults and about relevant research findings. Under the sponsorship of the U.S. Environmental Protection Agency, the committee also conducted a workshop on differential susceptibility of older persons to environmental hazards. The committee discussed data availability and research findings; identified critical issues; analyzed data (including Current Population Survey Data for March 2001) and issues; and formulated the findings, conclusions, and recommendations expressed in this report as follows.

Chapter 2 discusses what is known about the characteristics and retirement patterns of the older population and workforce, including an overview of their health status. Chapter 3 reviews the changing structure of the American labor market and the changing nature of work experiences. Chapter 4 reviews sources of disparities in older workers' work experiences and related health outcomes, presenting what is known about social and economic differences between older and younger workers.

Chapter 5 reviews what is known about the physical, cognitive, and social differences between older and younger workers and the psychological characteristics of older workers. Chapter 6 reviews overall health effects of workplace exposures, including consideration of biological, sociological, psychological, and economic effects, and examines their specific implications for older workers. Chapter 7 reviews labor laws, antidiscrimination laws, and wage and benefit protections that directly and indirectly affect an older worker's likelihood and choice of staying in or leaving the workforce. Chapter 8 presents intervention strategies to meet the safety and health needs of older workers. Approaches considered include accommodation through job design; alternative forms of work; vocational rehabilitation and return-to-work programs; access to preventive and restorative health care; community-based support services; physical aids; health promotion; employee assistance programs; physical fitness programs; and learning systems and retraining. Chapter 9 presents the committee's recommendations.

NOTE ON DATA TABLES IN APPENDIXES

In addition to the data tables contained in this report, two appendixes containing additional data tables (several of which are expansions of tables presented in the report) are provided on the National Academies Press internet site (website address www.nap.edu). References to the tables in the appendixes are included as appropriate in the report.

2

Demographic Characteristics
of the Older Workforce

DEMOGRAPHIC TRENDS OF OLDER PERSONS

The dominant population trend of the latter part of the 20th century results from a change in demographic structure known as population aging, brought about by a combination of lengthening life expectancy, decline in fertility, and an unusually large "baby boom" generation (Redburn, 1998; Moody, 2002). The aging of "boomers" is experienced in the workforce as a large number of older workers who are now beginning to retire. The effects this is going to have over the next 30 years both on the age distribution in the workforce and the size of the retired population is suggested by data presented in Figure 2-1. The aging workforce (portion of the population 45–64) and the increase in size and proportion of older adults (age 65 and older, most of whom will be retired) will have important effects for at least the next quarter century.

Interest in life after work has also increased in keeping with another significant 20th-century development—the striking improvement in life expectancy (Kinsella and Gist, 1995). Half a century ago, globally most people died before the age of 50. By 1995, the average life expectancy was more than 65 years, an increase of about three years from as recently as 1985. Life expectancy is now over 75 years in industrialized countries, 64 years in developing countries, and 52 years in the least developed countries. The

---

Appendixes A and B are not printed in this volume but are available online. Go to http://www.nap.edu and search for *Health and Safety Needs of Older Workers.*

number of countries having a life expectancy at birth of over 60 years increased from at least 98 (with a total population of 2.7 billion) in 1980 to at least 120 (with a total population of 4.9 billion) in 1995.

How Many Older Persons Are There?

Taking age 45 as the beginning age for inclusion, there are a large number of Americans in the age range of older workers, and they represent a large percentage of the population. In the year 2000, the U.S. civilian noninstitutionalized population, age 16 years and older, was 209.7 million (we shall refer to this group of mostly working-age people as the "population" in the following discussion). Close to half of this population (44 percent) were age 45 or over, with 15 percent over age 64 (Fullerton and Toossi, 2001). The number of women exceeds the number of men at all age groups, and the life expectancy of women exceeds that of men. At higher ages, the ratio of men to women declines from 92 percent in the 55 to 64 age range, to 82 percent in the 65 to 74 age range, to 69 percent in the 75 to 84 age range, and to 49 percent at older ages (U.S. Bureau of the Census, 1999).

Of the population, 174.4 million (83 percent) were white; 25.3 million (12 percent) were black; 10.1 million (5 percent) were Asian and other; and 22.4 million (11 percent) were of Hispanic origin (a category that overlaps the others). For each of these racial and ethnic groups, the number of women over the age of 50 exceeds that of men in the same age group in similar proportions for each racial and ethnic group. However, the racial and ethnic groups show significantly different proportions of older persons. Within the white population, 39 percent are over the age of 50; the percentage is 28 for blacks and only 20 for people of Hispanic origin (U.S. Bureau of the Census, 2000).

What Are the Past and Future Trends?

The year 2000 figures represent a continuing trend toward an increasing number of older persons constituting an increasing proportion of the population. Population pyramids for the years 1900, 1980, 1990, and 2000 show a historical trend away from the high proportion of younger people that created bottom-heavy distributions at the beginning of last century toward a more equal distribution of the population across age groups (see Figure 2-1, from Fullerton and Toossi, 2001). After World War II, the baby boom of 1946 to 1964 resulted in a prominent population bulge, with 75 million persons born. As they age, these baby boomers increasingly contribute to the growing proportion of older persons in the population, until, by the year 2060 or thereabouts, their numbers disappear.

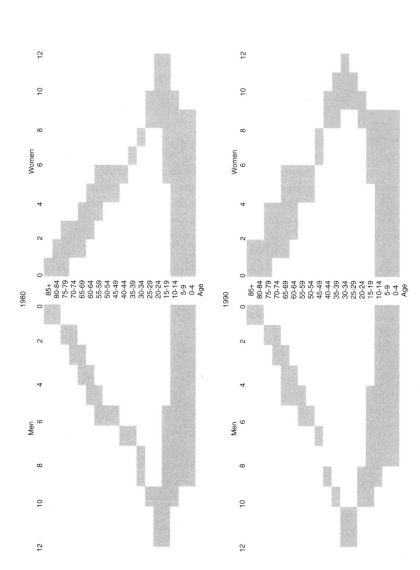

FIGURE 2-1 Population and labor force (in millions) by age, 1980 and 1990 (adapted from Fullerton and Toossi, 2001). NOTE: Shaded area represents population; unshaded area represents labor force.

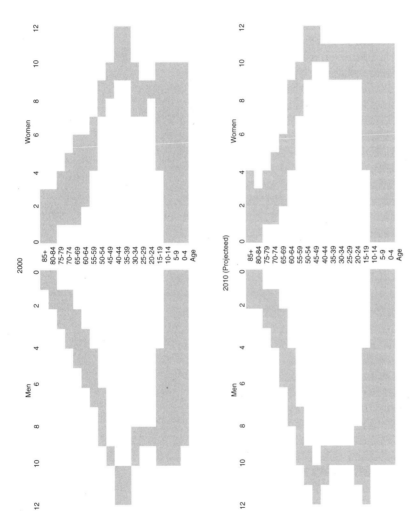

FIGURE 2-1 (Continued) Population and labor force (in millions) by age, 1980 and 1990 (adapted from Fullerton and Toossi, 2001).
NOTE: Shaded area represents population; unshaded area represents labor force.

Table 2-1 illustrates three major trends. First, there has been a significant increase in the general American population, from the year 1900 (50.1 million) to 2000 (209.7 million). Second, there has been a dramatic increase in the number and percentage of people age 45 and older (from 13.7 million in 1990 to 93.2 million in 2000, a shift from 26 percent to 44 percent of the population). Third, both the number of women age 45 and over and the proportion of the population they represent have shown a startling in-

TABLE 2-1 Trends and Projections for Numbers and Percentages of Older Persons (Over Age 44) in the United States

Year	1900		2000	
	Million	Percent[a]	Million	Percent[b]
Population[c]	50.1	100	209.7	100
Men and Women				
74+	0.9	2	14.9	7
65–74	2.2	4	17.8	8
55–64	4.1	7	23.6	11
45–54	6.5	13	36.9	18
Total	13.7	26	93.2	44
Women				
74+	0.5	1	9.0	4
65–74	1.0	2	9.7	5
55–64	2.0	4	12.4	6
45–54	3.0	6	18.9	9
Total	6.5	13	50.0	24
Men				
74+	0.4	1	5.9	3
65–74	1.2	2	8.1	4
55–64	2.1	4	11.3	5
45–54	3.5	7	18.0	9
Total	7.2	14	43.3	21

[a]Percent is of the population of persons for the given year who are over 15 years of age.
[b]Percent is of the noninstitutionalized civilian population for the given year who are 16 years of age and older.
[c]Population is, for the years 1900, 2020, and 2050, the population of persons for the given year who are over 15 years of age. For the years 2000 and 2010, population is the population of noninstitutionalized, civilian persons for the given year who are 16 years of age or older.

SOURCE: Data for years 2000 and 2010 are adapted from Fullerton and Toossi (2001: Table 2). Data for years 1900, 2020, and 2050 are adapted from U.S. Bureau of the Census (1993: Figures 1, 3, and 4).

crease: in 1900 the number of men in the population (7.2 million, 14 percent of the population) exceeded that of women (6.5 million, 13 percent); by 2000, the number of women over the age of 45 had grown to 50 million (24 percent of the population), exceeding the number and percentage of men in that age group (43.3 million, 21 percent). These trends are carried through at virtually all age groupings of older persons (45–54 years; 55–64 years; 65–74 years; and 75+ years).

2010		2020		2050	
Million	Percent[b]	Million	Percent[a]	Million	Percent[a]
233.7	100	258.8	100	309.0	100
16.3	7	21.9	9	43.6	14
20.6	9	31.6	12	35.2	11
34.8	15	42.0	16	42.7	14
43.9	19	38.2	15	43.4	14
115.6	50	133.7	52	164.9	53
9.8	4	13.0	5	24.9	8
11.2	5	16.6	6	18.1	6
18.2	8	21.6	8	22.0	7
22.4	10	19.5	8	22.3	7
61.6	27	70.7	27	87.3	28
6.5	3	8.9	3	18.7	6
9.4	4	15.0	6	17.1	6
16.6	7	20.4	8	20.7	7
21.5	9	18.7	7	21.1	7
54.0	23	63.0	24	77.6	26

These trends are projected, with some modification, to continue (see Table 2-1). Nearer-term projections by Fullerton and Toossi (2001) indicate that by 2010 the U.S. civilian, noninstitutionalized population 16 years of age and over will increase to 233.7 million, of whom fully 50 percent (115.6 million) will be age 45 or over. The percentage of the population who are women over age 45 will increase to 27 percent (61.6 million), continuing to exceed that of men, whose numbers and percentage of the population will, nevertheless, continue to grow as well.

Longer-term projections (U.S. Bureau of the Census, 1993: Table 2-1) suggest that these trends will continue through the year 2050, after which there is a projected leveling off of the increase of persons age 45 and over. The population over age 15 is projected to increase to 309 million by the year 2050. The number of those age 45 and older is expected to reach 170 million by the year 2050, representing 53 percent of the population.

DEMOGRAPHIC TRENDS OF OLDER WORKERS

Employment Trends of Men and Women in the 1980s and 1990s

The two most salient changes in the American labor force over the second half of the 20th century were the decline in the labor force participation rate of older men and the rise in the labor force participation rate of women. As nations become wealthier, part of that wealth is used to finance increased leisure. Costa (1998) argues that this growth in wealth in the U.S. population is behind the decline in the labor force participation rate of older men that she traces back to the late 19th century.

Table 2-2 reports labor force participation rates for men in the United States from 1940 to 2001 using cross sectional data from the U.S. Decennial Censuses of 1940 to 1960 and from the Current Population Survey (CPS) thereafter (Table A-1 in Appendix A expands Table 2-2 to include additional years and ages). Labor force participation is measured using questions about respondents' major activity in the week prior to the survey. Those who were employed or unemployed but looking for work are considered to be in the labor force. The labor force participation rate is the share of the relevant population that is employed, on temporary layoff, or actively looking for a job.

If the typical retirement age of men in a society is defined as the age at which only one-half of them remain in the labor force, then the typical retirement age occurred at about age 70 in 1940. After War World II the typical retirement age dropped in an irregular pattern, and, because of substantial increases in life expectancy after age 65, the length of time between retirement and death dramatically increased. In addition to increased personal wealth, post–World War II growth in private pension

TABLE 2-2 U.S. Labor Force Participation Rates of Men by Age, 1940–2001

Year	Age						
	50	55	60	62	65	66	70
1940[a]		93.8	85.5	80.0	70.0	68.1	48.6
1950[a]		90.6	84.7	81.2	71.7	67.1	49.8
1960[a]		92.8	85.9	79.8	56.8	49.0	37.2
1970	93.4	88.0	81.7	73.1	47.4	39.3	30.5
1975	91.0	86.0	79.0	68.8	41.9	32.6	25.7
1980	92.0	83.5	74.5	60.7	35.3	30.4	24.8
1985	92.2	84.3	70.8	50.6	32.2	25.8	20.5
1990	90.9	84.9	71.5	51.8	37.2	27.1	20.3
1995	88.7	81.8	71.6	47.9	33.6	32.9	20.0
2001	87.3	82.7	71.3	54.1	38.7	37.9	24.5

[a]Based on adjusted U.S. Bureau of the Census labor force participation data. The adjustment is based on the ratio of CPS figures and U.S Decennial Census figures in 1970.
SOURCE: Labor force participation figures for 1970–2001 are authors' calculations using March CPS Annual Demographic files.

plans and Social Security benefits allowed an increasing share of American workers to have financial resources available during a significant period of retirement at the end of their lives. By 1960, over one-half of men aged 66 were out of the labor force, and by 1970 the typical retirement age had fallen to 65. At that time, however, over one-fourth of older adults were also living in poverty (see Table 2-3; Table A-2 in Appendix A presents additional data for persons who work, persons who do not work, and

TABLE 2-3 Poverty Rate of Older Americans by Age Group, 1970–2000

Year	Age Group							
	45–49	50–54	55–59	60–64	65–69	70–74	75–79	80+
1970	6.6	7.6	9.5	13.6	19.1	23.7	29.0	31.1
1975	7.1	7.4	9.0	11.5	12.5	14.4	16.4	21.5
1980	7.3	8.2	8.7	10.4	12.0	14.4	17.8	22.5
1985	8.3	8.5	9.8	11.3	9.4	12.1	14.8	17.3
1990	7.3	8.4	9.0	10.3	8.4	11.3	13.3	18.6
1995	7.3	8.5	10.3	10.2	8.1	9.2	10.9	15.1
2000	6.2	6.7	8.8	10.2	8.3	9.6	10.8	12.5

percentage of age group at work). Over the next 15 years, labor force participation rates continued to fall, and by 1985 typical male retirement had dropped to age 62. What was notable about this period of rapid decline in the labor force participation rates of older men is that it came at a time when the poverty rate of older Americans was also dropping (see Table 2-3). On average, then, this generation of older men was able to both reduce its labor force participation and its risk of falling into poverty over its increasing years in retirement, in large part related to the rapid increase in the value of private pensions and social security benefits. (See Burkhauser et al., in press, for a discussion of the changes in the economic well-being of older persons over this period.)

The decline in labor force participation rates of older men over the post–World War II years was not confined to the United States. As documented by Gruber and Wise (1999) and most recently by the National Research Council (2001), the decline in the labor force participation of men since World War II occurred at various rates for most Organisation for Economic Co-operation and Development (OECD) countries. In many European countries this decline has been more rapid, and their typical retirement age has fallen below that for the United States.

A National Research Council report (2001: 66) argues that while social norms and the reduced demand for the labor of older men have played roles in this decline across countries, "changes in retirement patterns also depend heavily on the precise form of early retirement provisions in pension and social security plans, as well as on the structure of income support and welfare programs for older individuals" (see also Burtless and Moffitt, 1984; Quinn, Burkhauser, and Myers, 1990; Gruber and Wise, 1999). Clark, York, and Anker (1999) found that rising income and the growth of social security programs have also reduced male labor force participation rates in many developing countries.

The National Research Council (2001) report also argues that changing population age structures are compelling many national governments to create or revamp policies and programs that have encouraged early retirement. The report states: "The increasing financial pressure faced by public pension systems around the world is often attributed to demographic trends that have led to an aging population. But decreasing labor force participation rates for a given age structure also contribute to financial imbalances within pension programs, further increasing the number of retired persons relative to those in the workforce" (p. 8).

In the United States, major social security reforms in 1983 led to an immediate increase in payroll taxes; gradual increases in yearly benefits for those who postponed acceptance of benefits past age 65 to offset the loss in the lifetime value of social security benefits caused by such a postponement; a gradual increase in the age of eligibility for full social security retirement benefits from age 65 to age 67; and—beginning in 2000—a reduction in the benefits of those who began to take benefits at age 62. A new round of concerns over the long-term financial stability of the Social Security system has led to discussions of further increases in the early and full retirement ages as well as reductions in future benefits increases (see, for instance, Social Security Advisory Council Technical Report, 1997).

One of the six major recommendations of the National Research Council (2001: 4) report was "to encourage longitudinal research to disentangle and illuminate the complex interrelationship among work, health, economic status, and family structure" in order to inform governments of the consequences of public policy on the timing of retirement.

However, Table 2-2 suggests that the downward trend in labor force participation rates of U.S. men aged 62 and over ended in the mid-1980s. The labor force participation rates of men at most single ages above age 62 rebounded from their mid-1980s troughs. Quinn (2002) uses these data from the CPS to show that had the trend in early retirement over the period 1964 through 1985, which reduced the labor force participation rates of 60- to 64-year-olds by almost one-third (from 79 to 56 percent), continued at that same rate until 2001, labor force participation rates for men this age would have been dramatically below their actual levels, which are in fact higher than they were in 1985.

Post–World War II trends in the labor force participation rates of women have been quite different from those of men. Since World War II, more and more women have entered the labor force, and they have spent a considerably greater amount of their lifetimes in paid employment. As their work histories have become more like those of men, they have been affected by the same social structures—private and social security pensions plans— that have influenced the labor force participation of men.

As can be seen in Table 2-4, in 1970 the labor force participation rates of women were substantially below those of men at ages below the typical retirement age (Table A-3 in Appendix A expands Table 2-4 to include additional years and ages). For instance, only 49.4 percent of women aged 50 were in the labor force compared to 93.4 percent of males. But the labor force participation rates of younger women have increased dramatically since then. Thus, by 1995 over three-quarters of women aged 50 were in the labor force. Their labor force participation rate was 78.0 percent in 2000 compared to 88.7 percent of males. Like that of men, the labor force participation rate of women declines with age in cross-sectional data, but the increased percentage of women who were working as they approached the normal retirement age offset this decline in labor force participation with age in the 1970s and early 1980s. Hence, as Table 2-4 shows, the labor force participation rates of women aged 62 (the earliest age of eligibility for social security benefits) and older were relatively flat over this period.

TABLE 2-4 U.S. Labor Force Participation Rates of Women by Age, 1970–2001

Year	Age						
	50	55	60	62	65	66	70
1970	49.4	47.7	40.3	34.0	20.2	18.7	9.8
1975	57.4	52.3	42.3	36.2	20.9	14.7	10.0
1980	59.1	52.8	40.4	31.2	19.7	17.8	10.2
1985	63.3	59.7	41.5	32.7	16.1	14.3	8.3
1990	68.3	61.0	44.6	34.2	22.3	20.0	14.0
1995	75.2	62.5	47.2	38.4	22.3	19.2	10.5
2001	77.1	67.4	52.5	41.3	25.5	21.2	14.2

SOURCE: Labor force participation figures for 1970–2001 are authors' calculations using March CPS Annual Demographic files.

But as Table 2-4 also shows, after 1985 the labor force participation rates of older women had substantially increased. Quinn (2002) uses these data to show that, as was the case for men, labor force participation trend lines based on data before 1985 dramatically underestimate the labor force participation rates of older women between 1985 and 2001.

The reasons for this substantial change in the labor force participation rate trends of men and women since the mid-1980s are not fully understood. As noted by the National Research Council (2001) report, structural changes in the social security system put in place in the 1980s, the banning of mandatory retirement rules, and the shift from defined benefit to defined contribution retirement plans should all have increased the incentives to work at older ages in the United States over this period (Quinn et al., 1990; Bass, Quinn, and Burkhauser, 1995; Ghent, Allen, and Clark, 2002).

It also appears that older Americans are living longer and healthier. While there is no question that mortality rates at all ages are declining (National Research Council, 2001), some controversy remains about trends in the functional capacity of older workers. Manton, Corder, and Stallard, (1997) report declines in the trends in chronic disabilities among those over age 65 between 1982 and 1994. Crimmins, Reynolds, and Saito (1999) found significant improvements between 1982 and 1993 in the self-reported ability of men and women in their 60s to work. Improvement was noted by race and educational level, but level of self-reported health was lower to start for African Americans and those of lower educational attainment. It is still not clear whether these results gathered with cross-sectional data over relatively short time periods are part of a longer trend.

An alternative hypothesis is that the end of the decline in labor force participation rates of men since 1985 is simply a business cycle effect, and that the strong economy since the recession of 1992 explains most of the gains in the employment and labor force participation of older men and women over the period. There is substantial evidence that business cycles play an important role in the labor force participation of both men and women. Certainly overall employment rates rise and unemployment rates decline during business expansions, and the reverse occurs over business contractions. It is likely that older workers who have some alternative sources of income, if they are eligible for private pension plans prior to age 62 and for social security benefits after age 62, have a much greater choice than younger workers with respect to their decision to stay in the labor force in the face of a job loss. But the United States has experienced two complete business cycles over the 1980s and 1990s, and as we show below, the survival rates of older workers (the age-specific employment rates of workers who were working at age 50 at subsequent ages) did not decline in the 1990s when compared to the 1980s across the entire business cycle. In fact, survival rates appear to have slightly increased in the 1990s compared to the 1980s at most older ages.

Labor Market Exit Rates in the 1980s and 1990s

The business cycle of the 1980s began with a business cycle peak in 1979. The low point of the subsequent recession was 1982. The economy then grew continuously throughout the rest of the decade, peaking in 1989. The business cycle of the 1990s began with the peak year of 1989. The trough year was 1992. Continuous economic growth then occurred through the year 2000. Table 2-5 looks more closely at the transitions of older men and women out of work over the course of these two business cycles. It focuses on older Americans who work for others. Self-employed workers (about 9 percent of all adults who work and about 25 percent of those over age 65 who work; Bregger, 1996) are not included in the analysis.

Because the CPS surveys a subsample of its respondents in two consecutive March surveys, it is possible to follow the employment of this subsample over two years. This allows us to estimate age-specific employment exit rates for men aged 50 to 70 during these two business cycles. Table 2-5 reports the probability of men and women exiting the labor market at various ages. More formally, we use a Kaplan-Meier life table measure to look at the percentage of men and women who worked for at least 1,000 hours for someone else in year (t) who worked for no more than 100 hours in the next year (t+1) to estimate age-specific employment exit rates. We pool these workers over all pairs of years between 1981 and 2000 and then for 1981 to 1989 and for 1990 to 2000. This pooling technique provides

TABLE 2-5 Age-Specific Exit Rates from Employment for Men and Women Aged 50–70

	Men			Women		
Age	1981–2000	1981–1989	1990–2000	1981–2000	1981–1989	1990–2000
50	1.81	1.74	1.86	2.91	3.22	2.73
51	2.09	2.26	1.96	3.00	2.81	3.11
52	1.97	2.26	1.74	4.16	4.40	4.01
53	2.10	2.27	1.96	3.20	3.05	3.29
54	2.27	2.29	2.26	3.97	4.35	3.69
55	4.29	4.39	4.21	5.36	6.21	4.71
56	4.24	3.45	5.01	4.90	4.36	5.32
57	3.67	3.56	3.78	5.44	6.02	4.98
58	4.29	4.09	4.50	6.02	6.07	5.97
59	5.55	5.03	6.08	6.31	5.57	7.02
60	7.28	8.63	5.90	6.52	5.65	7.32
61	9.39	9.64	9.16	8.96	8.42	9.40
62	17.80	16.61	19.04	14.29	14.12	14.44
63	12.59	11.98	13.21	12.15	11.57	12.68
64	16.19	17.69	14.60	13.82	13.57	14.04
65	21.22	25.26	17.66	20.57	19.16	21.83
66	18.37	21.07	15.90	15.29	14.29	16.01
67	14.76	17.12	12.74	13.96	12.63	14.96
68	18.18	20.77	15.71	14.58	14.47	14.67
69	14.09	18.33	9.89	16.83	19.13	15.43
70	17.87	17.80	17.92	19.66	19.39	19.85

NOTE: Age and exit rate are based on year of exit (t+1) where an exit is defined as the percentage of workers who were employed for 1,000 hours or more in year (t) who are now employed for 100 or less hours.
SOURCE: Current Population Surveys 1981–2001.

greater sample size so that we can more precisely measure age-specific exit rates, but it also means that the resulting rates are a mixture of age effects and period effects.

Over the entire period (1981–2000), yearlong exits (less than 100 hours of work over the year) from employment are relatively rare for men before age 55—only about 2 percent of these younger men exit employment at each age. Yearlong exits between ages 55 and 59 increase to about twice that rate. They rise a bit more at ages 60 and 61. However, the exit rates are much higher thereafter but with two spikes. The first is at age 62, the earliest age of eligibility for social security retirement benefits. The second is at age 65, the age of eligibility for full social security benefits over this period.

Once we subdivide our sample to capture two different business cycles (1981–1989) and (1990–2000), we see that for men there has been a substantial change in the age-specific exit rates over the two periods. In the 1980s, the highest spike in exit rates was at age 65 with a somewhat smaller spike at age 62. In the 1990s the highest spike was at age 62. The exit rate at 65 is lower and not much different from the rates of its nearest age neighbors.

These exit rate patterns suggest that something different occurred in the 1990s with respect to men's age-specific exits. One possibility is the change in social security rules, fully phased in over the 1990s. The new rules no longer punish workers who postpone acceptance of social security benefits past age 65, as Social Security rules did in the 1980s. Another is the shift from defined-benefit to defined-contribution pensions for workers of these ages. This shift has reduced the retirement incentives that were contained in the eligibility rules of defined benefit pension plans (see Quinn et al., 1990, and Burtless and Moffit, 2001, for a discussion of the influence of defined pension plans on retirement age). Table 2-5 also shows, using the pooled 1981–2000 data, that women had similar age-specific exit rate patterns as those of men, but women's exit rates are somewhat higher than men's at younger ages (50–59) and somewhat lower thereafter. Women's peak exit rate years, however, are the same as those of men—ages 62 and 65. However, unlike men, women's exit rate spike at age 65 did not disappear in the 1990s.

Table 2-6 uses the exit rates from Table 2-5 to simulate the employment survival rate of men and women who were employed at age 50 in the 1981–2000 period, the 1981–1990 period, and the 1990–2000 period, as well as predicted employment rate of men and women at each age in these periods, assuming that no one who exits the labor force ever returns. The survival rates are simulated by following men and women who were employed at age 50 for the period of interest and then assuming that their probability of leaving employment at each age is the average exit rate for the period of interest. These survival rates simulate, for instance, that of the men who were employed for over 1,000 hours at age 50 over the 1981–2000 period, 88 percent would still be employed at least for 100 hours per year at age 55. The fraction employed would fall to 62 percent at age 61, and to 51 percent at age 62. High exit rates thereafter cut employment to 29 percent at age 65 and 12 percent at age 70. These rates blend the generally higher exit rates of the 1980s with the lower rates of the 1990s, especially past age 64. The survival rates are slightly higher in the 1990s, reflecting the lower exit rates over the period. The survival functions are lower for women at every age compared to men, but they are also slightly higher in the 1990s than in the 1980s.

TABLE 2-6 Age-Specific Employment Survival Functions and
Employment Rates for Men and Women Employed at Age 50

	Men					
	1981–2000		1981–1989		1990–2000	
Age	Survival Function[a]	Rate[b]	Survival Function[a]	Rate[b]	Survival Function[a]	Rate[b]
50	1.00	86.72	1.00	88.41	1.00	85.54
51	0.98	84.91	0.98	86.41	0.98	83.86
52	0.96	83.23	0.96	84.45	0.96	82.40
53	0.94	81.49	0.93	82.53	0.94	80.79
54	0.92	79.64	0.91	80.65	0.92	78.96
55	0.88	76.22	0.87	77.10	0.88	75.64
56	0.84	72.98	0.84	74.44	0.84	71.85
57	0.81	70.30	0.81	71.79	0.81	69.13
58	0.78	67.29	0.78	68.86	0.77	66.02
59	0.73	63.55	0.74	65.39	0.72	62.01
60	0.68	58.93	0.68	59.75	0.68	58.35
61	0.62	53.40	0.61	53.99	0.62	53.01
62	0.51	43.89	0.51	45.02	0.50	42.92
63	0.44	38.36	0.45	39.63	0.44	37.25
64	0.37	32.15	0.37	32.62	0.37	31.81
65	0.29	25.33	0.28	24.38	0.31	26.19
66	0.24	20.68	0.22	19.24	0.26	22.03
67	0.20	17.62	0.18	15.95	0.22	19.22
68	0.17	14.42	0.14	12.64	0.19	16.20
69	0.14	12.39	0.12	10.32	0.17	14.60
70	0.12	10.17	0.10	8.48	0.14	11.98

[a]Age-specific employment survival function is simulated based on exit rates in Table 2-5. It is the percentage of the workers age 50 who continued to be employed at subsequent ages.
[b]Based on estimated exit rates for those who were working at age 50. The employment rate at age 50 is the actual rate.
SOURCE: Current Population Surveys 1981–2001.

Our discussion of Tables 2-5 and 2-6 focuses on exit from employment. At older ages the difference between labor force participation outcomes and employment outcomes are small because the unemployment rate of older workers is very low. Most older workers who face significant spells of unemployment are likely to leave the labor force. Hence our definition of employment exit—not working for at least 100 hours in a given year—is likely to be very close to a definition of exit from the labor force.

Women					
1981–2000		1981–1989		1990–2000	
Survival Function[a]	Rate[b]	Survival Function[a]	Rate[b]	Survival Function[a]	Rate[b]
1.00	62.53	1.00	55.09	1.00	68.06
0.97	60.65	0.97	53.54	0.97	65.94
0.93	58.13	0.93	51.19	0.93	63.30
0.90	56.27	0.90	49.63	0.90	61.21
0.86	54.04	0.86	47.47	0.87	58.96
0.82	51.15	0.81	44.52	0.83	56.18
0.78	48.64	0.77	42.58	0.78	53.19
0.74	46.00	0.73	40.02	0.74	50.54
0.69	43.23	0.68	37.59	0.70	47.52
0.65	40.50	0.64	35.50	0.65	44.19
0.61	37.86	0.61	33.49	0.60	40.95
0.55	34.47	0.56	30.67	0.55	37.11
0.47	29.54	0.48	26.34	0.47	31.75
0.42	25.95	0.42	23.30	0.41	27.72
0.36	22.37	0.37	20.13	0.35	23.83
0.28	17.77	0.30	16.28	0.27	18.63
0.24	15.05	0.25	13.95	0.23	15.65
0.21	12.95	0.22	12.19	0.20	13.30
0.18	11.06	0.19	10.42	0.17	11.35
0.15	9.20	0.15	8.43	0.14	9.60
0.12	7.39	0.12	6.80	0.11	7.70

Differences in Outcomes by Employment, Ethnicity, and Education

Tables 2-5 and 2-6 assume no differences in exit rates within individual ages groups. However, exit rates vary widely in different industries and occupations. Figures 2-2 and 2-3 present simulated employment survival rates and employment rates of men and women, respectively, across industries for various ages. Table B-1 in Appendix B presents the data upon

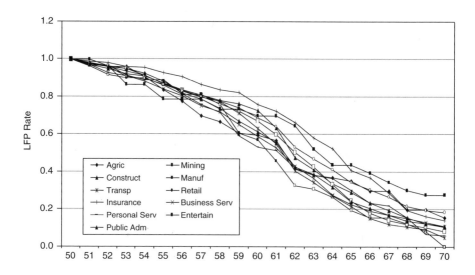

FIGURE 2-2 Survival function by industry for men.
SOURCE: Current Population Surveys, 1981–2001.

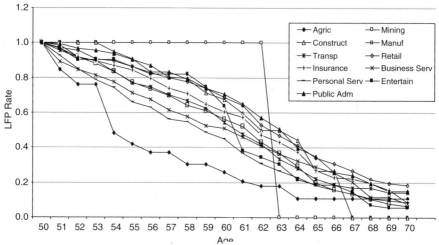

FIGURE 2-3 Survival function by industry for women.
SOURCE: Current Population Surveys, 1981–2001.

which the figures are based. Survival functions vary dramatically across industry. The average male working at age 50 in mining has a 45.6 percent chance of working at age 61. In contrast, the chance that the average worker, aged 50, in the insurance and real estate, banking, and other financial services industries is still working is 72.5 percent at age 61. By age 66 the implied employment rates are 15.5 percent and 36.9 percent, respectively. The chances of employment survival in the other industries fall somewhere in between. Similar differences are also shown for women.

Clearly there is an important correlation between the kind of industry at which one works and the speed at which one exits employment. But whether this difference is caused by the compensation package one receives in that industry (wages and salary, health benefits, pension plan), the demands of the job (e.g., level of cognitive skills or physical capacity required, the extent to which interactions with other workers and customers is critical to performance, worker control, range and breadth of tasks, etc.), the risks of the job to one's health and safety, and whether this is a contingent job cannot be determined with these data. Nor do the tables that we present confirm with certainty that changes in pension rules or social security rules are the driving force behind the ending of the decline in the labor force participation of older workers. Rather, these tables suggest that, on average, exit rates increase with age but that the resulting decline in employment varies tremendously across industry and, as we discuss below, across other individual dimensions.

Table B-2 in Appendix B repeats this exercise to show differences in work exit rates by occupation. We divide workers into white-collar, blue-collar, and service occupations separately for men and women. The variation across occupations is also substantial with, for instance 66.2 percent of white-collar male workers at age 50 still in the labor force at age 61, and 57.9 percent of blue-collar workers still employed at age 61. By age 66 the implied employment rates are 30.1 and 17.9 percent, respectively.

Table B-3 in Appendix B repeats this exercise by race. Figures 2-4 and 2-5 summarize the data for men and women, respectively. At age 61, 64 percent of white men who were working at age 50 are still working. For Hispanic men the chance of still working is 55 percent. For African American men it is 43 percent. The implied employment rates are 25, 20, and 11 percent, respectively, at age 66.

Figures 2-6 and 2-7 show differences in exit rates by education level for men and women, respectively. Table B-4 in Appendix B presents the data upon which the figures are based. At age 61, 72 percent of college or more highly educated men who were working at age 50 are still employed compared to 61 percent of high school graduates and 53 percent of those with less than a high school degree. At age 66 the implied employment rates are 41, 22, and 16 percent, respectively.

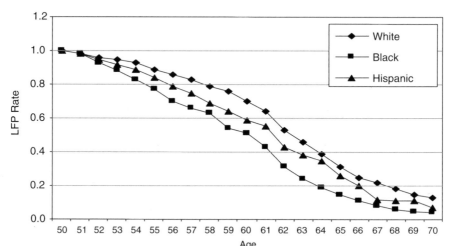

FIGURE 2-4 Survival functions by race for men.
SOURCE: Current Population Surveys, 1981–2001.

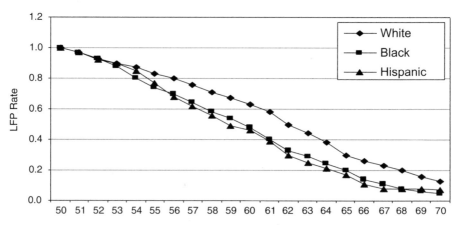

FIGURE 2-5 Survival function by race for women.
SOURCE: Current Population Surveys, 1981–2001.

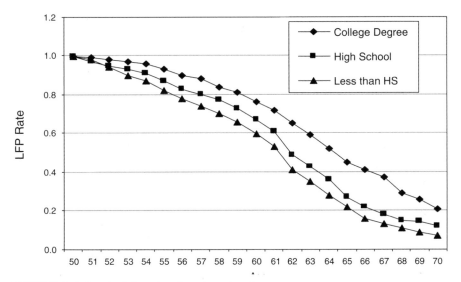

FIGURE 2-6 Survival function by education for men.
SOURCE: Current Population Surveys, 1981–2001.

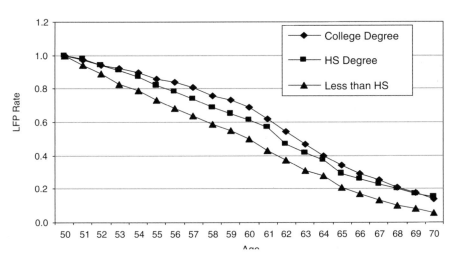

FIGURE 2-7 Survival function by education for women.
SOURCE: Current Population Surveys, 1981–2001.

The long expansion of the last decade of the 20th century is over, and a new business cycle has begun. At this point it is not clear how long the current downturn in the economy will last and how it will affect in the long-run employment of older workers. As Table 2-2 shows, the labor force participation rates of older men fell between 2000 and 2001; it is likely that they will continue to fall as the economy declines. While the declines thus far do not signal a return to pre-1985 trends, an important topic of future research will be how the employment of older workers changes over the current business cycle.

Need for Better Data

Tables 2-2 through 2-5 confirm that the decades-long decline in the labor force participation of older males has ended and the labor force participation rates of older females has substantially increased, at least over the 1990s business cycle. It is possible that this shift in work outcomes was partly caused by changes in the work incentives of our private pension and social security systems advocated by those who have suggested that such changes are necessary to preserve the financial integrity of these systems.

The tremendous differences in employment survival rates among people with different socioeconomic characteristics and who work in different industries and occupations are to some extent explained by differences in the retirement and other compensation packages provided to workers in these industries and occupations.

The National Research Council (2001) emphasized the importance of gathering information on these financial incentives so that researchers can provide policy makers with the information necessary to develop future evidenced-based employment and retirement public policies. This report singles out the Health and Retirement Study as an example of the type of multidisciplinary-based longitudinal data; linking these detailed financial aspects of jobs with a core set of social, economic, and health variables on workers and their families is necessary to provide needed data.

In addition to the detailed information that longitudinal surveys like the Health and Retirement Study have gathered on employment compensation in the form of wages, health coverage, and retirement pension rules, other aspects of the job should also be considered in detail. As we will discuss in subsequent chapters, there are significant differences in job demands that may differentially affect older workers as well as differences in the risks of accident or toxic exposure they may face. These job characteristics can have effects both on the health of older workers and on their retirement decisions.

As the U.S. government shifts Social Security policy to encourage greater employment at older ages, the consequences of this shift must be monitored across the diverse population of older workers it will affect. For instance, workers who would have been expected to leave the job under the old Social Security rules may now find it much less economically advantageous to do so. It is important to know if these changes in social policy, which encourage longer stays in the workforce, will have differential effects on the health of workers, especially on economically disadvantaged populations of workers and those in riskier or more demanding jobs. These questions can only be answered by more detailed information on the characteristics of the job (e.g., health and safety risks) linked to the powerful longitudinal data contained in datasets like the Health and Retirement Study.

Older-Worker-Intensive Industries and Occupations

We can expect to see differences in the distribution of older workers among the various industries and occupations in which they are employed. Determining which industries or occupations have the largest representation of older workers, however, depends on the way the question is asked. The actual count of older workers by industry or occupation allows a comparison of the sizes of the older workforces, male and female, across industries or occupations. Three proportional distributions add further information: We could be interested in (1) the overall proportion of older workers in the workforce who are employed in each industry or occupation; (2) the proportion of all older workers in the workforce who are employed in each industry or occupation; or (3) the proportion of the workforce in a specific industry or occupation who are older workers. The first proportion provides an indicator of the interaction between the size of the workforce of a given industry and the percentage of the workforce in that industry that are older workers. The second proportion allows a comparison across industries of what proportion of the older employed workforce are working in each industry. The third proportion allows a comparison across industries of the proportion of workers, male and female, who are older.

A separate question concerns projections of future trends. These projections include rate of growth or decline in employment predicted for industries, as well as projections of the numbers of older workers and their allocations to industries.

Older-Worker-Intensive Industries

Number of older workers. In which industrial categories are the greatest number of older workers employed, and which, therefore, employ the greatest percentage of older workers? The Current Population Survey (CPS) provides data on the employed population at any point in time. Table 2-7 uses data from the CPS for March 2001 to present overall employment by major industry category along with the total employment levels for workers age 45 and older stratified by sex. The greatest number of older workers are employed in manufacturing, retail, educational services, and finance/insurance/real estate services. When examined by sex, the same four industrial categories employ the greatest number of female older workers. For men, construction ranks third, and transportation and business services categories share fourth ranking, replacing educational services and financial/insurance/real estate services.

Proportionate distribution of older workers. What proportion of workers within a given industry are older workers? Proportional employment data

TABLE 2-7 Distribution of Older Workers Across Major Industrial Categories

Industry	Employed Workers Age 16 and Older		Employed Workers Age 45 and Older		
	Total[a]	Percent	Total[a]	Female[a]	Male[a]
Agriculture	2,940	2.2	1,230	340	890
Forest and fisheries	120	0.1	60	20	40
Mining	540	0.4	240	40	200
Construction	8,830	6.5	2,810	360	2,460
Manufacturing	19,570	14.5	7,650	2,540	5,120
Transportation	6,190	4.6	2,420	550	1,870
Communications	2,070	1.5	630	270	360
Utilities	1,420	1.0	590	110	480
Wholesale trade	5,240	3.9	1,910	570	1,350
Retail trade	22,220	16.4	5,770	2,980	2,800
Finance/insurance/realty	9,020	6.7	3,370	1,870	1,500
Personal services	910	0.7	340	320	020
Business, auto services	9,850	7.3	2,940	1,100	1,840
Other personal services	3,600	2.9	1,280	840	440
Entertainment	2,490	1.8	690	280	400
Hospital services	5,330	3.9	1,950	1,500	450
Other medical services	6,590	4.9	2,530	1,870	650
Educational services	11,870	8.8	5,510	3,850	660
Social services	3,550	2.6	1,290	1,000	290
Other professional service	6,510	4.8	2,750	1,280	470
Public administration	6,050	4.5	2,840	1,300	1,540

[a]Numbers in thousands.
SOURCE: CPS March 2001.

for workers over age 45 in 2001 are provided in Table A-4 in Appendix A, stratified by major industrial category, using the same CPS survey data for March 2001. The table includes the percentage of all employed persons who are older workers employed in the industry, the percentage of all older workers employed in the given industry, and the percentage of all workers in a given industry who are older workers.

A somewhat different picture is presented when the proportional distribution of older workers is examined. Of the four largest industrial categories by numbers employed, only educational services holds a rank amidst the four categories with the largest proportion of older workers overall. The three other top ranks by proportion are forestry/fishing/trapping, public administration, and mining. Greater differences in distribution by sex are seen in these proportional distributions. The four highest for women are all service industries: personal services, educational services, other medical services, and social services—although only educational services was among the highest overall. By contrast, for males the dominant industries were primarily physically demanding ones: mining, utilities, forestry/fishing/ trapping, communications, and agriculture.

Determining older-worker-intensive industries, then, is predicated on the question asked and whether gender is of interest. In addition, the industrial categories examined here are at the level of major categories; there may be differences (which should be researched to determine whether within-industry variance exceeds between-industry variance) at more detailed levels within categories.

Anticipated changes in employment for older workers. When examining older-worker-intensive industries, an important question concerns projections of future trends. Bureau of Labor Statistics projections are used to assess the likely trends in employment distributions in the future. These projections include rate of growth or decline in employment predicted for industries. The rates of change in employment projected for each industrial category through 2010 (see Berman, 2001) suggest the following:

• Of the industries with high current numbers of older workers, none, except business-auto services, rank in the top four in terms of projected employment growth. In addition, of the other three, only educational services has a projected growth rate above the median for industries.

• Of the industries with a high within-industry percentage of older workers, none ranks in the top four in terms of employment growth. Declines in employment in mining and forestry/fishing/trapping are projected; growth in educational services is projected to be above the median; and growth in public administration is projected to be below the median.

• The four industrial categories projected to show the greatest growth in employment through 2010 are business-auto services, other personal services, other (not hospital) medical services, and social services. Of these, a relatively high proportion of social service workers and educational service workers are older female workers, while only business-auto services has around the median proportion of older male workers; the rest are lower.

• The two industrial categories showing projected decline in employment (mining and forestry/fishing/trapping) are older-worker-intensive in that a relatively large percentage of workers in these industries are older workers (mostly males).

Overall, then, it can be predicted that older-worker-intensive industries will experience moderate growth in employment over this decade. On that account, and on account of the predicted growth in the older worker labor force over this period (with shifts also toward a greater percentage of workers being older workers), we can predict that there will be more older workers in the older-worker-intensive industries in 2010, and that (except for mining and forestry/fishing/trapping) there will not likely be dramatic change in employment in industries that are older-worker intensive.

The industries projected to show highest growth in employment through 2010 are all service industries: business-auto services, personal services, other (not hospital) medical services, and social services. These are, for the most part, not currently older-worker intensive (except social services for older female workers). These will have to be examined carefully in the future to determine whether their growth will prove important with respect to participation of older workers.

Older-Worker-Intensive Occupations

Number of older workers. In which occupational categories are the greatest number of older workers employed, and which, therefore, employ the greatest percentage of older workers? Table 2-8 uses data from the CPS for March 2001 to present overall employment by major occupational category along with the total employment levels for workers age 45 years and older stratified by sex. The four occupational categories with the greatest number of older workers are executive/administrative/managerial; professional specialty; sales; and administrative support. When examined by sex, the first two categories are still the largest for both sexes. Subsequently we see segregation of jobs by sex with the sales category high for males but not females and the administrative support category high for females but not for males. Reflecting similar findings when employment is examined by industry, the fourth important category for males is employment in jobs

TABLE 2-8 Distribution of Older Workers Across Major Occupational Categories

Industry	Employed Workers Age 16 and Older		Employed Workers Age 45 and Older		
	Total[a]	Percent	Total[a]	Female[a]	Male[a]
Professional specialty	21,610	16.0	8,490	4,530	3,970
Technicians	4,490	3.3	1,410	750	660
Sales	16,090	11.9	5,480	2,550	2,930
Administrative support	18,890	14.0	6,970	5,630	1,340
Private household service	820	0.06	310	290	20
Protective service	2,360	1.7	790	160	630
Other services	15,270	11.3	4,400	3,010	1,390
Precision production/craft/repair	14,670	10.9	5,110	500	4,610
Machine operators, assemblers, inspectors	6,910	5.1	2,480	1,080	1,400
Transportation and material moving	5,630	4.2	2,180	220	1,960
Handlers, helpers, laborers	5,220	3.9	1,190	330	860
Farming/forestry/fishing	3,020	2.2	1,270	300	970

[a]Numbers in thousands.
SOURCE: CPS March 2001.

requiring physical skills—production/craft/repair—while the fourth important category for females is service-related-other services.

Proportionate distribution of older workers. What proportion of workers within a given occupation are older workers? Proportional employment data for workers over age 45 in 2001 are provided, stratified by major occupational category, in Table A-5 using the same CPS survey data for March 2001. Table A-5 shows the percentage of all employed persons who are older workers employed in the occupation, the percentage of all older workers employed in the given occupation, and the percentage of all workers in a given occupation who are older workers.

Focusing on the overall older worker population, two of the four proportionately largest occupations for older workers—executive/administrative/managerial and professional specialty categories—are the same that were seen when numbers of older workforce were examined (Table 2-8). The other proportionately large categories are transportation and material moving, and farming/forestry/fishing. Stratified by sex, evidence for occupation segregation is again present—there are no overlapping categories. Females apparently make up an important proportion of one of the four largest occupational groups for older workers—professional specialty—

while the three other proportionately high occupational categories for females are all service-related (administrative support, private household service, and services–other). By contrast, males make up a large part of two different largest occupational groups for older workers: transportation and material moving, and farming/forestry/fishing. The two other highest proportion male occupations are new (precision production/craft/repair and protective services). Only one of the four is a service occupation.

Determining older-worker-intensive occupations is, as with industries, predicated on the question asked and whether gender is of interest, and some patterns emerge. In addition, the occupational categories examined here are broadly defined. There may be differences (which should be researched, particularly to determine the within-occupation variance) at more detailed levels within categories.

Anticipated changes in employment for older workers. Older-worker-intensive occupations can also be examined in terms of projections of future trends. BLS projections of growth or decline in occupational categories have been described by Hecker (2001). Examining the rate of change in employment projected for each occupational category through 2010 suggests the following:

• Of the occupations highlighted above on the basis of high current numbers of older workers the projected rate of employment growth is high only for professional specialty. The other three occupations have projected growth rates below the median.
• For the additional occupations highlighted above on the basis of within-occupation percentage of older workers (for older workers overall and for older male workers: transportation and material moving; for older female workers: private household service; and for older male workers: protective services) projected employment growth is among the highest. All but one are service occupations.
• The occupational categories projected to show the greatest growth in employment through 2010 are protective services, professional specialty, private household services, and other services. Each of these is highlighted as older-worker intensive by one or both of the questions posed above.

Overall, then, it can be predicted that older-worker-intensive occupations will experience high growth in employment over this decade. On that account, and on account of the predicted growth in the older worker labor force over this period (with shifts also toward a greater percentage of workers being older workers), we can predict that there will be more older workers in the older-worker-intensive occupations in 2010.

HEALTH AND JOB CHARACTERISTICS
AMONG OLDER WORKERS

It is important to have information on the current job activities of older workers to better understand on a population basis the nature and challenges of their workplaces, as well as worker health and functional status in these work environments. Several important national surveys offer many elements of this information, including databases supported and conducted by federal agencies. However, many focus on specific dimensions of this activity and do not contain information on work status, job characteristics, and health and economic status in the same individuals. One national survey that offers information on many of these domains is the Health and Retirement Study (HRS), an ongoing panel study of approximately 20,000 older Americans (Health and Retirement Study, 2004), sponsored by the U.S. National Institute on Aging. The HRS is a representative sample of the older American population with both telephone and in-person surveys conducted every two years.

The National Health Interview Survey (NHIS) offers some additional information about the age and health characteristics of workers; detailed work characteristics were obtained primarily in the survey supplement obtained in 1988. Since the NHIS survey covers all of the civilian noninstitutionalized population, it provides a somewhat different window through which to observe older workers.

In the following data from the 1998 HRS survey (detailed data are presented in Tables A-6 through A-10 in Appendix A), national prevalence estimates (expressed as percentages) are weighted to reflect oversampling of census tracts containing high minority populations and of the state of Florida; all information is based on self-report. The data show that about 40 percent of persons over 50 years of age are working, ranging from 65.4 percent among those 51–64 years, to 6.6 percent of those 75 years and older. Women over 50 years of age are much less likely to be working than men or to have never worked. Only about 1 percent are either temporarily off work or unemployed and looking for work.

Complementary estimates (Wagener et al., 1997), albeit with a different age distribution, reflecting earlier (1993) NHIS data are that of the overall adult population: 58 percent of women and 76 percent of men were employed at the time of the survey. Among women between the ages of 45 and 64, and age 65 and over, there were 62 percent and 10 percent, respectively, employed. For men the same age groupings had 80 percent and 17 percent, respectively.

The HRS data showing selected work characteristics among older workers indicated that nearly one-fourth were self-employed, and three-fourths were working full time (more than 35 hours per week). About a third had the ability to reduce their hours at their own discretion. Fewer than 20 percent were in supervisory positions. Considering reported job characteristics and demands reported by current workers, a substantial proportion of the jobs required physical effort, heavy lifting, and kneeling or stooping. Job physical demands were lower for workers at higher ages. Nearly all required good eyesight, intense concentration, and skills for interacting with people. Nearly half reported that the job was more difficult than it used to be, and over half reported a lot of stress. Despite this, nearly 90 percent reported that they enjoyed going to work.

Considering the functional status of current workers over 50 years of age, overall, the rates of reported difficulty with a wide variety of physical functions was relatively low, with rates of difficulty ranging from 2 percent for fine motor functions (e.g., picking up a dime from the table) to 27.3 percent for more gross motor functions (e.g., stooping, crouching, and kneeling). Rates of difficulty generally increased with age and were more prevalent among men than women. While not shown, these rates are somewhat lower than among nonworkers. In general, lower extremity difficulties were more common than upper extremity or fine motor difficulties.

The HRS data also indicated the prevalence rates for reported chronic illnesses or disorders, overall health status, difficulties with activities of daily living, and the presence of health insurance for both workers and nonworkers. With respect to major chronic illnesses or disorders, such as a history of heart attack, stroke, hypertension, diabetes mellitus, chronic lung disease or hip fracture, older workers clearly reported fewer than nonworkers, although two-thirds of the workers report at least one major condition. Overall self-assessed health status was also reported to be much better among workers than nonworkers, although about 15 percent of workers reported their health to be fair or poor. Few reported difficulty with activities of daily living (basic self-care activities such as dressing, bathing, and grooming), although the rates were higher among nonworkers. Nearly 16 percent of workers 51–64 years did not have health insurance, but nearly all of those 65 years and above did report insurance, largely because of Medicare coverage.

Overall self-reported health status of currently employed individuals is also provided by Wagener et al. (1997), who indicate that older women who are currently employed are more likely to report being in better health than males of equivalent ages.

The 1988 NHIS survey also collected details of work-related symptoms or disorders. Work-related back pain due to accidents was not common and was twice as likely to occur in men (4.4 percent of women and 9.2 percent of men) while work-related back pain attributed to repeated activities was much more common (20 percent of women and 28 percent of men). The prevalence of neither self-reported condition varied substantially by age. Those 65 or older, however, did have lower prevalence of work-related back pain due to repeated activities (Wagener et al., 1997). Job change, altered job activities, or ceasing work due to back pain, regardless of cause, occurred among approximately 20 percent of both women and men. Women were more likely to change jobs or stop working after age 65.

Combining HRS and NHIS data suggests, then, that the majority of Americans 51–65 years in 1998 were still working, although sometimes at a second career. A substantial proportion were continuing to work after conventional retirement ages of 60–65 years. Women were less likely to be working than men, but this may change in subsequent cohorts. Jobs among workers over age 50 were reported to contain many physical and emotional challenges and stresses, but most workers reported that they enjoyed going to work. As expected, older workers as a group were healthier and more functional than their nonworking counterparts, but a majority reported at least one chronic illness or disorder, suggesting that these conditions in general did not substantially interfere with job functions, but they did point to a higher risk of future illness or disorder and disability. About 15 percent of workers reported their health status as being fair or poor, possibly leading to risk of job loss and progression of illness or disorder. About 16 percent of workers 51–65 years reported that they did not have health insurance of any type; over 80 percent were receiving such insurance from their employers. This has implications for access to health services in this age group.

3

The Role of the Changing Labor Market and the Changing Nature of Work in Older Workers' Work Experiences and Health Outcomes

CHANGES IN THE LABOR MARKET

In the past century, the median income of Americans has increased substantially, many aspects of their working conditions have improved, and their average life span has increased (Council of Economic Advisors, 2002). Nevertheless, some recent economic and workplace trends raise concerns about the health and safety of older American workers. Income growth has been uneven across the income distribution, and while the health and safety conditions of workers in some occupations and industries have improved, this has not been the case for all workers. For instance, as we discuss in Chapter 6, changes in the nature of work (increases in stressful job characteristics and work organization) are associated with increased risk of cardiovascular disease and other illnesses or disorders commonly experienced at older ages. Unfortunately, there is limited evidence on how these trends are affecting the health and safety of older workers. More generally, there is controversy over the validity of the illness or disorder and injury data that we now collect to measure these trends (see Chapter 6).

Important changes in the structure of the American economy over the past several decades have affected older workers' occupational distribution, income, availability of retirement and disability benefits, job security, union membership, and, potentially, their health and safety. Employment in the United States has gradually shifted from the production of goods to the service-producing industries (U.S. Bureau of Labor Statistics [BLS], 2003). Employment relations have become more flexible, or more precarious, depending upon one's point of view (Kalleberg et al., 1997; Standing, 1999). Deregulation, increasing reliance on voluntary standards, privatization of government services, and an emphasis on market forces to meet societal needs are all key aspects of a new American economy, which has grown substantially and increased employment, especially over the last decade of the 20th century, but has resulted in workplaces that still contain substantial health risks for some workers (Levenstein and Wooding, 1997).

Shift to Service Industry Employment

In the mid-20th century, about a third of the American workforce was employed in manufacturing. Today, not much more than a tenth are so employed. About 80 percent of the workforce is in the service sector. In the economic downturn after 2000, about 10 percent of manufacturing workers lost their jobs—about 1.9 million workers. On the other hand, service industry employment has continued to increase by almost 2 percent (BLS, 2003).

Table 3-1 shows the occupations with the largest expected job growth between 2000 and 2010 (Hecker, 2001). The large, high-growth occupations include a disproportionate share of low-wage service sector jobs, and 60 percent of these high-growth occupations are in the lowest quartile of median hourly earnings. However, many smaller occupations that require advanced training and pay high wages will also expand. Hence, the skill distribution of the future workforce is likely to increase somewhat faster at the high and low ends than in the middle.

These trends have important implications not only for income but for benefits received by older workers, including health and retirement benefits. For instance, after substantial increases in employer pension coverage from the end of World War II to the 1980s, primarily obtained through collective bargaining, pension coverage has remained constant at about 50 percent for all workers. Also, a significant percentage of workers are still not covered by employer health insurance. The end of this trend toward growing pension and health coverage was due in part to the shift of jobs from more heavily unionized manufacturing industries to service industries.

Nonstandard, Alternative, and Precarious Employment

One aspect of increased employment flexibility is the rise in nonstandard, alternative, or precarious work arrangements. Such arrangements include employment for a temporary help agency or contract company, independent contracting, on-call work, day labor, and several forms of self-employment (National Research Council, 1999). Nonstandard workers typically receive lower wages (or salaries) and fewer health and retirement benefits than

TABLE 3-1 Occupations with the Largest Expected Job Growth Between 2000 and 2010

Occupation	Employment	
	2000	2010
1. Combined food preparation and serving workers, including fast food	2,206	2,879
2. Customer service representatives	1,946	2,577
3. Registered nurses	2,194	2,755
4. Retail salespersons	4,109	4,619
5. Computer support specialists	506	996
6. Cashiers, except gaming	3,325	3,799
7. Office clerks, general	2,705	3,135
8. Security guards	1,106	1,497
9. Computer software engineers, applications	380	760
10. Waiters and waitresses	1,983	2,347

[a]The quartile rankings of Occupational Employment Statistics annual earnings data are presented in the following categories: 1 = very high ($39,700 and over); 2 = high ($25,760 to $39,660); 3 = low ($18,500 to $25,760); 4 = very low (up to $18,490). The rankings were based on quartiles using one-fourth of total employment to define each quartile. Earnings are for wage and salary workers.
SOURCE: Constructed by Labor Research Associates from Bureau of Labor Statistics data.

workers with similar skills who work as full-time, regular employees (Houseman, 2001; Mishel, Bernstein, and Boushey, 2003). Older workers are more likely than younger workers to be employed as independent contractors and other kinds of self-employment (Houseman, 2001). On the other hand, workers between ages 45 and 64 are less likely than younger workers to be employed in a precarious forms of nonstandard employment, including employment as agency temporaries, day laborers, contract company workers, and temporary employees. Workers who are 65 and older are more likely to work in nearly all forms of nonstandard employment.

While available data suggest that nonstandard employment has been increasing in a number of advanced industrialized countries (Quinlan and Mayhew, 2000), the long-term trends are difficult to assess in the United States because comprehensive surveys such as the Contingent Work Supplements to the Current Population Survey are not available before 1995. During the economic expansion between 1995 and 2001 the proportion of

Change		Quartile Rank by 2000 Median	
Number	Percent	Hourly Earnings[a]	Education and Training Category
673	30	4	Short-term on-the-job training
631	32	3	Moderate-term on-the-job training
561	26	1	Associate degree
510	12	4	Short-term on-the-job training
490	97	2	Associate degree
474	14	4	Short-term on-the-job training
430	16	3	Short-term on-the-job training
391	35	4	Short-term on-the-job training
380	100	1	Bachelor's degree
364	18	4	Short-term on-the-job training

U.S. workers in all nonstandard work arrangements (including part-time employment) declined, falling from 25.3 percent to 23.0 percent among men and from 34.3 percent to 31.0 percent among women. However, the proportion rose during the following recession (Mishel, Bernstein, and Boushey, 2003). One possible indication of the longer-term trend in nonstandard work arrangements is the rising fraction of workers who are employed in the personnel supply services industry. The proportion of employees on nonfarm payrolls who work in this industry rose from 0.3 percent in 1973 to 3.2 percent in 2001, although, as noted above, workers between ages 45 and 64 are less likely than younger workers to obtain employment in this industry (Houseman, 2001; Mishel et al., 2003).

The increased use of temporary employees and the practice of contracting out pose challenges for the protection of worker health and safety. A study of contractors in the petrochemical industry showed substantial deficits in the health and safety practices applied to contract workers, deficits that may have played a part in the promulgation of the OSHA's Process Safety Standard (Wells, Kochan, and Smith, 1991).

Trade Union Density

Another feature of the U.S. labor market is the decline in trade union membership among nonagricultural employees from 24.1 percent in 1947 to 13.6 percent in 2000 (Hirsch, Macpherson, and Vroman, 2001). By 2001, only 9 percent of private sector workers were union members (BLS, 2000). This reduced the significance of negotiated work rules, including seniority rules. However, the net effect of the decline in unionization—and the consequently greater control over the workplace environment given to management—on the health and safety of older workers, especially their potential loss of seniority protection, is not clear and should be investigated (Standing, 1999; Weil, 1991).

Immigration

Because of its high level of immigration, the United States may have a relatively younger age structure compared to other industrialized nations (Gibson and Lennon, 1999). On the other hand, as immigrant workers grow older and settle in the United States, problems of racial and ethnic discrimination may be compounded by age discrimination. The lack of attention to the health and safety needs of minority workers may pose problems for U.S. industry (Azaroff and Levenstein, 2002). To the extent age dimensions of such problems have been studied, the focus has been on young workers.

Trends in Income and Income Inequality

The consequences of the changing labor market structure on family income are significant. While real median family income grew from 2.8 percent annually between 1947 and 1973, annual growth slowed to 0.2 percent per year between 1973 and 1995. Over the latter period income inequality also increased (Mishel et al., 2003). The United States has greater income inequality than other industrialized countries, and its level of in-equality rose sharply over the 1980s business cycle (1979–1989). However, the rise in income inequality was slower over the 1990s business cycle (1989–2000), as the growth of real income for low- and middle-income families outpaced that of upper-income families during the boom years of the late 1990s. Despite this economic boom, hourly wages for men in the bottom half of the income distribution were lower in 2001 than in 1979 (Mishel et al., 2003). In addition, income inequality began to rise again as the U.S. economy moved into an economic downturn after 2000.

A debate is now ongoing in the health literature with respect to the importance of income and income inequality on health outcomes. As discussed in more detail in Chapter 4, income is associated with health outcomes, and a health gradient has been found in many countries. (Lower income persons have worse health outcomes than higher income persons.) Hence, an increase in income over time should improve health outcomes. But if proportional increases in income occur at higher rates for higher income parts of the income distribution, they are also likely to increase inequality in health outcomes, others things equal. Furthermore, it is argued by some that income inequality itself has an independent negative effect on the health outcomes of lower income people. (See Kaplan et al., 1996, and Deaton, 2003, for divergent views on the relative importance of income, poverty, and income inequality on health outcomes.) It is difficult to disentangle the net effect of increases in income (in many groups) and in income inequality on the health outcomes of Americans in general and older Americans in particular. This is especially the case since serious questions have been raised about the validity of current (nonmortality-based) illness or disorder and injury data in the United States (see Chapter 6).

THE CHANGING NATURE OF WORK

Trends in Working Life

Throughout the developed world, economic growth has been accompanied by some of the same trends in income inequality and in the nature of work that are occurring in the United States. This phenomenon may be affecting the health of workers, particularly those with lower socioeconomic status (SES) (Deaton, 2003; Gabriel and Liimatainen, 2000; Landsbergis, 2003; Singh and Siahpush, 2002; Tuchsen and Endahl, 1999; Subramanian, Blakely, and Kawachi, 2003). A report of the National Research Council (1999) describes features of the changing nature of work such as organizational restructuring, downsizing, declines in unionization, flatter organizational hierarchies, increasing job insecurity and instability, teamwork, and nonstandard work arrangements. The report noted that these changes appear to lead to decreased employee morale, but the report did not examine health and safety effects of the changing nature of work. While initially developed in manufacturing, new forms of work organization are increasingly seen in other sectors of the economy (Landsbergis, 2003; Landsbergis, Cahill, and Schnall, 1999; "The Tokyo Declaration," 1998). These trends have been described by NIOSH (National Institute for Occupational Safety and Health, 2002) and are summarized in "The Tokyo Declaration," a 1998 consensus document produced by occupational health experts from the European Union, Japan, and the United States. Research is needed to determine to what extent and how these changes in work organization affect the health and safety of older workers. For further information, see the website: http://www.workhealth.org/news/tokyo.html.

Trends in Work Hours

Average weekly and annual hours worked fell for many decades in the United States through the early 1970s, but they have largely stabilized since then. However, the proportion of women who work for pay and who are employed in year-round jobs has continued to rise (Rones, Ilg, and Gardner, 1997). Between 1976 and 1993, total annual hours for men increased by 5.5 percent and for women by 18.0 percent. After age adjustment, these increases were 3.4 percent and 14.9 percent, respectively (Rones et al., 1997). Between 1979 and 2000, for married couple families with children, with heads of household aged 25–54, total annual hours increased by 11.6 percent (Mishel et al., 2003).

It is certainly true that employed Americans are engaged in paid work for more hours each year than is the case in most other industrialized countries. Only workers in Japan are typically employed for approximately as many hours as Americans, and the average work week and work year in Japan have recently been falling. International Labour Office (ILO) statistics suggest that Americans now have a longer work year than workers in other rich countries (ILO, 2001). For example, employed Americans work about 200–400 more hours (or 5–10 more weeks) per year than workers in France, Germany, Sweden, or Denmark (OECD, 2002). The growing gap between typical hours in the United States and in other rich countries is mainly the result of declining average hours in the rest of the world. While greatly excessive working hours have been associated with adverse health outcomes, it is not known how many hours are too many. A better understanding of the age-specific effects of working hours over short (weekly) and long (annual) intervals will require better information on trends in different patterns of working hours by age, gender, race, and socioeconomic status.

The trends in employment rates and in weekly hours at work among older Americans are displayed in Table 3-2. The top panel in the table shows hours and employment trends among adults of both sexes. Columns 1 and 4 show average weekly hours among employed persons who reported working at least one hour per week in March 1979 and March 2001, respectively. Columns 2 and 5 show the percentages of all adults in each age category who worked at least one hour per week; columns 3 and 6 show the actual percentages holding a job. (Because of vacations or sickness, some employed people did not work during the survey week.) Columns 7 and 8 show the change in weekly hours and the change in the fraction of people who were employed between 1979 and 2001. The top panel in the table shows little consistent trend in the average weekly number of hours worked by older Americans, except among workers past the age of 65, where there is a consistent pattern of increase in weekly hours. However, the proportion of older Americans in employment has increased noticeably, particularly for adults between ages 45 and 59. As shown in the bottom two panels of Table 3-2, the rise in employment was driven by a substantial increase in the fraction of older women who work, which more than offset a smaller decline in employment among 45- to 64-year-old men. Moreover, the average work week of employed women also rose, fueled by a decline in the proportion of working women who are employed on part-time schedules. The most significant trend revealed in Table 3-2 is the marked convergence of men's and women's life-cycle pattern of labor supply. American women are now far more likely to hold jobs through the traditional job-leaving age than they were in 1979. In contrast, male employment rates have modestly declined. While average weekly hours have been stable, between 1976 and 1993, an increasing proportion of men (from 14.7 percent to 20.6 percent), age 55 or older, were working long work weeks (49 hours or more). For older working women, the proportion increased from 4.9 percent to 7.9 percent (Rones et al., 1997). Whether this trend is continuing needs to be determined.

Trends in Job Characteristics

Workers in developed countries have experienced substantial changes in psychosocial job characteristics over the past generation. In Europe, surveys indicate increases in time constraints (i.e., time pressures or workload demands) between 1977 and 2000 (European Foundation, 2000). Similarly, in the United States, increases between 1977 and 1997 were reported for "working very fast" (from 55 percent to 68 percent) and "never enough time to get everything done on my job" (from 40 percent to 60 percent) (Bond, Galinsky, and Swanberg, 1997). U.S. findings are based on the 1977 Quality of Employment Surveys (Quinn and Staines, 1979) and the 1997 National Surveys of the Changing Workforce (Bond, Galinsky, and Swanburg, 1998). Somewhat increased job decision latitude or job control was also reported in these surveys. In Europe, the proportion of workers reporting a measure of autonomy over their pace of work increased from 64 percent in 1991 to 72 percent in 1996 (Walters, 1998). In the United States, "freedom to decide what I do on my job" increased from 56 percent in 1977 to 74 percent in 1997 and "my job lets me use my skills and

TABLE 3-2 Employment and Average Hours of Work Among Older Americans, March 1979 and March 2001

| Age Group | March 1979 | | |
	Average Hours Last Week at All Jobs for Those With at Least One Hour of Work	Percentage of Population With Positive Hours	Percentage of Population Employed
Both sexes			
45–49	41.1	71	74
50–54	40.7	67	70
55–59	40.6	59	62
60–64	38.5	44	46
65–69	30.7	19	21
70–74	25.8	11	12
75+	24.3	5	5
Male			
45–49	44.7	86	90
50–54	44.4	83	87
55–59	43.6	75	78
60–64	41.5	57	61
65–69	32.7	26	28
70–74	27.3	17	19
75+	24.9	8	9
Female			
45–49	36.1	56	58
50–54	35.4	52	54
55–59	36.1	46	48
60–64	33.7	32	34
65–69	27.7	14	15
70–74	23.2	7	8
75+	23.2	3	3

SOURCE: Tabulation of March 1979 and March 2001 Current Population Survey files.

March 2001			Change 1979–2001	
Average Hours Last Week at All Jobs for Those With at Least One Hour of Work	Percentage of Population With Positive Hours	Percentage of Population Employed	Change in Average Hours per Week Among Employed Population	Change in Fraction of Population Employed
41.4	79	82	0.3	8
41.5	75	78	0.8	8
40.4	65	67	−0.2	5
37.4	46	48	−1.1	2
31.6	23	24	0.9	4
27.1	14	15	1.3	2
29.0	5	5	4.7	0
44.2	84	87	−0.5	−4
44.4	82	85	0.0	−2
43.2	72	74	−0.4	−4
40.5	52	56	−1.0	−6
34.1	28	30	1.4	2
29.1	17	18	1.8	0
30.2	8	9	5.3	0
38.4	74	77	2.3	19
38.3	70	73	3.0	19
37.3	58	61	1.2	13
33.8	40	42	0.1	8
28.0	18	19	0.3	4
24.7	11	12	1.5	4
26.6	3	3	3.4	0

abilities" increased from 77 percent in 1977 to 92 percent in 1997 (Bond et al., 1997).[1]

A combination of high job demands and low job control has been called job strain or high-strain work—an important risk factor for hypertension and cardiovascular disease (Schnall et al., 2000), a common cause of disability among older workers (Ilmarinen, 1997). In theory, since job control appears to buffer or moderate the effects of job demands on risk of stress-related illness or disorder, increases in job control reported in the European and U.S. surveys might compensate for the increases in job demands. On the other hand, there may be a limit to the buffering effects of job control. Job strain was not analyzed in the U.S. surveys. In Europe, increases in autonomy were not sufficient to compensate for increased work intensity. The proportion of high-strain jobs in Europe increased from about 25 percent in 1991 to about 30 percent in 1996 (European Foundation, 1997).

European Foundation surveys in 2000 show continuing increases in work intensity and job demands (working at very high speed and to tight deadlines); however, increases in job control or autonomy before 1995 have leveled off or are declining slightly (Paoli and Merllié, 2001). This suggests that the prevalence of job strain has continued to increase in Europe, a trend with the potential effect of increasing risk of hypertension and heart disease.

These trends may also vary by social class, although very little data are available to test this hypothesis. Analyses of national Swedish surveys that combine questions on hectic and monotonous work, as a proxy measure for high-demand, low-control work or job strain, show only a slight increase, from about 9 percent to 11 percent, between 1992 and 2000 for all workers. During 1992, the Swedish economy experienced a major recession. Between 1992 and 2000, among low-income and blue-collar workers, prevalence of hectic or monotonous work increased to a much greater degree, from about 12 to 20 percent (Vogel, 2002). Unfortunately, there are few data available on trends in job characteristics by age group in Europe or the United States.

---

[1]A number of limitations of the 1997 Work and Families Institute Survey suggest that it may underestimate the increase in job strain since 1977. First, the survey excluded anyone who did not have a phone, and the response rate was much lower than the 1977 survey. Only three demands and six decision latitude items were available, not the full Job Content Questionnaire (Karasek et al., 1998). More importantly, the 1977–1997 comparison data file excluded self-employed, contract, or contingent workers—it included only wage and salary workers. The self-employed contingent group was larger in 1997 than 1977. That group was also more likely to have job strain, leading to underestimates of increases in job strain. In addition, today, there are many more undocumented immigrant workers in the United States doing hazardous, high-strain work, a group not likely to have participated in the surveys.

The negative effect of increases in job strain have not been reflected in measures of injuries and illnesses or disorders in the workplace calculated each year by the BLS (see Chapter 6) or by measures of impairment or function in more general datasets that are used to track heath outcomes of older Americans (Manton, Corder, and Stallard, 1993, 1997; Crimmins, Reynolds, and Saito, 1999). Also, they have not been sufficient to offset the factors that are improving age-constant mortality rates, such as improvements in medical care, increasing income for many groups, and exportation of hazardous industries. However, BLS data greatly underestimates the extent of work-related illnesses or disorders (National Research Council, 1987; Landrigan and Baker, 1991; Biddle et al., 1998; Rosenman et al., 2000). In addition, as noted in Chapter 6, the extent of underreporting injuries and illnesses or disorders may be increasing (Conway and Svenson, 1998; Azaroff and Levenstein, 2002). Analysis of data on impairment of function is only currently available through 1994. Therefore, it is unclear to what degree the negative trends in job characteristics and work organization discussed are offset by improvements in other risk factors, both within and outside the workplace, which may even be leading to reductions in overall rates of injuries and illnesses or disorders. Since stress-related chronic diseases such as cardiovascular disease and hypertension take years to develop, it will be necessary to improve existing data systems in order to provide valid data on trends in work-related injuries and illnesses or disorders.

Development of New Systems of Work Organization

Paralleling these trends in work hours and job characteristics, new systems of work organization have been introduced by employers throughout the industrialized world to improve productivity, product quality, and profitability. Such efforts have taken a variety of forms and names, including lean production, total quality management (TQM), team concept, cellular or modular manufacturing, reengineering, high-performance work organizations, and patient-focused care (Landsbergis, 2003; Landsbergis et al., 1999). These new systems have been presented as reforms of Taylorism and the traditional assembly-line approach to job design (Womack, Jones, and Roos, 1990). About half of U.S. manufacturing facilities use some innovative work practice, such as job rotation, work teams, quality circles (QCs), or TQM (Osterman, 1994).

Manufacturing

While these new systems increase worker productivity and contribute to economic growth, they are likely to contain features that increase job stress and that may affect worker health. Lean production combines diverse elements of Japanese production management (Babson, 1995); it is an attempt to reduce impediments to the smooth flow of production through continuous improvement in productivity and quality, just-in-time (JIT) inventory systems, and elimination of wasted time and motion (Appelbaum and Batt, 1994). Small teams of hourly workers, or quality circles (QCs), meet to solve quality and productivity problems.

A 1990 report (Womack et al.) argued that in the best Japanese auto companies, by rotating jobs and sharing responsibilities, multiskilled workers can solve quality problems at their source and boost productivity; that this results in freedom to control one's work, which replaces the "mind-numbing stress" of mass production; that armed with the skills they need to control their environment, workers in a lean plant have the opportunity to think proactively to solve workplace problems; and that this creative tension makes work humanly fulfilling. If such claims of increased worker skills and decision-making authority are true, then such programs could reduce job strain and stress-related illness or disorder.

Lean production provides for more job enlargement, cross training, and problem-solving opportunities than traditional manufacturing job design (Appelbaum and Batt, 1994). However, QCs are not online autonomous work teams, nor are they empowered to make managerial decisions, in contrast to self-directed or semi-autonomous work teams typical of Scandinavian sociotechnical systems design (Appelbaum and Batt, 1994). Lean production also leaves traditional organizational hierarchy and the assembly line essentially unchanged (Appelbaum and Batt, 1994; Babson, 1993, 1995). Cycle time for job tasks typically remains very short (often one minute or less in auto assembly). Mandatory procedures require that workers follow highly standardized steps at narrowly defined tasks (Berggren, Bjorkman, and Hollander, 1991; Bjorkman, 1996). Reliance is placed on industrial engineering, time studies, and predetermined standards to ensure maximum workloads (Adler, Goldoftas, and Levine, 1997). JIT inventory systems remove the stock between operations that acts as buffers in the system and also removes any free time the worker may have previously enjoyed while the machine ran through its cycle (Delbridge, Turnbull, and Wilkinson, 1993: 66), leading to more strictures on a worker's time and action (Klein, 1991). Thereby, workers' personal time and flexibility become the buffers (Delbridge and Wilkinson, 1995; Johnson, 1997; Lewchuk and Robertson, 1996).

In Canadian and U.S. studies of lean production in auto manufacturing, job demands were often reported to be elevated (Lewchuk and Robertson, 1996). For example, at a Michigan assembly plant, in 1991, 73 percent of workers surveyed reported "I will likely be injured or worn out before I retire" (Babson, 1993). British auto parts employees reported slightly less workload if they participated in the implementation of a lean system, but a significant increase in workload if they did not participate (Parker, Myers, and Wall, 1995). Lean production practices may lead to reduced availability of lighter duty jobs for older workers (Lewchuk and Robertson, 1996).

Low or decreasing decision authority was also reported in many cases, including a decline in participation in decisionmaking and influence over the job over time as new systems were implemented (Babson, 1993; Parker and Sprigg, 1998; Robertson et al., 1993). The promise of producing highly trained, multiskilled workers was also challenged by Canadian and U.S. (Babson, 1993; Robertson et al., 1993) and British (Parker and Sprigg, 1998) survey data.

Some alternative new work systems, jointly bargained for by management and labor, have been labeled high-performance work organizations. However, little research has been conducted on the health and safety effects of such systems. One example is a Michigan auto plant where 71 percent of workers report having benefited from the team concept and, on average, report a slight decrease in perceived stress since the program began (Kaminski, 1996). Workers provided input to the design of the new system before it was put in place, team leaders were elected, teams could schedule personal and vacation time, the union monitored overtime and seniority rights, and the new system was written into contract language and ratified overwhelmingly (Kaminski, 1996).

In the U.S. garment industry, the traditional (and still widely used) production process is the bundle system (Bailey, 1993; Berg et al., 1996). Inventories are stored in bundles of about 30 cut garment parts each. Operators perform one task, such as sewing a hem, on each piece in the bundle, which often takes only a few seconds (Bailey, 1993; Batt and Appelbaum, 1995). The fragmented, repetitive work combined with piece-rate payment leads to high rates of work-related musculoskeletal disorders (WRMDs) (Brisson et al., 1989; Punnett et al., 1985; Schibye et al., 1995). In a new work system known as modular manufacturing, teams of multi-skilled operators assemble an entire garment with reduced supervision and are involved in quality control, machine maintenance, and sometimes in setting and meeting group goals (Bailey, 1993). Piece-rate wages are replaced by an hourly wage with a group bonus (Berg et al., 1996). Modular workers reported greater skill use, but also increased perceived stress and no difference in job satisfaction compared to bundle workers (Berg et al., 1996). Worker teams or job redesign (to create more task identity and significance) were significantly associated with satisfaction; however, increased workload or stress or both were associated with reduced satisfaction. There was no net gain in satisfaction for modular workers (Batt and Appelbaum, 1995). Notably, 38 percent of textile sewing machine operators are 45 years of age or older, greater than the average of 34 percent for all jobs (Dohm, 2000).

Similar new work systems have also been implemented outside of manufacturing in industries such as telecommunications and health care.

Telecommunications

Little effect of self-managed teams on unionized customer service work has been found. However, unionized installation and repair workers reported significantly more job satisfaction, autonomy, coworker support, days of training, and advancement opportunities relative to workers in traditionally managed, highly skilled craft jobs. Their job satisfaction was significantly associated with online participation (e.g., greater autonomy) but not with offline participation (e.g., quality of work life, TQM, problem-solving teams) (Batt and Appelbaum, 1995). Forty-nine percent of telephone installers and repairers are 45 years of age or older, greater than the average of 34 percent for all jobs (Dohm, 2000).

Health Care Industry

In the U.S. health care industry, two forms of work restructuring introduced in the 1990s have been studied. First, patient-focused care, based on TQM, uses cross-trained multiskilled teams, with fewer individual job categories, decentralized ancillary services, and computers to reduce case recording time. Registered nurses (RNs) manage teams, but fewer RNs are needed because lower paid, unlicensed generic health care workers undertake some direct care (Richardson, 1994; Sochalski, Aiken, and Fagin, 1997). Second, operations improvement seeks rapid cost savings by reducing the number of RNs and replacing them with nurses' aides (Greiner, 1995). These two new approaches are replacing a system developed in 1970s, known as primary nursing (Brannon, 1996), professional nurse practice models, or magnet hospitals. These older models featured RN autonomy and control over clinical practice and decentralized decisionmaking (Aiken, Sloane, and Klocinski, 1997; Kramer and Schmalenberg, 1988; McClure et al., 1983). Cost containment efforts have led to longer hours of work and increased stress among nurses and have contributed to a nursing shortage (Joint Commission on Accreditation of Healthcare Organizations, 2002). Thirty-nine percent of registered nurses are 45 years of age or older, greater than the average of 34 percent for all jobs (Dohm, 2000).

As discussed above, it is unclear to what degree the increased health and safety risks associated with some new systems of work organization (further detailed in Chapter 6) will affect more general trends in health and safety in the workplace or in the overall (nonmortality-based) health of Americans. Current data are insufficient for us to know if the specific negative outcomes are of sufficient importance in the general economy to significantly affect overall (nonmortality) injury and illness or disorder trends.

Monitoring Job Conditions

Several decades ago the U.S. Department of Labor sponsored the Quality of Employment Survey (QES), which used a nationally representative sample of the workforce to characterize and track features of work. NIOSH added a module to these surveys in 1977 to assess job stress (Murphy, 2002). The surveys offered a unique resource for policy and for research. For example, Karasek et al. (1998) used the survey instrument and findings to develop the Job Content Questionnaire, an instrument that has gained international acceptance as a primary tool used to measure job demands, job decision-making authority, job skill use, and supervisor and coworker social support (Karasek et al., 1998). The availability of a tool to characterize these risk factors has led to a large body of research studying the association between work and cardiovascular disease as well as other disease endpoints, as discussed above and in Chapter 5. Although there have been a number of dramatic changes in the workplace since 1977, the Department of Labor has not sponsored nationally representative surveys since that time. Consequently changes in organizational practices and production technologies as well as changes in the structure and composition of jobs held by a more gender-balanced and multicultural workforce are not reflected in data available to understand the modern workforce.

In contrast, the European Foundation began carrying out a related survey of working conditions in 12 European nations beginning in 1990 using a prototype survey with only 20 questions. After the pilot survey, the survey was expanded to over 80 questions; it has been repeated every five years, with 15,800 workers surveyed in January 1996 and 21,700 in 2000 (Paoli, 1997; Paoli and Merllié, 2001). This is a questionnaire-based survey, involving face-to-face interviews conducted outside the workplace. The survey permits evaluation of time trends and working conditions that are standardized for a wide variety of workplaces and different cultures. As a result, a number of reports on trends for working condition factors have been published. Groups of factors affecting working conditions include physical environment of the workplace; organization of work; social and psychosocial environment; management of human resources; and labor law, collective agreements, and systems of industrial relations. As an example of the survey findings, the European Foundation is able to report (http://www. Eurofound.ie/working/working_knowledge.htm):

> that problems related to health, the pace of work and working time continue to rise in European workplaces. One main conclusion of the survey is that the phenomenon of work intensification has become an established

reality for European Union workers over the last decade. Employees may be working somewhat shorter hours but their pace of work has increased, in certain cases markedly. One in three workers complain of backache related to their job. Nearly half complain of working in a painful/tiring position while over half are working at very high speed to tight deadlines for one quarter of their working day.

In 2000 NIOSH sponsored a limited effort to fill the long gap in knowledge about the distribution of working conditions in the workforce (Murphy, 2002). Its approach was to add a module on quality of work life to the 2002 General Social Survey, a biannual, personal interview survey of U.S. households conducted by the National Opinion Research Center (NORC). A quality-of-work-life module was developed by NIOSH with advice from a multidisciplinary panel, but space constraints limited the size of the module to one-quarter the size of the 1977 QES. Results are still being tabulated.

4

The Social and Economic
Context of Work for Older Persons

Older Americans live their daily lives embedded in a larger social context. Their health and safety needs as workers reflect not only their individual life course histories, but also factors related to socioeconomic status, gender, race, ethnicity, and recent changes in the labor market and nature of work. The effects of these factors are intertwined in a complex web (Dressel et al., 1997; Moen, 2001), making them challenging to study; the implications for older workers have been underresearched. Studies of the health and safety needs of older workers stand to benefit greatly from a better understanding of the social factors influencing older workers' work opportunities, patterns of employment, experiences on the job, and access to health care and other health-relevant resources.

A good springboard for such research already exists. During the past two decades, a voluminous research literature has developed around the theme of health disparities—systematic health differentials within populations that seem to parallel social divisions based on socioeconomic position, race, ethnicity, and gender (Evans, Barer, and Marmor, 1994; Marmot, 1985; Black et al., 1988; Carr-Hill, 1987; Bunker, Gomby, and Kehrer, 1989; Wilkinson, 1986). This body of research addresses how health inequalities are produced and what they imply for efforts to prevent illness or disorder and injury, both generally and in relation to occupational health and safety.

One theme in this research focuses on ways in which race and class disadvantages can contribute to higher exposures to health hazards in the living and working environment, as well as limit access to needed health care (Institute of Medicine, 1999; Bryant and Mohai, 1992; Friedman-

Jimenez, and Claudio, 1998; Bullard, 1990, 1996). Another theme deals with the social gradient, exploring the health relevance of the social hierarchy (Singh and Siahpush, 2002; Steenland, Henley, and Thun, 2002; Pappas et al., 1993; Marmot et al., 1991; Marmot and Shipley, 1996). Other authors have examined populations defined by race, ethnicity, or gender, identifying their health needs and risks for preventable illness or disorder (Frumkin and Pransky, 1999; Centers for Disease Control [CDC], 1997; Polednak, 1989; Molina and Aguirre-Molina, 1994; Braithwaite and Taylor, 1992). Interrelationships among the social factors that influence health have also been the subject of research (Krieger et al., 1993; Kirkpatrick, 1994). Studies focused on work-related illness or disorder and injury within these populations remain relatively sparse; however systematic disparities in occupational health have been found to be related to race, class, and gender (Santiago and Muschkin, 1996; Burnett and Lalich, 1993; Robinson, 1984, 1989).

Older workers should not be regarded as a uniform population. Within the population of older workers, there are disparities related to social class, race, ethnicity, and gender, all of which have implications for how best to conduct research and develop policy for protecting older workers' health. Although health research traditionally has used the individual as the unit of analysis, this methodological approach leaves societal-level factors unexamined (Schwartz, 1994; Needleman, 1997). The social context of exposure and health—the relevant history, cultural values, social networks, behavioral norms, economic and power relationships, and access to health-relevant resources—should be considered. For example, analyzing data on individuals' social class as a static personal attribute is not the same as seeking insight into how the social system itself is stratified and the ways that individuals at different class levels interact. Examining individuals' race and gender as personal attributes is different from studying the processes by which societal norms regarding race and gender can develop and change, differentially shaping work opportunities and health outcomes. To understand causes and possible solutions for health disparities within the aging workforce, it will be important to conduct research not only on detecting patterns among individual-level variables, but also on clarifying ecological, system-level variables having to do with social meanings, institutions, relationships, and interactions.

SOCIOECONOMIC POSITION

Social Gradient and Health

An examination of a social gradient for health is important for the older worker for at least five reasons. First, the nature of the work may play an important part directly in generating social inequalities in health. Second, for most people, before retirement the job is the principal determinant of income level and general standard of living. Third, the job is an important shaper of self-identity and a means through which personal growth and development are realized, or not. Fourth, occupation is an important criterion of social stratification. These are all potentially important for health. Fifth, the other side of having a job is not having one, or having insecure employment. This is relevant for health because of direct effects of unemployment and job insecurity and because these will be related to the wider aspects listed above.

There is by now a general agreement that health follows a social gradient. Studies from both the United Kingdom and the United States illustrate that the social gradient in health is not confined to poor health for those at the bottom of the social hierarchy and good health for those above a threshold of absolute deprivation. This is true for morbidity as for mortality. Figure 4-1 shows mortality rates from the original Whitehall Study of British Civil Servants, with men classified according to their employment grade, which is a precise guide to their position in the occupational hierarchy

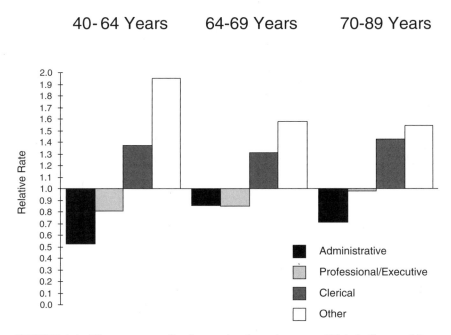

FIGURE 4-1 All-cause mortality by grade of employment: Whitehall men, 25-year follow-up.
SOURCE: Marmot and Shipley, 1996.

(Marmot and Shipley, 1996; van Rossum et al., 2000). Even at the oldest age, there is a social gradient in mortality.

Figure 4-1 also shows that the occupational classification continues to predict mortality long after these men left the workforce. The relative differences in mortality are slightly less at ages 70–89, but the absolute differences are greater because overall mortality is higher. In addition, there is a substantial social gradient in morbidity that continues well into retirement. Figure 4-2 presents results from a follow-up of the original Whitehall cohort, 29 years after the original baseline examination. At the time of resurvey, two-thirds of participants were over age 75. Employment grade continues to predict mental and physical health and disability after retirement (Breeze et al., 2001). The Whitehall II study, in a cohort studied 20 years after the original Whitehall cohort, documented persisting social gradients in morbidity (Marmot et al., 1991, 1997).

Investigations as longstanding and robust as the Whitehall studies are not available from the United States. However, there is evidence to suggest a similar social gradient effect on health exists in the United States. Figure 4-3 presents the mortality gradient for older adults according to household income. The data are from the Panel Study of Income Dynamics (PSID), a household survey (McDonough et al., 1997). Those with poorest house-

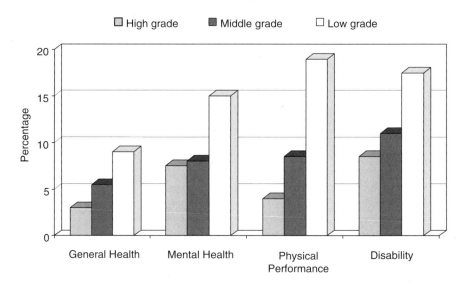

FIGURE 4-2 Morbidity (percent) at resurvey by baseline grade, median age 77 (range 67–97): Whitehall men 1997–1998.
SOURCE: Breeze et al., 2001.

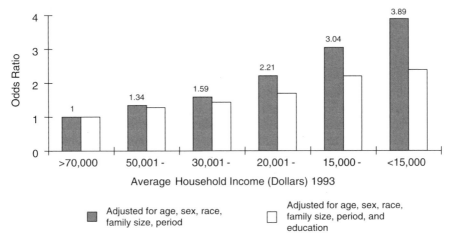

FIGURE 4-3 Mortality PSID: United States, ages 45–64 years.
SOURCE: Mcdonough et al.; AJPH, 1997.

hold income had highest mortality rates, but for people at each level of income, mortality rates were higher than for those above them in the hierarchy. The PSID graph also shows that even after adjustment for education the relation between income and health remains.

A National Center for Health Statistics report (1988) with a special focus on health disparities shows that a gradient in life expectancy according to income exists at age 45 and at age 65. The gradient is steeper for men than for women. As a result, the male-female difference in life expectancy is greater for low-income people than it is for high-income people. It is true also for blacks and whites. There is also a racial disparity: at any given income category blacks have lower life expectancy than whites.

In addition, inequalities in mortality by measures of socioeconomic status (SES) have been increasing in the United States. One study used an area-based classification of socioeconomic level. It showed clear social gradients in all-cause mortality. The slope of the gradient increased between 1969 to 1970 and 1997 to 1998. For example, in 1969 the odds ratio between the bottom quintile of low SES and the top quintile for men was 1.4. From 1997 to 1998 this odds ratio had increased to 1.7. For women the odds ratio had increased from 1.3 to above 1.5 (Singh and Siahpush, 2002). Another study reports a comparison of two American Cancer Society cohorts, 1959–1996, and shows increasing mortality according to education for a range of diseases (Steenland, Henley, and Thun, 2002). Using the 1986 National Mortality Followback Survey and the 1986 National Health Interview Survey, Pappas et al. (1993) showed that disparity in mortality rates according to income and education had increased over a 26-year period.

The main markers that have been used to measure socioeconomic position—education, income, and occupation—are likely to relate to health and to one another in complex ways. For example, if education, income, and occupation are entered into a multivariate equation with health as the outcome and education drops out of the model as a predictor, this does not mean that education is unimportant. Indeed the lack of education may lead to ill health because people with low education are likely to end up in low-paying jobs, and hence to have low occupational status and low income. Conversely if occupation stays in and the others drop out, it does not mean that it is the job itself that is the cause of social inequalities in health. For the reasons set out above, occupation may be a measure of soecioeconomic position, in addition to being a guide to the nature of work. For economists, the unit of analysis is the individual. When economists speak of income inequalities they commonly use a metric such as the Gini coefficient, which measures the degree of unevenness of income among individuals. When public health people speak of health inequalities or health disparities, they most usually refer to inequalities between social groups, or racial/ethnic groups, which are probably closely related. These are quite different questions; the determinants of individual differences in illness or disorder may be different from the determinants of the differences between social groups and, more particularly the social gradient in health and illness or disorder.

In the Whitehall II study, low control at work and imbalance between efforts and rewards are both related to incidence of coronary heart disease and mental illness or disorder (Bosma et al., 1997, 1998; Stansfeld et al., 1999; North et al., 1996). These psychosocial work characteristics, particularly low control, make an important contribution to explaining the social gradient in these two illnesses or disorders (Marmot et al., 1997).

As people move from work to retirement the relative importance for health, and specifically for health inequalities, of work and nonwork factors will change. As noted above, resurvey of men from the original Whitehall study 29 years later showed that employment grade continues to predict mental and physical health and disability after retirement (Breeze et al., 2001). It is less likely that this is a direct effect of work than it is a result of the correlation between employment grade and other aspects of socioeconomic position.

The results of the Whitehall studies related to worker health are likely to be generalizable to other populations. For example, in a general population case-control study in the Czech Republic, low control in the workplace was strongly related to myocardial infarction risk and appeared to be an important mediator of the social gradient in chronic heart disease (Bobak et al., 1998).

The Whitehall studies related to retirement may be less generalizable, because they will relate to the circumstances of the British Civil Service and the nature of its pension scheme. Three sets of factors were related to early retirement. First, men and women in high grades were more likely to retire early. Qualitative interviews suggest that they had more options for an interesting postwork life. Second, those with worse health were more likely to retire early. Third, those with lower job satisfaction were more likely to leave early. In multivariate analysis, these three factors were independently related to early retirement (Mein et al., 2000). Material problems tended to keep people working.

The Role of Work

In the Whitehall studies, employees were classified according to their position in an occupational hierarchy. The Panel Study of Income Dynamics makes clear that classifying people by income or education would also reveal a social gradient in mortality. This raises the question of how important work is. Do men and women at different points in the occupational hierarchy have differing patterns of health and illness or disorder because of their occupation or because of other factors associated with their social position?

Work is a major source of income and life chances. This is of particular relevance to older workers. When people leave work, incomes generally decline, and so does access to social participation that is associated with the world of work. But this scenario is likely to differ according to occupational level. A high-status worker who leaves formal employment is more likely to pursue a portfolio career of paid and unpaid work than is a low-status worker. When one is employed, one's income is strongly related to position in the hierarchy. Illustrating this point, Table 4-1 shows that financial difficulties are clearly related to grade of employment (lower positions are denoted by higher category numbers): the lower the position, the greater the difficulty.

Work is a major definer of social and personal roles. The acquisition of appropriate education and development of appropriate skills is of great relevance to younger workers. For older workers the application of these skills may define the extent to which the workers see themselves as playing an important social role and are seen to be doing so by others. For an older worker, lack of work or change to tasks with less responsibility may influence mental and physical health. As Table 4-1 shows, people of higher status have more active social networks beyond the family. They are more

TABLE 4-1 Characteristics of Men and Women (Aged 35–55) by Grade of Employment in the Whitehall II Study (Age-Adjusted)

Characteristics (in percent, except for hostility score)	Sex	Employment Category					
		1	2	3	4	5	6
Married or cohabiting	M	89.2	88.5	84.7	76.4	74.6	57.0
	F	58.8	56.1	50.9	51.4	56.4	67.6
Current smokers	M	8.3	10.2	13.0	18.4	21.9	33.6
	F	18.3	11.6	15.2	20.3	22.7	27.5
No moderate or vigorous exercise	M	5.1	5.4	4.9	7.5	16.2	30.5
	F	12.0	14.7	10.8	13.2	19.7	31.1
High control	M	59.3	49.7	43.1	31.6	24.7	11.8
	F	51.2	45.4	47.1	31.2	20.1	10.2
Varied work	M	70.5	52.1	41.9	27.1	18.2	3.9
	F	71.2	55.2	40.5	31.7	14.0	4.7
High satisfaction	M	58.2	38.7	34.1	29.5	29.4	29.8
	F	57.5	42.2	40.3	36.6	41.6	47.7
See at least 3 relatives per month	M	22.1	24.8	29.0	27.2	29.7	30.6
	F	18.9	23.7	21.1	24.1	30.4	44.9
See at least 3 friends per month	M	65.3	61.3	58.5	58.6	56.4	50.2
	F	71.1	62.8	67.1	63.6	52.9	49.0
No hobbies	M	12.4	12.9	12.7	15.0	23.0	25.4
	F	12.5	15.4	11.3	11.9	18.3	27.5
Negative aspects of support	M	25.0	28.4	31.3	30.9	38.1	39.0
	F	33.0	32.5	28.3	36.4	28.3	33.8
Two or more major life events	M	29.6	31.6	35.1	37.9	39.9	41.9
	F	41.1	43.6	35.5	42.8	46.5	49.2
Sometimes not enough money	M	7.0	12.6	21.5	26.4	34.4	37.2
	F	7.7	6.9	9.6	13.2	24.4	34.4
Some difficulty paying bills	M	11.0	16.2	22.8	24.7	29.6	29.6
	F	15.2	13.2	11.8	15.7	18.1	26.9
Hostility score	M	9.7	10.2	10.9	11.3	12.7	14.7
	F	9.5	9.5	9.4	10.1	10.4	12.3

SOURCE: Marmot et al. (1991) study of health inequalities among British civil servants (the Whitehall II study).

likely to be married, to have hobbies, and to be physically active in leisure time. They are also less likely to experience stressful life events.

Occupation is one definer of social status. Research on health inequalities suggests that relative position in the hierarchy may be important for health in addition to the material conditions of life that go with that relative position.

Work is a major source of pain and pleasure, frustration and fulfillment, demands and rewards. These are in addition to any positive or negative effects of physical exposures in the workplace. Table 4-1 also illustrates differences by grade of employment in psychosocial work characteristics.

In sorting out the importance of work for the health of the older worker, we have to take into account both the wider set of influences to which people in different occupations are subject and differences that people bring with them to work. Table 4-1 shows that smoking is strongly related to position in the hierarchy. Similarly, there is a social gradient in hostility. Running through each of the ways that the wider aspects of work can affect health is the crucial distinction for older workers of working versus not working.

As discussed in Chapter 3, the nature of work has been changing. In 1900, about 1 in 6 of the U.S. workforce were in professional, managerial, clerical, and service occupations. In 1980 it was 6 in 10 (National Research Council, 1999). The changing nature of work has led to increasing polarization in work according to education. People with higher education tend to be in jobs requiring a higher level of skills compared to those with less education. There are cohort effects, such that older workers are somewhat less likely to have higher educational qualifications. Cross-sectional data from the Current Population Survey 2000 show that older people have had less experience of higher education. This means there will be some tendency for older workers to be underrepresented in jobs requiring higher education. This has implications for their experience of work. The Gantz Wiley Research WorkTrends™ Survey (National Research Council, 1999) examines attitudes toward work of a national sample of workers. In general, the higher the status of the job in which they are employed the more likely are workers to report high satisfaction, good use of skills and abilities, greater participation in decision making which affect work, opportunities to improve skills, and trust in management.

The MIDUS survey (Americans at Midlife) provided an opportunity to confirm these trends and examine interactions with age (Marmot et al., 1998; Grzywacz, personal communication to M.G. Marmot, 2002). MIDUS did indeed confirm the link between education and experience of work. The higher the level of education, the less likely people were to be classified as having low autonomy at work and low use of skills or variety. However, the relation between education and these characteristics of work did not differ according to age, though, interestingly, for a given level of education women had less autonomy on the job than men.

Another important way that age and social position can be related to work is in risk of unemployment. Job displacements are closely linked to educational and occupational status. The higher the education the lower the risk of job displacement defined as loss of job through plant closure, cessation of trading, and layoffs (Newman and Attewell, 1999). The age group at highest risk of job displacement is the youngest—new entrants to work—followed by the oldest workers. Four year retention rates by age are 29 percent (at age 16–24), 57 percent (age 25–39), 67 percent (age 40–54), and 45 percent (age 55 and older) (National Research Council, 1999).

Unemployment and Job Insecurity

The unemployed have worse health than the employed. There are three principal reasons that may account for this:

(1) Unemployment may lead to ill health.
(2) People who are ill may be less likely to find or retain a job.
(3) Low education and low skills render some people more liable to unemployment and to ill health. The relation of unemployment to illness or disorder may be spurious.

All three of these may be operating. Their relative importance may differ by age. The evidence suggests that higher mortality of the unemployed cannot simply be explained by health selection (i.e., recruitment of sick people into the ranks of the unemployed). Were this to be true, one would predict that the health disadvantage of the unemployed would diminish the longer they were followed. This does not appear to be the case. Further, the 1958 birth cohort in the United Kingdom showed that mental health deteriorated consequently upon a period of unemployment (Montgomery et al., 1999). This could not be accounted for by mental illness or disorder preceding unemployment. The 1958 birth cohort did show the expected relation between prior social disadvantage and periods of unemployment, but the worse health of the unemployed could not be attributed to this relationship.

For older workers particularly, ill health may well be a reason for being out of the workforce. Administrative arrangements may blur the distinctions between unemployment, retirement, and being out of work through sickness or disability. There is good evidence that the benefits system influences the degree to which people are categorized administratively as unemployed or out of work due to disability. In addition, an older worker with some illness or disorder may appear a less attractive proposition to an employer, quite apart from whether, in fact, the illness or disorder would interfere with ability to perform the job, or the job would affect the illness or disorder.

There is also evidence that job insecurity has an impact on mental and physical health. The other side of labor market flexibility, which is thought to be good for companies and the economy, is job insecurity, which has an adverse impact on the health of workers.

From an international perspective, it is clear that labor force participation for older workers differs markedly among countries. A study by Gruber and Wise (1999) examined how pension arrangements affected labor force participation. These researchers calculated implicit taxes and benefits of an extra year of work. If an extra year of work meant no increase in the level of pension but one lost year from the total number of years of pension received, this represented an implicit tax on working. If a further year of work resulted in a higher level of pension, this was an implicit benefit. The study showed that the taxes implicit in pension arrangements had a marked impact on labor force participation. The study did not deal directly with the question of whether continued labor force participation of older workers was beneficial to their health or good or bad for the economy, and to what degree. At least in part, answers to this question will depend on the nature of the work.

GENDER

There have been significant changes in the gender composition of the older workforce (see Chapter 2). Among women between 55 and 64 years of age, labor force participation rates have increased steadily from 42 percent in the mid-1980s to 52 percent in 2000. According to the Bureau of Labor Statistics (BLS), this participation rate is expected to increase to 61 percent by 2015 (GAO, 2001). Similar increases are anticipated among women age 65 and older, whose labor participation rate was about 7 percent in the mid-1980s, 9 percent in 2000, and is expected to grow to 10 percent by 2015. The labor force participation rate of men over 55 is similarly expected to increase in the future, although this rate has remained relatively stable in recent years. In 2000, 67 percent of men aged 55 to 64 were in the labor force, and this rate is expected to increase to approximately 69 percent by 2015. Among men over 65, labor force participation rates in 2000 were at 17 percent, expected to rise to 20 percent by 2015. As these figures illustrate, despite the rapidly increasing labor force participation of older women, men are more likely than women to be in the labor force in their later years.

These patterns underscore the importance of taking gender into account as an important social determinant of the work experiences of and related health outcomes for older workers. Men and women differ in their earlier lifetime experiences and in the broader contexts of social and historical change that have shaped gender roles (Moen, 1996). It is necessary not only to analyze work experiences and health outcomes for gender, but also to understand gender as an organizing structural force, that is, to examine the role of gender as an independent variable influencing the work experiences and related health outcomes of older workers, as well as a factor in itself that needs examination (Moen, Robison, and Dempster-McClain, 1995; Umberson, Wortman, and Kessler, 1992; Walsh, Sorensen, and Leonard, 1995). Gender is important for the health and safety concerns of older workers for several reasons, including its influence on the types of jobs men and women hold, the resulting work-related exposures, the patterns of work over the life course, consequent income differentials, and differences in men's and women's experiences of retirement. Each of these is discussed below.

Gender influences the nature of work experiences. The sex segregation of the labor market has decreased in recent years but continues to structure the nature of work for men and women alike, although it is most notable in the types of jobs women hold. In 1980 about 80 percent of women were employed in the 20 leading occupations for women. By 1996, this proportion was reduced by about half, but those 20 occupations remain a considerable force influencing women's work experiences (Walstedt, 2000). As a consequence of the segregation of the labor market, men and women are exposed to different types of demands, strains, and hazards. Men are more likely than women to report hazardous work exposures. For example, approximately 39 percent of working men report that they have been exposed to substances at work that they believe were harmful if breathed or placed on the skin, compared to 23 percent of working women. Similar proportions of workers aged 45 to 64 reported these exposures (22 percent of women and 33 percent of men), although reported exposures were less common among workers over age 65 (Centers for Disease Control and Prevention, 1997). Women's occupations may, nonetheless, have unnoticed adverse health effects (Messing, 2000). An example is prolonged standing, common among such female-dominated occupations as bank tellers, grocery cashiers, restaurant workers, and sales clerks; prolonged standing may cause back, leg, and foot pain (Seifert, Messing, and Dumais, 1997). Women are reported to have higher rates of occupational musculoskeletal disorders than men; a large proportion of this difference may be attributable to ergonomic exposures (Punnett and Herbert, 1999; Zahm, 2000). Female-dominated jobs are also more likely than male-dominated occupations to be characterized by low pay, low levels of autonomy, low levels of authority and power, low levels of complexity and high levels of routinization, and responsibility for providing care and support for others (Bulan, Erickson, and Wharton, 1997; Marshall, 1997; Pugliesi, 1995; Ross and Mirowsky, 1992; Starrels, 1994; Wright et al., 1995).

Gender and age have intersecting influences on patterns of workforce participation. Although the percentage of employed persons working part-time increases with age, the proportion of women working part-time is consistently higher, across the working years, than that for men. Among workers over 55 years of age in 1997, 19.4 percent of men compared with 35.4 percent of women worked part-time (National Center for Health Statistics, 1998). Whether women are choosing to work part-time or are unable to find full-time work is unclear (Hill, 2002). Working part-time may have the salubrious result of reduced potential for hazardous exposures, or alternatively may place workers at risk of lower income and fewer work benefits.

Gender influences income, and hence the standard of living, as well as access to resources that may permit the choice of retirement or the necessity of working later in life. Women earn less than men. In 2000, women earned on average 76 percent of what men earned (U.S. Department of Labor, 2001). This earning differential is more pronounced among older workers. Among workers 55 to 64 years of age, the female-to-male earning ratio was 68.5 percent. In contrast, among those 25 to 34 years of age, women earned 81.9 percent of what men earned. Men earn more than women despite the fact that women have higher educational levels in similar occupations (Marini, 1980; McGuire and Reskin, 1993). Women are 70 percent more likely to spend their retirement in poverty than are men (Parsons, 1995). Women also are more likely than men to work at jobs that lack pension coverage (Richardson, 1999). Socioeconomic disadvantage and irregular career trajectories experienced by women in their middle years influence the availability of pensions and savings in later life (Moss, 2000).

Financial strain is a particular concern for older women. With age, women become increasingly at risk for poverty, reflecting the fact that women tend to earn less than men and that women are more likely than men to work at jobs without pensions (Richardson, 1999). Systematic inequalities in retirement policies further place women at a disadvantage; for example, women who divorce prior to 10 years of marriage are not eligible for dual Social Security entitlements. Women who receive Social Security benefits based on their own work records average $151 per month less than men (Logue, 1990; Richardson, 1999). While women comprise about 58 percent of the population over 65, they constitute about 75 percent of the elderly poor (U.S. Bureau of the Census, 1991). Among those aged 56–65, 27 percent of women and 17 percent of men have been poor at least once, and for women aged 66–75, that number rises to 35 percent (Duncan, 1996). Women from ethnic and racial minority groups are especially likely to be poor. For example, older African American women are twice as likely as older white women and five times as likely as older white men to be poor (Richardson, 1999). Risk of economic strain is also heightened among women who live alone or are widowed. Evidence indicates that widowhood is associated with approximately an 18 percent reduction in women's standard of living (Bound et al., 1991). Umberson et al. (1992) reported that financial strain was the primary variable accounting for higher levels of depression among widowed women relative to married women.

Not surprisingly, gender also plays an important role in retirement patterns. While the average age of retirement has declined in recent years among men, it has shown less of a decline in women. The traditional conceptualization of retirement is based on the presumption of a linear work path that results in a point of retirement representing the cessation of paid employment (Richardson, 1999). For many women who work intermittently or part-time in order to balance work and home responsibilities or who have few retirement benefits on which to rely, it may be necessary to either continue working or return to work. Indeed, retirement does not always signal the end of employment; one-third of older workers become reemployed after retirement, and this is especially true among women who have been intermittently employed before retirement (Han and Moen, 1998; Marshall and Clarke, 1998). Nonetheless, several researchers have concluded that although poverty may be a real threat, the personal and non-economic aspects of women's lives, such as family situations and previous labor force attachment, may be even more influential than economic factors in determining whether older women worked or not (Haider and Loughran, 2001; Hill, 2002; Honig, 1985). For women, there is a strong correlation between labor force participation early and later in life (Pienta, Burr, and Mutchler, 1994).

Men's and women's differing experiences of retirement are further shaped by socioeconomic position and race. For example, for low-income African Americans who lack private pensions and other sources of income during retirement, it may be necessary to work periodically in their later years (Gibson, 1991). Studies of retirement must therefore consider the qualitatively different experiences of differing subgroups as they face retirement. Understanding differences by gender and social class in the experience of retirement requires that we examine differing work histories, patterns of movement in and out of the workforce, shifting family responsibilities, occupation, and available financial resources for retirement (Moen et al., 1995).

The situation and experiences of older men and women today do not necessarily predict what future generations of older workers will experience. For example, many women in the current cohort of older workers either did not work outside the home or had discontinuous work patterns that excluded them from pensions or other retirement benefits. In recent years, women have experienced rapid changes in their status and roles. These changes may influence the very definition of work. As increasing numbers of women move into the labor force, work that has traditionally been in the private sphere without financial compensation, such as housework, is increasingly being done for pay (Messing et al., 2000). Likewise, changes in the extent to which men and women share responsibilities for childcare and work in the home will have consequences for future generations of workers of both genders.

Future research on the health of older workers needs to control for gender and also needs to examine the roles that gender may play in the health of older workers. Men and women often work in different types of jobs, both in their later years and throughout their working lives, and consequently they experience differing exposures to work-related hazards. Their patterns of work differ across the life course, in part because women generally have greater household and caregiving responsibilities than men. Women consequently earn less money and are more likely to be economically disadvantaged than men in their later years. Understanding these variations in the work experiences of men and women across the life course provides an important departure point for planning future research and informing social policy.

RACE AND ETHNICITY

In contemporary American society, race is a key determinant of social identity and access to resources. Many minority older workers have been exposed to adverse social circumstances throughout their life courses, including deficits in education and health care during childhood and experiences of poverty, discrimination, and other forms of exclusion during adulthood. The research literature suggests that many of these challenges persist into old age and shape the opportunities and outcomes for minority elders. Although there has been little research specifically on occupational health and safety concerns for older minority workers, an understanding of factors that influence the general health of the minority elderly provides a useful point of departure and raises important questions for future research.

Traditional interest in minority elders has been dominated by studies of black and white differences. However, there is growing recognition that the minority elderly are racially and ethnically diverse, and that there are important intergroup and intragroup differences within these populations. In recent decades, there has been dramatic growth in both the number and proportion of older persons. The number of ethnic minorities is increasing at a faster rate than the white population. In the year 2000 non-Hispanic whites were the largest percentage of the total population of older persons, representing 84 percent of those older than 64 and 78 percent of those between ages 45 and 64. Their percentages are projected to decline by the year 2050 to 64 percent for those over age 64 and 55 percent for those between the ages of 45 and 64 (U.S. Bureau of the Census, 2000; Federal Interagency Forum, 2000). In 2000, 8 percent of those over the age of 64 were non-Hispanic black, 6 percent were Hispanic, 2 percent were Asian and Pacific Islander (API), and 0.4 percent were American Indian/Alaska Native. The corresponding percentages were higher for those in the 45–64 age range: 10 percent non-Hispanic blacks, 8 percent Hispanics, 4 percent APIs, and 1 percent American Indians.

The population of Hispanic elderly is growing particularly rapidly and is estimated to increase by the year 2050 to 16 percent of those over age 64 (21 percent of those between ages 45 and 64). In the year 2050, 12 percent of those over the age of 64 are projected to be non-Hispanic blacks, 6.5 percent APIs, and six-tenths of a percent American Indians. The percentages are predicted to be higher for those in the 45–64 age range: 15 percent non-Hispanic blacks, 10 percent APIs, and 1 percent American Indians. By 2050, over one-third of those over the age of 64 (and close to half of those between the ages of 45 and 64) will be black, Hispanic, or Asian.

There is considerable racial variation among minority elderly in years of formal education. For example, among persons aged 65 and older, almost six out of every ten blacks and seven out of every ten Hispanics have not completed high school; whites 65 years and older have rates of high school graduation that are more than twice that of Hispanic elders and 1.7 times that of blacks. Compared to whites, Asian American elders are overrepresented at both extremes of the educational distribution. The API elderly are more likely than whites to not have completed 12 years of education or to have a bachelor's degree or more (U.S. Bureau of the Census, 1996). The pattern for Hispanics reflects the impact of immigration, with large numbers of Latinos being raised outside of the United States in the context of lower educational opportunities compared to their U.S. born counterparts. The black-white differentials reflect the unequal educational opportunities and lack of investment in education for blacks that characterized U.S. society during the time period when today's black seniors were growing up.

Patterns of poverty also differ by race and ethnicity. During the latter half of the 20th century, there was a steady decline in the poverty rates among the aged of all races. At the same time, rates of poverty have remained relatively high among the elderly. One-fourth of all black elders, one-fifth of Latino elders, one-tenth of white elders, and one-eighth of API elders reside in households that fall below the federal poverty line (U.S. Bureau of the Census, 2001). The level of poverty for American Indian elders resembles that of blacks (John, 1996). Data on poverty tell only a part of the story of economic vulnerability, however, given the large number of persons who are only slightly above the poverty level. Data from the 2000 census show that combining the poor (annual income below the poverty threshold) and the near-poor (annual income above the poverty threshold but less than twice the poverty level), 30 percent of the American elderly are economically vulnerable (12 percent are below the poverty level). Among those over the age of 64, 35 percent of non-Hispanic whites, 56 percent of blacks, and 56 percent of Hispanics fall into this vulnerable group; among those between the ages of 45 and 64, the corresponding percentages are 14 for non-Hispanic whites, 35 for blacks, and 37 for Hispanics (U.S. Bureau of the Census, 2001).

Race and socioeconomic position are related but nonequivalent concepts. For example, although the rate of poverty is three times as high for the black compared to the white elderly, two-thirds of the black elderly are not poor, and two-thirds of all poor elderly are white. There are important variations within these categories. For example, although the overall rate of poverty among Hispanic elders was 22.5 percent in 1990, the rate for Puerto Ricans was 31.7 percent (Chen, 1995).

Beyond the issue of poverty per se, other large racial differences are apparent in income across elderly groups. The 1998 median income for elderly whites ($22,442) was 1.6 times that of elderly blacks ($13,936) (U.S. Bureau of the Census, 1999). There are also striking differences in the sources of income by race and ethnicity. In 1998, income from Social Security provided at least half of the total income for 63 percent of the beneficiaries (Social Security Administration, 2000). Minority elders depend more heavily on Social Security than their majority peers. For example, 33 percent of black and Hispanic and 30 percent of American Indian elders, compared to 16 percent of whites, depend on Social Security for all of their income (Hendley and Bilimoria, 1999).

Research is needed to understand the role of several key factors likely to influence the health of older minority workers. It is important to explore the role of acculturation and length of residence in the United States. Across a broad range of health status indicators, research suggests that foreign-born Hispanics have a better health profile than their counterparts born in the United States; for example, rates of cancer, high blood pressure, and psychiatric disorders increase with residence in the United States (Vega and Amaro, 1994). It is also important to clarify the intersections between race and socioeconomic position, given that the minority elderly are overrepresented among lower income groups. Research is needed to examine the effects of racism. This concern is especially notable for the African American elderly population. Although many groups have suffered and continue to experience prejudice and discrimination in the United States, blacks have always been at the bottom of the racial hierarchy and the social stigma associated with this group is probably greatest (Massey and Denton, 1993; Lieberson, 1980). It is also important to understand the role of specific work experiences. For persons over the age of 45, a higher proportion of white males and females participate in the labor force than their black and Hispanic counterparts, with one exception: the labor force participation rate for white men does not exceed that for Hispanic men in the 45 to 64 age range (Siegel, 1996; Fullerton, 1999). Research reveals that even after adjusting for education and work experience, employed blacks are more likely than their white counterparts to be exposed to occupational hazards and carcinogens (Williams and Collins, 1995). Additional research is needed to better understand how lifelong job-related exposures combine with specific work experiences in later life to affect the health and well-being of minority elders.

AGE DISCRIMINATION

Legal protections are provided to older workers to prevent discrimination on the basis of age (see Chapter 7 for a detailed discussion of laws pertaining to age discrimination). Nonetheless, a recent survey of older workers found that over two-thirds of workers over 45 years of age were concerned that age discrimination was a barrier to their advancement and well-being at work (American Association of Retired Persons, 2002). Evidence of age discrimination may be found in the length of time it takes to find employment, the wage loss experienced by many on reemployment, and the size of award as a result of reported discrimination (American Association of Retired Persons, 2002).

Inequalities in work opportunities, experiences, and health outcomes may be the consequence of discrimination on the basis of age, gender, race/ ethnicity, social class, sexual orientation, or disability (Krieger, 2000; Minkler and Estes, 1999). For many older workers, the accumulated effects of discrimination related to race or gender, for example, have persistent influences on work experiences, retirement patterns, and health outcomes in the later years (Dressel et al., 1997). Between-group comparisons that focus solely on aging, ignoring the intersections of other social determinants, are likely to mask the important roles of other factors (Dressel, 1988). For example, focusing on the effects of age discrimination for older African American women who have experienced poverty, racism, and sexism throughout their lives must account for the long-term consequences of social inequalities resulting from multiple forms of discrimination (Dressel et al., 1997; Dressel and Barnhill, 1994; Hill, 2002). Social inequalities on the basis of race, social class, gender, and age represent interlocking systems of inequality.

The theory of political economy of aging, which has been applied to the field of gerontology as "critical gerontology," provides a useful lens for understanding age-based discrimination (Estes, 1999; Minkler and Estes, 1999). This perspective describes the experiences of older persons as socially and structurally produced through the distribution of material and political resources, as defined by social policy. Public policy reinforces the life chances of individuals based on social class, gender, race/ethnicity, as well as age. Accordingly, the status and resources of older persons are conditioned by their location within the social structure. The political economy approach has been criticized for its emphasis on structural disadvantage at the expense of a focus on individual agency and for a lack of attention to cultural change (Bury, 1995). Nonetheless, the perspectives offered by the theory of political economy highlight the important roles of social structure in shaping older workers' experiences, which might be balanced with the dynamic approaches provided by life course perspectives.

Discrimination is likely to be of particular concern for minority older workers due to the consequences of lifelong differences in opportunity. Among persons over 65 years of age in 1996, for example, 31 percent of whites, 57 percent of blacks, and 70 percent of Hispanics had less than a high school education (U.S. Bureau of the Census, 1996). These differentials reflect the historically unequal educational opportunities and lack of investment in education for blacks that was prevalent in the United States when these older persons were growing up (Williams and Wilson, 2001). The consequences of racism thus persist throughout a lifetime, and have clear implications for the work opportunities and retirement possibilities for older African Americans. Reflecting the dual discrimination of ageism and racism, a recent survey of older workers found that African Americans were more likely than other older workers to view ageism as a problem for older workers and were also most likely to report that their employers treated them worse than other workers because of their race (American Association of Retired Persons, 2002).

Discrimination may constrict work opportunities, influence overall economic well-being, and ultimately influence health outcomes. Research on the health effects of discrimination is a new but growing field of study. Krieger (2000) outlines five potential pathways whereby discrimination may influence health outcomes: economic and social deprivation, including residential and occupational segregation; increased exposures to toxic substances and hazardous conditions, resulting from residential or occupational environments; socially inflicted trauma, with consequent physiologic responses; targeted marketing of legal and illegal psychoactive substances, including marketing of pharmaceuticals to older persons; and inadequate health care. Although much research on these pathways has focused on effects of racial discrimination, age discrimination may follow similar pathways to influence the health of older workers and must be studied as well.

THE NATURE OF WORK

The preceding sections suggest that work, or its lack, plays an important part in people's lives and may have a profound effect on health. The nature of the work itself may also be crucial (see Chapter 6). As advanced industrial economies move increasingly away from heavy industry toward the service sector, the nature of work hazards changes. For office workers, some physical hazards of work may be less important, in terms of population-attributable risk of ill health, than are psychosocial hazards. Even for blue-collar workers, these loom large.

There is no strong suggestion from the literature that the relation between psychosocial working conditions and ill health differs by age. It has been reported from Sweden that control at work tends to increase with age, because of increasing seniority. This peaks at age 55. Thereafter degree of control may decline.

UNPAID WORK ROLES

The health and safety needs of older workers arise not only from their paid employment, but also from their unpaid work roles, including participation in volunteer work, caregiving responsibilities, and other household responsibilities. Volunteer work may provide important health benefits for older men and women. Moen, Dempster-McClain, and Williams (1992) found that volunteer work on and off through adulthood was positively associated with health; memberships in clubs or organizations were associated with women's longevity (Moen, Dempster-McClain, and Williams 1989; Moen et al., 1992). Preference, choice, and level of autonomy may be important elements in linking these roles to health (Moen et al., 1992). Volunteer work may likewise provide increased social ties, recognition, reduction in anxiety and self-preoccupation, and social support (Moen et al., 1992). Of course, it is possible that older workers who enjoy good health are more likely to engage in volunteer work in the first place, but even for already-healthy workers, volunteerism seems to hold potential for benefits.

Housework and caregiving responsibilities tend to be structured by the overall division of labor by gender. Multiple roles may take a toll on health while also offering potential health benefits. There are health risks associated with multiple roles. Employed women spend about 50 percent more time than men on domestic tasks (Canadian Advisory Council on the Status of Women, 1994). Several studies show that although the total amount of time spent on paid and unpaid work is comparable for men and women, women do more of the unpaid work characterized by low schedule control that is associated with psychological distress (Barnett and Baruch, 1987; Barnett and Shen, 1997). Psychological and physical health problems may additionally result from efforts to balance work and family (Moss, 2000). Women are more likely to experience role strain and overload as a consequence of family responsibilities in combination with work-related stress

(Arber, 1991). These stressors may be either compounded or alleviated by material well-being (Arber, 1991).

Women, including daughters and daughters-in-law, are primarily responsible for providing care to elderly family members (Starrels et al., 1997; Walker, Pratt, and Eddy, 1995). About 55 percent of women between the ages of 45 and 59 with one parent living can expect to provide some level of care to a parent in the next 25 years, and with increases in life expectancy, this percentage has been estimated to increase to as high as 74 percent (Himes, 1994). Caregiving is associated with higher rates of depression and lower levels of self-rated health (Moen et al., 1992; Schulz, Visintainer, and Williamson, 1990). Caregiving may also pose particular strains for employed women. Among caregivers, women are more likely than men to miss work due to responsibilities in caring for an older family member (Anastas, Gibeau, and Larson, 1990). Among female caregivers, there is no difference in the amount of care provided between those employed and not employed (Stone and Short, 1990). To cope with elder care, working women may rely on rearranging schedules, job flexibility, and leave (Bird, 1997). Such flexibility and the resources available to provide this care clearly differ by socioeconomic position. For example, poor- and working-class women are more likely than their middle- and upper-class counterparts to provide hands-on care and less likely to function as a care manager (Archibold, 1983). Additionally, the cost of leaving the workforce to care for a family member is highest for those in low paying jobs with few fringe benefits, for whom the loss of a job signals further reductions in income and pension benefits (Sidel, 1996).

On the flip side, despite the risks posed by multiple roles, participation in a range of social roles may also provide resources that have been associated with older workers' health (Marshall, 2001). For example, in one study women in their 50s and 60s who were currently caregiving reported a higher sense of mastery than women not currently caregivers (Moen et al., 1995). Men and women with more roles tend to be in better health (Hopflinger, 1999), although the healthy worker selection effect may partially explain these findings. Women who successfully manage multiple roles over their life course seem to benefit in terms of increased confidence and self-esteem later in life (Moen et al., 1992; Thoits, 1995). By contrast, men who avoided household responsibilities in their younger years may experience reductions in instrumental activities of daily living. For example, a Swiss study of men and women over age 75 found that 5 percent of older women and 29 percent of older men were not able to prepare a meal (Stuck et al., 1995). Compared to older men, older women also have more social contacts and are more involved in neighborhood activities and family networks (Hopflinger, 1999). Occupying multiple social roles augments an individual's social network, power, prestige, resources, and emotional gratifications (Moen et al., 1992). Compared to men, women have more inti-mate relationships and receive more support from these relationships (Turner and Marino, 1994; Umberson et al., 1996). Social support provides an important buffer against the negative health effects of stress (Cohen, 1988).

WORK AND THE WIDER CONTEXT

The issue of the health of older workers has to be set in a socioeco-nomic context. Both the nature of work and the wider implications of work will be important for the health of older workers. The balance of gains and losses associated with work versus retirement will be influenced by wider social and economic forces. The number of lifetime hours in paid employ-ment has been diminishing as the number of discretionary hours has been increasing; monetary income from paid work probably represents a minor-ity of total benefits; and the egalitarian challenge for the future is equaliza-tion of spiritual resources (Fogel, 2000). These resources include self-fulfill-ment, family ties, social cohesion, and control over life circumstances. It is important to put work in this context. For some older people, work will be a source of these spiritual and psychosocial opportunities. For others the reverse will be the case. The health of older workers will be influenced by where the balance lies.

5

Physical and Cognitive Differences
Between Older and Younger Workers

Older workers differ from their younger counterparts in a variety of physical/biological, psychological/mental, and social dimensions. In some cases these reflect normative changes of aging (e.g., presbyopia); in others they represent age-dependent increases in the likelihood of developing various abnormal conditions (e.g., coronary artery disease). In some cases these age-related differences (whether normative or pathologic) are disadvantageous to the older workers because their work performance is diminished relative to that of younger workers. For example, older workers are likely to have decreased capacity to sustain heavy physical labor for extended periods. In other cases these age-related differences are disadvantageous to older workers because their susceptibility to environmental hazards is increased. For example, Zwerling et al. (1998) reports that poor eyesight and hearing are associated with occupational injuries among older workers. In still other cases, however, changes associated with age may actually enhance capabilities and performance at work. For example, crystallized knowledge (that which has accumulated and is stored, often contrasted with fluid knowledge, which refers to the flexible solution of novel problems) and its positive impact on work is likely to be greater in 50-year-old than 20-year-old workers.

This chapter examines these age-related differences in function, capacity, and vulnerability, investigating the physical, psychological, and social characteristics that distinguish older from younger workers and how they affect differences in function, capacity, and vulnerability.

WELL-BEING OF OLDER WORKERS AND CHANGES WITH AGE

Because of changing workplace environments, job opportunities, and national and regional economic circumstances, maintaining the health and safety of older workers will become increasingly challenging as the number and proportion of older workers continue to grow. It is also likely that there will be important changes in the health status of succeeding cohorts of older workers in ways that may not be fully predictable. For example, overall health status and mortality of successive cohorts of Americans has been improving, but some persons with previously fatal diseases are now surviving to older adulthood and participating in the workforce. Thus, successive cohorts will require special consideration vis-à-vis future workplace threats to older workers. This section briefly reviews population and gerontological concepts relevant to aging, health, and work; delineates the current health and social characteristics of older workers; contrasts these characteristics with those of nonworking age mates; and defines a selected set of important issues related to maintaining optimal health in the face of age-related health changes.

Biological and Gerontological Perspectives on Age-Related Changes and Older Worker Health and Safety

Understanding the health of a given cohort of older workers is aided by important gerontological theory. Particularly important is the life course perspective on aging (Baltes, 1997), also discussed in previous chapters. The life course perspective suggests that a vast array of biological, social, and environmental factors that occur in child and adult development, beginning from conception, all play important roles in the nature and trajectory of aging. This concept acknowledges that the health, function, and survivorship of each older worker cohort will depend in part on exposures and events that occurred in the remote past, in addition to environmental exposures concurrent with aging—the subject of continuing epidemiological research. This trajectory may only be partially overcome by various clinical, social, and environmental interventions. Also, it is axiomatic that there is great interindividual variation in early developmental, genetic, and social factors within a particular birth cohort, and so it is not surprising that there are important differences among persons after 40 to 50 years of age in the capacity for various kinds of workplace activities and challenges. That is not to diminish the role of the social, political, physiochemical, and economic environment facing older workers, but only to point out that many determinants of aging outcomes are already in place.

It is likely that among the most important determinants of health and aging for older workers are the prior work experiences, in turn related to the levels of environmental exposures and hazards as well as the social and health care opportunities created by work, with their effect on overall socioeconomic status, which is an extremely powerful determinant of the future occurrence of diseases, illnesses or disorders, disability, and death (Adler and Newman, 2002). The intimate association between types of work and the socioeconomic context in which that work takes place makes understanding the health impact of various workplace exposures extremely complex. In addition to prior and current workplace exposures, the trajectory of health and aging will be substantially affected by nonwork-related environmental, physiochemical, and social exposures, such as recreational and other avocational activities, intentional and unintentional injuries, communicable diseases, and unhealthy hygienic behaviors such as tobacco, alcohol, and other substance abuse, careless automobile driving habits, inadequate exercise, unhealthy diets, and many other risk-taking behaviors.

The nature and causes of age-related changes in individuals and populations are complex and in general beyond the scope of this volume. While theories abound, no one has identified a unique cause or biological process that is pure aging. Rather, there are a very large number of age-related changes that involve every bodily system and function to a greater or lesser extent. To the extent that these individual changes have been investigated, age-related change rates in individual bodily organ and system functions do not necessarily track at the same pace. The difference between the mechanisms of aging and disease pathogenesis may also be more apparent than real, with many common causes and opportunities for interdiction. For example, cigarette smoking accelerates the age-related decline in lower extremity function (Bryant and Zarb, 2002) as well as causing lung cancer and coronary heart disease.

Thus, removing or limiting many toxic environmental exposures, particularly the intensive ones that can occur in the workplace, may lead to lower disease rates and improved maintenance of general human function, irrespective of whether the intervention affects aging or disease pathogenesis. Disease phenomena, particularly the large number of chronic conditions that increase in frequency with age, have very important implications for health status and outcomes, including among older workers, but distinguishing a disease from other aging manifestations is often arbitrary or one of degree. Thus, it may be useful to consider aging as age-related change, in reality a large set of important but at least partly malleable processes and functions that are not necessarily biologically obligate or fully predetermined (Arking, 1998).

Observations from the gerontological and geriatric literature enhance the understanding of age-related change. Importantly, this approach avoids attributing older worker performance or function to aging, which may convey an erroneous prospect of immutability or nonpreventability. An example may be lower extremity pain or dysfunction, often related to degenerative arthritis, an entity that is at least partly preventable and susceptible to treatment and rehabilitation. Many important age-related changes may begin in youth or midlife, which can allow early detection with physiological or other performance testing. Regardless of the causes of these early changes, early physiological abnormalities or behavioral changes can predict later overt dysfunction and disease (Whetstone et al., 2001), allowing the observational and experimental studies of possible interventions. However, not all age-related changes occur in slow, continuous decrements. Not only do acute changes in health and function occur with certain diseases and conditions, such as with injury and acute infectious diseases, but also with the rapid emergence of chronic diseases such as cancer, heart disease, and stroke (Ferrucci et al., 1996). This highlights the role of clinical disease prevention in deterring what might in populations be seen as age-related functional decline.

It is useful to invoke a phenomenon that is well described in the biology of aging literature: homeostasis (Pedersen, Wan, and Mattson, 2001). This refers to the observation that older human beings (as well as older organisms in other species) may function at a normative level, but when a large stress occurs, whether a disease, illness or disorder, injury, or social occurrence, the ability, *ceteris paribus*, to return to one's prior health and functional status is impaired when contrasted with that of younger adults. This may have import for older workers, who may be able to function under usual environmental circumstances, but who have more severe consequences after an acute medical insult, such as a given amount of trauma, a respiratory infection, a toxic exposure, or an unusual climatic condition. Thus, there may be some circumstances where older workers may require more enhanced protection from environmental insults than younger workers, because the consequences of those insults may be greater, and there may be greater premium placed on prevention. When a certain acute insult occurs in the face of existing, if controlled, chronic illness or disorder, the consequences may be more devastating. However, little research has been conducted in this area.

It is important to always consider the role of mental illness or disorder among older persons, including older workers. Mental conditions take a substantial toll on health status, and while major mental illnesses or disorders may have their onset in young adulthood, they often persist into old age. Mental illnesses or disorders such as various psychoses, major depression, bipolar disorder, and substance abuse often have important functional, social, and health consequences and can be related to workplace performance, absenteeism, and the risk workplace-related conditions. Pharmaceutical treatments of some of these conditions may also place some workers at increased risk of work-related injuries, but whether this is a special problem for older workers is uncertain.

Whatever the nature of aging and age-related change, it is axiomatic in gerontology that most general physiological and biological functions in older persons tend to have greater variation than in younger persons, related to greater variation in age-related change, the selective occurrence in subpopulations of specific medical conditions, varied availability of and access to optimal treatments and rehabilitation for these conditions, varied individual capacity to cope with and adapt to these changes and conditions and the nature, compatibility, and adaptability of the social and work environments. It is this variation that provides the basis for the observation that function and performance often do not correlate very well with chronological age (Masuo et al., 1998). Much of this variation may be modified by the social environment outside of work.

Another general characteristic of older populations, including older workers, is the presence of comorbidity (Gijsen et al., 2001; Brody and Grant, 2001). This refers to the distribution and co-occurrence of medical conditions that may affect health status, health risk, and adaptability to the work environment. While some active conditions may limit or preclude employment, many prevalent conditions in older workers are well controlled and do not have a substantial functional impact on worker performance. Comorbidity may, however, affect the use and timing of medical care utilization or encompass treatments that may alter workplace activities, such as somnolent or other psychoactive drugs. However, there has not been very much research on the effects of various workplace exposures on health in the presence of even controlled clinical conditions or their treatments. Also, further evaluation is needed to determine the role of comorbidity as an indicator of increased risk to various workplace exposures, requiring administrative action such as altered job placement.

In addition to acquired comorbidity and the heterogeneity in age-related change is the increasing number of children and young adults with substantial disabilities due to congenital, inherited, or acquired conditions that manifest themselves in childhood or early adulthood. Due to improved medical and rehabilitative care, as well as specialized social support, many more of these individuals are now surviving into late adulthood; some may at certain points be eligible for certain types of productive employment under certain circumstances. How their trajectories of age-related illness or disorders and dysfunction compared to others in the population has not been well characterized and should be one focus of future research in order to determine the suitability for various workplace environments.

However, as noted above, it may be difficult to predict the health and functional status of subsequent cohorts of older populations and older workers. For example, there is emerging evidence that in recent decades each succeeding cohort of older populations, from whom older workers are drawn, have overall better levels of physical and cognitive function than the prior ones (Manton, Corder, and Stallard, 1997; Schoeni, Freedman, and Wallace, 2001; Freedman, Aykan, and Martin, 2001). The issue is complex and sometimes disputed. However, if true, general, and persistent, this trend could have a positive impact on the net health and function of older workers and their responses to workplace challenges.

Defining Age-Related Health and Functional Changes: Epidemiological Findings and Implications

In general, almost all physiological and mental functions change with increasing age, even if at varying rates and intensities, including internal organ function, physical movement, and sense organ functional characteristics. However, as noted above, the causes for these changes are often unclear, and the consequences for complex activities such as individual job performance are even more uncertain because of personal adaptations and selective forces over time. Nor is it clear how many of the measurable changes are preventable or modifiable, but an increasing literature on intervention studies suggests that some mutability is possible.

When objectively evaluating and measuring the function and performance of older workers, several observations pertinent to assessing age-related physiological and metabolic changes should be considered in order to understand the impact of past or present work exposures on health and functional status:

(1) While the rates of age-related change are highly variable by organ, organ system, and anatomic region, in general the slope declines at a greater rate with increasing age. Thus, an important research and clinical problem is that older workers may need more frequent assessments to characterize the impact of work-related exposures. Also, it should be noted that many studies infer age-related change from cross-sectional population measurement, an inference that may not always reflect the reality or trajectory of longitudinal change (for example, see Louis et al., 1986).

(2) Age-related changes in workplace performance, particularly using job-related production measures, may not be due to age-related anatomic or physiological changes alone. Rather, there may be other social and psychological factors that impinge more prominently on that performance, such as caregiving chores, altered motivation, and social discord among workers. At least potentially, this may also be true of even more abstract physiological assessments. For example, the impact of social stress on immune function is well documented (Kiecolt-Glaser et al., 2002).

(3) There may be great differences between subtle physiological measures of organs and organ systems and their effects on complex human performance. It is often uncertain whether physiological or biochemical

measures adequately mirror the diverse challenges and functions of many occupations.

(4) Physiological and metabolic tests also may not adequately reflect cognitive, adaptive skills that come with experience and extensive training, to meet job challenges and changes.

(5) As noted above, in many instances it may not be possible to distinguish the various causes of laboratory-measured decrements in function. Candidate causes of these changes include genetic forces, modifiable environmental exposures, and nascent clinical illnesses or disorders; the implications for maintaining worker health and functions are very different for each of these factors.

(6) Although maximum capacity to function may be important in certain instances, most occupations do not usually require performance at full individual capacity. Thus, workplace or other exposures may cause decrements in function from full capacity without affecting work performance or function at usual levels. At the level of national economies this is particularly true since there has been a decline in the proportion of physically demanding blue-collar jobs in many industrialized countries. Conversely, there has been an increase in cognitively demanding occupations.

(7) Age-related decrements in bodily physiological functions may be related to the duration as well as the number and intensity of symptoms and acute responses to physiological work stresses that almost all persons experience. That is, functional decrements may relate to temporary symptoms and conditions that alleviate over time but may be more common among older workers. For example, certain stereotypic work activities may lead to painful muscles and joints, which are not different among older or younger persons in their onset but may take longer to dissipate in older workers. Similarly, common upper respiratory infections may have longer courses among older persons, including older workers. Age-related decrements may be related to the permanent performance decrements, but only to varied persistence of temporary acute stresses.

Age-Related Changes in Various Organ Systems and Relevance to the Job Experience

Despite the cautions and conceptual issues noted above, there is substantial data on organ system-specific physiological and functional changes with age. While the various causal and contributing factors are uncertain, they are likely to include environmental exposures (including those in the workplace); genetic factors; positive and negative health behaviors; as well as medical and preventive services. The following is a brief overview of important age-related changes in organ systems that are possibly important to job exposures among older workers and the job experience:

Skeletal Muscle

With increasing age, there is a gradual loss of muscle mass, and muscles become weaker (McArdle, Vasilaki, and Jackson, 2002). Specific contractile proteins undergo alteration, and contraction itself becomes more disorganized (Larrsson et al., 2001). Age-associated changes in muscle strength occur earlier in women, who also appear to have greater loss of muscle quality (Doherty, 2001). Also, with increasing age, the time it takes to repair damaged tissue increases (Khalil and Merhi, 2000), possibly having implications for high-level physical occupational activities among older persons. Because of age-related loss of muscle strength and cardiac capacity, maximal exercise capacity and oxygen consumption clearly decline with age, even in apparently healthy persons (Fielding and Meydani, 1997). In an excellent review of age and work capacity, de Zwart, Frings-Dresen, and van Dijk (1995) noted that physical work capacity clearly declines with age, but whether physical work demands are different for older versus younger workers has not been well documented. Age-related muscle loss may have an important effect on other organs, such as respiration (Franssen, Wouters, and Schols, 2002), joint function and mobility, and vocal function.

However, while the causes of age-related muscle changes are often uncertain, it is likely that lack of continued physical training (i.e., poor exercise habits or deconditioning) plays an important role (Franssen et al., 2002). Not only may aging decrease the capacity of workers for some exertional tasks, but an increased risk of falls and balance maintenance are possible secondary consequences, suggested to occur among frail elders (Rigler, 1996). However, little research of this issue has been conducted among older workers. Weight-bearing exercise improves muscle glucose and lipid uptake, as well as strength and exercise endurance (Mittendorfer and Klein, 2001), suggesting a possible role for exercise activity in older worker health promotion programs.

Vision

Visual functions clearly undergo decrements with increasing age, with important implications for many workplace activities (West and Sommer, 2001). Age-related changes in visual function are often due to a variety of diseases and conditions that have been subject to treatment, such as hypertensive retinopathy, diabetic retinopathy, glaucoma, and cataract. Some late-occurring conditions, such as macular degeneration, may be subject to only modest treatment effects. Some of these conditions are related to systemic illnesses or disorders that themselves need detection and treatment in order to help maintain optimal vision. Ocular injuries are a well-recognized occupational hazard, and preventive programs should be part of worker health programs for all ages. However, some elements of visual function are not altered with age (Enoch et al., 1999), and a substantial proportion of these sense organ decrements, such as myopia, hyperopia, and accommodation loss, are correctable with appliances or surgical procedures, with the expectation of improved function.

Hearing

Age-related hearing loss, known as presbycusis, is very common, and can occur in 20 to 25 percent of persons 65 to 75 years of age (Seidman, Ahmad, and Bai, 2002). The causes are not well understood, and a variety of genetic and environmental factors have been suggested. There are apparently substantial differences in presbycusis among populations defined geographically or socioeconomically, suggesting the importance of nonoccupational noise and other environmental factors. Among the most important occupational causes is noise exposure, and considerable effort has been spent understanding the mechanisms and management (Prince, 2002). Other toxic exposures, including exposures to chemicals and medications, have been linked to progressive hearing loss and may have occupational implications. Some of these factors may be synergistic with occupational noise exposure.

Occupational hearing loss is an important cause of monetary compensation in the United States (Dobie, 1996). Severe hearing loss is often related to systemic illness or disorder and cochlear disease, which may have concomitant balance, communication, and other health problems that can impair worker function. While some traumatic and infectious causes of hearing loss are treatable, most occupational hearing loss is not curable, and rehabilitation must be made available (Irwin, 2000). This highlights the importance of the availability of general safety and prevention programs throughout a worker's career. There is relatively little research into the functional and health consequences to workers of mild to moderate hearing loss.

Pulmonary Function

Physiological aging of the lung is associated with dilation of the alveoli, enlargement of airspaces, decrease in exchange surface, and loss of supporting tissue for peripheral airways. These changes result in decreased elastic recoil and increased residual volume and functional residual capacity (Janssens, Pache, and Nicod, 1999). Most dimensions of pulmonary function, measured using physiological testing methods, decline with age, due to a variety of clinical, climatic, and other factors (Babb and Rodarte, 2000). How much of this is attributable to normal aging is uncertain because of varied exposure to environmental lung stresses—occupational and non-occupational—including cigarette smoke, air pollution, various allergens, and occupational gases, fibers, and particulates. The role of cardiac and other nonpulmonary systemic conditions is also important is assessing lung function. A large number of specific occupational lung diseases have been documented; they are beyond the scope of this report. In addition, the aging lung is susceptible to increasing risk of infection, due at least in part to structural and immune alterations, increasing the importance of immunization programs for older workers and others (Petty, 1998). Less clearly understood is the impact of ongoing pulmonary occupational exposures on existing or developing lung conditions such as chronic obstructive pulmonary disease and emphysema, and the effect of well-established occupational pulmonary pathogens when exposure begins at a later age. These exposures and related medical conditions may have an effect on general human function and hence on work capacity. The net impact on the older worker will depend on the job demands and environment, as well as on individual clinical illnesses or disorders, exercise, and other hygienic habits.

Bone Health and Fracture Risk

Bone anatomy and function are not often related to occupational conditions and the older worker, but they have an important role. For example, bone may be a repository for occupational exposures, such as heavy metals and certain chemicals. Synergy of bone structure with marrow activity may be important for immune and hematological status (Compston, 2002). Older persons have decreasing bone density and increased rates of traumatic fractures; this is particularly more common among postmenopausal women than in men (Riggs, 2002), but fracture rates also vary by ethnicity and other risk factors. Lower bone density may be a risk factor for degenerative arthritis (Sowers, 2001), the leading cause of disability among older persons within industrialized countries. Poor quality maxillary and mandibular bone may lead to the need for more dental prostheses and may contribute to poorer nutritional status, leading to other health problems (Bryant and Zarb, 2002).

In job situations where the risk of falls and other unintentional injury is high, older workers will likely sustain more fractures for a given amount of trauma, due to age-related increases in bone fragility and architectural changes (Seeman, 2002). Several approaches to preventing age-related osteoporosis, other bone loss, and fractures are possible, including increasing calcium and vitamin D intake, maintaining an active exercise program, and screening and treatment for osteoporosis. The emphasis on bone health is not often prominent in worker health promotion programs, but with an increasing number of older workers, this may become more important.

Hormone replacement therapies have received attention in both women and men and may have implications for bone, muscle, skin, and other organ systems if successfully applied on a widespread basis. However, their adverse effects have not been fully evaluated.

Skin Aging

A wide variety of occupationally related skin conditions have been described, with many pathogenic mechanisms (Peate, 2002). Skin aging may be thought of as intrinsic and extrinsic, with many genetic and environmental determinants and altered cellular and biochemical activity (Jenkins, 2002). A particularly important cause of extrinsic skin aging is related to sun exposure, which in some circumstances may have occupational dimensions. This in turn leads to wrinkling, blotching, dryness, and leathering (Schober-Flores, 2001), as well as important skin cancers. Photo-aged skin, of whatever origin, is anatomically thinner and acquires increased permeability, becoming at least potentially a poorer barrier to chemical and related exposures (Elias and Ghadially, 2002). This may have implications for the rates of absorption of occupationally associated chemical and biological agents, possibly exacerbated by occupations where major or minor skin injuries occur, although little work has been done in this area. Age-related decreases in the rate of skin wound healing may also be important in certain workplaces, although there is likely to be an important role for comorbid conditions in wound healing (Thomas, 2001). As research progresses, it may be possible to add skin topics to health promotional programs in occupational settings.

Metabolism

Many changes in intermediary and xenobiotic metabolism occur with age, and these undoubtedly have great import for the older worker. For example, with increasing age, mitochondria produce less adenosine triphosphate (ATP), the body's main metabolic source of energy, and higher levels of reactive oxygen species, which have been related to several human diseases as well as DNA instability (Wei and Lee, 2002). The aging liver is characterized by a reduction in oxidative functions, including oxidative drug metabolism (Jansen, 2002). However, the impact of age on pharmacodynamics and pharmacokinetics may be difficult to predict, suggesting that more studies among elders are needed (Klotz, 1998). These observations and others have implications for the general determination of whether the metabolism, toxicology, and disposition of workplace chemical exposures differ between older and younger workers as well as for understanding the impact of polypharmacy (common among older persons) on organ function and metabolism of environmental agents. In the experimental setting, there may be age-related declines in rodent xenobiotic metabolism (Williams and Woodhouse, 1996), including the hydroxylation of benzene, possibly due to age-related changes in xenobiotic action on liver microsomes (Sukhodub and Padalko, 1999). Cigarette smoke has an age-related differential effect on pulmonary xenobiotic metabolizing enzymes (Eke, Vural, and Iscan, 1997).

Immunity

Aging is associated with general changes in immune function, although the relation of these changes to disease occurrence and survival is uncertain (Meyer, 2001), and more research is needed. An example from animal experimentation is the observation that exposure to certain immuno-suppressive xenobiotics leads to greater *T. spirilas* infection rates among older than younger animals (Leubke, Copeland, and Andrews, 2000). It is possible that these age-related changes impair responses to vaccines, leading to lesser protection from preventable infections (Ginaldi et al., 2001). It is possible that infection risk is altered by overtly nonimmune mechanisms—there is evidence that metal fume exposure may alter the risk of community-acquired pneumonia (Palmer et al., 2003). These observations have two immediate implications for the older worker. One is the possibly increased risk of clinical infections and the need for clinical prevention to maintain worker health. The other is the potential for increased infection risk among older workers exposed to special biological agents in the work environment. An additional potential implication is that the altered immune function among older workers may diminish the response to and protection by various vaccines (Murasko et al., 2002). Much more research is needed in this area.

Thermoregulation

Age-related changes in thermoregulatory function may be important for older workers. Older people have seasonally higher mortality rates at both high and low extremes of temperatures. Older persons, particularly those over 60 years, have a lower capacity to maintain core temperature during a cold challenge and have a reduced thermal sensitivity and a reduced thermal perception during cooling (Smolander, 2002). Thermogenesis under situations of cold stress appears to decline with age (Florez-Duquet and McDonald, 1998). Similarly, reflex sweating to heat exposure may be diminished in older persons, making them more heat sensitive, and mechanisms for this have been suggested (Holowatz et al., 2003). Whether these phenomena are important for actual job exposures to temperature extremes should be further evaluated. Worker selection factors and the modulation of temperature extremes through environmental controls may mitigate most challenges. Response to more extreme temperatures in the workplace may also be affected by other factors, such as the presence of chronic illness or disorder, as well as level of training and physical fitness (Kenney, 1997).

MENTAL HEALTH ISSUES FOR THE OLDER WORKER

There has been increasing recognition of the work-related mental health, psychosocial, and organizational issues among older workers, (Griffiths, 2000), in addition to the emphasis on physiochemical workplace hazards. This recognition may be due in part to a shift in the United States and most industrialized countries from a manufacturing to a service economy, where interpersonal issues are more apparent. As shown in the data from the Health and Retirement Survey (see Chapter 2), older workers are over-represented in many service occupations as well as in part-time work situations. It is likely that among older persons, workers are less likely than nonworkers to have serious or severe mental illness or disorder because of the debilitating nature of these conditions. Also, not all work-related mental health problems are age-related, and some approaches to assessment, prevention, and management may be suitable for all ages. Yet, as shown in the data from the Health and Retirement Study, certain workplace situations— such as ageism, increasing physical and cognitive demands, and pressure to retire—may have disparate effects on older workers' mental health.

Mental health problems with job implications include the consequences of work-related stress, clinical depression, and a variety of other psychological problems such as burnout, alcohol and other substance abuse, unexplained physical symptoms, and chronic fatigue as well as the secondary consequences of these conditions, such as higher injury rates (Hotopf and Wessely, 1997). In many instances older workers bring to the workplace mental health problems that may have long histories and origins outside the job setting. Common or severe mental conditions such as depression may cause stress, conflict, poor productivity (Goetzel et al., 2002), and potentially threats to individual safety and health related to the conditions or their treatments. The following discussion highlights some of the more important mental health issues for older workers and summarizes results of selected relevant studies on these issues.

Complaints of Work-Related Stress

One important issue is the proportion of older and younger workers who suffer from job-related stress. There is evidence that work-related stress impairs worker satisfaction and productivity and may cause long-term physical diseases and conditions, as well as increase the costs of absenteeism and low productivity (Tennant, 2001). In the Netherlands, occupational health surveys are conducted every three to five years, querying workers from various occupational and demographic groups about health complaints, health care treatment, working conditions, and work demands. With increasing age, a general increase in health and stress complaints was seen for almost all item categories, although the relationship to age was only modest. In general, women reported relatively higher complaint levels than men in almost all survey domains (Lusk, 1997). The high levels of perceived job stress by older American workers, reported in the Health and Retirement Survey, were shown in Chapter 2.

In Great Britain in 1997, mental and behavioral disorders such as stress-related symptoms were one of the most prevalent types of claim for incapacity benefit. Incapacity benefit figures reveal the number of people of working age who are unavailable for work because of ill health (Griffiths, 2000). As part of the British Labour Force Survey, a stratified random sample of 40,000 people who were working or who had worked were surveyed in 1990. When surveyed again in 1995, the prevalence rates for most illness or disorder categories had fallen, but rates of work-related stress, anxiety, depression, and musculoskeletal disorders had increased (Griffiths, 2000). Compared to younger workers, twice as many cases of psychological ill health (stress, depression, and anxiety) were reported by workers between 45 years and retirement age. However, very few cases were found in the postretirement population. This pattern was consistent between two surveys. There is some but not full support for the hypothesis that older persons who are working and also serving as caregivers have more role conflict and role overload (Edwards et al., 2002).

The relationship between job stressors and mental health also has been documented for health workers (Sutherland and Cooper, 1992). In Japan, Shigemi and colleagues (2000) conducted a prospective cohort study to investigate the effect of job stressors on mental health, using the General Health Questionnaire. It was found that workers who complained of perceived job stressors had a greater risk of mental illness or disorder than those not reporting job stressors. Specific items from the job stressors questionnaire, such as "poor relationship with superior" and "too much trouble at work" were particularly associated with higher mental health risk. While such studies do not prove that perceived job stressors cause mental illness or disorder, they point to direction for further research on the causes and potential interventions for such problems.

Depression

Several studies have examined depressive disorders and symptoms in the workplace, and an estimated 1.8 to 3.6 percent of the U.S. workforce has major depression (Goldberg and Steury, 2001). Druss, Rosenheck, and Sledge (2000) examined data from the health and employee files of 15,153 employees of a major U.S. corporation who filed health claims in 1995. Over 70 percent of people with major depression were thought to be actively employed, and employees treated for depression incurred annual per capita health and disability costs of $5,414, significantly higher than the cost for treating hypertension. Employees with depressive illness or disorder and any other medical condition cost 1.7 times more than those with the comparable medical conditions alone.

Depressive symptoms have also been reported to be common after work-related injuries, such as in the case of claims for cumulative trauma disorders (Keogh et al., 2000). Physiochemical workplace exposures should be considered as potential causes of some depression and other mental disorders. For example, suicide rates among electric utility workers exposed to electromagnetic fields have been reported to be increased (van Wijngaarden et al., 2000), and depression rates were reported increased among women occupationally exposed to organophosphate pesticides (Bazylewicz-Walczak, Majczakowa, and Szymczak, 1999).

The relationship between work-related stress or pressure and depression has been explored in several work settings. In a review of this issue, Tennant (2001) concluded that specific, acute work-related stressful experiences contributed to depression, and that enduring structural factors in some institutions lead to various psychological problems. For example, in nurses, Feskanich et al. (2002) found that the relation between self-reported work stress and suicide was U-shaped, after adjusting for age, smoking, coffee consumption, alcohol intake, and marital status. When stress at home was also considered, there was an almost fivefold increase in risk of suicide among women in the high-stress category. However, few studies of the association between job stress and depression report the age at onset of clinical depression in study subjects. When age was studied, it was usually used for adjustment in multivariate models (e.g., Druss et al., 2000).

It is unclear how retirement affects an individual's psychological states, including self-esteem and depression. Work gives individuals not only financial security but also can provide identity and roles. Some researchers believe that retirement creates an identity crisis, given the prominent role of work (Reitzes, Mutran, and Fernandez, 1996). Others, such as Atchley (1974), argue that individuals occupy multiple roles and can proceed to imply family, friendship, and religious roles into retirement that would prevent an overall negative consequence. Reitzes et al. (1996) followed 826 workers for two years to explore the social and psychological consequences of retirement. When comparing workers who retired to those who continued to work, depression scores declined for workers who retired, while the self-esteem scores did not change in either group. In general, depression and depressive symptoms decline with retirement in most studies, but this may differ by gender and reason for retirement (e.g., voluntary versus forced by health or job circumstances). Cohort studies that follow individuals of both genders through retirement offer an important opportunity to explore the role of the workplace in depression among older workers.

Several methodological issues are apparent when studying depression among older workers. Occupations vary in stress generation, and there may be individual differences in response to conflict and stress. In many studies, depression and depressive symptoms are not rigorously defined, and, as noted above, age-at-onset is rarely considered. Patients with major depression often have substantial psychiatric comorbidity, such as mania or alcoholism, and the effects of drug or other psychotherapeutic regimens should be considered in assessing health or economic outcomes. Identification of depression may be problematic in any population, including workers, and may depend in part on worker mental health benefits and the attitudes and programs of employers.

Sleep Problems

A substantial number of older persons report sleep problems, including difficulty in initiating sleep, early awakening, and daytime sleepiness (Foley et al., 1999). Sleep problems among certain occupational groups such as health care workers and truck drivers have been well recognized. In one study, approximately 20 percent of truck drivers had undiagnosed sleep disorders affecting their overall functioning (Stoohs et al., 1995). Sleep disturbances caused by shift work have been shown to affect work productivity and social functioning (Regestein and Monk, 1991). Results from the study on mental health status of female hospital workers in the Paris area showed that 32 percent of the sample had symptoms of fatigue (e.g., waking up tired, working despite exhaustion) (Estryn-Behar et al., 1990); about a third of these subjects also had sleep impairment. Sleep problems were more frequent among older women and those with higher numbers of children at home.

Sleep problems have a strong relationship with both mental and physical health in general. A study by Manocchia and colleagues (2001) indicated a strong association between sleep problems and the psychological wellness of older individuals. These data, on patients with chronic illnesses or disorders from the Medical Outcomes Study, showed that 45.6 percent of the sample reported mild to severe levels of sleep problems. Sleep problems were significantly associated with a higher percentage of respondents reporting losses in work productivity and quality. Further, sleep problems were strongly associated with worse levels on the mental health scale of the

SF-36, an instrument summarizing several dimensions of health-related quality of life.

One of the consequences of sleep disturbances is dependence on prescription and over-the-counter (OTC) sleep medications. It was found that older adults and females use greater amounts of sleep medication in order to manage their sleep problems (Ohayon, Caulet, and Lemoine, 1996; Pillitteri et al., 1994; Mullan, Katona, and Bellew, 1994). Individuals who do not seek formal care for sleep problems tend to overmedicate their condition using OTC drugs.

Chronic Fatigue Syndrome

In recent years, chronic fatigue syndrome (CFS) has become increasingly recognized as a common clinical problem (Sharpe et al., 1997). The causes of CSF are unknown, but there are many variables that appear to predispose individuals to develop CFS, including various lifestyle behaviors, personality traits, and work stress. Also, CFS may make individuals more susceptible to illnesses or disorders such as viral infection and worsen existing illnesses or disorders such as sleep problems and depression. Older individuals with a declining general health may be more susceptible to developing CFS. The relationship between CFS and work factors such as workload and hours and job-related stress, as well as home stress, should be investigated further for older workers.

Alcohol and Substance Abuse

It is reported that 70 percent of current illegal drug users are employed, and approximately 7 percent of Americans employed in full-time work report heavy drinking (Roberts and Fallon, 2001). Individuals who use alcohol or other drugs in the workplace are estimated to cost business $81 billion annually in lost productivity; 86 percent of these costs are attributed to alcohol use. Ruchlin (1997) used the 1990 Health Promotion and Disease Prevention supplement to the National Health Interview Survey to determine prevalence data on alcohol use among older adults. Close to half of the sample reported having consumed alcohol during the survey year. According to Rigler (2000), one-third of older alcoholic individuals developed problem drinking in later life, while the remainder grew older sustaining the medical and psychosocial consequences of early-onset alcoholism. However, the prevalence of problem drinking and alcoholism among older workers is not known. The reported prevalence of alcohol problems among older adults in the general population ranges from 1 to 22 percent. In all age groups, the rates are lower in women than in men. In any case, the consequences of alcohol abuse are known to be more serious among the elderly. The problem of alcohol and drug abuse at work is predicted to increase as the baby boomer cohort grows older, because this cohort had higher rates of substance use, including alcohol, than previous generations.

Of course, not all individuals with a history of alcohol abuse exhibit serious problems with drinking. A substantial number seem to be managing their lives while engaging in controlled drinking or repeating a pattern of abstinence and remission. There are few studies on effects of controlled drinking and the abstinence-remission pattern of drinking on health and function of older adults, including older workers. It is likely that many middle-aged and older adults continue to function well enough to sustain employment. Researchers point out that the currently used criteria for alcohol or substance abuse may not be sensitive enough to screen older adults who exhibit a pattern of symptoms different from those exhibited by younger drinkers. For example, many older workers may be asymptomatic cases of alcoholism. Also, a different intervention approach may be needed to help older workers who have been drinking for decades. An important research direction is to explore the relation between job stressors and alcohol abuse, for example, whether job stressors triggers alcohol abuse among abstaining individuals. Also, there is a great need to better understand later life onset of alcoholism (Liberto and Oslin, 1995).

Another underevaluated area for the future research is problems associated with medication abuse among older women. There are few studies on alcoholic women, since the prevalence of alcoholism is lower in women across all age groups. However, older women are more problematic users of prescribed psychoactive drugs than men, and a prevailing comorbidity among older women alcohol abusers is depressive disorder (Gomberg, 1995).

PSYCHOLOGICAL CHARACTERISTICS OF OLDER WORKERS

Effects of Normal Aging on Psychological Functioning

Among the major psychological characteristics of individuals are their personality or psychological adjustment and their mental (or cognitive) functioning. Relatively little change with age has been found in the level of most personality traits (see Ryff, Kwan, and Singer, 2001, and Warr, 1994, for reviews). However, increased age has been found to be associated with reports of greater happiness, less negative affect, reduced amounts of occupational stress (e.g., Mroczek and Kolarz, 1998), and lower levels of depression and anxiety (e.g., Christensen et al., 1999; Jorm, 2000). At least one study has also reported that older workers have slightly higher levels of occupational well-being than younger workers (Warr, 1992). This latter trend is illustrated in Figure 5-1. The average ratings from the question-

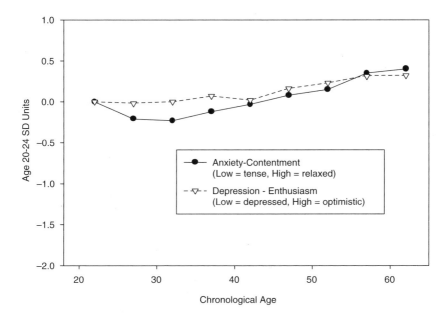

FIGURE 5-1 Occupational well-being.
SOURCE: See Warr, 1992.

naires are expressed in standard deviation units of young adults to provide a common scale for all variables. Use of this group as the reference distribution allows comparison levels of adults of different ages entering the workforce. Although young adults are only a subset of the total sample (and hence the estimate of the standard deviation from this subset may not be as precise as when the entire sample is used as the reference group), young adults may offer a more meaningful comparison when there are large age effects on the variable of interest because some of this variability will be due to effects of age. As is apparent in Figure 5-1, occupational well-being increases slightly across a 40-year age range, but the total effect is small, corresponding to less than .5 standard deviations of the reference distribution of young adults.

In contrast to the small and generally positive effects of age on variables related to personality or adjustment, age-related effects on many measures of cognitive functioning are large and negative. Figures 5-2 and 5-3 illustrate age trends in several cognitive variables from nationally representative samples used to establish norms from recent standardized cognitive test batteries (i.e., Wechsler, 1997a,b; Woodcock, McGrew, and Mather, 2001).

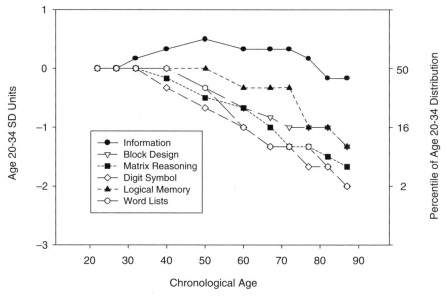

FIGURE 5-2 WAIS III and WMS III test results by age.

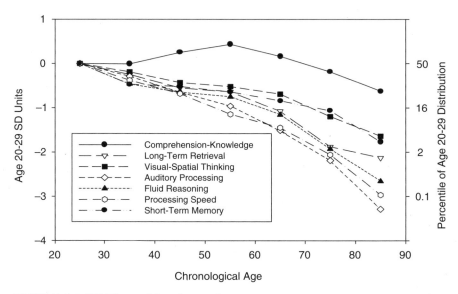

FIGURE 5-3 WJ III cognitive clusters by age.

There is a slight increase up to about age 50 for measures of knowledge of word meaning and general information, but a continuous decline beginning in the 20s for variables representing memory, reasoning, and spatial abilities. The magnitude of these latter effects is about 1.5 to 2 (young adult) standard deviations between 20 and 70 years of age, which means that the average 70-year-old on these tests is performing at a level lower than that of over 90 percent of the young adults in the reference distribution. A similar pattern is evident in normative samples for other standardized tests (e.g., the WAIS, WAIS-R, WJ-R, K-BIT, and KAIT), as well as many studies examining a mixture of standardized tests and specially designed experimental tasks in convenience samples (e.g., Park et al., 2002; Salthouse, 1991, 2001; Salthouse and Maurer, 1996).

The distinction between two types of cognitive variables based on different age trends has been recognized since the 1920s. The most familiar labels for the two types of cognition are fluid and crystallized, but these terms are not very descriptive, and other labels have been proposed such as mechanics and pragmatics, or process and product. In each case the first type of cognition broadly refers to the efficiency of processing at the time of assessment, and the latter to the cumulative products of processing that occurred at earlier periods in one's life. A considerable body of research has established that there are nearly continuous declines from early adulthood in the effectiveness of fluid, mechanics, or process cognition, as reflected in the detection and extrapolation of relationships, novel problem solving, memory of unrelated information, efficiency of transforming or manipulating unfamiliar or meaningless information, and real-time processing in continuously changing situations. In contrast, the research indicates that there are increases at least until about age 50 in crystallized, pragmatics, and product cognition, as assessed by measures of acquired knowledge. However, the true relation between age and knowledge may be underestimated in standardized test batteries, because in order to have broad applicability the assessments have focused on culturally shared information rather than idiosyncratic information specific to a particular vocation or avocation. It has therefore been suggested that continuous increases until very late in adulthood might be found if more comprehensive individualized assessments of knowledge were available (e.g., Cattell, 1972; Salthouse, 2001).

Although the group trends described above are firmly established, there is considerable variability at every age even in variables with large average age-related declines. That is, some people in their 60s and 70s perform above the average level of people in their 20s, and some people in their 20s perform below the average level of people in their 60s and 70s. The reasons for the across-person variability are still not well understood, but it is important to recognize that trends apparent at the group level may not apply at the level of specific individuals.

Two basic questions can be asked with respect to psychological aging in the context of health and safety in work. The first concerns the effects of psychological aging on safety and productivity in the workforce, and the second concerns the effects of work on the mental abilities of older workers.

Effects of Psychological Aging on the Productivity, Health, and Safety of Workers

As noted earlier, in many respects older workers appear to have higher levels of personality or emotional stability than young adults. There are consequently no reasons to expect adverse effects on health and safety related to the personality or psychological adjustment of older workers.

In contrast, negative relations might be expected between age and work performance, because cognitive abilities are important for work, and, as indicated above, increased age is associated with declines in certain aspects of cognitive functioning. However, reviews of research on aging and work performance have revealed little overall age trend in measures of job performance (e.g., Avolio, Waldman, and McDaniel, 1990; McEvoy and Cascio, 1989; Salthouse and Maurer, 1996; Waldman and Avolio, 1986; Warr, 1994). Although the reviews suggest that there is little relation between age and job performance, one should be cautious about any conclusions at the current time, because of weaknesses in many of the empirical studies. For example, most studies can be criticized for having a limited age range with few workers over the age of 50; questionable validity and sensitivity of the job performance assessments; and little control for selective survival such that only the highest performing workers may have continued on the job to advanced age (Warr, 1994). Furthermore, it is worth noting that moderate to strong negative relations between age and performance have been reported in certain cognitively demanding occupations, such as air traffic controllers (e.g., Becker and Milke, 1998) and pilots (e.g., Taylor et al., 2000), and in the magnitude of performance improvements associated with job training (Kubeck et al., 1996).

One explanation for the lack of stronger negative relations between age and work performance is a positive relation between age and job-relevant experience. Warr (1994) has speculated about a possible interaction of age and experience for performance in different types of jobs, based on hypothesized patterns of age-related and experience-related influences. He suggested that negative age relations would be expected in only a few jobs, and not in the jobs that involve knowledge-based judgment with no time pressure, relatively undemanding activities, or skilled manual work. Warr's speculations are intriguing, but there is currently little understanding of the demands of particular jobs in terms of the relative involvement of process (or fluid or mechanics) and product (or crystallized or pragmatics) abilities,

and of the effects of experience on these abilities or on actual job performance. It is also possible that the specific effects of age and experience
could vary depending on changes that occur in the workplace. For example,
Hunt (1995: 18) has suggested that "aging increases the value of a workforce when the workplace is static, but it may decrease the value of the same
workforce if the methods and technology of the workplace are changing."

   Little information is currently available about the relations between age
and quality of work or about possible differences in how a given level of
work is achieved by adults of different ages. Some insights on this latter
issue may be available from research on driving, which is an activity with
many parallels to work. Age-related declines in abilities related to driving,
such as vision, reaction time, and selective and divided attention, have been
well documented. However, as illustrated in Figure 5-4, there is no evidence
of age-related increases in crash frequency when the data are expressed
relative to the number of drivers of a given age.

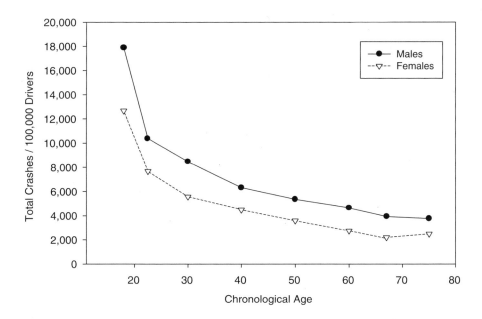

FIGURE 5-4 Automobile crashes by age.
SOURCE: Table 63, *Traffic Safety Facts 1999*, National Highway Traffic Safety
Administration, U.S. Department of Transportation.

Brouwer and Withaar (1997; also see Withaar, Brouwer, and van Zomeren, 2000) introduced a distinction among three aspects of driving that may help explain the absence of expected age-related increases in crashes (when crash rates are not adjusted for distance driven). In their classification scheme, operational aspects refer to control of the car in reaction to continuously changing traffic conditions; tactical aspects refer to voluntary choice of cruising speed, following distance, and maneuvers; and strategic aspects refer to choice of travel mode, route, and time of traveling. It is possible that older drivers rely on their stable or increasing strategic and tactical knowledge acquired through experience to minimize dependence on operational abilities that may be declining.

In fact, when crash rates are adjusted for distance driven they do start to increase with age after age 65, and it is reasonable to expect that they would increase to an even greater extent if it were also possible to take into consideration when the individual is driving and under what conditions (e.g., during the day or at night, in the middle of the day or during rush hour, etc.). The applicability of the strategic-tactical-operational distinction to occupational contexts is not yet known. However, it is certainly possible that increased age is associated with declines in operational abilities in many work situations, but that the consequences of these declines are offset by age-related increases in strategic and tactical knowledge. Furthermore, to the extent that safety is positively associated with quality or quantity of tactical and strategic knowledge, the safety of older workers may be at least as great as that of young workers because an age-related increase in job-relevant knowledge (Warr, 1994).

Certain adaptations may be required on the part of the older worker, and possibly some accommodations on the part of the employer in order to maximize the capabilities of older workers. However, there appears to be little reason to expect age-related changes in cognitive functioning to adversely affect the health, safety, or productivity of workers who are continuing in the same job and are performing familiar activities.

Experience and Expertise

Examination of the physical, psychological, and social differences between older and younger workers indicates that aging processes tend to lower some functional capacity. Increased age, however, is also associated with increased experience that tends to raise experience-related functional capacities. These two aspects of age may trade off, particularly when experience leads to skill and expertise, a point stressed in some of the earliest literature in this field (e.g., Welford, 1958).

Is there evidence that experience or expertise can mitigate general age-related declines in basic mental abilities? The reason for being concerned by declines in general cognitive abilities is that in metanalysis studies these abilities are strong predictors (r = 0.5) of initial job performance and of job-related training performance (Schmidt and Hunter, 1998). Job experience typically correlates about r = 0.2 with job performance, with the best prediction achieved with experience levels below three years and for low complexity jobs (McDaniel, Schmidt, and Hunter, 1988). If experience compensates for age-related declines in mental ability, then older workers may not have special needs relative to younger ones. By virtue of longevity in a workplace, they might be expected to have acquired the knowledge and skills to work safely and productively.

The literature on how acquired skill may compensate for negative age-related changes is somewhat limited in scope (see reviews by Salthouse, 1990; Bosman and Charness, 1996). Research has focused on representative cognitive abilities such as spatial ability, as measured by psychometric test instruments, and memory ability, as measured by experimental tasks. Although experience and expertise usually covary, they may be only loosely connected (e.g., Charness, Krampe, and Mayr, 1996). Practice aimed at improving performance (deliberate practice) appears to be necessary for acquiring high levels of skill (Ericsson and Charness, 1994).

Experimental studies of age and skill in domains such as playing instrumental music (Krampe and Ericsson, 1996; Meinz, 2000; Meinz and Salthouse, 1998) show that experience does not fully mitigate age-related memory decline on domain-related tasks such as recalling briefly presented music notation segments. However, there is some compensation for domain-relevant measures such as performance of music by pianists or violinists in the case of maintained practice schedules.

Studies on typing (Salthouse, 1984; Bosman, 1993, 1994) indicate that older skilled typists may compensate for normative age-related slowing in response time by using greater text preview to maintain high typing rates. The Bosman studies also indicate that for very skilled older typists there may be no need for compensation for typing the second character in a digraph.

Studies by Charness on chess playing (1981a,b) and bridge playing (1983, 1987) indicated that observed age-related declines in memory function were not predictive of game-related performance by older players. There were no age effects on problem-solving performance, just an effect of skill.

Cross-sectional studies by Salthouse and colleagues on architects and engineers showed similar rates of decline in spatial abilities for professionals whose work required spatial reasoning as for control professionals not working in environments demanding spatial reasoning (e.g., Salthouse, 1991). Archival data sources have been used to trace life-span performance in professions (e.g., Simonton, 1988, 1997). They typically show a sharp rise in performance from the teen years to the early adult years followed by a peak in performance in the decades of the 30s followed by a slow decline. Career age seems to be the better predictor of this function than chronological age. A similar inverted backward j-shaped function can be seen for longitudinal Grandmaster performance in chess (Elo, 1965). The age of peak performance varies depending on the profession with earlier peaks observed in mathematicians and later ones in historians. The shape of the function depends on initial productivity rate, as seen in longitudinal publication patterns by psychologists. There is an earlier age of decline for higher-level performers (Horner, Rushton, and Vernon, 1986).

Studies by Morrow (Morrow, in press; Morrow et al., 1993, 1994, 2001) investigating pilot performance show that experience does not fully compensate for age-related decline when considering memory-related navigation activities such as plotting a route, read-back of air traffic control messages, answering probes about current position, and recall of the route. However, when pilots were allowed to take notes (Morrow et al., in press), minimizing the need to use internal memory, older and younger pilot accuracy was equivalent. A recent study by Guohua et al. (2003) suggests that crash rates among professional pilots do not increase as the pilots age from their 40s to their late 50s and, after age adjustment, increased flight experience was associated with markedly lower crash rates. A "healthy worker effect" may partly explain the absence of an age effect.

A concern with many of these studies (except typing, chess, and career performance) is that few had well-validated measures of expertise. Experience was used as a proxy for expertise. However, in the workplace it is also true that few firms can claim validated measures of employee expertise.

On balance, these studies suggest that acquired experience, while improving performance, may not fully compensate for age-related declines in component abilities (for instance, memory and spatial abilities), though acquired skill may play such a role for domain-related performance. As the workforce does become older, and more older adults in the higher age ranges are working, there are likely to be some issues related in the management of cognitive impairment. However, studies that attempt to address the links between basic abilities, knowledge, and professional performance specifically for older adults are relatively sparse and need to be expanded. To the extent that such laboratory behavior generalizes to the workplace, accommodative strategies would seem necessary to try to maintain and improve productivity in an aging workforce.

Effects of Work on Personality and Mental Abilities of Older Workers

The impact of work on psychological characteristics of older workers has been difficult to investigate because type of work is typically confounded with other factors such as intellectual ability, socioeconomic status, exposure to stressors, lifestyle, and diet. However, at least two categories of work-related influences on mental abilities can be identified. One concerns effects attributable to physical aspects of the work environment, such as exposure to toxins. An example of this type of research is a report by Schwartz et al. (2001) in which age-related declines in measures of cognitive functioning were greater for workers with a history of lead exposure than for workers without prior lead exposure. Exposure effects may be more pronounced for older workers than for younger workers because (a) the effects are often cumulative, and older workers typically have had a greater period of exposure; (b) some effects could have a long latency and may not be apparent for 10 to 20 years after the exposure when the workers are older; and (c) older adults may be more vulnerable to many types of biochemical stressors.

The second category of work-related influence on mental ability concerns the psychological nature of the work. The most relevant research within this category is a project by Schooler, Mulatu, and Oates (e.g., 1999) investigating the effects of the substantive complexity of work (based on characteristics such as closeness of supervision, variety, ambiguity, and decision making) on ideational flexibility (a form of fluid intelligence, based largely on examiner ratings). Reciprocal relations have been reported between the two constructs, such that higher ideational flexibility was associated with greater complexity of work, and more complex work was associated with less negative, or more positive, changes in ideational flexibility. The latter direction is particularly intriguing because it suggests that psychological aspects of the nature of work might influence the direction and magnitude of age-related change in cognitive ability.

Although the Schooler et al. (1999) results are encouraging, they should be viewed cautiously because some other evidence appears to be inconsistent with a positive influence of lifestyle or activity on cognitive functioning. For example, college professors, who might be assumed to have highly cognitively stimulating lives, have been found to exhibit age-related declines in cognitive abilities similar to those found in the general population (Christensen et al., 1999; Sward, 1945). Furthermore, although there are some reports of smaller age-related cognitive declines for people with more self-reported cognitive stimulation (e.g., Wilson et al., 2002), other studies have failed to find this pattern (e.g., Salthouse, Berish, and Miles, 2002), including studies focusing specifically on crossword puzzle experience, which is often recommended as a form of mental exercise (Hambrick, Salthouse, and Meinz, 1999).

Perhaps because of the difficulty in characterizing and isolating relevant dimensions of work, there has been relatively little research in which psychological characteristics have been considered as dependent variables reflecting the impact of work conditions on the individual. This is unfortunate because measures of psychological adjustment and of cognitive functioning could prove to be informative outcomes relevant to issues of health and safety in the workplace.

6

Effects of Workplace Exposures on Older Workers

EFFECTS OF CHEMICAL, PHYSICAL, AND BIOLOGICAL EXPOSURES

For the most part, the information available on workplace injuries and illnesses or disorders is derived from employer injury and illness reports required by the Occupational Safety and Health Act (OSHA) and analyzed by the Bureau of Labor Statistics (BLS), U.S. Department of Labor. The BLS reported that a total of 5.2 million workplace injuries and illnesses or disorders were reported in private industry during 2001, the most recent year for which survey data are available from the BLS.[1] The injury and

---

[1]"The Survey of Occupational Injuries and Illnesses is a federal/state program in which employer reports are collected from about 179,800 private industry establishments and processed by state agencies cooperating with the Bureau of Labor Statistics .... The survey measures nonfatal injuries and illnesses only. The survey excludes the self-employed; farms with fewer than 11 employees; private households; federal government agencies; and, for national estimates, employees in state and local government agencies.

"The annual survey provides estimates of the number and frequency (incidence rates) of workplace injuries and illnesses based on logs kept by private industry employers during the year. These records reflect not only the year's injury and illness experience, but also the employer's understanding of which cases are work related under current recordkeeping guidelines of the U.S. Department of Labor" (BLS workplace illness and injury summary December 19, 2002).

It should be noted that the September 11, 2001, events may have impacted the 2001 BLS data, but the BLS survey design did not permit any estimate of such an effect.

illness or disorder rate of 5.7 cases per 100 equivalent full-time workers was the lowest rate since BLS began reporting in 1973 (Table A-11 in Appendix A presents incidence rates of occupational injuries and illnesses for private industry by selected case types, for 1973–2001). Of the 5.2 million total nonfatal injuries and illnesses or disorders, about 2.6 million (2.8 cases per 100 full time workers) were lost workday cases, requiring recuperation away from work or restricted duties at work, or both. These injuries and illnesses or disorders occur in a wide range of industries and occupations (see Table 6-1) as a result of exposure to a wide range of hazards (see Table 6-2).

Of the 5.2 million nonfatal occupational injuries and illnesses or disorders in 2001, 4.9 million were injuries. Eight industries accounted for about 1.4 million injuries, or 29 percent of the total (see Table 6-3). There were about 333,800 newly reported cases of occupational illnesses or disorders

TABLE 6-1 Incidence Rates of Nonfatal Occupational Injuries and Illnesses by Selected Industries, 2001

Industry	Incidence Rate per 100 Full-Time Workers of Occupational Injuries and Illnesses	Range
Agricultural production	7.6	4.8-12.5
Agricultural services	7.1	5.6-9.1
Forestry	6.4	4.7-7.7
Fishing, hunting, trapping	3.9	—
Mining	4.0	2.3-6.9
Construction	7.9	3.5-9.8
Manufacturing, durable goods	8.8	1.8-24.4
Manufacturing, nondurable goods	6.8	0.9-20.0
Transportation and public utilities	6.9	0.9-14.4
Communications	2.9	1.6-5.8
Wholesale trade	5.3	2.6-11.2
Retail trade	5.7	0.9-8.9
Finance, insurance, real estate	1.8	0.3-5.4
Personal services	3.1	1.1-6.0
Business services	2.7	0.8-5.4
Auto repair, services and parking	4.5	3.4-5.2
Hospital services	8.8	—
Other medical services	—	1.2-13.5
Educational services	2.9	1.0-3.1
Social services	5.9	2.9-9.4

SOURCE: U.S. Bureau of Labor Statistics, adapted from *Industry Injury and Illness Data—2001*, Table 1.

TABLE 6-2 Effects of Workplace Exposures

Type of Exposure	Examples of Exposure	Effects

Chemicals	Neurotoxins: e.g., organic solvents
	Asphyxiants: e.g., carbon monoxide
	Carcinogens: e.g., benzene, asbestos
	Allergens and sensitizers:
	  e.g., isocyanates
	Irritants: e.g., chlorine, ammonia
	Reproductive toxins: e.g., lead
	Cardiovascular toxins: e.g., methylene
	  chloride
		Peripheral neuropathy
		Encephalopathy
		Mesothelioma
		Lung cancer
		Pneumoconiosis
		Asthma
		Contact dermatitis
		Toxic hepatitis

Biological agents	Bloodborne pathogens Airborne infections Zoonoses	Hepatitis B, HIV Tuberculosis Rabies
Radiation	Ionizing: e.g., x-ray Non-ionizing: e.g., sunlight (UV)	Leukemia Malignant melanoma
Musculoskeletal stressors	Repetitive motion Awkward posture High force movements Vibration: segmental and whole body	Nerve compression Tendinitis
Other physical hazards	Noise Heat and cold Physical exertion Working at heights Working around powered machinery	Hearing loss Heat stroke Fractures Amputations
Occupational stress: psychosocial factors and work organization	Shiftwork and overtime work High-demand/low-control jobs Organizational change Interpersonal conflicts Role ambiguity	Hypertension Emotional distress
Workplace violence	Worker on worker Other	Homicide

in private industry in 2001. Manufacturing accounted for more than 50 percent of these cases (Table A-12 in Appendix A presents BLS data indicating the number of nonfatal occupational illnesses by industry division and selected case types for 2001). Disorders associated with repeated trauma, such as carpal tunnel syndrome and noise-induced hearing loss, accounted

TABLE 6-3 Number of Cases and Incidence Rates[a] of Nonfatal Occupational Injuries for Private Sector Industries with 100,000 or More Cases, 2001

Industry[b]	SIC Code[c]	Total Cases (in Thousands)	Incidence Rate
Eating and drinking places	581	283.7	5.2
Hospitals	806	265.7	8.2
Nursing and personal care facilities	805	192.9	13.0
Grocery stores	541	175.1	7.8
Department stores	531	145.3	7.7
Trucking and courier services, except air	421	134.9	8.3
Air transportation, scheduled	451	116.3	13.6
Motor vehicles and equipment	371	102.7	10.9

[a]The incidence rates represent the number of injuries per 100 full-time workers and were calculated as (N/EH) × 200,000, where N = number of injuries; EH = total hours worked by all employees during the calendar year; 200,000 = base for 100 equivalent full-time workers working 40 hours per week, 50 weeks per year.
[b]Industries with 100,000 or more cases were determined by analysis of the number of cases at the 3-digit SIC code level.
[c]Standard Industrial Classification Manual, 1987 Edition.
SOURCE: Bureau of Labor Statistics.

for 65 percent of the 333,800 total illness cases. Sixty-five percent of the repeated trauma cases were in manufacturing industries.

Of 2.6 million lost workday cases, 1.5 million required actual days away from work, while the rest resulted in restricted activity at work. Ten occupations accounted for nearly one-third of the 1.5 million lost workday cases that actually involved time away from work (Table A-13 presents BLS data indicating the number of nonfatal occupational injuries and illnesses involving days away from work by selected occupation and industry division for 2000). More than 4 out of 10 of these 1.5 million were sprains or strains, most often involving the back. (Table A-14 presents BLS data indicating the number of nonfatal occupational injuries and illnesses involving days away from work by selected injury or illness characteristics and industry division for 2000). Men accounted for nearly two out of three of the 1.5 million cases, a proportion somewhat higher than their share of the hours worked. The risk of workplace injury or illness or disorder varies substantially by industry and occupation (Table A-15 presents BLS data indicating incidence rates for nonfatal occupational injuries and illnesses involving days away from work per 10,000 full-time workers for selected characteristics and industry division for the year 2000). For example, there is a tenfold difference in incidence rate for falls to a lower level between workers in finance, insurance, and real estate (4.2 per 10,000) and those in construction (40.0 per 10,000).

The U.S. Department of Labor defines work-related musculoskeletal disorders (WMSDs) as injuries or disorders of the muscles, nerves, tendons, joints, cartilage, and spinal discs, not including disorders caused by slips, trips, falls, or motor vehicle accidents. Unfortunately, the OSHA reporting system and the BLS survey do not have a single category for WMSDs. For example, cases caused by exposure to repetitive trauma, such as carpal tunnel syndrome (but not including back disorders), are grouped as illnesses together with occupational hearing loss. All back disorders, whether caused by repetitive trauma or sudden trauma, are grouped with injuries. BLS has estimated that when all WMSDs are aggregated they totaled more than 575,000 in 2000, more than 33 percent of all lost workday cases (U.S. Bureau of Labor Statistics, 2002).

A more detailed assessment of WMSDs has been undertaken by the Washington State Department of Labor and Industries, using worker compensation data. Of approximately 250,000 workers' compensation claims accepted every year in Washington State, more than 65,000 or nearly 30 percent were for nontraumatic, soft-tissue WMSDs. The annual medical and wage replacement costs for these claims is more than $410 million, with additional indirect costs increasing the total impact to $1 billion. While these problems have been identified in substantial numbers in all industry sectors, industries can be rank ordered by the rate and number of WMSDs to determine where the greatest impacts and opportunities for prevention exist. Those industries with the highest combined ranking of WMSD rates and numbers include nursing homes, trucking and courier services, masonry, carpentry, roofing, concrete work, sawmills, and grocery stores. The highest risks are in those industries characterized by manual handling and forceful, repetitive exertions (Washington State Department of Labor and Industries, 2000, 2002). The National Research Council report (2001), *Musculoskeletal Disorders in the Workplace*, provides informative detail on the topic.

Over the past several years there have been approximately 6,000 fatalities annually from workplace injuries as counted by the BLS Census of Fatal Occupational Injuries (CFOI).[2] The numbers and risks vary by industry and

---

[2]"The Census of Fatal Occupational Injuries, part of the BLS occupational safety and health statistics program, provides the most complete count of fatal work injuries available. The program uses diverse state and federal data sources to identify, verify, and profile fatal work injuries. Information about each workplace fatality (occupation and other worker characteristics, equipment being used, and circumstances of the event) is obtained by cross-

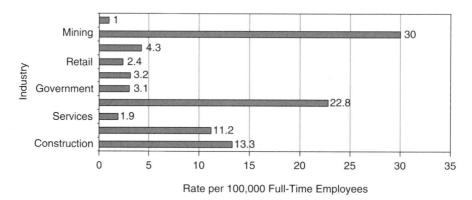

FIGURE 6-1 Rate of workplace fatal injuries, 2001.
SOURCE: Bureau of Labor Statistics

occupation (see Figure 6-1). The number and rate of workplace fatalities have been declining steadily for more than 40 years. However, the longest continuous data series is limited to death certificate information and only dates back to 1980 (see Figure 6-2). The most complete data are from CFOI but only date back to 1992 (see Figure 6-3).

This summary of occupational injury and illness or disorder reporting should be placed in the context of the generally accepted understanding that workplace injuries and illnesses or disorders are substantially under-reported. For example, the BLS survey measures the number of work-related illness or disorder cases that are recognized and reported by employers during the year, but long-term latent illnesses or disorders caused by chemical exposure are difficult to relate to the workplace and are not adequately recognized. Gaps in the training and awareness of medical pro-

referencing source documents, such as death certificates, workers' compensation records, and reports to federal and state agencies."

"Data . . . include deaths occurring in 2001 that resulted from traumatic occupational injuries. An injury is defined as any intentional or unintentional wound or damage to the body resulting from acute exposure to energy, such as heat, electricity, or kinetic energy from a crash, or from the absence of such essentials as heat or oxygen caused by a specific event, incident, or series of events within a single workday or shift. Included are open wounds, intracranial and internal injuries, heatstroke, hypothermia, asphyxiation, acute poisonings resulting from short-term exposures limited to the worker's shift, suicides and homicides, and work injuries listed as underlying or contributory causes of death. Information on work-related fatal illnesses is not reported in the BLS census . . . because the latency period of many occupational illnesses and the difficulty of linking illnesses to work make identification of a universe problematic" (BLS National Census of Fatal Occupational Injuries summary, September 25, 2002).

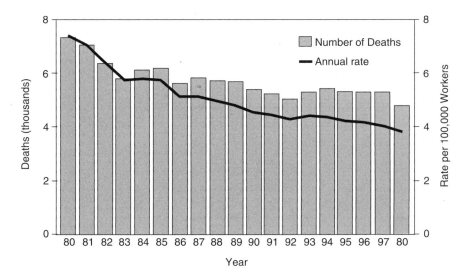

FIGURE 6-2 Distribution and rate of traumatic occupational fatalities by year, United States, 1980–1998.
NOTE: All data for 1998 exclude New York State.
SOURCE: Fatality data are from the National Traumatic Occupational and Fatalities Surveillance System, National Institute for Occupational Safety and Health. Employment data are from the Current Population Survey, Bureau of Labor Statistics.

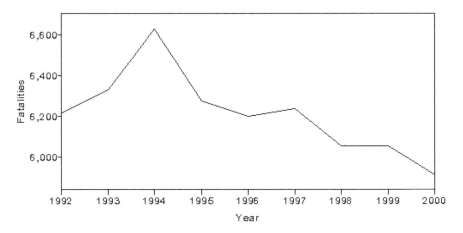

FIGURE 6-3 Number of occupational fatalities.
SOURCE: Bureau of Labor Statistics Census of Fatal Occupational Injuries.

viders contribute to underreporting. There are also significant disincentives to reporting workplace problems. For medical providers these include reluctance to participate in contentious workers' compensation proceedings. For workers these include fear of discrimination and income loss.

Several studies have found this underreporting to be of significant magnitude. A National Research Council panel evaluated the BLS system for occupational injury and illness or disorder reporting in 1987 and concluded that it had significant shortcomings for both statistical and administrative purposes (National Research Council, 1987). While noting substantial reasons and incentives for underreporting, particularly with regard to long-latency occupational illness or disorder, the panel was unable to determine the extent of reporting errors. The panel found it startling that the nation did not even have an agreed method to estimate a phenomenon as basic as traumatic death in the workplace. The subsequent development of the BLS CFOI system to count these traumatic deaths addressed this, but most of the other sources of underreporting have yet to be corrected.

There are a number of factors that might result in underreporting of occupational injuries and illnesses or disorders. Those who experience economic insecurity appear to have increased concern about job loss (Minter, 1996). Union membership among nonagricultural employees has been falling (Dunlop, 1994; Hirsch, Macpherson, and Vroman, 2001; BLS, 2002). Contingent work has been growing, and the U.S. General Accounting Office (GAO) estimated that by the year 2000, contingent workers comprised 30 percent of the country's workforce (GAO, 2000). The growing immigrant worker population includes those lacking documentation (Schmitt, 2001). Few reliable data are available on the growth of traditional safety incentive programs. Medical diagnosis of occupational illness or disorder depends on access to medical care, which has been declining among the workforce (Hoffman and Schlobohm, 2000; Holahan, 2000). Landrigan and Baker (1991) estimated that there are 50,000 to 70,000 deaths yearly from workplace diseases and that these are typically not correctly diagnosed because they mimic nonoccupational illnesses or disorders and because most physicians are not adequately trained to recognize them. Biddle and colleagues (1998) concluded that workers' compensation databases also undercount workplace illness, estimating that between 9 percent and 45 percent of workers with known or suspected cases actually file for benefits. Acute conditions were no more likely to lead to claims than chronic conditions with long latency. Rosenman et al. (2000) similarly found that workers' compensation claims were filed by only 25 percent of workers whose WMSDs had been reported by physicians according to the Michigan State occupational disease reporting law.

Most recently Azaroff and Levenstein (2002) have evaluated obstacles to the reporting of occupational injuries and illnesses in the BLS survey, workers' compensation systems, employer medical programs, and physician reporting systems. They identify numerous barriers (filters) to reporting in each of these systems and note that these barriers "particularly block documentation of health problems affecting populations especially vulnerable to workplace hazards, including immigrant and low-wage workers." None of these analyses, however, specifically address reporting among older workers.

The BLS undertook an evaluation of current injury and illness reporting in an effort to understand the declining trend in injury and illness reports (Conway and Svenson, 1998). This analysis did not suggest that rates fell because of a shift in industry composition of the labor force, but it did note that major legislative changes in workers' compensation systems at the state level may have had an effect on reports of injuries. They suggested on the basis of anecdotal evidence that the trend may result from increasing awareness and recognition of occupational hazards among all parties. At about the same time, the BLS commissioned an annual audit of its own reporting system (Lexington Group and Eastern Research Group, 2002). The results suggest that over the four-year period, there have been generally consistent results with over 90 percent of the sample providing accurate reports. In this administrative audit, employer reports to OSHA were matched with internal company records. Consequently no interviews with workers are reported, nor is there an effort to develop independent estimates of occupational injury and/or disease. A comprehensive analysis of the trend in injury reporting, therefore, has yet to be done.

IMPAIRMENTS, INJURIES, AND ILLNESSES OR DISORDERS AMONG OLDER WORKERS

Workers 45 years and older accounted for 494,000 of the 1.6 million lost workday cases reported by BLS for the year 2000 (30 percent of the cases and 32 percent of the hours worked; Table A-16 presents BLS data indicating the number of nonfatal occupational injuries and illnesses involving days away from work, by selected worker characteristics and industry division for the year 2000). While the numbers of cases among workers less than 45 years old dropped steadily from 1992 to 2000, the number of cases among older workers slowly rose over the same period (see Figure 6-4). Also, the median duration of absence from work due to a work injury increased consistently with age, from 4 days among those age 24 and younger to 10 days for those age 55 and older (BLS, 1996). BLS identified two reasons for this age differential. First, a higher proportion of injuries among older workers are more severe in nature; fractures, for example, make up 11 percent of injuries among workers 55 years and older but only 5 percent of injuries among workers under age 55. Second, for the same

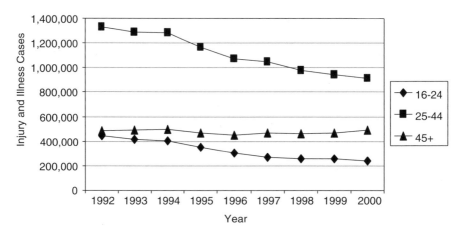

FIGURE 6-4 Number of lost workday injury and illness cases by age group in the years 1992–2000.
SOURCE: Bureau of Labor Statistics.

condition older workers lose more workdays; fractures result in a median 30-day absence among older workers but 18 days among younger workers.

Assessment of differences in employment and employment characteristics over time could contribute to a better understanding of the changes in rates of workplace injuries and age. Current BLS data reports lack adequate denominator information for this purpose although it has been demonstrated that application of CPS age-specific employment information could be used to estimate rates for many BLS data now available only as counts (Ruser, 1998). A complementary system of self-reported work-related injury data is provided by the National Center for Health Statistics annual surveys, the National Health Interview Survey in particular. Detailed information about work and work exposures, however, has only been collected once (1998). The NHIS 1988 supplement provided a single snapshot of data; changes in employment and risk patterns should be followed prospectively to provide information about whether, for example, the increased number of cases among older workers is due to increased numbers of older workers, or whether older workers are exposed to more or different workplace hazards now than previously.

Although WMSDs are the most common work-related disorders, little is known about their age distribution. Numbers of WMSDs (but not rates) by age and industry are available from the Washington State workers' compensation system (Table A-17 presents a summary of workers' compensation claims for work-related musculoskeletal disorders for Washington

State, from 1992 through 2000). Twenty-two percent of the WMSD claims occur in workers age 45 and older, ranging from 17 percent in construction to 37 percent in public administration. The greatest number of claims among those age 45 and older was in the service sector, with 23,612 claims for the years 1992–2000. This was 29 percent of all claims in this older age group, only slightly greater than the 26 percent of claims among all ages for this sector. Only for public administration was the percentage of claims among the older workers (7.6 percent) substantially greater than the percentage of claims among all workers (4.5 percent).

In 2001, 2,665 or 45 percent of the 5,900 total fatalities counted by CFOI were accounted for by the 35 percent of all workers who were 45 years or older (Table A-18 presents BLS data indicating the number and percentage of occupational injuries, by selected worker characteristics, for 2001). The fatal injury rate is higher for self-employed than for wage workers, and differences increase with age (Personic and Windau, 1995).

Older workers experience relatively high rates of workplace fatality and high injury severity compared with younger workers (Kisner and Pratt, 1999; Myers et al., 1999). A recent analysis (Bailer et al., 2003) of the National Traumatic Occupational Fatality database confirmed that the rates of fatal occupational injuries increase with age and noted that this trend is especially marked for machinery related fatalities. Agnew and Suruda (1993) noted that the rates of work-related fatal falls increased among older workers and that a relatively large percentage of these fatalities were associated with the use of ladders. Possible reasons include enhanced susceptibility, lower baseline function, or the effects of cumulative exposures.

Older workers also experience relatively low overall rates of work-related injury and illness or disorders compared with younger workers. The reasons for this are not entirely clear but possible explanations include experience and expertise, motivation, and survivor or healthy-worker effects.

The prevalence of disability in the workforce has long been known to increase with age (Kraus and Stoddard, 1991; Blanck et al., 2000). The National Health Interview Survey (1994) shows that the percentage of workers with work-limiting disabilities increases with age, starting at 3.4 percent for workers aged 18 to 28 years, increasing to 8.4 percent for workers aged 50 to 59, and to 13.6 percent for workers aged 60 to 69. The increased prevalence of impairments among older workers and the growth of our older workforce will increase the number of workers who bring impairments into the workforce with them.

This increased prevalence of impairments among older workers is of concern because of recent research (Zwerling et al., 1997, 1998; Zwerling, Sprince et al., 1998) suggesting that workers with a broad spectrum of impairments are at higher risk for occupational injuries. This increased risk was seen among older workers in the Health and Retirement Study

(Zwerling et al., 1998; Zwerling, Sprince et al., 1998), as well as among workers of all ages surveyed in the National Health Interview Survey (Zwerling et al., 1997). Similar results were recently found among Taiwanese workers as well (Chi, Chen, and Lin, 2001).

In the United States, controversy over the risk of injuries to older workers dates back at least to the 1920s, when a purported increased risk of occupational injuries among older workers was used as justification to exclude them from the workforce (Kossoris, 1940). Using data from the states of Wisconsin and New York as well as from Switzerland and Austria, the BLS (Kossoris, 1940) concluded that "older workers were injured less frequently than younger workers; but once injured, they experienced proportionately more deaths and permanent impairments than did younger workers. Similarly, their healing periods in temporary disability were, on the average, longer." Although these data had a number of limitations—underreporting of injuries, absence of occupational data, and inaccuracy of reported ages, to name just three—the results have stood the test of time.

Over the years, substantial data have accumulated suggesting that older workers have a decreased risk for nonfatal occupational injuries than that of their younger colleagues. This has been seen both in national databases (Root, 1981; Leigh, 1986) as well as in studies of single industries (Mueller et al., 1987; Jensen and Sinkule, 1988; Oleske et al., 1989). In the 1988 National Health Interview Survey Supplement on Occupational Health and Safety, men 50 years of age and older averaged 2.65 lost workday injuries per 100 person-years compared to men aged 30–49 years who averaged 5.78 per 100 person-years (Landen and Hendricks, 1992). In part, this difference may be related to differences in occupations of younger and older workers. Mitchell (1988) addressed this issue in a multivariate analysis of U.S. national data. She found that for injuries causing only temporary disability, 81 percent of the variance was explained by occupation, but age explained 11 percent of the variance after accounting for occupation and industry. A recent review of the literature (Laflamme and Menckel, 1995) concluded that older workers have a lower risk of nonfatal occupational injuries than that of their younger colleagues.

Pransky et al. (2000) reviewed possible explanations for the lower rate of occupational injuries among older workers. These included increased experience, safer behavior, and less physically demanding jobs. They also considered potential reporting bias, with some occupational injuries being attributed to nonoccupational causes by worker health care providers. However, the literature provides little evidence to support any of these explanations.

Although older workers are less likely to be injured at work, there is considerable evidence to suggest that the consequences of those injuries are greater than those suffered by younger workers. Since 1940 (Kossoris), the

BLS has reported evidence that older workers had longer periods of disability than their younger colleagues. More recent data (Personick and Windau, 1995; BLS, 1996) show that the median number of workdays lost per occupational injury increases monotonically from 4 at age 20 to 10 at age 55 and over (see Figure 6-5). Since this prolonged disability can be seen in specific industries as well as across broader jurisdictions, it is not likely that it can be explained by industry, occupation, or specific job exposures (Laflamme and Menckel, 1995; Landen and Hendricks, 1992; Kossoris, 1940). The most frequently mentioned explanation for the difference in duration of disability has been a presumed decrease in recuperative powers among older workers (Personick and Windau, 1995; Nicholson, 1995). The prolonged period of disability among injured older workers suggests the importance of return-to-work programs to hasten the recovery of these older workers.

Although occupational injuries are less common among older workers, when they do occur they are more likely to result in death than among younger workers. This was clear in the statewide databases of the 1930s (Kossoris, 1940), and it is still seen in the National Traumatic Occupational

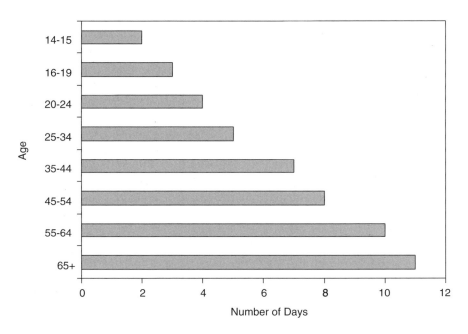

FIGURE 6-5 Median days away from work due to workplace injury, 2000.
SOURCE: U.S. Bureau of Labor Statistics, Issues in Labor Statistics, April 1996.

Fatality database (Kisner and Pratt, 1997) and in the Census of Fatal Occupational Injuries (Personick and Windau, 1995). In the 1980s, workers aged 65 years and older had a workplace fatality rate 2.6 times that of workers aged 16 to 64. Using a multivariate analysis, Mitchell (1988) found that 80 percent of the variance in occupational fatalities was related to age, even when occupation and industry are entered in the model.

HEALTH EFFECTS OF WORK ORGANIZATION

Downsizing has been associated with increased rates of fatal occupational injuries in the United States (Richardson and Loomis, 1997) and absenteeism in Finland. In the health care industry, studies have suggested that downsizing, understaffing, and stress (American Nurses Association, 1995) are associated with occupational injuries among nurses (Shogren and Calkins, 1997) and back injuries among aides in nursing homes (Service Employees International Union, 1995; Institute of Medicine, 1996). Needlestick injuries have been associated with organizational restructuring that increases stressful working conditions in U.S. hospitals (Aiken and Fagin, 1997) and with understaffing and poor organizational climate (Clarke, Sloane, and Aiken, 2002). Thirty-nine percent of nurses are 45 years of age or older (Dohm, 2000).

A higher incidence of injury and illness has been reported among subcontractors (Quinlan and Mayhew, 2000). For example, the outsourcing of maintenance in the U.S. petrochemical industry has led to serious safety and health problems, including several catastrophic explosions (Rebitzer, 1995). In Australia, outsourced (largely home-based) garment workers reported three times more injuries and more work-related violence than those working in factories. In addition, self-employed workers, especially those in agriculture, road transport, and construction, face a significantly higher risk of serious injury or death (Quinlan and Mayhew, 2000). A study in Finland also observed a greater risk of mortality among temporary employees compared with permanent employees, primarily from alcohol-related causes and, for men, smoking-related cancer (Kivimäki et al., 2003).

Extended work hours have been associated with work accidents and injuries (Daltroy et al., 1991; Hanecke et al., 1998; Leigh, 1986; Lowery et al., 1998; Spurgeon, Harrington, and Cooper, 1997). For example, Hanecke et al. (1998), examining 1994 national German injury data, found a greatly increased injury risk beyond the ninth hour at work during a workday. For evening and night shifts, risk increased greatly past the eighth hour of work. Similarly, Lowery et al. (1998), examining data from construction contracts at Denver International Airport, 1990–1994, found that contractors with overtime payrolls had a two to three times higher injury rate than those without overtime payrolls. Recent reviews of studies on organiza-

tional factors have found lower injury rates to be associated with empowerment of the workforce; good relations between management and workers
(Hale and Hovden, 1998; Shannon, Mayr, and Haines, 1997); autonomy;
efficacy; delegation of control; low stress; low grievance rates (Hale and
Hovden, 1998); and encouragement of long-term commitment of the workforce (Shannon et al., 1997).

Musculoskeletal injuries and pain have been associated with organizational downsizing in Finland (Vahtera, Kivimaki, and Pentti, 1997), reengineering in a Canadian hospital (Shannon et al., 2001), low staff density
combined with high nursing-unit workloads (Larese and Fiorito, 1994;
Yassi et al., 1995), lean production in the automobile industry in the United
States and Canada (Landsbergis, Cahill, and Schnall, 1999), contingent or
temporary work (European Agency for Safety and Health at Work, 2002),
and overtime work (Bergqvist et al., 1995; Bernard et al., 1994).

A substantial body of research has linked WMSDs to stressful aspects
of work organization, such as machine-paced work, inadequate work/rest
cycles, wage incentives, time pressure, overload, low job control, low social
support, repetitive work, and lack of task variability (Ahlberg-Hulten,
Theorell, and Sigala, 1995; Bergqvist et al., 1995; Bernard et al., 1994;
Bongers et al., 1993; Kerr et al., 2001; Krause et al., 1997; Leino and
Hanninen, 1995; Moon and Sauter, 1996; National Research Council,
2001; Warren, 2000; Warren et al., 2000). It has been suggested that the
dramatic increase in the number of reported WMSDs in the United States,
beginning in the mid-1980s, resulted in part from work intensification. For
example, the U.S. meat packing industry, in response to global competition,
had increased line speed, introduced machine pacing, and fragmented jobs
(Novek, Yassi, and Spiegel, 1990), which contributed to dramatic increases
in WMSDs (National Institute for Occupational Safety and Health [NIOSH],
1994).

The NIOSH Musculoskeletal Disorders Working Group has determined
that "research is needed in the areas of task assignment and work/rest
schedules, job rotation, job enlargement, and length of the workday" (NIOSH,
2001: 11) and has called for studies on "the impact of downsizing, labor
shortages, or increased overtime on the occurrence of MSD" (NIOSH,
2001: 17). Additional evidence for the importance of such research comes
from studies of the effects of long-term employment in piecework jobs.
Garment workers in Quebec were found to have a doubling of risk of severe
disability associated with employment for more than five years in jobs paid
according to a piecework system. The association was strongest for disability due to musculoskeletal disorders but also present for cardiovascular
disease (Brisson et al., 1989; Brisson, Vezina, and Vinet, 1992). Vineyard
workers in France were found to have a doubling of risk of hand

paresthesias associated with piecework paid jobs in vine pruning (Roquelaure et al., 2001).

Downsizing has also been associated with minor psychiatric disorders among English male government employees (Ferrie et al., 1998). Long work hours have been associated with psychological distress, including burnout (Spurgeon et al., 1997), psychological symptoms (Sparks et al., 1997), and unhealthy behaviors (Westman, Eden, and Shirom, 1985).

The International Labour Office (ILO) of the United Nations recently reported on workplace mental health issues in Finland, Germany, Poland, the United Kingdom, and the United States. It noted that "in all five countries, the incidence of mental health problems [particularly depression] has risen in the past decade [and] . . . while the origins of mental instability are complex and the workplace practices and income and employment patterns differ widely among the countries studied, a number of common threads appear to link the high prevalence of stress, burnout, and depression to changes taking place in the labor market, due partly to the effects of economic globalization" (Gabriel and Liimatainen, 2000: 4).

The strongest evidence that recent trends in working life may be having an impact on workers' health comes from studies of chronic diseases, such as cardiovascular disease (CVD), CVD risk factors such as blood pressure (BP), and the job characteristics and job schedules that are associated with CVD and BP. CVD is the number one cause of morbidity and mortality in the United States (American Heart Association, 1998). Hypertension in the United States is very common, with a prevalence of about 75 percent among African Americans and 50 percent among whites aged 60–74. The cost of work-related CVD in the United States is estimated at $10 to $20 billion annually (Leigh and Schnall, 2000).

We commonly label chronic diseases or conditions (e.g., hypertension, CVD, adult-onset diabetes), as diseases of aging, implying that they result from some natural biological process. However, essential hypertension (the 95 percent of hypertension cases without an organic cause such as kidney disease), adult-onset diabetes, and heart disease are quite uncommon in nonindustrialized populations (Carvalho et al., 1989; Cooper, Rotimi, and Ward, 1999). A major cross-cultural study of adult BP in 84 groups worldwide found virtually no rise in BP with age and no hypertension among hunter-gatherers, herders, or traditional family farmers (Waldron et al., 1982). This study also found substantial ($r = 0.46–0.67$) and significant associations between BP and involvement in a money economy even after controlling for salt consumption and, for men, after controlling for body mass index (BMI) (Waldron et al., 1982).

Such studies suggest that the primary causes of these diseases are stressful living and working conditions, shaped by a socioeconomic status hierarchy in developed societies. Therefore, prevention of these diseases, or accommodation of older workers who have these diseases, involves identifying and altering those conditions.

Few studies have examined the effect of new organizational practices on cardiovascular outcomes. Danish bus drivers transferred to another bus company showed increases in urinary cortisol, glycated hemoglobin, and systolic BP at work during the year following transfer (Netterstrom and Hansen, 2000). In a study of English male government employees, downsizing was associated with increases in BP (Ferrie et al., 1998). However, other studies have shown only temporary increases in BP following reorganization (Pollard, 2001) or downsizing (Schnall, Landsbergis et al., 1992).

In contrast, a larger body of research exists examining the effect of task-level risk factors that have been increasing in prevalence: excessive work hours and stressful job characteristics. Job strain, defined as high psychological job demands and low job control (Karasek and Theorell, 1990), is the most widely studied job stressor; it has been increasing in prevalence in Europe in the past decade (European Foundation, 1997) and may be increasing in the United States. As of 2000, there have been 24 studies of job strain and CVD among men (Belkic, Landsbergis et al., 2000), and six studies among women (Brisson, 2000), most with significant positive associations. Some studies, while not examining the full demand/control model, have shown that low job control predicts cardiovascular disease (Bosma, Peter, Siegrist, and Marmot, 1998). There is also evidence that low control in the workplace increases risk of depression (Stansfeld et al., 1999) and rates of sickness absence (North et al., 1996).

The link between job strain and CVD appears to be mediated in part by BP. While few studies of job strain and casual clinic BP have shown significant associations (Schnall, Landsbergis, and Baker, 1994), strong evidence of an association is found in studies where BP is measured by an ambulatory (portable) monitor (Belkic, Schnall, and Ugljesic, 2000). Ambulatory BP (AmBP) is a better predictor of target organ damage and CVD than is casual clinic BP (Verdecchia et al., 1999). Most cross-sectional studies of job strain and AmBP in men (Belkic, Landsbergis et al., 2000) and in women (Brisson, 2000) show significant positive associations, with an effect of job strain in the range of 4–8 mm Hg systolic AmBP. In the only long-term prospective study of job strain and AmBP, New York City men with chronic exposure to job strain over three years had 11 to 12 mm Hg higher systolic work AmBP than the group unexposed at both times (Schnall et al., 1998). In addition, those reporting job strain at entry into the study but no job strain three years later exhibited a significant decrease in systolic AmBP of 5.3 mm Hg at work and 4.7 mm Hg at home (Schnall et al., 1998). This decrease suggests that early detection and prevention strategies should be effective, especially for older workers who are more likely to have elevated BP.

On-the-job BP monitoring while employees are working holds promise as a surveillance technique to detect hidden work-related hypertension, characterized by normal casual clinic BP and elevated work BP (Schnall and Belkic, 2000). Such surveillance programs can trigger both individual treatment and workplace prevention programs for older workers, including job redesign (Belkic et al., 2001). Siegrist's (1996) effort-reward imbalance model has as its basis the notion of reciprocity: appropriate reward for effort expended. Reward may be income, esteem (including self-esteem), and status, including career opportunities. The hypotheses is that emotional distress that accompanies inadequate reward for effort expended activates biological pathways that increase risk of cardiovascular disease. The effort-reward imbalance model relates not only to a particular workplace, but also to the operation of the labor market. Careers may be blocked, and hence rewards diminished, by lack of occupational opportunity in the labor market. Studies in Sweden (Peter et al., 2002) and the United Kingdom (Bosma et al., 1998) have shown that low control and effort-reward imbalance are independently related to coronary heart disease. The Whitehall II study has shown that effort-reward imbalance is related to functioning, using the SF-36 measure (Stansfeld et al., 1998).

A number of studies have suggested that long working hours may increase the risk of heart disease (Alfredsson, Spetz, and Theorell, 1985; Russek and Zohman, 1958; Theorell and Rahe, 1972; Falger and Schouten, 1992; Liu, Tanaka, and The Fukuoka Heart Study Group, 2002; Sokejima and Kagamimori, 1998). Two recent Japanese studies also found evidence linking overtime work with elevated BP among men working more than 55 hours per week (Hayashi et al., 1996; Iwasaki et al., 1998), with the second study finding an association only among men greater than 50 years old.

Increased risk of CVD has also been seen in threat-avoidant vigilant work (Belkic et al., 1992). For example, professional drivers, particularly urban transport operators, have been consistently found to have high risk of CVD and hypertension (Belkic, Emdad, and Theorell, 1998). Fifty-four percent of all U.S. bus drivers are 45 years of age or older (Dohm, 2000).

The amount of CVD that can be attributed to work stressors may be substantial. Conservative estimates of population-attributable risk (PAR percent) are 7 to 16 percent in Sweden (Karasek and Theorell, 1990) and 6 to 14 percent in Denmark (Kristensen, Kronitzer, and Alfredsson, 1998). Based on data from the New York City blood pressure study, roughly 25 to 40 percent of hypertension among men can be attributed to work stressors (Landsbergis et al., 1994). Few studies have examined the combined or synergistic effect of workplace stressors along with other work exposures.

The effect of job strain is more consistent and stronger for blue-collar men than for men with higher socioeconomic status (SES), both for CVD (Belkic, Landsbergis et al., 2000) and BP (Landsbergis et al., 2003). Among women, similar (though not completely consistent) patterns were seen in the Framingham Heart Study (Eaker, Pinsky, and Castelli, 1992; Eaker, Packard, and Thom, 1989; Haynes and Feinleib, 1980; LaCroix, 1984). These findings suggest that increased efforts at early detection and prevention of work-related CVD and hypertension are especially required among lower SES workers. There has been a large decline in the death rate from CVD over the past 40 years in the United States (Liao and Cooper, 1995), and studies suggest that CVD incidence was also declining during the 1960s and 1970s (Elveback, Connolly, and Melton, 1986; Gillum, Folsom, and Blackburn, 1984; Pell and Fayerweather, 1985). However, more recent U.S. studies show little or no decline in CVD incidence over the past 20 years (Derby et al., 2000; Goldberg et al., 1999; Kostis et al., 2001; McGovern et al., 2001; Rosamond et al., 1998, 2001). There has been remarkable progress in treating CVD (and reducing mortality), but little recent success in preventing this disease.

This is surprising given declines in the prevalence of smoking and cholesterol levels (Johnson et al., 1993; Sytkowski et al., 1996). There is conflicting evidence regarding trends in the prevalence of hypertension (Brody, 1994; Burt et al., 1995; Kannel, Garrison, and Dannenberg, 1993). While some risk factors, such as obesity and diabetes, are increasing in prevalence (Harris et al., 1998; Kuczmarski et al., 1994), there is increasing recognition that psychosocial stressors may also be contributing to maintaining stable CVD rates (Gornel, 1999).

In the context of declining mortality rates for all SES groups, there is a growing gap between higher and lower SES groups in the United States in death rates from all causes, according to data from 1959 through 1996 (Steenland, Henley, and Thun, 2002) and death from CVD, according to data from 1969 through 1998 (Singh and Siahpush, 2002). For example, for men 45 years or older, the disparity in heart disease mortality rates between the highest and lowest educational groups during 1959 to 1972 was only 22 percent but rose to 62 percent during the 1982 to 1996 period. For women 45 years or older, the disparity rose from 48 percent during 1959 to 1972, to 73 percent during 1982 to 1996 (Steenland et al., 2002). There are no U.S. data on incidence of CVD by social class; however, growing SES differences in incidence of heart disease have been observed in Sweden between 1971 and 1994 (Hallqvist et al., 1998) and in Denmark between 1981 and 1993 (Tuchsen and Endahl, 1999).

Since chronic diseases such as CVD and hypertension take years to develop, we may only be observing the initial stages of the health impact of increasingly stressful working conditions. Further research is needed to test the hypothesis that increasingly stressful job characteristics, especially among lower SES workers (Vogel, 2002), and increasing income inequality may be contributing to the observed increases in health inequality and to the failure of CVD rates to decline.

Effects of Job Characteristics on Learning and Psychological Functioning Related to Health and Health Behaviors

Karasek's job demands-control model of work stress also describes the adult socialization of personality traits and behavior patterns that occur at work. Chronic adaptation to low-control/low-demand situations (passive jobs) can result in reduced ability to solve problems or tackle challenges (Karasek and Theorell, 1990), feelings of depression (Karasek, 1979), and learned helplessness. Conversely, when high (but not overwhelming) job demands are matched with greater authority and skill, more active learning occurs, enabling individuals to develop a broader range of coping strategies. For example, decreases in smoking prevalence were observed among New York City men whose job control increased over three years (Landsbergis et al., 1998). In Sweden, workers whose jobs became more passive over six years reported less participation in political and leisure activities. In contrast, workers in jobs that became more active participated more in these activities (Karasek and Theorell, 1990). In the United States, increased intellectual flexibility, nonauthoritarianism, capacity to take responsibility for one's actions, and participation in intellectually demanding leisure time were observed among workers with greater occupational self-direction, a concept similar to decision latitude (Kohn and Schooler, 1982). These findings were replicated in 20 years of follow-up, with an effect significantly greater among older workers (Schooler, Mulatu, and Oates, 1999). Similarly, participation in complex leisure-time activities increases intellectual functioning among older workers (Schooler and Mulatu, 2001).

There is "a substantial amount of evidence documenting the continued learning capacity of older workers. . . . Interventions designed to increase the feelings of self-direction and the control of older persons (such as teaching them effective coping skills) result in improved cognitive problem-solving ability. . . . In terms of the workplace, efforts to enhance the autonomy and decision latitude of older workers might well result in heightened levels of psychological well-being and performance" (Robertson and Tracy, 1998: 89). "Jobs that are stimulating or that enhance skill development over time may positively affect productivity, while jobs that are simple or highly routine may over time produce workers who are unchallenged, bored and eventually poor performers" (Robertson and Tracy, 1998: 89; Avolio and Waldman, 1987). In a prospective study of a representative sample of Danish employees, early retirement was predicted not only by ergonomic exposures, but also by poor possibilities for development at work, mediated by monotonous repetitive work (Borg, Burr, and Christensen, 1997). Thus, work organization acts not only as a potential source of stress and increased disease risk for older workers, but also potentially as a key factor in the promotion of physical and mental health and the development of creative potential, effective coping, and social involvement outside work.

Differential Health Effects of Work Organization by Age

There is limited evidence that physical workplace stressors can impact the health of older workers to a greater extent than younger workers. For example, shiftworkers over 40 years of age seem to sleep worse than younger workers after night (but not after morning) shifts (Haermae, 1996). There is also limited evidence that psychosocial workplace stressors can produce an even greater risk of injury and illness or disorders among older workers than younger workers. For example, in Finland, the effect of downsizing on absenteeism and musculoskeletal disorders was found to be greater for older workers than younger workers (Vahtera et al., 1997).

Older workers also appear to be less likely to tolerate tight time constraints and assembly work (Molinie and Volkoff, 1994). In a New York City study, the effect of job strain on ambulatory blood pressure (AmBP) was greater among men aged 51–60 (15 mm Hg) and 41–50 (9 mm Hg) than among 31- to 40-year-old men (Schnall, Schwartz, Landsbergis, Warren, and Pickering, 1992). Similarly, in a Japanese study of white-collar men, an effect of overtime on BP was seen only in men over 50 years old (Iwasaki et al., 1998). These studies are consistent with an effect of cumulative lifetime exposure to work stressors (represented by age). A less likely alternative explanation is that older workers are somehow more vulnerable to the effects of work stressors, independent of their previous work-life exposures. This question needs to be resolved through further research.

Older workers may find some job schedules and characteristics more challenging, such as night work, tasks that rely heavily on working memory, muscular strength and joint flexibility, or require high levels of cardiovascular fitness, fast reaction times, and fast information processing (Griffiths, 1997). Such tasks could result in performance deficits in older people, as well as an increased risk of accidents or other acute or chronic health problems (Czaja and Sharit, 1993; Haermae, 1996). Thus, "any efforts to keep older people at work will clearly have to pay particular attention to minimizing work stress, musculoskeletal disorders and cardiovascular disease" (Griffiths, 1997: 199), which are common conditions experienced by older workers (Ilmarinen, 1997; Tuomi, Ilmarinen, Martikainen, Aalto, and Klockars, 1997).

In contrast to the BP studies cited above, studies of job strain and CVD have provided mixed findings when stratified by age. Some studies do find stronger associations of job strain among older workers and CVD among older Swedish white-collar men (Johnson, Hall, and Theorell, 1989); coronary heart disease (CHD) symptoms among older Swedish white-collar workers (Karasek, 1990); and CHD among older Framingham, Massachusetts women (LaCroix, 1984).

However, two case control studies of myocardial infarction (MI) in Stockholm found a greater relative risk in younger workers: 40- to 49-year-olds versus 50- to 64-year-olds in one study (Alfredsson, Karasek, and Theorell, 1982) and 45- to 54-year-olds versus 55- to 64-year-olds in the other (Theorell et al., 1998). In the more recent Stockholm study (Theorell et al., 1998), decreasing job control during the three years preceding the MI was a much stronger risk factor in the 45–54 age group than in the 55–64 age group. The authors speculated that, in this younger group, "decreased job status could be seen as a major threat. Previous studies in industrialized countries have shown that working men can expect rising levels of decision latitude (Beilin and Puddey, 1993), especially during the first years of their working career. During the period after 55 years of age, this development is halted, and no further increase in decision latitude may then be expected in most men. When men are approaching retirement age, such a loss of status may not be perceived as equally threatening" (Theorell et al., 1998: 387).

An important concept called *work capacity* or *work ability* has emerged from research in the Nordic countries. A recent review points out that the concept of work capacity requires that the productive potential of workers not be thought of only in terms of the capabilities of a person, but also in terms of the nature of the work itself, specifically work demands and other factors such as work content and work organization. This is an "innovative and promising line of research on the relationships among age, health, and the productivity of older workers" (Robertson and Tracy, 1998: 91). The World Health Organization (WHO) conceptualizes work capacity as "a comprehensive term covering all the capacities necessary to perform a given type of work . . . [and] therefore including physical, mental, and social functioning capacities" (WHO, 1993: 3).

The Finnish Institute of Occupational Health conducted the largest study of the work capacity of older workers, an 11-year follow-up (1981–1992) of 6,259 municipal workers, aged 44–58 at the beginning of the study (Tuomi, Ilmarinen, Martikainen et al., 1997). The researchers developed a work ability index (WAI) that "represents a composite of standard measures of health status, such as the number of diagnosed diseases and the number of sick days within the past year, in combination with more subjective measures, such as estimations of present work ability in relation to physical and mental work demands (as a function of the nature of the work itself) and personal psychological resources" (Ilmarinen, 1994, cited in

Robertson and Tracy, 1998: 92). The WAI of this cohort in 1981 was a strong predictor of retirement on disability pension or death by 1992 (Tuomi, Ilmarinen, Seitsamo et al., 1997).

Work content, work environment, and work organization were found to predict accurately both the reported decline in work capacity and the observed rate of retirement due to disability over the first four years of the study (Ilmarinen, 1994). Demanding physical features of work content accounted for significant decreases in work capacity, including static muscular work, use of muscular strength, lifting and carrying, sudden peak loads, repetitive movements, and simultaneously bent and twisted work postures (Ilmarinen, 1994). This implies the need for ergonomic improvements in the workplace to reduce these risk factors. Aspects of the work environment that contributed to the deterioration of work capacity were dirty and wet workplaces, accident hazards, hot or cold workplaces, and changes in temperature during the workday (Ilmarinen, 1994), implying the need to improve environmental conditions. Work organization risk factors in the Finnish study included role conflicts; unsatisfactory supervision and planning of work; fear of failure and mistake; time pressure; lack of freedom of choice; lack of influence on own work; lack of professional development; and lack of acknowledgment and appreciation (Ilmarinen, 1994; Robertson and Tracy, 1998). Such risk factors are consistent with the job demands-control model of occupational stress and health as described by Karasek and Theorell (1990). Older workers appeared to be more vulnerable to these risk factors than their younger colleagues (Griffiths, 1997: 206).

Major factors associated with improving work ability over 11 years of follow-up were improvement in the supervisors' attitudes, decreased repetitive work movements, and increased vigorous physical exercise during leisure time (Tuomi, Ilmarinen, Martikainen et al., 1997; Tuomi, Ilmarinen, Seitsamo et al., 1997). The major positive components of supervisors' roles were a positive attitude to the process of aging, team-based cooperation with employees, and taking age-related changes into account in the design and management of work (Tuomi, Ilmarinen, Seitsamo et al., 1997). Predictors of decreasing work ability included lowered recognition and esteem, increased standing at work, poorer workrooms, and decreased vigorous exercise during leisure time (Tuomi, Ilmarinen, Martikainen et al., 1997; Tuomi, Ilmarinen, Seitsamo et al., 1997). Adverse effects "may also be partly due to the rationalization of jobs and to the increase in the total amount of work, required by individual workers, that prevailed generally in the 1990s" (Tuomi, Ilmarinen, Martikainen et al., 1997: 70).

HIGH-RISK JOBS FOR OLDER WORKERS

High-risk jobs for older workers, now and in the future, are jobs that present exposure to relatively common work risks. These risks have already been characterized, but their prevalence among older workers bears review. The National Health Interview Survey supplement in 1988 provides an estimate of common types of risks and their prevalence by age. The most common risks are biomechanical. (Table A-19 in Appendix A shows biomechanical risks that occur for specific work activities engaged in four or more hours per day.) Among women, 10 percent of those surveyed report repeated strenuous physical activity; almost a quarter report repeated bending, twisting, or reaching; more than one-third report bending or twisting of hands or wrists; but only 3.5 percent report hand operation of vibrating machinery. The prevalence of these biochemical risk factors was higher among men, although the reported difference for bending or twisting of hands or wrists four or more hours per day was similar (40 percent) to that of women. When examined by age of worker the prevalence is somewhat lower for those 45–64 years for each of the biomechanical risk factors; however, even for those 65 and older there is a substantial amount of bending or twisting of hands or wrists of four or more hours (22 percent of employed women and 25 percent of employed men), as well as repeated bending and twisting or reaching (12 percent of employed women and 20 percent of employed men).

The survey also assessed exposures to substances believed to be harmful if breathed or contacted by the skin, and radiation exposure (Table A-20 shows data indicating number and percent distribution of employed adults reporting exposure to substances or radiation at work in 1992). Less than 5 percent of the employed population of women and only 6 percent of employed men reported radiation exposure, with slightly lower percentages among those aged 45 to 64 and even less among those 65 or older. Combining reported harmful exposures, the prevalence is much higher (23 percent for women and 39 percent for men). The prevalence among women is stable for all age groups until 65 or older. Among men, while the exposures decrease for those aged 45 to 64, over one-third still report such exposure. These exposures are almost 20 percent, even among men 65 or older.

In Chapter 2 we identified industries and occupations that are older-worker-intensive. Among those industries the following appear to represent higher risk for both biomechanical and other hazardous exposures: manufacturing, transportation, medical services, mining, utilities, agriculture, and forestry/fishing/trapping. With the exception of mining and forestry/fishing/trapping, each of these industries is projected to experience at least moderate growth in employment.

Among those occupations identified as older-worker-intensive the following appear to represent higher risk for biomechanical exposures and, in some cases, additional hazardous exposures: administrative support, production/craft/repair, transportation and material moving, farming/forestry/fishing, private household services, protective services, and services–other. Most of these occupations are projected to experience moderate to high growth in employment.

EFFORTS TO ASSESS BURDEN OF OCCUPATIONAL DISEASES

The ILO estimates that injuries and diseases together cause over 1.2 million fatalities globally per year; workers suffer more than 250 million accidents; and more than 160 million workers fall ill due to workplace hazards and exposures (International Labour Organization, 2004). Anan (1997: 59) estimated that the economic burden of such disease and injury amounted to "4 percent of the world's gross national product; in terms of shattered families and communities, the damage is incalculable."

The WHO is currently assessing the global burden of disease and death from approximately 20 risk factors, among which are those factors that result in the burden associated with work. Leigh and colleagues provide a summary assessment of the approach being taken (Leigh et al., 1999). The methodology includes consideration of age-specific disease and injury risks, although they have age-adjusted their data to achieve their objectives. In order to arrive at age-adjusted estimates, they have relied on data from countries where conditions are reported by age and sex (Finnish Institute of Occupational Health, 1994; Worksafe Australia, 1995). This approach suggests it may be possible to assess age-specific burdens in the United States if age-specific risk information from other developed countries is used.

Leigh et al. (1999) note that efforts to estimate rates of occupational illness in any jurisdiction are constrained by the fact that most work-related illnesses have multiple potential causes and long latency periods. Work-related events (injury or illness) with rapid onset are easier to identify, but even among these the reporting methods emphasize the most severe and significant events. Other limitations of the available evidence include the general lack of training of health care providers in recognizing occupational illness or disorder and the mix of approaches to data collection used, even within a country with information derived from death records, hospital records, workers' compensation claims, cancer registry records, workplace records, surveys, and sentinel reports. All of these limitations apply to assessment of occupational illness or disorders and injury burden in the United States.

Within the limitations of available data, Leigh and Schnall (2000) have produced an estimate of the economic burden of occupational illness or disorder and injury in the United States. The study is the first comprehensive estimate that uses national data, though without adequate age-specific data; their report does not consider the problems of older workers. They estimated that there were 13,337,000 occupational injuries in 1992, including 6,371 fatalities. The total estimated cost of those injuries was $132.8 billion. They estimated the occupational illnesses in 1992 to be 1,184,000 and deaths from occupational illness to be 60,290. The total cost of morbidity and mortality from occupational illness was estimated to be $22.8 billion. In 1992, the total loss from occupational injury and illness amounted to approximately 2.5 percent of Gross Domestic Product. Researchers in the United Kingdom and Denmark have made similar estimates of national product lost to occupational illness or disorders and injury.

7

Programs and Policies Related to the Older Workforce and Safe Work

LEGALLY MANDATED INTERVENTIONS

Public policy interventions affect the ability of older workers both to continue to work safely and to exit from the workforce. This chapter describes these interventions. The first section provides a description of the general legal regulation of employment. There are three basic components to this general context in the United States: first, the current status of the common law employment-at-will doctrine; second, the status of rights to collective organization and negotiation; and third, the patchwork nature of regulation of employment that results in variance among jurisdictions as well as holes in coverage for important groups of workers and firms.

Following this general contextual overview, the second section describes the more specific laws that govern older workers' ability to remain safely in the workforce and to design appropriate exit strategies from the labor market. These laws mandate (or fail to mandate) key interventions that directly affect aging workers. This inquiry is divided into three general areas: occupational safety and health protections designed to encourage or mandate safe workplace practices; antidiscrimination laws that protect designated subgroups of workers from less advantageous treatment; and mandated interventions that regulate or encourage leaves of absence and accommodations at work (influencing the ability of workers with chronic illness or disability to move into and out of the workforce).

The final section very briefly describes the availability of nonwage benefits for older workers that affect their decisions regarding when and how to exit the labor market. Government intervention in this area consists of both the direct provision of social benefits and the legal regulation of private benefit programs.

Certain elements of relevant public policy are simple to articulate. For example: age-based discrimination against workers over age 40 is illegal; all workers who participate in the Social Security system have some guaranteed health insurance, disability and retirement income protections, at least after specified periods of participation in covered employment. Beyond this, the terrain becomes more difficult. There are few special legal protections for aging workers. In general, employment policies must be age-neutral (although actuarially derived age-based benefit designs are generally permissible). That is, employers are required to treat older workers in the same manner as otherwise equivalent younger workers would be treated. The key question is whether the laws that mandate intervention in employment provide adequate protection to workers as they age, so that they can continue to work safely or so that they have the necessary economic security to exit at the appropriate time from the workforce. As noted in other sections of this report, the answer to these questions is not the same for all workers, in all industries. Moreover, there has been remarkably little study of the effectiveness of these mandated interventions in relation to older workers' health and safety needs.

THE LEGAL CONTEXT

Employment at Will

The employment-at-will doctrine is at the core of the U.S. legal code governing the private sector employment relationship. Originally articulated in a 19th-century legal treatise, this doctrine allows an employer to discharge an employee "at will" (Wood, 1877). The employer is under no obligation to articulate a reason for the discharge. This is most often described as the right of an employer to discharge someone for a good reason, a bad reason, or no reason at all. In the pure application of the doctrine (as it existed in the early 20th century), an employer could legally discharge an employee because the employee was unproductive, too old, African American, an immigrant, a woman, disabled, simply because of dislike, or based upon any stigma or prejudice.

Within the context of dominant American common law, the at-will relationship between worker and employer results in a contractual relationship that can be terminated by either party without notice at any time. As a practical matter, this means that an employer may also change the specific elements of the bargain with a worker without notice: If the employee continues to work, he or she is generally deemed to have accepted the new terms. Unwillingness of employees to work, or work for the proffered terms, would therefore be the sole restraint on the employer's managerial control.

Obviously, this is no longer true. The terms of this at-will "agreement" can be, and have been, modified in several ways: by legally enforceable individual contracts;[1] by common law limitations on the at-will doctrine that have been developed by the courts;[2] by collective agreements; and by legislation at the state or federal level. Nevertheless, the at-will doctrine remains the default rule for private employment in almost every American jurisdiction: If there is no specific applicable exception to the rule, then the default rule applies. In contrast, almost all public sector employees have considerably more protection from both constitutional guarantees and civil service laws.

Collective Bargaining

In unionized workplaces, employers are required to bargain with representatives of the employees in a bargaining unit. For the covered employees, almost all of the resulting collective bargaining agreements set wages and benefits, establish progressive disciplinary procedures, require employers to have "just cause" to discipline or terminate an employee, and establish rights to job allocation and retention based, at least in part, on seniority.

Several areas of bargaining are of particular concern to aging workers. Wages and benefits tied to longevity and skills may tend to encourage workers to remain in the workforce. Disciplinary provisions and protections against arbitrary discharge shield older workers from dismissals that may be tied to both age-related stigma and minor loss of productivity attributable to aging. Safety and health contract provisions and union safety committees established through collective bargaining result in more attentiveness to risks and increased enforcement of occupational safety and health requirements (Weil, 1991). There is, however, no literature that suggests that unions exercise the right to bargain over health and safety by seeking heightened protections for older workers. Union safety committees, often established under collective bargaining agreements, may, however,

---

[1]Courts have consistently held that individual written contracts for a set term are enforceable. Less commonly, courts have also enforced implied or oral contracts in cases involving individual employees. In fact, however, relatively few employees have individual contracts that provide continuing entitlement to wages and benefits or other significant protections.

[2]The judicial erosion of the employment-at-will doctrine has occurred at the state court level and generally reflects an application of modern ideas of "public policy" that are used to restrict employers' unilateral right to discharge when the discharge violates legally articulated public policy that can be found in statutes or prior case law.

assist aging workers in adapting appropriately to job demands. This may be particularly effective when the union is assisting older workers, due to the just-cause contractual requirements and the privileges associated with greater seniority.

Seniority systems may be the most effective protection for older workers. Employers that choose among workers based upon seniority are likely to retain workers as they age, even if their work capacity declines. Seniority also enables older workers to obtain transfers to preferable positions that become vacant based upon bidding procedures. In addition, seniority is viewed as superior to any rights to accommodation of disabled workers when vacant jobs are filled (*U.S. Airways, Inc. v. Barnett*, 122 S. Ct. 1516 [2002]). As long as older workers are capable of doing their jobs, they will be protected by seniority systems from reassignment demands made by disabled employees who may be less senior or less qualified.

In fact, however, few workers are protected in this way. First, and most importantly, only about 9 percent of the private sector workforce is covered by collective bargaining agreements. Particular subgroups of disadvantaged workers, most notably immigrants, are even less likely to be unionized.

In addition, there are significant limitations to the degree of protection offered by union contracts to aging or disabled workers. The general principles of seniority do not benefit disabled or aging workers based upon age or disability directly, and most arbitrators will uphold the right of an employer to discharge an employee who is medically unfit to continue working (Gross and Greenfield, 1985). Although seniority in general benefits older workers, this is not always true: Older workers are not necessarily the most senior, and individuals in need of special health and safety protection may not always be the oldest workers. Moreover, unions owe a duty of fair representation to all members of a bargaining unit; any effort to create advantage for one subgroup raises the potential specter of a claim that a relatively disadvantaged group will sue the union. Finally, unions are often unable to represent the interests of current retirees effectively; any issue for people who have already retired (as opposed to active workers) is not a mandatory subject of bargaining for employers (*Allied Chemical and Alkali Workers of America, Local Union No. 1 v. Pittsburgh Plate Glass Co., Chemical Division*, 404 U.S. 157 [1971]).

Inconsistency in Mandated Interventions

In looking at the legal interventions that are of concern to aging workers, it is also important to recognize the patchwork nature of all employment regulation. Independent contractors and self-employed workers are excluded from almost all protective employment laws and collective bargaining agreements. Also excluded are people who do not report their wages—who work "under the table." Most protective statutes exclude small employers, although the specific size of covered employers may vary (e.g., most federal antidiscrimination laws cover employers with 15 or more employees; the Age Discrimination in Employment Act, 29 U.S.C.A. §621 et seq., requires 20 employees; the Family and Medical Leave Act of 1993, 29 U.S.C.A. §1601 et seq., requires 50 employees). Some statutes include a workforce connection test that requires the employee to have worked for a covered employer a certain amount within a specified time period (e.g., the Family and Medical Leave Act). Eligibility for some social insurance requires labor market participation over specified periods of time (e.g., Social Security, Unemployment Insurance). Private benefits may only be available to full-time permanent employees. The result is that many contingent or part-time workers are excluded from the interventions that are discussed here.

Enforcement of laws also varies. Reports of noncompliance with basic labor legislation, including overtime, child labor, and occupational safety have been common (Kruse and Mahony, 2000; Conway and Svenson, 1998). As noted above, enforcement has been reported to be more effective in unionized than in nonunionized workplaces, but few private sector workers are unionized.

Tension between federal and state regulation further complicates the terrain. States control both the common law governance of the employment relationship and the compensation programs for occupational injuries and illnesses (with some limited exceptions such as the federal Black Lung and the Energy Employees Occupational Illness Compensation programs). The federal government controls private sector unionization rights and generally preempts the right of states to govern private employee benefit plans (including pension and health). Federal mandates set floors for legal interventions involving status-based discrimination and occupational safety and health. The result is that in key areas of interest to aging workers, the legal rules may vary depending upon the state in which the worker lives and works. In addition, legal rights are often asserted under state laws. Little attention has been paid in the legal and sociolegal literature to this trend.

SPECIFIC AREAS OF LEGAL INTERVENTION

The following provides a brief overview of the existing laws and legal interpretations that may directly affect the work and health outcomes for aging workers. Laws and public policy merely set the minimum standards for employers. Noncompliance by employers with these requirements is always possible; more protective voluntary or collectively bargained programs also occur. Attention to areas of mandated intervention means that areas in which there is no mandated intervention are less prominent in this discussion. These include, for example, the lack of any national standard that governs ergonomic risks in workplaces; the lack of any requirement for job accommodation for individuals who do not meet the high standard for disability set out in the Americans with Disabilities Act (ADA); and the lack of seamless social benefits, including health insurance.

Occupational Safety and Health Protections

The Occupational Safety and Health Act (OSHA), 19 U.S.C. §651 et seq., is the primary intervention to promote health and safety of workers under U.S. law. OSHA covers the vast majority of private establishments in general industry, but it excludes all public sector employers. Federal employees are covered by presidential Executive Order 12196, which extends the broad health and safety protection to the federal sector, with the exception of the military. In addition, many states have specific laws that extend OSHA or equivalent health and safety protection to state and local public employees. Employers and workers in the mining industries are covered by the Mine Safety and Health Act (MSHA) of 1977, 30 U.S.C. §801 et seq., a law that generally provides more protective coverage for workers in these industries than is available under OSHA.[3] A variety of other laws that are less well known provide some health and safety coverage to workers in specified industries.

The stated purpose of OSHA is to "assure as far as possible every working man and woman in the Nation safe and healthful working conditions" (29 U.S.C.A. §651[b]). Similar language requires the Occupational Safety and Health Administration to set health standards at levels that most adequately ensure, to the extent feasible, on the basis of the best available evidence, that "no employee will suffer material impairment of health or functional capacity." Employers are obligated to comply both with standards and with the general duty clause that creates an obligation for every employer to "furnish to each of his employees employment and a place of employment that are free from recognized hazards that are causing or are likely to cause death or serious physical harm to his employees" (29 U.S.C. §654[a][1]).

This statutory language suggests either that workers are due protection from health hazards on an individualized basis or that every standard should provide protection for every worker, even those at greatest risk. Judicial

---

[3]For example, MSHA requires quarterly inspections of all underground mining facilities and allows compliance officers to shut down operations that pose immediate danger to workers. In contrast, OSHA has no specific requirement for worksite inspections, and many are never inspected. OSHA compliance officers can only shut down imminently dangerous operations by seeking an order from a federal district court.

interpretations of the statute, however, put a heavy burden on the agency to prove that a standard is "reasonably necessary and appropriate to remedy a significant risk of material health impairment" (*Industrial Union Dept., AFL-CIO v. American Petroleum Institute*, 448 U.S. 607 [1980]). In the promulgation of any standard designed to regulate physical agents or toxic substances, OSHA must "make a threshold finding that a place of employment is unsafe—in the sense that significant risks are present and can be eliminated or lessened by a change in practices" (Id.). There is no precise definition of "significant" in the case law, but the Supreme Court has noted that all workplaces need not be without risk for all persons. Standards involving health risks therefore reflect a generalized assessment of risk and, conversely, an acceptance of some degree of risk for some individuals.

The health and safety standards successfully promulgated under OSHA do not vary exposure limits based upon the age, gender, or physical capacity of workers. Instead, the standards set limits on exposures or safety standards that are the same for all workers, with the theoretical goal of protecting all workers to the extent required by the statute. The standards, however, have not been based on the special needs of workers whose risk is substantially heightened by personal characteristics.

As noted in Chapter 6, reported injuries have declined steadily and substantially in recent years, but questions have been raised regarding the accuracy of these data. Due to funding limitations, the Occupational Safety and Health Administration has never been able to employ a sufficient number of enforcement officers to conduct regular field inspections of most workplaces (Shapiro and McGarity, 1993; Shapiro and Rabinowitz, 2000). Unlike MSHA, which requires quarterly worksite inspections, OSHA includes no such requirement. As a result, the agency has moved increasingly to voluntary compliance.

The Occupational Safety and Health Administration has also encountered significant barriers to the promulgation of new or revised permanent health standards (Shapiro and McGarity, 1993). Critical health hazards remain unregulated under OSHA. Attempts to promulgate regulations have met with high levels of judicial scrutiny as well as congressional resistance. As noted elsewhere in this report, work-related musculoskeletal disorders are common and debilitating for older workers. Due primarily to direct congressional action, including invocation in 2001 of the Congressional Review Act to stop a final published regulation, OSHA has been unable to issue a standard that addresses these risks. Instead OSHA has attempted to use what is known as the *general duty clause* to regulate serious hazards that can cause work-related musculoskeletal disorders in some workplaces (*Pepperidge Farm*, 17 OSH Cases 1993 [Rev. Comm'n 1997]; *Beverly Enterprises*, 19 OSH Cases 1161 [Rev. Comm'n 2000]). The general duty clause both depends on discretionary enforcement activity and fails to provide specific notice to employers regarding their obligations to reduce hazards that can cause work-related musculoskeletal disorders.

There is evidence that workplace injuries decline following OSHA inspections (Scholz, 1990). It is nonetheless debatable whether the aggregate declines in reported injuries can be attributed to the regulatory and enforcement activities that are authorized under OSHA. No studies directly support this broader conclusion.

It is also impossible to measure the normative effects of laws on behavior. But to the extent that voluntary compliance is not assured, compliance with OSHA's mandate cannot be certain. As the cohort of current workers ages, the number and percentage of workers with aging-related physical impairments will also rise. On the other hand, there will also be increasing heterogeneity within these aging cohorts. It is not clear what the implication of these trends is for health and safety regulation. Ultimately, the critical question regarding older workers is this: To what extent do current regulations provide adequate protection to prevent morbidity in aging workers and to protect aging workers who remain in the workforce? Finding the right balance is difficult: Specific protections aimed at workers at greater risk, including in some cases older workers, are likely to result in increased exclusion of these workers from the workforce; increased general protection may be too costly or too extensive to survive legal challenges. In fact, little is known regarding the effectiveness of the laws governing health and safety to protect this population.

Antidiscrimination Laws

Age Discrimination

The Age Discrimination in Employment Act (ADEA), 29 U.S.C. 621 et seq., specifically prohibits any discrimination by employers with 20 or more employees against workers who are 40 years old or older. Generally, mandatory retirement policies are unlawful unless public safety is implicated. As recently as the early 1970s, about half of all American workers were covered by mandatory retirement provisions that required them to leave their jobs no later than a particular age, usually 65. In 1978, the earliest age for mandatory retirement was raised from 65 to 70, and in 1986 mandatory retirement was outlawed entirely, except for a range of jobs that most commonly involve public safety. In addition, under the Older Workers Benefit Protection Act of 1990 (amending the ADEA), an employer may not legally reduce or terminate an employee's fringe benefits because of the employee's age. In addition to the federal law, state fair employment practice laws often have provisions similar to those in the ADEA that may cover smaller employers.

The ADEA and related laws are designed to prevent discrimination against people over 40, not to provide special protections to people as they age. The problem these laws were designed to correct was a problem of exclusion, rooted in stigma, stereotypes, and economic incentives to exclude more expensive workers. Studies prior to the enactment of the laws suggested that older workers who lost their jobs were less likely to be reemployed than younger workers and that durations of unemployment were longer (Miller, 1966). Explicit employment rules mandated retirement at particular ages or prevented hiring of workers over an established age. A review of the literature exploring the reasons for exclusion may be found in Neumark (2001). The age discrimination laws created no rights to training, job redesign, accommodation, or reassignment for aging workers with specific needs.

The extent to which these laws may or may not assist aging employees in prolonging their working lives is not well studied. One review of the literature analyzing the effectiveness of the ADEA suggests that age discrimination laws may marginally increase employment rates for workers over 60, but that there is little evidence of a positive effect on hiring. The increased employment rate appears to be likely due to a reduction in retirement, resulting in a net increase in employment (Neumark, 2001).

Age discrimination claims filed under the ADEA with the U.S. Equal Employment Opportunity Commission (EEOC) grew 34 percent between 1989 and 1993 and nearly 200 percent over the 1980 to 1984 period (Jolls, 1996; Patel and Kleiner, 1994). These claims accounted for approximately 25 percent of the caseload of the EEOC from 1984 to 1988, peaked at approximately 27 percent in 1992, declined somewhat during the 1990s to a low of 18.3 percent in 1999, and rose again to 23.6 percent in 2002. The absolute numbers of claims has also increased, so that the total number of age-related claims filed reached its highest level of 19,921 in 2002 (EEOC, 2003). The majority of these cases involve claims of job loss, often involving group layoffs, brought by people not protected by seniority systems.

Not all of these claims of discrimination ultimately succeed, however. To qualify for protection, workers must be able to demonstrate that they are as qualified for employment (in every respect) as a younger worker who is treated more beneficially. The worker must be able to show that direct age discrimination—not longevity or lack of skills or health impairment—was a factor in the adverse employment decision that she or he is challenging (*Reeves v. Sanderson Plumbing Products, Inc.*, 530 U.S. 133 [2000]). Employers can defend these actions by showing that the decision was based on any factor other than age; that relative youth was a bona fide occupational qualification for the job; or that the older individual was unable to meet the demands of the job.

There is substantial evidence that older workers tend to earn higher wages, and that the ADEA legitimizes this practice (Jolls, 1996). Not surprisingly, job loss leads to significant earnings losses for older workers (Chan and Stevens, 2001; Haider and Stephens, 2001). ADEA cases that do not involve mass layoffs are most likely to be filed by relatively privileged workers, predominantly white males from managerial, professional, or white-collar backgrounds in order to challenge discharges, layoffs, and involuntary retirement (Eglit, 1997). In general, litigation over discharges is successfully pursued predominantly by employees who have been relatively economically privileged (Summers, 1992; Neumark, 2001). Moreover, in the majority of employment discrimination cases filed, employees who do prevail are unlikely to regain employment. The persistent consistency of these litigation results suggests that the ADEA is not likely to be a useful tool for aging workers in nonmanagerial employment who are most likely to confront health and safety risks at work and who want to remain employed.

Disability Discrimination

The Americans with Disabilities Act (ADA), 42 U.S.C. §§ 12101–12213 is, in contrast to the ADEA, specifically designed to provide special protection to workers who meet the Act's definition of disability and who can achieve success at work if they can overcome stigma and prejudice or are provided "reasonable accommodation." State laws generally provide equivalent protection. The ADA defines "disability" as:

(A) a physical or mental impairment that substantially limits one or more major life activities of an individual, as, for example, walking, talking, seeing, hearing, or caring for oneself;

(B) a record of such an impairment; or

(C) being regarded as having such an impairment (42 U.S.C. § 12102[2]).

> Only the first part of this definition, covering individuals with current and actual impairments, has specific relevance to the requirement that employers provide a healthy and safe working environment for employees. On its face, the ADA gives heightened protection at work to individuals with chronic health conditions, including those caused or exacerbated by work. In order to qualify for accommodation, an individual must be able to prove that she or he has a qualifying disability but is able to perform the essential functions of the job with reasonable accommodation.

For those workers who qualify under the disability definition, the ADA's definition of reasonable accommodation is quite broad and includes:

(A) making existing facilities used by employees readily accessible to and usable by individuals with disabilities; and (B) job restructuring, part-time or modified work schedules, reassignment to a vacant position, acquisition or modification of equipment or devices, appropriate adjustment or modifications of examinations, training materials or policies, the provision of qualified readers or interpreters, and other similar accommodations for individuals with disabilities (42 U.S.C. § 12111[9][A] and 29 C.F.R. § 1630.2[o]).

The ADA is intended to encourage employers to accommodate disabled workers by undergoing an individualized process of determining the needs of the employee, identifying the essential functions of jobs, and providing necessary, reasonable accommodation to the disabled employee. If a disabled person cannot perform the essential functions of his or her own job, that employee may be entitled to reassignment to another vacant job. Since reported work disability increases substantially with age, the ADA provides a potential source of significant protection for aging workers.

A series of U.S. Supreme Court decisions have clarified the scope of employers' obligations under this statute. In 1998, the Court held that individuals who are HIV positive qualify as "disabled" and therefore are entitled to protection under the law (*Bragdon v. Abbott*, 524 U.S. 624 [1998]). The following year, the Court rejected claims from individuals claiming disability discrimination in three cases. Although none of these decisions specifically involved older workers or work-related issues, all three have some bearing on the development of the law under the ADA.

In two of these cases the court concluded that "a person whose physical or mental impairment is corrected by medication or other measures does not have an impairment that presently 'substantially limits' a major life activity" (*Sutton v. United Airlines*, 527 U.S. 471 [1999]; *Murphy v. United Parcel Service*, 527 U.S. 516 [1999]). In Sutton, the court rejected the claims of individuals whose myopia was corrected with lenses. In Murphy, UPS had terminated the employment of a worker with hypertension. The Court applied the ruling in Sutton and held that Murphy did not meet the definition of disability set out in the statute. Therefore, his termination was legal. Under these decisions, older workers with chronic disease, including hypertension and diabetes, may not be considered "disabled" within the meaning of the ADA, unless they can demonstrate that they continue to be substantially impaired in the performance of a major life activity despite treatment.

Second, in *Albertson's, Inc. v. Kirkingburg*, 527 U.S. 555 (1999), the plaintiff was rejected for reemployment after undergoing a return-to-work physical following an absence for an unrelated work injury. The examining physician determined that he did not meet required vision standards due to monocularity. The Supreme Court rejected any per se rule that would hold that monocularity constituted a disability within the meaning of the ADA, but suggested that some monocular individuals might meet a more individualized inquiry regarding whether their impairment substantially limited a major life activity. In all three of these cases, the Court emphasized the need for individualized inquiry into the nature and extent of the plaintiffs' impairments. In *Albertson's,* the Court also held that the employer could rely on Department of Transportation safety rules for visual acuity to justify exclusion of the returning employee, foreshadowing the decision in the next critical case (*Toyota Motor Manufacturing, Kentucky, Inc. v. Williams,* 534 U.S. 184 [2002]).

In this first decision to specifically address the claims of an individual with work-related injuries, the Court held that the definitional terms in the ADA "need to be interpreted strictly to create a demanding standard for qualifying as disabled." (In this case, the plaintiff claimed that she was substantially limited in performing manual tasks, housework, gardening, playing with her children, lifting, and working due to musculoskeletal injuries sustained at work. In sending the case back down to the lower courts, the Supreme Court made several observations regarding disability that may significantly limit the ability of the ADA to provide legal protection to aging workers with physical impairments. Noting that the severity of impairment due to carpal tunnel syndrome can vary, the court held:

> [T]o be substantially limited in performing manual tasks, an individual must have an impairment that prevents or severely restricts the individual from doing activities that are of central importance to most people's daily lives . . . the manual tasks unique to any particular job are not necessarily important parts of most people's lives. As a result, occupation-specific tasks may have only limited relevance to the manual task inquiry. In this case, "repetitive work with hands and arms extended at or above shoulder levels for extended periods of time," the manual task on which the Court of Appeals relied, is not an important part of most people's daily lives. The court, therefore, should not have considered respondent's inability to do such manual work in her specialized assembly line job as sufficient proof that she was substantially limited in performing manual tasks. . . . In addition, even after her condition worsened, she could still brush her teeth, wash her face, bathe, tend her flower garden, fix breakfast, do laundry, and pick up around the house. The record also indicates that her medical conditions caused her to avoid sweeping, to quit dancing, to occasionally seek help dressing, and to reduce how often she plays with her children, gardens, and drive long distances. But these changes in her life did not amount to such severe restrictions in the activities that are of central importance to most people's daily lives that they establish a manual-task disability as a matter of law.

Employers may also raise safety concerns as a defense against a disabled worker's claim for continued employment. Special health and safety protection for these workers might have been available as a part of the accommodation requirement under the ADA and related fair-employment practice laws at the state level. But employers have successfully argued that there is a tension between the legal obligation to continue the employment of employees who are disabled and the obligation to provide a safe work-place for all employees, mandated by OSHA. Employers can defend them-selves from liability under the ADA if they can show that the work sought by the person with a disability is a direct threat to the safety of employees and if alternative accommodation would not eliminate the safety concern. The statute defines direct threat to mean "a significant risk to the health or safety of others that cannot be eliminated by reasonable accommodation" (42 U.S.C. § 12113[b]). The EEOC regulations provide that the significant risk must be a "significant risk of substantial harm" to either the individual worker or to others, based on an assessment of "the individual's present ability to safely perform the essential functions of the job" (29 C.F.R. § 1630.2[r]).

Where the work is viewed as potentially dangerous to the employee, the employer may be relieved of its obligation to continue to employ the aging worker at all. EEOC regulations specifically allow an employer to exclude a susceptible worker from a job that may put him or her at significant risk. In *Chevron U.S.A. Inc. v. Echazabal*, 536 U.S. 73 (2002), the U.S. Supreme Court relied on OSHA to uphold this regulation. In this case, Chevron's doctors said that the plaintiff Echazabal's liver disease (hepatitis C) would be exacerbated by continued exposure to toxins at the oil refinery. Chevron argued that its obligation under OSHA to provide a safe workplace was controlling, and that therefore Chevron should not be required to continue the employment of a disabled employee in a job that put him at significant risk. The Supreme Court, in a unanimous decision by Justice Souter, concluded:

> Chevron's reasons for calling the regulation reasonable are unsurprising: moral concerns aside, it wishes to avoid time lost to sickness, excessive turnover from medical retirement or death, litigation under state tort law, and the risk of violating the national Occupational Safety and Health Act . . . . [F]ocusing on the concern with OSHA will be enough to show that the regulation is entitled to survive. Echazabal points out that there is no known instance of OSHA enforcement, or even threatened enforce-ment, against an employer who relied on the ADA to hire a worker will-ing to accept a risk to himself from his disability on the job. In Echaza-bal's mind, this shows that invoking OSHA policy and possible OSHA liability is just a red herring to excuse covert discrimination. But there is another side to this. The text of OSHA itself says its point is 'to assure so far as possible every working man and woman in the Nation safe and healthful working conditions," §651(b), and congress specifically obligat-ed an employer to "furnish to each of his employees employment and a

place of employment which are free from recognized hazards that are causing or are likely to cause death or serious physical harm to his employees,"§654(a)(1). Although there may be an open question whether an employer would actually be liable under OSHA for hiring an individual who knowingly consented to the particular dangers the job would pose to him . . . , there is no denying that the employer would be asking for trouble: his decision to hire would put Congress's policy in the ADA, a disabled individual's right to operate on equal terms within the workplace, at loggerheads with the competing policy of OSHA, to ensure the safety of "each" and "every" worker.

While this decision endorses the general principle that employers have an obligation to provide a safe and healthy working environment for each and every worker, it also underscores the fact that public policy does not guarantee job security to individual workers with underlying chronic illness who are at risk at work. This recent Supreme Court decision has potentially significant importance to the continuing employment of older adults with chronic conditions. Under *Chevron*, if a worker poses substantial safety risks to self or others, and the employer does not have an open job to which the disabled worker can be reassigned, the employer may terminate the employee. In fact, under general employment law, an employer is free to terminate any worker, including an aging worker, who is at risk or who poses a safety threat to himself or herself. The *Chevron* decision endorses this practice in the case of individuals with disabilities.

The disability discrimination statutes require employers to accommodate the needs of disabled workers through job redesign or reassignment. To the extent that these interventions are effective, the ability of aging workers to remain in the workforce will obviously be enhanced. Job accommodation has unquestionably been shown to successfully extend a worker's working life for a period of years (Burkhauser, Butler, and Kim, 1995; Daly and Bound, 1996; Strunin, 2000). Despite the narrow reading of the ADA by the courts, ADA advocates maintain that the changing treatment of disabled employees may simply not be mirrored in the visible litigation of claims, but rather is lodged in changing norms that encourage employers to accommodate workers.

On the other hand, the impact of the Supreme Court decisions has been far-reaching. Individuals who cannot meet the Court's strict interpretation of the meaning of "disability" are not entitled to any protection under the act. In litigated ADA cases in the lower courts, it has been difficult for workers to meet the burden of showing that they are qualified disabled persons under the ADA. Judges have tended to dismiss ADA cases at a high rate (Colker, 1999, 2001). Individuals with common occupational disabilities are often unable to prove their entitlement to protection under the act (Rabinowitz, 2002). Workers who need accommodation at work but who are outside the scope of the definition of disability as adopted by the Supreme Court have no claim under the ADA.[4]

Current research also suggests that employment of people reporting disabilities that affected their ability to work did not rise during the 1990s (Burkhauser, Daly, and Houtenville, 2001). This was the economic boom period that followed the effective date of the ADA. Some researchers have further suggested that the ADA has actually contributed to the failure of the labor market to absorb disabled workers during this period (Bound and Waidman, 2000; DeLeire, 2000).

Although the ADA has been the subject of considerable evaluation, no study has focused on its effects for older workers. EEOC charges show a much higher correlation between claims filed under the ADEA and claims under the ADA: A higher percentage of ADA claims have companion age-discrimination claims than other discrimination suits. This is not surprising; the majority of these claims involve challenges to job terminations. More study is needed to explore the effectiveness of the ADA and the correlation between age and disability discrimination claims.

Non-ADA Interventions Involving Leaves of Absence, Job Redesign, and Job Accommodation

The strongest public policy endorsement of workplace accommodation is unquestionably found in the ADA and related state statutes. The ADA suggests that employers are required to provide a broad range of accommodations to workers with qualifying disabilities. But many aging workers, including many with health impairments, are not disabled within the meaning of the ADA. Older workers are not per se entitled to accommodation or reassignment simply because they have age-related health impairments, unless those impairments are sufficiently severe to create qualifying disabilities. One must therefore ask: To what extent is there public policy endorsement of accommodation of older workers outside of the ADA?

In addition to ADA policy, there appears to be a general public endorsement of light duty and return-to-work programs for occupationally injured employees. Outside of the disability discrimination laws, however, specific requirements regarding effective job redesign are fuzzy. In workers'

---

[4]Notably, some state courts have begun to reject the federal interpretation of the ADA and to interpret state disability laws more favorably for disabled workers (e.g., *Dahill v. Police Department of Boston*, 748 N.E. 2d 956 [Mass. 2001]; *Stone v. St. Joseph's Hospital of Parkersburg*, 538 S.E. 2d 389 [W.Va., 2000]; *Wittkopf v. County of Los Angeles*, 209 Cal. Rptr 2d 543 [Ct. App. 2001]).

compensation programs, there is often little oversight by public agencies of attempts to accommodate injured workers.

Transfers to different jobs are an alternative mechanism for guaranteeing that a worker with physical limitations can remain at work. Both the health and safety laws and workers' compensation programs provide legal bases for reassignment. OSHA/MSHA rules, as well as ADA guidelines, suggest that this is an appropriate way to provide safe work for aging workers. For example, under the Mine Safety and Health Act, coal workers with evidence of developing pneumoconiosis have a permanent right to transfer from dusty jobs. The implementation of this section has been fraught with difficulty, but it is a process that has been successfully used by older coal miners to transfer from heavy jobs with dust exposure to lighter jobs with less dust (Spieler, 1989; 30 U.S.C. §843[b]; 30 C.F.R. §90). OSHA rules at this point only provide for transfers for workers suffering from respiratory disease due to cotton dust exposure (29 C.F.R. §1910.1043) and for temporary transfer for individuals with acute health problems (e.g., 29 C.F.R. §1910.1025 [lead]; 29 C.F.R. §1910.1028 [benzene]). Temporary transfers are of little benefit to aging workers with progressive or chronic conditions.

Workers' compensation programs do not specifically mandate job transfers. Many programs are, however, designed to encourage employers to provide light duty assignments to injured workers. To the extent that this encourages appropriate return to work and job reassignment, this may be of considerable value to older workers.

Regarding leaves of absence, older workers may need to leave work for a period of time or may need particular job accommodations at work in order to remain in the active workforce and to continue to work safely at their jobs.

In addition to the ADA's allowance for leave as a reasonable accommodation, the Family and Medical Leave Act (FMLA), 29 U.S.C. §§2601-2654, provides that employees who meet minimum work duration requirements and whose employers employ more than 50 employees are entitled to take 12 weeks of unpaid leave in each calendar year; the leave can be continuous or intermittent. Leave is granted if the employee needs to care for a family member with a serious health condition or if the employee needs time off because of his or her own serious health condition. The employer must guarantee reinstatement to the prior job at the end of the leave, unless the employee is a high-level manager. Rabinowitz (2002) provides a full description of the FMLA in the context of occupational safety and health concerns. In addition, workers with job-related injuries may be entitled to time off from work while they are collecting workers' compensation benefits. Not all states guarantee that an individual on workers' compensation is entitled to return to work after the injury, however. Moreover, in most states, once an injured employee has recovered as much as she or he can, if she or he is unable to perform the pre-injury work, most states will not require an employer to reinstate the employee.

Accommodation and return to work have been a driving force in the cost-containment strategies in the management of workers' compensation programs. Most state workers' compensation programs require injured workers to accept an offer to return to work and may provide for termination of temporary wage replacement benefits if the worker refuses a return to work offer.

It is not clear whether the current policy governing leaves is either consistent or adequate to meet the needs of aging workers. There has been no evaluation of these rights that focuses on this issue.

WAGE AND BENEFIT PROTECTION TO ENABLE WORKERS TO EXIT RISKY WORK

Income Replacement

Differentials in health status and disability correlate with education and socioeconomic status. Those with less education are more likely to be employed in more physically demanding occupations and less able to adapt to their disability by shifting to less physically demanding employment. For workers who are disabled, there are several important policy questions. To what extent are people forced to work due to their need to maintain income despite excessive health risks of the available work? How do we define "excessive" health risks in this situation? To what extent are they enabled to exit the workforce because there are adequate wage replacement programs that cushion their exit? What is the appropriate balance between providing more protective working environments in order to allow for continued work and enabling labor market exit through the availability of income replacement schemes? Do we know the extent to which some subsets of workers are essentially abandoned, unable to continue to work but unable to access income replacement schemes?

As noted above, the current federal policy regarding workplace regulation makes no special provision for accommodation of workers based on age when combined with disability, and it specifically permits the termination of a worker if the employer can show that the worker is at significant personal risk in the job. Implementation of health and safety preventive policy does not directly address the needs of older workers. The ability of a worker to exit the workforce due to the availability of income replacement is therefore critical to the well-being of workers who are at risk at work.

The programs that provide labor market exit cushions are of two types. First, there are direct income replacement programs that provide cash payments to workers who cease work due to age or disability.[5] These include the Social Security disability and old-age programs, workers' compensation, Supplemental Security Income, and private disability insurance plans. Unemployment insurance benefits may also provide a temporary cushion after an older worker loses a job and before she or he becomes discouraged and chooses to exit the labor market permanently. Second, there are benefit plans that provide essential nonwage benefits. The key benefit for older and disabled workers is health insurance.

Each of these programs is complex and cannot be comprehensively described here. Below is a very brief overview of key aspects of some of these relevant programs.

Income Replacement Programs

Social Security Disability Insurance (SSDI)

SSDI provides benefits to employees who have participated in the Social Security system and who are totally disabled. Notably, growth in the SSDI rolls in the 1990s appears to correlate with the lack of expansion in the employment of people with disabilities (Bound and Waidman, 2000). To qualify, workers must establish that they are totally disabled for at least 12 months; eligibility cannot begin until six months after onset of total disability. There is a special, more lenient eligibility standard for manual workers over 55 years old with limited education, providing a safety net for the most at-risk aging workers. Although SSDI is a critical cushion for many workers, its eligibility requirements suggest that it is most often utilized by workers who have lost their jobs and are unable to reenter the labor market successfully. Benefits are lower for lower wage earners or for earners with fewer quarters of earnings; this means that people who have not been consistently in the workforce may be ineligible or receive lower benefits. As a result, female workers receive lower benefits than males.

Workers' Compensation

Workers' compensation programs provide cash and limited medical benefits to workers who are injured or made ill by their work. These systems are state based and controlled and vary substantially from one state to another. In general, they provide: weekly benefits while a worker is

---

[5]Of course some workers exit fully voluntarily and receive retirement income or rely on personal assets; these workers are not the subject of this discussion.

recovering from an acute injury (most commonly, these temporary benefits are capped as to both duration and weekly payment amounts); temporary partial disability benefits to workers who return to work at reduced wages (similarly capped); permanent partial disability benefits that are paid for either wage loss or impairment and may be paid after the worker has returned to work; and permanent total disability benefits to workers who are permanently unable to return to work. Medical benefits are provided for the compensable injury or illness only.

There has been very limited study of the adequacy of workers' compensation benefits for older workers. While frequency and duration of benefits associated with injuries may rise with age, earnings replacement rates for permanent disability appears to decline, at least for the post-injury period that has been studied (Biddle, Boden, and Reville, 2001). Further, tightened eligibility standards, reductions in permanent disability benefits, and changes in rules regarding compensability (particularly exclusions of disabilities that have ambiguous or complex etiology) may seriously and adversely affect the benefits of older workers with underlying chronic conditions (Burton and Spieler, 2001). Workers' compensation rarely provides a safety net for workers who need to exit the workforce permanently. Awards of permanent total disability are quite rare, averaging 6 per 100,000 workers in the 42 states for which data are available (National Council on Compensation Insurance, 2002). The decline in these long-tailed benefits in most state programs further aggravates the economic problems of aging, disabled, displaced workers who are unable to find alternative employment due to a combination of disability and stigma.

Recent review of the literature suggests that workers' compensation fails to replace long-term earnings losses of injured workers. Further, the availability and level of benefits vary substantially among states (Mont et al., 2002; National Academy of Social Insurance, 2003). The combined data suggest that state workers' compensation systems are not designed to provide long-term economic security to aging workers with occupationally caused health conditions. It is likely that many of these workers seek benefits from the SSDI and SSI systems, but data are not available to explore this question fully.

Supplemental Security Income (SSI)

SSI provides limited cash benefits to individuals who meet strict needs tests and who can show disability sufficient to meet the standards for SSDI. Disabled individuals with limited historical attachment to the workforce may collect limited SSDI benefits and additional SSI benefits. For those who qualify only for SSI because they are not qualified under the work requirements of the Social Security program, medical benefits are generally obtained through a state's Medicaid program, which provides medical benefits to the indigent. SSI cash benefits are substantially lower than SSDI or workers' compensation benefits.

Social Security Old Age (SSOA)

The SSOA program provides monthly benefits to older workers who have worked a sufficient number of quarters during their lifetime in covered employment, or to their spouses and dependent children. As in the SSDI program, benefit amounts are dependent on wages earned, with higher replacement rates for lower waged workers. The SSOA program is most frequently cited as the program responsible for preventing poverty among older Americans.

Social Security is now the main source of cash income of households headed by someone 65 or older. The program provides slightly more than 40 percent of the total cash income received by the aged. Among aged households in the bottom 60 percent of the elderly income distribution, Social Security provides over three-quarters of the total cash income. Until 1941, Social Security provided no income at all to the aged. Today the program replaces about 42 percent of the final wage earned by a full-career single worker who earns the average wage and claims a pension at age 65. If the worker has a nonworking dependent spouse, the benefit replaces 63 percent of the worker's final wage. Benefits are clearly large enough to be economically significant in influencing the choice of retirement age.

Most workers can choose to collect Social Security starting at age 62, and many do. One reason that many people must retire in order to collect a Social Security check is that the program imposes an earnings test in calculating the annual pension. Workers who are at least 62 but less than the age for unreduced pensions and who earn more than $11,280 a year lose $1 in annual benefits for every $2 in earnings they receive in excess of $11,280. Until recently, workers between 65 and 69 lost $1 in benefits for every $3 in annual earnings in excess of $17,000. At one time the earnings limits were much lower, discouraging pensioners from work and possibly encouraging them to postpone claiming a pension until they were confident their earnings would remain low.

Social Security old age pensions are no longer growing more generous. Workers who retired between 1950 and 1980 retired in an environment in which Social Security benefits were rising, both absolutely and in relation to the average earnings of typical American workers. Most workers received pensions that were higher than those they would have obtained if their Social Security contributions had been invested in safe assets.

The maturation of the Social Security program meant that fewer workers who retired after 1985 received windfalls from the program. The Social

Security amendments of 1977 and 1983 brought an end to a four-decade expansion and liberalization of benefits. In fact, the amendments trimmed retirement benefits in order to keep the program solvent.

Congress has changed Social Security rules and the pension formula to make work more attractive later in life. The amount of income a recipient can earn without losing any Social Security benefits has been increased, and the benefit loss for each dollar earned over the exempt amount has been reduced. For pensioners between 65 and 69, the earnings test has been eliminated altogether. In the 1977 and 1983 Social Security amendments, Congress also increased the reward that workers receive for delaying initial benefit receipt past the normal retirement age (NRA). Instead of penalizing work after the NRA, Social Security is becoming more age-neutral. When this formula change is fully implemented, for workers attaining age 62 after 2004, the adjustment for delayed benefit receipt will be approximately fair for retirements up through age 70. It is nearly so today. There will be no retirement penalty for delaying retirement beyond the normal retirement age.

Private Pension Plans

No law requires any employer to provide a pension plan. For private employers who choose to provide them, the funding and governance of the employer-sponsored pension plans are regulated under the Employee Retirement Income Security Act (ERISA) and tax code provisions. Over the past decade, there has been a sharp increase in the relative importance of defined-contribution pension plans and a continuing decline in the importance of defined-benefit plans. Defined-contribution plans specify only the amount that is contributed and set general rules regarding the withdrawal of money from the plan. In contrast, defined-benefit plans set out the specific amounts that will be paid to the beneficiary at particular ages and create financial incentives for workers to retire. Defined-contribution plans are age-neutral by design, and therefore they have none of the age-specific work disincentives that are common in traditional defined-benefit plans. As a growing percentage of workers reaches retirement age under defined-contribution plans, there will be less reason for workers to leave their jobs to avoid a loss in lifetime retirement benefits. On the other hand, the ability of workers to leave their jobs will be affected by the performance of the stock market or other assets held in the plan. Thus, the recent downturn in the value of assets has created pressure on many workers to remain in the workforce because of reduced retirement income potential.

Many employer-sponsored pension plans are structured similarly to Social Security pensions. Workers who are covered under a defined-benefit plan earn pension credits for as long as they work for the employer that sponsors the plan (sometimes up to a maximum number of years). The longer they work under the plan, the higher their monthly pension. Most defined-benefit plans are structured to encourage workers to remain with the employer for a minimal period—say, 10 years—or until a critical age—say, age 55. Workers who stay for shorter periods may receive very little under the plan. On the other hand, workers who stay in the job too long may see the value of their pension accumulation shrink. This would happen if the plan offered benefits to workers starting at age 55 but then failed to significantly increase the monthly benefit for workers who delayed retirement after age 55. This is effectively a pay cut, which might seem illegal under U.S. age discrimination laws but is perfectly legal as long as the pay cut is reflected in reduced lifetime pensions rather than reduced money wages. Many employers find this kind of pension formula to be an effective prod in pushing workers into early retirement.

Earned Income Tax Credit (EITC)

Although not a program that provides wage replacement for nonworking people, the EITC can provide significant income enhancement to low-wage earners. The EITC provides direct cash benefits to low-wage earners, with the amount of the benefit dependent on earnings (such that the amount increases with wages at the lower end and then declines to zero). Older workers who are unable to continue in full-time work but who do not end their participation in the labor market may derive significant benefit from this program. Nevertheless, as can be seen in Table 7-1, the number of income tax returns in which EIC is claimed declines with age.

Health Insurance

Unlike most other industrialized countries, the United States does not provide universal health insurance to its citizens. Instead, most working-age Americans receive health insurance coverage as part of an employer's compensation package. In 1995, 72 percent of American workers between ages 18 and 64 had health insurance coverage under an employer-based plan, either through their own employer or through the employer of another family member. Some workers obtain insurance through publicly provided Medicaid or privately purchased health plans, but 18 percent of American workers were left uninsured.

Some employers offer continuing health insurance to their workers, even after they leave the firm. In 1995, of those full-time employees in medium and large firms who had health insurance on their jobs, 46 percent also had retiree health coverage before age 65, and 41 percent had retiree coverage at ages 65 and older. The percentage of the labor force employed

TABLE 7-1 Tax Year 2000 Individual Income Tax Returns

Age of Primary Taxpayer	All Returns (Number)	Returns with EIC		Percent with EIC
		Number	Amount ($1,000)	
Total	129,373,500	19,277,189	32,296,296	14.90
Under 20	10,228,193	298,374	577,450	2.92
20–24	13,852,522	2,091,239	4,183,606	15.10
25–29	12,561,493	3,327,527	5,467,367	26.49
30–34	13,047,186	3,371,755	5,857,202	25.84
35–39	13,566,201	3,381,064	6,061,293	24.92
40–44	13,524,963	2,767,624	4,685,172	20.46
45–49	12,187,100	1,737,479	2,732,748	14.26
50–54	10,206,288	1,028,659	1,336,117	10.08
55–59	7,927,979	640,515	743,882	8.08
60–64	5,986,207	463,924	421,293	7.75
65–69	4,620,811	114,354	153,139	2.47
70–74	4,172,432	31,202	42,247	0.75
75 or older	7,492,125	23,474	34,780	0.31

NOTE: All data are estimates based on samples.
SOURCE: Adapted from unpublished table from the preliminary Statistics of Income File for 2000.

by firms offering such protection is shrinking, and many employers now require their retired workers to pay for more of the cost of these plans (Fronstin, 1997). Health insurance is particularly important for workers who are past middle age but not yet eligible for Medicare, because many of them face high risk of incurring heavy medical expenses. Workers with health insurance on the job who would lose it if they retire have an obvious incentive to remain on the job, at least until age 65 when they become eligible for Medicare. Those with postretirement health benefits have less incentive to remain employed, although how much less depends on how the insurance costs after retirement are shared between the employee and employer.

ERISA does not regulate coverage, payment provisions, or funding of private health insurance plans and preempts the rights of states to regulate these matters in many instances. As a result, the specifics of self-funded health plans are not highly regulated. ERISA's rules governing employer-provided benefit plans are restricted to the following: Plan administrators must meet fiduciary responsibilities to beneficiaries; plans may not deprive beneficiaries of promised benefits under the plan; employers may not terminate employees in order to deprive them of rights under a plan; and states may not in general regulate ERISA plans. State health insurance laws may create specific requirements for insured health plans, but these laws are inapplicable to self-funded ERISA plans. The ADA prohibits the singling out of specific disabilities for limitations on coverage, but it does not prevent actuarially based plan designs that limit coverage more generally (EEOC guidance). Private health insurance also plays a hidden role: It creates incentives for some workers to stay at their jobs due to the lack of insurance coverage if they were to exit, and it creates incentives for employers to terminate older workers who may add substantially to the cost of employer-based group health plans.

Although older workers are among those most likely to have health insurance, the consequences of lack of insurance in this age group create significant risks for both economic loss and downwardly spiraling health. Moreover, if a worker needs to exit the workforce before reaching age 65, she or he may be presented with a considerable dilemma. Current accounting rules require employers to fully prefund the future costs of any health insurance promises made to future retirees. As costs for health care have increased for people over 50, the cost of this coverage in the private market has risen, and the availability of coverage has declined. Attempts to intercede in the small group and individual market, theoretically mandated under the Health Insurance Portability and Accountability Act (HIPAA), have been largely unsuccessful.

For those workers who qualify, the federal Medicare program provides health insurance to everyone over 65 years old and to SSDI recipients after two years of income replacement eligibility. The plan provides full hospitalization coverage, less comprehensive outpatient coverage, and no coverage for prescription drugs consumed outside of hospitals or for chronic long-term care. Although it provides critical coverage to those in the retirement age group, Medicare fails to protect workers who must exit the workforce prior to the presumptive retirement age. The two-year waiting period after qualification for SSDI means that workers with disabilities may have periods during which they have no access to health insurance.

Finally, for the very poor, or for those who have depleted their savings, Medicaid will provide coverage for both personal health services (including prescription drugs) and long-term care. Medicaid eligibility is determined under state rules, although states receive federal assistance (at varying levels based upon poverty incidence). Because of the strict income and assets eligibility requirements for Medicaid eligibility in many states, Medicaid is a program that is primarily beneficial to workers after they have been forced to deplete savings as a result of job loss and adverse health events. Medicaid eligibility accompanies eligibility for SSI income benefits.

Table A-21 in Appendix A summarizes the availability of different sources of health insurance to age cohorts over the age of 45. Not surprisingly, due largely to the availability of government programs that cover 97 percent of those 65 and older, 99 percent of these individuals are covered by some type of insurance. Private insurance coverage declines as workers age: 80 percent for individuals 45 to 54, 76 percent for those 55 to 64, 61 percent for those 65 and older (for whom private insurance is generally a supplement to government programs). Employment-based coverage similarly declines over time: 75 percent for those 45 to 54, 68 percent for those 55 to 64, 34 percent for those 65 and older. The critical observation from the standpoint of the health and safety of older workers is that close to one-third of workers over 55 do not have health insurance provided by their employers. As chronic health conditions increase with age, the lack of health insurance (and the accompanying barriers to access to health care) may significantly impact the ability of these workers to remain in the workforce.

There is considerable evidence that health insurance coverage before and after retirement has an important influence on individual retirement decisions. Gustman and Steinmeier (1994) found, for example, that the effects of insurance plans are similar in nature to those of employer-sponsored pension plans. If workers can become eligible for retiree health benefits only after a delay, the availability of the plan tends to delay workers' retirements until they gain eligibility. After eligibility has been achieved, the availability of retiree health benefits encourages earlier retirement than would occur if no benefits were offered. Quinn estimates that men and women in career jobs in 1992 were 8 to 10 percentage points less likely to leave their jobs over the next four years if they would lose health insurance coverage by doing so (Quinn, 1999). Inferring the overall effect of health insurance incentives on retirement patterns is not straightforward, however. A number of components of employee compensation, including wage rates, pension coverage, health insurance, and retiree health benefits, tend to be highly correlated with one another. This makes it difficult to distinguish statistically between the separate effects of each component of compensation. Nonetheless, the rising importance of health insurance coverage to older Americans suggests that the evolution of the public and private health insurance system may have had a sizable impact on retirement patterns.

8

Interventions for Older Workers

Earlier chapters have examined the evidence indicating that more older workers are expected to be on the job over the next 20 or more years and that the workplaces and working relationships they face are changing. These discussions have also reviewed how the physical and cognitive resources of older workers are likely to match these workplace demands. We now turn attention to the range of interventions that might best enhance this matching of older workers and the working environment.

It was suggested in Chapter 1 that intervention and research needs might be approached from either of two perspectives. The first is that insofar as older workers, especially those with high skill levels, may be necessary to meet basic needs of the national economy, our society has a strong interest in retaining older workers. From this perspective our policy and research agenda should focus on the characteristics that predict which older workers are most likely to work most productively and on the best incentives and methods to encourage and enable the most productive workers to stay.

The second perspective focuses on the needs of aging workers and their families. The goal would be to maximize opportunities for workers to make informed decisions about work and retirement that are not unreasonably constrained by economic conditions. The accompanying policy and research agenda should develop information and resources that would assist older workers in making successful choices and also support initiatives to ensure equal protection for older workers on the job.

Both perspectives anticipate significant numbers of older workers and the need for research and policies that will help accommodate their needs and enhance their safety and productivity. The American Association of Retired Persons states: "If employers are to reap the benefits of the work ethic and experience of older workers, they must design the workplace of the future to meet their needs." We consider interventions from the premise that it is generally preferable to accommodate the working environment to anticipate and meet the needs of older workers than to attempt only changing the aging workers themselves to adapt to their environments. There are two sources for such a premise. The first is pragmatic and finds expression in the science and practice of human factors engineering. It is recognition that human beings are imperfect.

> Everyone, and that includes you and me, is at some time careless, complacent, overconfident, and stubborn. At times each of us becomes distracted, inattentive, bored and fatigued. We occasionally take chances. We misunderstand, we misinterpret and we misread. As a result of these and still other completely human characteristics, we sometimes do not do things or use things in ways that are expected of us. Because we are human and because all these traits are fundamental and built into each of us, the equipment, machines and systems that we construct for our use have to be made to accommodate us the way we are, and not vice versa. (Chapanis, 1985)

The second source is ethical and legal and finds expression in the Occupational Safety and Health Act (OSHA) of 1971: "The Congress declares it to be its purpose and policy . . . to assure so far as possible every working man and woman in the Nation safe and healthful working conditions . . ." (P.L. 91-596). These workplace protections apply equally to every worker. But all workers are not the same. There are notable differences in size, strength, age, sex, health status, genetic makeup, and other factors that affect people's risk from hazards on the job. Since Congress intends to protect workers equally across this varied spectrum of characteristics, including age, it follows that workplaces must adapt and change to accommodate a reasonable range.

OSHA's approach to workplace accommodation and worker protection has been based on the hierarchy of controls concept. This concept in its simplest form holds that workers should be protected by controlling hazards as close to the source as possible. For example, designing a job so that a dangerous chemical is not necessary is preferable to providing a worker with a respirator, which in turn is preferable to training the worker to be as careful around the chemical as possible. Some version of a control hierarchy has been observed by virtually all safety and health professional associations and organizations for more than 50 years. Many OSHA standards require efforts to utilize feasible engineering or administrative controls before personal protective equipment or worker training may be considered. A more fully elaborated version of the hierarchy of controls places protective measures in the following order of preference:

(1) engineering controls (e.g., elimination, ventilation, mechanical guarding);
(2) administrative controls (e.g., safe job procedures, job rotation);
(3) personal protective equipment (e.g., respirators, ear plugs);
(4) individual behavior (e.g., safe lifting techniques); and
(5) warnings (e.g., labels, bells).

While these hierarchies vary in their detail, they tend to share at their core the notion that methods of protection that do not rely primarily on individual employee behavior alone are preferred to those that do.

Extending the legal and ethical perspective and the goals of maintaining a safe and healthful work environment, however, leads inevitably to varying interpretation of the extent to which health promotion, treatment, and rehabilitative services—crucial to the general health status of older workers—should be provided at or through the workplace. This is in addition to worker education and training, retraining for changing job tasks, and the many other activities that are offered at or through the workplace. A wide variety of employee interventions to maintain and improve health and safety have been established over many decades, albeit usually not universal in coverage, and new delivery and experimental programs are continually appearing.

The Americans with Disabilities Act (ADA) is one law that anticipates and addresses the hierarchical approach by requiring job interventions and accommodations. The ADA protects workers if they have a disability that substantially limits one or more major life activities but they are able to perform the essential functions of the job with reasonable accommodations. Accommodations under the ADA require that employers make existing facilities readily accessible and usable, and that they restructure jobs or modify work.

While older workers are more likely than younger ones to have disabilities covered by the ADA, the need to accommodate older workers goes well beyond these covered limitations. This chapter considers accommodations in the broadest fashion. For example, Burkhauser, Butler, and Kim (1995), using a proportional hazards analysis with data from the 1978 Survey of Disability and Work, found that provision of an accommodation, defined broadly, slowed worker withdrawal from the workforce and delayed the beginning of SSDI payments. Potential recall bias in these studies might be addressed in a longitudinal study, using data now available from the Health and Retirement Study. No studies have examined whether workplace accommodations lower the risk of occupational injuries found by Zwerling et al. (1998a) among older workers with various impairments.

We adopt here the control hierarchy as an approach to beginning a discussion of the current status of intervention strategies to meet the safety and health needs of older workers. While there is some specific evidence to support this approach, it is limited (e.g., older adults are more likely to read warnings but less likely to comprehend warning signals [Rogers and Fisk, 2000]). Therefore, we use the concept as a useful way to structure and present ideas for accommodating the needs of older workers without arguing for a rigid order of preference. Interventions relevant to all workers, but particularly for older workers, also include workplace design and redesign; worker training; learning systems and retraining issues; alternative forms of work; the relation of the workplace to community service support; worksite health promotion and illness or disorder prevention programs; and employee assistance programs, including return-to-work programs.

JOB DESIGN AND REDESIGN

In keeping with the breadth of potential workplace interventions noted in the introduction to this chapter, we now consider job design, including redesign and engineering, to improve the accommodations for older workers. There are many well-documented cross-sectional studies and some longitudinal ones outlining normative changes in vision, hearing, physical strength, and flexibility with age, as examples for requisites for many work environments (see Chapter 5). Some data derive from representative national samples. These age-related changes can be expected to affect older workers if they cannot compensate for such changes. Nonetheless, to the extent that work in the future requires maximal performance rather than typical performance, and if older adults retire later or return to part-time work after retirement, design interventions will probably become necessary.

Design Interventions to Accommodate Normative Changes in Vision

There are a variety of normative changes in vision with increased age (see Fozard and Gordon-Salant, 2001, for a review). Prominent among these are loss of accommodative power for the lens (near-vision focus), yellowing of the lens that weakens color discrimination, scattering of light in the eye due to debris in the vitreous humor, and inability to expand the pupil fully (senile miosis). Most of these changes result in less light being admitted to the eye—about one-third as much light comparing a 65-year-old to a 20-year-old in low light conditions. Due to increased scattering of light, there is also greater susceptibility to glare from light sources. There are also changes due to loss of cells in the visual cortex that reduce the likelihood that correction via lenses will restore youthful vision.

Disease processes also contribute to the increased risk of loss of visual function with age. These nonnormative changes include glaucoma, macular degeneration, and cataract. Some of these diseases are linked to high blood pressure and diabetes. Cigarette smoking is also a well-established risk factor (Smith et al., 2001). Not well understood is the extent to which these changes are related to work environment factors. Lifetime exposure to ultraviolet light, which is higher for outdoors (blue-collar) than indoors (white-collar) work, has been found to be a risk factor for development of lens opacities (e.g., Hayashi et al., 2003). There is also evidence of higher risk of age-related maculopathy for blue-collar compared to white-collar professions (Klein et al., 2001).

Corrective Lenses

Eyeglasses are a potentially effective intervention for protecting against UV exposure and for accommodating to age-related changes in near-distance vision. An increase in computer-related work (e.g., Chan, Marshall, and Marshall, 2001, who reported 4–5 hours per day of computer work at a large corporation) means that instead of reading from paper sources people will increasingly be required to access information from computer monitors. Most monitors are placed about 40 to 60 cm from the user. This is a distance that, similar to vehicle instrument panels, falls between typical near-and far-focus distances and therefore leads to difficulty for older workers in their early forties and beyond. Potential solutions involve prescribing gradient lenses (progressive bifocals) and specialized lenses just for computer work. There are empirically validated ergonomic guidelines for the positioning of monitors, keyboards, and pointing devices (e.g., a computer mouse) that can minimize strain when working with these tools (e.g., Occupational Safety and Health Act, 2002). Whether these guidelines need to be modified to better accommodate older workers is not known.

Road Signs

For those working in the transportation sector, particularly those driving vehicles, age-related changes in vision and visual attention (e.g., shrinkage of the useful field of view, Owsley et al., 1991) can have a direct impact on safety and productivity. There are several studies demonstrating that signs can be redesigned to make them more visible, particularly by changing spatial frequency characteristics to improve contrast (Kline, Ghali, and Kline, 1990; Kline and Fuchs, 1993). There are many suggestions for redesigning the road environment to improve safety for older drivers (and pedestrians) as evidenced by the new guidelines for older drivers (Federal Highway Administration, 2000). Because automobile crashes are quite infrequent for the average driver, with a probability of 0.1 per year (Evans, 1991), it is sometimes difficult to show the effects of an intervention, such as changing signage, on crash rates. There is considerable evidence that older drivers (age 55 and older) adapt their driving patterns to compensate for weaknesses, such as reducing night driving and rush hour traffic exposure (Ball et al., 1998). Such strategies may not be considered acceptable by those working under time pressure, such as professional drivers.

Lighting

Aging processes diminish the sensitivity of the visual system. One simple intervention is to increase the amount of light in the environment, particularly for work-related tasks. Care must be taken to avoid increasing glare in the process by controlling the light sources and the work surfaces. Field studies show that light levels in many U.S. office environments generally meet recommended levels for reading tasks of about 100 cd/m^2 (Charness and Dijkstra, 1999). However, there is a dearth of information about optimal light levels for older workers. Some evidence suggests that legibility of print can be boosted differentially for older office workers by increasing light levels beyond existing guidelines (Charness and Dijkstra, 1999). Information about the effects of print size, contrast level, and luminance levels on print legibility for older adults is beginning to accumulate (Steenbekkers and van Beijsterveldt, 1998). It would be useful to extend this work to applied settings using typical clerical tasks and to assess the impact of contrast for monitor-based reading tasks.

Design Interventions to Accommodate
Normative Changes in Hearing

Hearing capabilities decline normatively with age (Fozard and Gordon-Salant, 2001). Pure tone thresholds decline with age, particularly for higher frequency tones and more so in men than women. Speech comprehension shows noticeable changes (for monosyllabic words) after age 50. Older adults show more masking of signals by noise. Speech compression (e.g., in automated voice mail systems) and rapid speech rate affect older adults more than younger ones (e.g., Stine, Wingfield, and Poon, 1986). Most of these changes can be attributed to loss of hair cells in the cochlea and loss of cells in auditory areas in the brain as well as to general age-related slowing in comprehension processes.

The extent to which such loss is driven by exposure to noise versus normal aging is a matter of dispute. Losses are linked to noise exposure as well as to factors such as cardiovascular disease, smoking, and dietary factors. There are a number of approaches to remediating hearing loss. In general, hearing aids have not been particularly functional in fully restoring hearing acuity because they boost both signal and noise.

Given that some have estimated that normative hearing loss is at least partially attributed to noise exposure in the workplace (e.g., Corso, 1981), prevention is a potentially useful approach. One important source of noise exposure is aging equipment. Farmers using older tractors can be exposed to noise levels in excess of 100 dB (Pessina and Guerretti, 2000). Also, hearing loss is strongly associated with livestock-related injuries for farmers (Sprince et al., 2003). Noise reduction engineering and promotion of safe practices in inherently noisy environments, such as the use of noise reduction devices (e.g., ear protective equipment such as earplugs), may be important components in preventing problems.

Given that hearing loss may pose a significant problem (particularly for older male workers), redesign can be an important tool in preventing hearing impairments from becoming disabilities. One such design change is to make use of other less-impaired sensory channels, described below, to signal important information (such as warnings).

Use of Redundant Channels and Substitution of Channels

There are many examples of using redundant channels to compensate for hearing loss. It is possible to provide both visual and auditory warnings (flashing lights with sound). Perhaps the best-known example is the use of a warning sound (beep) to indicate when a vehicle is backing up (moving in the unexpected direction). Other examples can be found in catalogs of assistive devices, such as those that supplement normal sound channels with tactual feedback (e.g., a vibrating cell phone). For those with profound hearing loss, substitution of vision for hearing is sometimes possible (flashing lights for a doorbell, closed captioning on television). Vanderheiden (1997) offers specific recommendations on redesigning to accommodate those with disabilities.

Minimizing Background Noise

Several studies show greater comprehension impairment for older adults than younger ones at the same signal-to-noise ratios, compared to the case of detection of pure tones in quiet surroundings. Minimizing background noise should aid older workers differentially for comprehension tasks. Simply increasing signal strength, e.g., shouting over noise, results in diminishing returns (Crocker, 1997).

Design Interventions to Accommodate Physical Changes

The Canada Fitness Survey (Kozma, Stones, and Hannah, 1991) showed cross-sectional linear decline on most fitness and flexibility variables with age, though sometimes gender interacted with age; men typically showed faster decline than women. A main effect on fitness and flexibility was shown for activity level as well, an effect that did not interact with age. Because of changes in the cohort structure of the workforce, particularly the shifts in minority composition from large influxes of Hispanic workers, current data on anthropometry (e.g., Kroemer, 1997; Peebles and Norris, 2003; Steenbekkers and van Bijsterveldt, 1998) may not predict characteristics of future cohorts of older workers. Such data are useful for designing functional workplaces. Anthropometric data typically encompass size, strength, and flexibility ranges for people's bodies. An example would be extent of reach from a seated position. If a given worker has a shorter-than-average reach, he or she may become inadvertently handicapped and possibly suffer musculoskeletal disorders (MSDs) in work environments designed for those with a longer reach.

Arthritis, which affects flexibility and dexterity, increases in prevalence with age and affects older women more than men (Verbrugge, Lepkowski, and Konkol, 1991). Arthritis can make many manual tasks difficult to perform. Women tend to be differentially employed in clerical positions that require typing (Chan et al., 2001), implying that some accommodations may be particularly critical for them. Also, arthritis has recently been shown to be a risk factor for occupational injury, for instance, in farmers who are injured by livestock (Sprince et al., 2003).

Changes in the mechanisms supporting balance may be an important factor to consider, given the data on age-related increases in death from falls in construction and manufacturing industries (Agnew and Suruda, 1993; Bailer et al., 2003).

Shephard (1995) reviewed research on physically demanding work and suggested changes to accommodate older workers (women and men). A central concern is the likelihood of fatigue in a physically demanding task that exceeds a threshold for cardiorespiratory capacity of 33 percent maximal oxygen intake. If aerobic capability declines from about 12 to 14 metabolic units (METS) in young adults to 7 METS in the average 65-year-old, many older workers would not be expected to be able to perform other than light physical work. Given that women typically average two-thirds the aerobic power of men at all ages, older women are most at risk for excessive demands from physically demanding jobs.

There are similar problems with age-related declines in muscular strength in the general population. Guidelines for strength demands typically recommend that median load be less than 10 percent of maximal load and that peak load be less than 50 percent of peak force. Strength benchmarks are usually set for the case where at least 75 percent of women and 99 percent of men can meet job requirements safely. In practice, there are few cases of aerobic and muscular limitations found in the workplace. This may be due to physical stressors on the job that increase fitness, or because job shifts and disability remove those who cannot meet job requirements. Job redesign is a safe way to reduce physical workload to acceptable levels.

OECD Job Redesign Studies

Marbach (1968) described a set of case studies of redesign of jobs to accommodate older workers. There was little formal evaluation of the effect of redesign, so these cases are more illustrative than scientifically informative. Most of the examples involved substituting machines (cranes, conveyor belts, forklifts) for human effort on lifting and moving tasks, as well as shifting workers to sitting instead of standing positions. Some involved changing the nature of the work task by shifting heavy physical tasks to other team members and having an older worker assume lighter tasks. In another case with computer equipment assembly, instructions were provided aurally via audiotape and headphones instead of with written instructions, eliminating eyestrain and freeing workers' hands. In many cases the older workers at risk (because of work-related injuries or development of arthritis) were able to continue work in cases where they may have otherwise been forced to leave. As Marbach comments, there are probably numerous cases of small but important modifications that have been made to accommodate older workers that were not reported in the OECD survey forms. This approach of gathering examples of best practices seems promising.

Design for Safety: Providing More Effective Warnings

Given high rates of job turnover in modern labor markets, workers are less likely to remain at the same job site over their entire career than they have during prior historical periods. Accidents are most likely to occur in the first year of employment at a new job setting (Root, 1981). Hence, there is a need to prevent injuries through effective warnings, training, and redesign of existing tools and settings.

A recent review suggests methods to improve the design of warning systems (Rogers, Lamson, and Rousseau, 2000). As that review noted, older adults demonstrated poorer ability to notice warnings and to comprehend warning symbols. Hancock, Rogers, and Fisk (2001) showed that older adults were more likely to report that they read warnings but were also less likely to comprehend warning symbols. There did not appear to be much literature pertaining to age differences in compliance with warnings. If one assumes that appropriate warnings are already posted in workplaces, older workers may be heeding them better, given their lower rate of accidents. The medication adherence literature also suggests that older adults are more compliant with medication routines than middle-aged adults (Park et al., 1999).

Ergonomic Design Interventions and Musculoskeletal Disorders

In addition to training approaches discussed below, there have been studies to assess the effectiveness of engineering, administrative, and individual-focused interventions at the workplace in the prevention of musculoskeletal disorders (MSDs). Due to ongoing changes at most workplaces unrelated to planned interventions, it is difficult to use formal epidemiology studies to determine whether ergonomic interventions are effective. A review by Westgaard and Winkel (1997) noted this problem in an assessment of the efficacy of different workplace intervention studies for MSDs. The review examines problems in the current intervention literature, ranging from lack of statistical analysis to failure to include control groups to confounders such as inadvertent changes in the psychosocial climate. Interventions they classified as mechanical exposure interventions unaccompanied by organizational change were generally unsuccessful. Production system interventions based on changing the organization of work also failed to show much benefit. Intervention studies that attempted to change the organizational culture of a work environment achieved relatively good results. So too did modifier interventions that attempted to change the capabilities of a worker through physiotherapy or exercise interventions. These latter approaches involve both targeting of risk factors for workers and intervention at the level of the individual worker. It is recognized, however, that it is difficult to isolate the modifier intervention from parallel changes, including psychosocial improvements.

More recently published studies support more optimism about the effectiveness of workplace interventions to prevent MSDs. Several studies have reported a positive impact of ergonomic interventions on low back and other MSDs among workers performing lifting and related manual material handling tasks (Evanoff, Bohr, and Wolf, 1999; Brophy, Achimore, and Moore-Dawson, 2001; Marras et al., 2000; Yassi et al., 2001). Others have found positive effects among workers using video display units (Aaras et al., 2001; Brisson, Montreuil and Punnett, 1999; Demure et al., 2000; Ketola et al., 2002). Positive outcomes of comprehensive interventions, including job redesign and organizational change, have also been reported for MSDs among hospital workers (Bernacki et al., 1999; Carrivick, Lee, and Yau, 2002), sign language interpreters (Feuerstein et al., 2000), and office workers (Nelson and Silverstein, 1998). Negative results were found among a small group of assembly workers after jobs were redesigned to be more varied, less repetitive, and more autonomous (Christmansson, Friden, and Sollerman, 1999). A review of interventions aimed at reducing exposure to mechanical stressors concluded that there were significant benefits (Lötters and Burdof, 2002). A review of studies for carpal tunnel syndrome suggested the need for better-designed intervention investigations (Lincoln et al., 2000). In three recent intervention studies, ergonomically modified jobs have also been associated with more rapid return to work after work related MSDs (Crook, Moldofsky, and Shannon, 1998; Loisel et al., 1997; Arnetz et al., 2003).

The most recent comprehensive review of intervention effectiveness was completed by a National Academy of Sciences committee (National Research Council and the Institute of Medicine, 2001), which evaluated 20 years of formal studies along with results from a best-practices symposium sponsored by the National Institute for Occupational Safety and Health (NIOSH) in 1997 (NIOSH Effective Workplace Practices and Programs Conference, Chicago, 1997). In addition to examining reviews published through the mid-1990s, the committee identified 17 recent intervention epidemiology studies along with 40 case studies from the Chicago conference. The committee arrived at a positive conclusion about the benefits of interventions directed at reducing exposure to mechanical and psychosocial stressors. It concluded that

> [T]he weight of the evidence justifies the introduction of appropriate and selected interventions to reduce the risk of musculoskeletal disorders of the low back and upper extremities. These include, but are not confined to, the application of ergonomic principles to reduce physical as well as psychosocial stressors. To be effective, intervention programs should include employee involvement, employer commitment, and the development of integrated programs that address equipment design, work procedures, and organizational characteristics (pp. 9–10).

Psychological Climate

A less researched area is the influence on safety-of-job factors such as degree of empowerment and feelings of insecurity. Metanalysis has shown significant negative impacts of job insecurity on mental and physical health in the range of r = −0.1 to −0.2 (Sverke et al., 2002). Probst and Brubaker (2001) indicated that self-reported accidents increased as a function of the extent to which food-processing workers considered their jobs to be insecure. The effect, as assessed by path modeling, was not direct; it operated through job satisfaction and safety motivation.

Increased degree of empowerment of teams was a strong negative predictor of accidents ($r = -0.51$) and of unsafe behaviors ($r = -0.48$) among chemical plant workers where the worksites had undergone significant reductions (Hechanova-Alampay and Beehr, 2001). Given trends toward lean production (Landsbergis, Cahill, and Schnall, 1999) that increase the probability of layoffs, and given that older workers perceive themselves to be potential targets, they may be particularly at risk for serious injury at work. This is because older workers who see their jobs to be at risk to layoff may be tempted to rush work using unsafe behaviors that lead to injury. They also suffer, on average, more serious injuries than their younger counterparts. However, research is needed to evaluate the pathways from job insecurity to accidents specifically for older worker populations.

Countering the reported trend toward increased feelings of job insecurity is the finding that older workers usually exhibit higher job satisfaction (e.g., Warr, 1992). There is a need to evaluate what characteristics of job environments are particularly important for older worker safety and whether there are interventions that improve job climate differentially for older workers.

The earlier discussion on health and job class (see Chapter 4) shows that job class, a measure of socioeconomic status, is an important predictor of present and future health status for civil servants. Work empowerment interventions may be a useful way to decrease the risk of negative health outcomes for lower SES workers.

Work Organization, Job Redesign, and Cardiovascular Health

The effectiveness of a limited number of interventions to improve work organization and job design, reduce job stressors, and create a more healthy work organization have been documented (International Labour Office, 1992; Landsbergis et al., 1997; Murphy et al., 1995; Parker and Wall, 1998; Parkes and Sparkes, 1998). These include (1) action plans by Swedish civil servants carried out to reduce work stressors, resulting in a significant decrease in apolipoprotein B/AI ratio in the intervention group but not in the control group (Orth-Gomer et al., 1994); (2) interventions on an inner-city bus line in Stockholm designed to diminish time pressure and promote traffic flow, resulting in a significant decline in systolic BP (-10.7 mm Hg) among bus drivers (Rydstedt, Johansson, and Evans, 1998); and (3) among Swedish autoworkers, a more flexible work organization with small autonomous groups having greater opportunities to influence the pace and content of their work, which resulted in lower systolic BP, heart rate, epinephrine, and self-reported tiredness than that of workers in a traditional auto assembly line (Melin et al., 1999).

There have been no published job redesign studies in the United States that have examined cardiovascular disease outcomes per se. However, some American job redesign programs have examined other stress-related health outcomes, providing valuable guidance (Cahill and Feldman, 1993; Israel, Schurman, and House, 1989; Smith and Zehel, 1992). In addition to job redesign, legislative, regulatory (Warren, 2000), and collective bargaining (Landsbergis, 2000) approaches have been attempted. A promising development in this area is recent state legislation in the United States, which provides minimum staffing levels and limits on mandatory overtime for health care workers. U.S. policy makers may find valuable legislature models in Scandinavia, the European Union (Levi, 2000), and Japan (Shimomitsu and Odagiri, 2000) that regulate work organization and job stressors as health hazards.

ISSUES IN TRAINING FOR WORKER HEALTH AND SAFETY

Training can be an important intervention for the workplace if it is placed in the proper context of environmental interventions and its limitations are properly understood. This section examines how training can be used to promote safe, healthy, and productive work for aging workers. As people age, the balance between their capabilities and the demands of the workplace may shift, requiring training and design interventions. The field of human factors and ergonomics has been influential in advocating the use of both training and design to improve the productivity, safety, and comfort of people in both work and nonwork environments. Reviews underline the importance of human factors approaches specifically for older workers (e.g., Charness and Bosman, 1992; Czaja, 2001; Rogers and Fisk, 2000). However, establishing guidelines for training and design is challenging. Variability in older worker capabilities (see Chapter 5), diversity in workplace settings, and the changing nature of work (Hunt, 1995; Landsbergis, 2003) contribute to this difficulty.

It is useful to outline some of the assumptions underlying our reasoning about the role of training and design. People tend to *satisfice* (Simon, 1969) when problem solving; that is, they choose good enough, rather than optimal, solutions. Hence, most workplaces are not likely to be optimally designed for safety and productivity. For similar reasons, training packages are unlikely to be optimized for a given set of participants. Because knowledge about the types of normative changes that occur as people age is not widespread, we expect that most workplaces will not be optimized for an aging workforce. Finally, we do not expect older workers or their peers and supervisors to be passive inhabitants of a workplace. Workers do change jobs to yield better fits between their abilities and job demands (e.g., Swaen et al., 2002). There are probably many cases of accommodative activities in place throughout the workforce.

The existing scientific literature has significant limitations intrinsic to population surveys, field studies, and laboratory experiments. We often rely on metanalytic studies, for example, to help ensure better inference, but these have weaknesses, for instance, the choice of rules for inclusion and exclusion of studies in the analysis and the fact that studies with nonsignificant findings tend not to be published. However, metanalyses do provide an efficient way to estimate effect sizes across studies (e.g., Schmidt, 1996).

An important theme is the need to consider increased age as contributing to counterbalancing trends. Aging processes tend to lower overall general functional capacity. Increased age is also associated with increased experience that tends to raise experience-related functional capacities. These two aspects of age may trade off, particularly when experience leads to skill and expertise, a point stressed in some of the earliest literature in this field (e.g., Welford, 1958).

Training and Retraining

Training and retraining seem particularly relevant for older workers, who are likely to be the most distant from initial professional training and from initial job training (Sparrow and Davies, 1988). Whether older workers are particularly in need of training and retraining can be addressed from the perspective of two outcome criteria: productivity and safety. To the extent that age discrimination exists in work settings, it may be driven by perceptions that older workers are less productive.

Productivity

Cross-sectional metanalyses show no relation between age and job productivity (McEvoy and Cascio, 1989; Waldman and Avolio, 1986). This outcome is surprising in view of the ubiquitous laboratory-based findings of age-related declines in basic perceptual and cognitive abilities and in problem-solving performance on novel tasks (see Chapter 5). Productivity is typically measured using work output measures or peer and supervisor ratings of performance. One explanation for the apparent lack of an association between age and productivity is that, as mentioned previously, increased age is associated with the acquisition of job-specific knowledge and skills that compensate for age-related declines in general abilities (Salthouse and Maurer, 1996).

Another possibility is that the cross-sectional comparisons involve a mix of younger workers with varying skills and older workers with established skills, given that younger workers move out of jobs much more frequently than older ones (Swaen et al., 2002). It is also possible that typical jobs do not demand continuous maximal performance to the same extent as laboratory-devised tasks. Older workers may find ways to accommodate to changes in capabilities that enable them to continue performing at satisfactory levels. An example would be the adoption of reading glasses to enable them to compensate for normative development of presbyopia (inability to focus on near objects). However, future findings about the relation of age to performance may change to the extent that the demand for new, nonpracticed abilities increases in the workplace. If current trends toward later retirement strengthen, and if there is increased job mobility, we may expect to see some narrowing in the gap between lab and life findings.

An important limitation on the conclusions about age and productivity is the insensitive measures of productivity. For example, in psychological literature productivity is often defined in terms of simple output. In economic analyses, a firm that produces the same number of goods and services using fewer inputs than a competitor is considered more productive. As a group, older workers are usually paid more than younger workers. Examined cross-sectionally, income tends to peak in the late 40s and early 50s compared with earlier and later ages (U.S. Bureau of the Census, 2002). Even if they show equivalent product output, older workers would be more costly to employ (or less cost-effective) by virtue of their higher salaries (and possibly by the higher cost of their benefits). But, cross-sectional analyses neglect the issues pertaining to lifetime costs and benefits to a firm and to a worker for an employment contract. Current higher wages paid to older workers may be explicable by delayed payment contract models (e.g., Hutchens, 1986). Such models argue that single-period accounting of the relative costs of labor do not fully capture the lifetime nature of labor contracts and the value of workers to their firms over their complete tenure.

So there is mixed news on the productivity question. Older workers appear to be as capable (or incapable) as younger ones in performing their jobs. However, older workers may appear to be less efficient than younger ones. Hence, there would appear to be a strong incentive to provide training and retraining to increase job productivity and efficiency. Or there may be an incentive to replace costly but equally productive (for output) older workers with younger, less expensive ones, should replacement prove less expensive than investing in training.

An important prerequisite for productivity is being available for work. Absenteeism, differentiated into voluntary (e.g., calling in sick when not sick) and involuntary (true illness or disorder or injury) types, does show age-related differences. Martocchio's (1989) metanalysis used frequency of absence to index voluntary absenteeism and time loss to index involuntary absenteeism. It indicated that older workers tend to have fewer absences of each type than younger workers, though the relationship is slight (r values between age and absenteeism were in the −0.1 to −0.2 range). The study also showed that gender moderated the relationship for voluntary absence: Women showed a near zero relation to age compared to the negative one for men, possibly due to nonlinear relationships for women.

Is there reason to believe that older workers would benefit as much from training as younger workers? A metanalysis showed that older adults benefit less than younger ones from training (Kubeck et al., 1996), with the correlation between age and training outcome being r = −0.26, and with training taking longer for older adults (r = −0.42). However, an important constraint on this conclusion is that a substantial subset of the training studies reviewed involved novel tasks. Some recent research that involved retraining (learning a second word processing software package) has shown a divergence in outcomes for novices versus experienced adults (Charness et al., 2001). There were strong age-related deficits in performance during and following training with novices and minimal (speed-related) or no declines in the performance of experienced middle-aged and older adults. However, in agreement with the metanalysis, this study also showed older adults, both experienced and inexperienced, taking longer to complete self-paced training sessions.

Safety

Are older workers less safe than younger ones, hence in need of better workplace design and training? It is important to distinguish injury probability and injury outcome as well as to differentiate injuries that are the result of a single episode or that are incurred by long-term exposure. Generally, the industrial accident literature indicates that acute injuries are most likely to be incurred by inexperienced workers in their first year at a new job and that older workers are much less likely to incur accidents (see Chapter 6; Sterns, Barrett, and Alexander, 1985).

Workers age 45 and older are much more likely to die as a result of a fall (e.g., Agnew and Suruda, 1993). Similarly, older workers are more likely to incur more serious nonfatal injuries (e.g., Layne and Landen, 1997).

The vehicle crash literature offers a model task environment for examining accident probability and injury as a function of age, particularly for North American workers who usually drive to work settings. About 42 percent of fatal occupational injuries are associated with transportation (NIOSH, 2002a). About 90 percent of all trips taken in the United States are taken in personal vehicles, with some 70 percent of those involving self-driving (e.g., Stutts, in press). Older drivers are more at risk for crashes per mile driven than middle-aged drivers, though this is not seen until after age 65, and the risk becomes pronounced for those in their 80s. However, consistent with an age-positive experience effect, even 85-year-old drivers are less likely to suffer a crash (per mile driven) than 16- to 19-year-old drivers. Consistent with an age-negative effect on physical and physiological functioning, older drivers are more likely to be killed in a crash due to their greater fragility (Li, Braver, and Chen, 2003). When crash intensity is controlled statistically, there is still a greater likelihood of death for older adults and also for women (Evans, 1991). The latter finding points to the importance of body size and composition in absorbing impact forces.

Size of workplace is likely to be an important factor in opportunities for training and design intervention. Smaller workplaces are less likely to be regulated and less likely to have the resources to do effective training and design. Perhaps as a result, workplace fatalities tend to be concentrated in workplaces employing fewer than 10 workers (NIOSH, 2002b). Finding ways to disseminate relevant information to workplaces employing fewer than 10 employees is an important challenge.

The literature on productivity and safety, then, indicates that older workers are at somewhat greater risk for negative outcomes than younger ones. The literature on fatal falls (Agnew and Suruda, 1993) suggests that this increased risk first appears in incidence figures in the 45- to 64-year-old age range. Therefore, we can justify advocating training and retraining interventions, as well as design interventions, to improve productivity and safety of older workers. In the next sections we examine in more detail literature that points to possible guidelines for training and design.

Training Principles

There is an extensive literature on training (e.g., Salas and Cannon-Bowers, 2001). Training studies often focus on the individual, ignoring organizational and motivational factors that may be important mediators or moderators of training outcome. A review by Cohen and Colligan (1998) of literature on training for occupational safety and health makes a similar point about the effectiveness of interventions in workplaces: "Management's role/support of safety training and its transfer to the jobsite, setting goals and providing feedback to motivate use of the knowledge gained, and offering incentives or rewards for reinforcing safe performance all seemed crucial to attaining a positive result" (p. 6).

With some exceptions (e.g., Noe and Wilk, 1993; Colquitt, LePine, and Noe, 2000), the same is true for the literature on training older adults and particularly for training older workers. The emphasis in the age and training area has been on training individuals. Although team training and collaborative performance tasks are more likely to be the norm in work settings, there is a need for a better-developed literature on team training and aging. We focus here on individual differences in outcome for individually based training.

A useful way to partition the training literature is to differentiate broadly versus narrowly focused training. For instance, many white-collar jobs in the economy are advertised as requiring a college or university undergraduate degree, an example of broad training. Others require a specific domain-related training program (e.g., nursing).

Similarly, when considering interventions to help older adults, some interventions are very specific, aimed, for instance, at fall avoidance (e.g., Hauer et al., 2001). Others are broad-based, aimed at improving general abilities. An example of the latter is exercise intervention to improve general cognitive functioning. Recent research shows that certain exercise may be associated with modest improvements in cognitive abilities, particularly those defining so-called executive functions such as planning (Kramer et al., 2001). Earlier studies with older adults focused on training reasoning and spatial orientation abilities (Willis and Schaie, 1986). Those studies found that short-term training effects were equivalent to seven-year longitudinal declines in ability, but that there were very narrow transfer effects, with only trained abilities showing significant improvement. Narrow generalization of training has been replicated with a recent clinical trial (Ball et al., 2002).

The general literature on skill acquisition and on expert performance gives little reason to expect broad transfer effects for training. The classic educational research by Thorndike (1924) suggested that teaching Latin was not likely to show transfer effects to general reasoning and thinking skills. Such work led to his law of identical elements, that transfer can only be expected to occur when there are identical elements in the training and transfer tasks. More recent work refines the methods for assessing identical elements and bears out this conclusion (Singley and Anderson, 1989). Work on expertise shows that the skilled memory of the expert is limited to domain-related material, not to a generally superior memory (e.g., Chase and Simon, 1973). Education and training interventions often appear to ignore this fundamental finding.

Similar transfer findings are obtained for physical work situations. As an example, waste management workers exhibited no better aerobic capacity than the general population, though they did show greater shoulder muscle strength (Schibye et al., 2001). Older waste management workers showed the usual age-related declines in aerobic capacity (compared to younger workers and young and old controls), though they maintained shoulder strength. Lifting and moving waste containers is more likely to improve specific shoulder muscle strength than general aerobic capacity.

Although it runs counter to the notion of satisficing described earlier, advocates of human factors approaches have argued for a "good, better, best" approach to design (Fisher, 1993). However, for whom should training and design be optimized? A fundamental issue is whether a good design or training program for the young will apply equally well to the old (and vice versa). Here we are concerned with age by treatment interactions.

Training Type

There is little disagreement that good training is better than poor training or no training. What is still unresolved is whether some forms of training work particularly well for older compared to younger adults (workers). Early research strongly advised using discovery learning as the best procedure to train older workers in new tasks (Belbin, 1969). In this format, learners are allowed to explore the task environment and try out different methods. Evidence supporting the value of discovery learning compared to traditional training methods for samples of older workers was positive, though weak. Others noted that differences in training method tended to overshadow differences in performance as a function of age (e.g., Czaja and Drury, 1981a,b). However, in the latter studies, training method did not interact with age. Interactions with age (greater gains for older adults) have been found for procedural (action) versus conceptual training for automated teller machine (ATM) use (Mead and Fisk, 1998) and for web search training (Mead et al., 1997).

Forced Pacing vs. Self-Pacing

The training literature frequently argues that training and production environments should be self-paced rather than forced pace for older workers (e.g., Belbin, 1965). This makes sense given the general nature of age-related changes in speed of processing (e.g., Salthouse, 1996), but a differential benefit for older adults has not been reported often. Word processing training studies tend to confirm the advantage of self-pacing for both older and younger adults (e.g., Charness, Schumann, and Boritz, 1992).

Even with self-paced training, older adults may not perform as well as younger ones. Charness et al. (2001) showed that older adults were less able to profit from three days of word processing training if they were novices. In a second experiment experienced older adults also learned more slowly in self-paced training. Although different interface types (keystroke, menus, menus plus icons) affected learning there was no interaction between age and training interface. Better interfaces resulted in parallel improvements in performance in young, middle-aged, and older adults. Across the two samples of participants, prior word processing experience and type of interface were strong predictors of both speed and accuracy, as were, in some instances, psychometric measures of ability.

Experimental tests of pacing in work-related tasks are infrequent. Czaja and Sharit (1993) used realistic work tasks such as data entry, file modification, and inventory management with novice young, middle-aged, and older adults. These tasks were taught over three days, a unique departure from typical one-hour laboratory experiments. One training manipulation that yielded an interaction with task type and age was forced pacing versus self-pacing. Forced pacing tended to reduce older adult performance variability and age-related differences in performance, particularly for the data entry task. However, a checklist measuring perceived fatigue showed that forced pacing resulted in higher levels of fatigue for older adults compared to self-pacing. Generalizing from this study, older individuals might achieve greater output rates if forced to quicken their pace, but the cost might be greater fatigue and possibly greater error rates over an extended workday. Errors related to safety would bear a particularly high cost.

Amount of Training

When people practice a skill over an extended period of time, their improvement function typically follows the power law of practice (e.g., Newell and Rosenbloom, 1981). This means that each successive interval unit of improvement requires a log unit increase in practice. The exact shape of the function (e.g., logarithmic, exponential, hyperbolic) depends on whether averaged group data or individual functions are modeled (Heathcote, Brown, and Mewhort, 2000).

Depending on the task and outcome measure, older adults exhibit equivalent or less improvement with practice than younger adults. Czaja and Sharit (1998) showed that older adults required more training than younger adults before showing improvement in a data entry task. In another study, Czaja (2001) did not find any interaction of age and training with output quantity or quality measures for a database query task (customer service environment).

Because of such mixed findings, the conservative conclusion to be drawn is that the rate of improvement with practice will differ marginally between younger and older adults, and when it does it will favor younger adults. A faster acquisition rate parameter for younger adult groups is a typical finding in analyses that involve fitting power functions to trial blocks, both for tasks with complex procedures (e.g., Touron et al., 2001) and for simple search tasks (e.g., Strayer and Kramer, 1994).

An implication from power law improvement functions is that older experienced workers can be expected to outperform younger inexperienced workers on routine (practiced) tasks, despite any age-related slowing in processing speed. However, on new tasks that incorporate few elements from already-learned tasks, younger workers will be expected to outperform older ones given their slightly faster rate of learning. Indeed, the rule of thumb for predicting how long an older adult will take to complete a laboratory task, compared to a younger one, is to multiply the young adult time by about 1.5 (e.g., Hale and Myerson, 1995).

Motivational Barriers to Training

Many reviews (e.g., Belbin and Belbin, 1972; Warr, 2001) have noted that older workers are less likely to be offered training than younger ones and also less likely to volunteer or show up for training when it is offered. The reluctance to offer older workers training may stem from a diverse set of causes. In the case of government-sponsored programs to assist unemployed workers, the U.S. General Accounting Office (GAO) recently reported that there was reluctance to enroll older workers when programs were assessed on factors such as reemployment and salary levels for fear that older workers who are unemployed longer and who take greater pay cuts when reemployed would hurt program evaluation (GAO, 2004). Also, managers' beliefs about aging and its effect on learning new skills may make them reluctant to offer training to older workers (Barth, 2000). Career orientation changes with age and history of success may affect receptivity toward training (Bray and Howard, 1983). The work environment and its reward structure may not motivate older adults to seek training (Noe and Wilk, 1993). Older workers may perceive training opportunities as irrelevant to their goals at work (e.g., for advancement in an organization). Some of the reluctance by older workers may be related to low self-efficacy both pre- and post-training (Colquitt et al., 2000). That is, older workers may see themselves as less capable of being trained successfully or of having benefited less from training. These beliefs may be driven by negative stereotypes about aging that show younger adults evaluated more positively than older adults, particularly from field-related work settings (Kite and Johnson, 1988).

Advantages of Training Older Workers

As some reviews have stressed (Barth, McNaught, and Rizzi, 1996), older workers may be advantaged compared to younger workers, given their lower likelihood of voluntary absences, their lower likelihood of moving from a workplace, and their greater experience levels. Training costs are more likely to be recovered for older workers who are less likely to change jobs. A study by McNaught and Barth (1992) involved a case study of room reservation takers for a U.S. hotel chain. It showed that older workers were somewhat longer on a call (perhaps exhibiting slowing with age) but more likely to book a caller. Taking into account employment costs and revenues, older workers were as economically productive as younger ones. Further, because of lower turnover rates, the annualized cost of recruiting and training showed a nearly three-to-one advantage for an older worker ($618 compared to $1,752). A British chain of home and houseware stores found that a store staffed entirely by workers age 50 and over was 9 percent more profitable than the storewide average (Barth et al., 1996).

Health and Training

Another important outcome measure for work is health status. Workplaces can influence both physical health and mental health (see Warr, 1998, for a model of the effects of age and work on mental health). Physical health can be impaired when workers incur accidents or illnesses or disorders that are a function of short- or long-term exposure to hazardous materials or working conditions. For example, night-shift work seems to increase morbidity as a function of increasing age in those who have had to leave that type of work, compared to those who stay or those who have never performed such work (Volkoff, Touranchet, and Derriennic, 1998). This selective attrition result resembles a Darwinian survival-of-the-fittest model, usually termed the healthy worker effect.

Cross-sectional research suggests that musculoskeletal complaints increase with age of worker, and particularly for women in occupations that require heavy physically demanding work (e.g., de Zwart et al., 1997). However, a review of gender differences in musculoskeletal disorders (MSDs) suggests that existing studies have a variety of weaknesses that make it difficult to determine the causal factors (Punnett and Herbert, 2000). For example, observed differences may depend on a large set of factors: the form of assessment (self-report, injury records, strength assessment), workplace risk exposure, work-task strategy, psychosocial environment, home-risk exposure, willingness to seek help, and gender-specific factors such as muscle strength, connective tissue differences, and hormonal differences.

On the positive side, work can contribute to physical fitness to the extent that injuries can be avoided. Professional athletes who have not been forced to retire because of injury undoubtedly exhibit much better physical fitness than the general population. Similarly, work can have both negative and positive effects on mental health. Lack of work (unemployment) is a serious risk factor for morbidity in older workers and for poor mental health (Gallo et al., 2000), with different patterns of outcome for men who tend to show higher levels of substance abuse and women who show higher levels of major depression and anxiety disorders (Avison, 2001). One notable outcome, depression, may in turn prolong unemployment (Vinokur and Schul, 2002). Stressful work can contribute to both poor mental and poor physical health.

Also, longitudinal studies show that intellectually challenging work shows reciprocal relations to intellectual functioning with stronger relationships evident for older workers (Schooler, Mulatu, and Oates, 1999: 483). One study with a representative sample showed minimal relationships between work, health, and well-being (Herzog, House, and Morgan, 1991) and an unexpected relation for those ages 65 and over, where greater physical work stress led to higher ratings of health and well-being. (This may fit with the healthy worker effect explanation above.) In general, having choice in the type and amount of work leads to greater well-being and self-reported health.

As mentioned earlier, much of the training in work settings has concerned productivity and safety. Sometimes these two outcome measures show opposite patterns when organizations introduce changes, though safety training is usually effective (e.g., Kaminski, 2001). However, work settings also offer opportunities for health protection through interventions such as treating drug addiction (Silverman et al., 2001) and providing tobacco cessation programs (Sorenson, 2001).

The United States is unique among industrialized nations in not providing government-sponsored universal health care. Employers provide much of the health insurance coverage for the working-age population in the United States (see Chapter 7). Therefore, private employers have an incentive to provide such coverage and to support workplace health interventions if they wish to maintain a healthy, productive workforce.

Physical Fitness and Training

Several approaches have been used to characterize work ability in order to make recommendations about fitness for a particular job. Fleishman and Quaintance (1984) review a large set of potential taxonomies for describing human performance including job performance. The more recently developed Finnish Work Ability Index (Ilmarinen, 1994) solicits worker self-report ratings on a seven-item scale. It has been used to predict work disability and is sensitive to factors such as age, gender, and type of work. Longitudinal investigations show that factors such as high physical demand (requirement for muscular strength), stressful work environments (e.g., temperature extremes), and role pressures at work can degrade work ability in aging workers.

Ilmarinen and Louhevaara (1999) summarize a number of innovative Finnish intervention studies, some lasting a year, that were aimed specifically at older workers. Some interventions (ergonomic) involved training better work postures (e.g., on production lines, for cleaning staff, for municipal workers). These interventions significantly lowered the frequency of poor postures, reduced cardiac strain, and lowered perceived exertion. Other interventions involved physical fitness training that resulted in significant gains in musculoskeletal fitness and cardiovascular fitness, both of which were associated with improvements in the work ability index. Some studies used both types of intervention. The pattern of results from this project makes it clear that physical fitness training is a potentially important intervention to improve musculoskeletal and cardiovascular functioning and to improve fitness to work. Similarly, this project provides good evidence that ergonomic training interventions can have significant effects on work postures.

Whether the positive results of such interventions can be maintained over longer intervals and subsequently can affect the incidence of MSDs and particularly work-related illnesses or disorders and injuries, requires longitudinal investigations. One relatively rare clinical trial that was not focused specifically on older workers showed no effect of an educational intervention (three hours of initial training and booster sessions over subsequent years) on reducing low back injuries in postal workers within a five-and-a-half year interval (Daltroy et al., 1997).

The difference in results between the Finnish studies and the clinical trial may have much to do with the type of outcomes measured: postures or fitness that are somewhat easier to change and injuries that are relatively rare and difficult to prevent. Training can act similarly to expertise in mitigating normative age-related declines in work-related capabilities, perhaps prolonging the useful work life of older adults engaged in physically demanding jobs. General training programs may not be effective for reducing injuries.

Despite the general utility of these training principles and experiences, there has been a relative paucity of studies on health and safety training for older workers. However, over the past 20 years, a large number of innovative programs have been developed for providing occupational safety and health education to workers in general. These programs have been based on participatory methods of training, such as small-group interactive methods, worker and union input regarding needs assessment, materials and evaluation measures, worker empowerment goals, and use of peer trainers (Deutsch, 1996; Fernandez, Daltuva, and Robins, 2000; Kurtz, Robins, and Schork, 1997; McQuiston et al., 1994; Merrill, 1995; Wallerstein and Weinger, 1992).

Recent ergonomic intervention studies have indicated effectiveness in reducing discomfort in video display unit (VDU) workers via training and education (Ketola et al., 2002), injuries and costs of compensation claims in cleaning staff (Carrivick et al., 2002), and MSDs for staff who lift and transfer hospital patients following installation of ceiling lifts (Ronald et al., 2002). However, these studies do not look specifically at the effects of interventions on older workers. If one views aging as engendering increased fragility, and given that cumulative exposure to stressors is likely to be greater with increased age, efficacy of interventions might be expected to be greater for older workers. Countering this prediction are the anticipated effects of selective attrition for older workers (the healthy worker effect).

Training: Research Needs

In recent evaluation studies, interviews with participants 3 to 21 months posttraining provided examples of the positive impact of education. Results included correction of workplace safety and health problems; successes at changing programs, procedures or equipment at work; improved handling of emergency response incidents; improved management communication; training of coworkers after returning to work; and positive evaluations of worker-trainers (Cole and Brown, 1996; Fernandez et al., 2000; McQuiston, 2000).

The innovative programs described above appear to provide adult learners, including older workers, with relevant tools and problem-solving skills, the confidence needed to use those tools, and the motivation to remain active participants in improving occupational safety and health conditions at work. However, which of these methods works best for older workers and yields measurable gains in health and safety outcomes such as injury frequency and injury severity remains to be explored. It is also uncertain what the appropriate intervals are for retraining and maintenance of health and safety gains.

HEALTH PROMOTION AND DISEASE AND ILLNESS OR DISORDER PREVENTION FOR OLDER WORKERS

Work environments may have important influences on health promotion and disease prevention among older workers. First and foremost, employer policies affect direct work experiences and environments. They also have immediate and long-term effects on workers, their families, and their communities through both direct and indirect mechanisms. Direct mechanisms include interventions on specific worker behaviors, conduct, and exposures; delivering general health promotional programs to individual workers; providing and structuring health and disability insurance programs; and, in appropriate circumstances, intercepting and controlling community environmental hazards such as air and water pollution.

There are indirect mechanisms as well. Among older workers, as others, sufficient work income in itself may provide resources for improving one's general environmental health and safety; monetary resources can be used to purchase needed health services, both preventive and therapeutic. Worksites may also provide social contacts and networks that create additional opportunities for workers to receive information relevant to maintaining healthy lifestyles and avoiding health threats.

Proactive worksite health promotion and disease prevention activities may be thought of in two general categories: those aimed at promoting better safety and health directly related to job functions and those related to exposures and improvement. These two activities are of course interrelated and refer to policies, programs, and interventions that may not all pertain to or occur at the physical worksite. Health education may be provided at the worksite, or they may be take-home informational programs studied at worker convenience. Health promotion may be enhanced through the employee benefit structure. For example, one benefit to workers may be respite care or flexible leave policies that allow workers to attend to ailing parents and, in the process, may help decrease worker stress and maintain worker health status (Bornstein and Shultz, 2002). Similarly, tobacco-control efforts may be delivered on the jobsite, potentially improving worker function and long-term health outcomes that continue throughout life, or worker health insurance could provide for smoking cessation counseling, medications, and other treatment as part of the basic benefit structure.

Health promotion programs may also encompass direct worker interventions, such as individual or group counseling, or provision of recreational resources. Or they may alter the social or policy environment, for example, creating smoke-free work areas or payment incentives for cessation.

Given the great range of direct health promoting programs available, it is difficult to determine how many workers receive job-related health promotion programs. In one recent survey, 90 percent of employers with at least 50 employees reported that they offered at least one worksite health promotion program in the last year (NIOSH, 2002b). However, data for specific age groups and job types, as well as for those self-employed or working in small businesses, are difficult to find, and more surveys of access to health promotion programs among employed populations would be of great value. Based on a review of the literature, it appears that most health promotion programs not related to specific job functions and safety are devoted to the modification of general, health-promoting behaviors, such as cigarette smoking cessation, diet and nutritional improvement, optimal physical exercise, leisure, recreational activity, and body weight maintenance. Companion activities focus on controlling risk factors for cardiovascular disease and various cancers. In some instances, workplace programs have used health risk appraisal instruments that address prevention of other conditions and other risk behaviors such as seatbelt use and caries prevention.

Evaluating Workplace Health Promotion Programs:
Conventional Content and Methodological Issues

A large number of general workplace health promotion programs have
been attempted. In addition to addressing the health behaviors noted above,
approaches have been attempted less commonly for problem alcohol drinking, illicit drug use, and other mental health issues. Programs related to
these latter mental health issues are important though difficult to conduct,
since they directly relate to high rates of worker morbidity, absenteeism,
and lower productivity (Williams and Strasser, 1999). Workplace health
promotion programs have had varying participation and success rates. What
constitutes success with respect to participation often is not specified, especially since these programs are almost all voluntary by nature, raising the
difficult question of whether the workers who would benefit most are
actually those most likely to participate. Similarly, what constitutes successful program outcomes should be viewed in light of many factors, including
the domains under intervention; the theoretical foundations behind such
programs; programmatic quality and resource expenditures; worker accommodations for program participation such as scheduling; the demographic and health characteristics of participants; and comparable program
outcome experiences in nonworksite venues.

The evaluative scientific literature for many of these programs is particularly problematic with regard to older workers. Most health promotional programs are directed at all adult age groups, and many do not
describe the age distribution of the study populations; even when age data
are available, many do not contain large numbers of older workers. Other
methodological problems are common to many of these studies: small
sample sizes, self-selection into programs, low participation rates in the
evaluation efforts, lack of credible experimental designs, inclusion of many
persons who are at low risk for the outcomes of interest, inability to determine long-term outcomes, and lack of breadth of job types included in the
interventions—especially those in small businesses. Particularly relevant to
this discussion, many health promotion programs do not necessarily adapt
to the special needs of various age, literacy, or cultural groups. In many
occupations and job settings, circumstances sometimes do not allow ran-
domization or other rigorous study designs, for several reasons:

(1) Many sites have frequent employee turnover, and it is hard to
follow those going to other geographic areas or diverse work situations.

(2) Some programs are not made available during normal employee
work schedules, and attending them may be difficult for many workers.
The same problem may exist for workers who are geographically and tem-

porally distributed from the program site. There may also be differences in access to programs, depending on job category and socioeconomic status.

(3) The extent of the problem being addressed may depend on the presence and intensity of preemployment screening and health problem monitoring by the employer. For those (uncommon) worksites where medical care is provided, a focus on health promotion may be in part redundant or at least more complex. The issue of employment prescreening is a sensitive matter to many workers, who may wish to withhold personal health information and histories both from employers and their health insurers. This dilemma is exemplified by mandatory and unannounced screening for illicit drug use (Bush and Autry, 2002), and the potential prospect of genetic screening to determine who may be at greater risk of adverse effects of workplace exposures.

(4) Communication between the worksite program and the workers' usual sources of medical care may be inadequate. Confusion over the overlapping or redundant approaches to the same problem may result in an inefficient or harmful program.

(5) In cross-sectional or short-term evaluative studies, the workers who might benefit most from health promotion programs may be underrepresented because they have lost their employment status due to illness or disorder and disability.

(6) Some workplace-sponsored health promotion programs are available to retired workers. This may be useful for assessing program impact on older persons, but it does not necessarily address issues related to the interventions in the occupational environment.

In addition to these issues, there is a set of challenges for all behavioral interventions that pertain to the workplace: inadequate resources, external interventions that contaminate the programmatic experiment (e.g., general community tobacco control activities), and varying levels of personal susceptibility to behavioral change. In addition, the intervention applied may not be effective. Thus, there are many potential issues that do not preclude full program evaluation, but many conceptual and study design issues that require consideration before credible studies can be conducted.

Health Promotion Programs for Older Workers

In general, scientific evidence suggests that older workers are potentially able to benefit from the same health promotion themes as younger workers, such as cigarette smoking cessation, obesity management, nutrition enhancement, blood cholesterol lowering, problem drinking interventions, and hypertension management. In fact, it is possible that for many successful interventions, there may be greater decrements in preventable disease rates per unit of resource expenditure toward older workers, in part because chronic disease rates are higher at older ages. However, there are potentially many cautions when carrying out health promotion interventions among older adults that are of much less concern for younger persons. Some examples are provided in Box 8-1. This is not to imply that these programs should not be invoked, but rather that their objectives and content should be tailored to meet older workers' special needs.

As noted elsewhere in this chapter, some hazardous aspects of the work environment may lead to negative changes in health with prolonged exposure, and interventions to mitigate these exposures should be considered important examples of health promotion. For example, Drudi (1997) demonstrated a striking increase in repeated trauma disorders (now called MSDs) occurring in private industry in the 1990s. Changing the nature of work by automating repetitive tasks (e.g., providing machines to perform stressful repetitive work movements) may help to stem the increase. Prevention of work-related injury and disease is an important goal that may be accomplished through job design and redesign as well as through training, and it should be thought of as a component of general health promotion. Approaches may vary depending on whether injury or disease is the target for prevention, as well as whether the disease is chronic or acute.

The following potential health promotion programs for older workers are areas that have not generally been explored but may merit consideration in future health promotion program design. These derive largely from geriatric practice, and they serve to highlight considerations that—though not usually applied for the broad range of working adults—merit consideration:

(1) *Education in providing caregiving skills.* Many older workers have aging parents or other family members or friends who require intensive supportive care in the household setting. This care ranges from providing transportation and general supervision and guidance to assistance with the most basic chores and activities of daily living. These caregiving activities can be extremely distracting, and the related stresses have been associated with worsening quality of life for the caregiver (Bell, Araki, and Neumann, 2001). Employee benefit structures, such as self-guided schedule flexibility and insurance for chore services, may or may not be available, but worksite programs that provide instruction and skills in caregiving may be very helpful in maintaining older workers on the job and may have important health-promoting value.

(2) *Nutritional and dietary interventions for older workers.* Tailored nutrition counseling for older workers may be helpful for health promotion in addition to the guidance provided by general nutrition education pro-

BOX 8-1
Special Considerations for General Health
Promotion Interventions in Older Workers

Intervention	Potential Problems	Examples
Low-fat diet	Denture problems; taste and smell deficiencies	Some older persons may not enjoy changed recipes; problems with chewing raw vegetables
High-calcium diet	Some high-calcium foods may cause adverse effects	High-calcium dairy products may provoke lactose intolerance
Promotion of community recreational resources	May require more night driving	Headlight glare may discourage night driving to recreational facilities
Vigorous aerobic exercise	Limited exercise capacity; decrements in balance; prior illness or disorder such as arthritis, stroke, or diabetes	Vigorous aerobic activity may lead to increased falling and injury
Blood pressure control	Hygienic interventions often insufficient	Worksite interventions requires coordination and follow-up with medical management

grams. Differences in programmatic emphases are important. For example, for some older persons, caloric sufficiency is as important as excess caloric intake. In some instances, higher caloric intake needs to be encouraged for optimal weight and muscle strength (Evans, 1998). In addition, herbal dietary supplements and products are very popular among older persons. Calcium intake recommendations are increased in postmenopausal women (Nordin et al., 1998) to maximize bone density and optimize fracture prevention. Since medication use is more common at higher ages (see below), even modest levels of alcohol intake may cause unwanted drug interactions that require attention (Lieber, 2000). Education as to possible interactions with existing medications and possible adverse effects may be beneficial. Lactose intolerance increases with age, and special knowledge of the identification and prevention of this condition can help maintain better health status (Swagerty, Walling, and Klein, 2002).

(3) *Polypharmacy and therapy management programs.* For both preventive and therapeutic purposes, older persons take more medications, prescription and nonprescription, than younger persons (Williams, 2002). This is because of the higher prevalence of chronic illnesses or disorders and of risk factors for them. Medication aimed at mitigating chronic illness or disorder risk factors target such issues as hypertension, hypercholesterolemia, low bone density, osteopenia and osteoporosis, and degenerative arthritis. Managing these medications and various treatments may make regular employment schedules and execution challenging. While this generally is a shared responsibility between the patient, health professionals, and pharmacists, educational programs to facilitate work and medical therapy may improve job performance and satisfaction. In addition, there may be value in considering workplace disease management programs for categorical conditions such as Type II diabetes (Berg and Wadhwa, 2002) or asthma, as long as coordination with standard medical care sources is available. These might be more clinically intensive than usual health promotion programs, but they may offer standardized effective programs that keep workers healthier.

Along these lines, workplace pharmacological prevention programs may be of value for older workers and others. With increasing age, primary and secondary chronic disease prevention may include routinely consumed medications for preventive purposes. For example, regular low-dose aspirin consumption can prevent heart attack and stroke (Anonymous, 2002), and control of blood lipids is increasingly common (Lipsy, 2003). It is even possible that over time some anti-inflammatory drugs or other drug categories may be taken to deter the occurrence of Alzheimer's disease (Breitner and Zandi, 2001). While such programs may require active medical supervision, they may yield important preventive outcomes. In the future, there may be useful and safe interventions that help deter degenerative states such as osteoarthritis and cognitive impairment.

(4) *Tailored exercise interventions.* The value of habitual exercise programs in disease prevention, weight control, and general well-being is unquestioned, and many such programs have been provided or encouraged in the work environment. However, in addition to the general health benefits imparted, such as improved muscle strength and aerobic capacity, exercise programs may be tailored for other goals among older workers, such as improving balance and coordination to prevent falls (Cumming, 2002), and to provide relief from degenerative arthritis, such as of knees (Fransen, McConnell and Bell, 2002). These programs may require special techniques and equipment, but these are generally not more costly than standard approaches.

(5) *Disease screening for older workers.* Many conditions increase with age. In some of them, early and asymptomatic detection will lead to better disease control, less long-term disablement, and decreased early mortality. There are many screening interventions that are indicated only for older adults, including bone density screening for osteoporosis detection and fracture prevention; mammographic screening for breast cancer; and fecal occult blood determination, sigmoidoscopy, and colonoscopy for colon cancer detection. All of these have proven value (Williams and Wilkins, 1996), although optimal timing and target groups remain an area for research. Provision of worksite screening clinics or programs, leading to referral when abnormalities are found, can, on balance, preserve health and function and lead to longer, more functional, and productive lives. It may also be possible to provide medical advice and care for preventive interventions that could decrease morbidity, such as anti-inflammatory or anti-coagulant medications and immunizations.

An Example of Workplace Health Promotion: Preventing Cardiovascular Disease

Cardiovascular disease (CVD) is a common source of disability for older workers. In order to manage and prevent CVD and reduce such disability, the team approach common in the field of occupational medicine is recommended: clinicians, health educators, ergonomists, epidemiologists, and other health professionals work to identify high-risk workplaces and occupations, facilitate the provision of clinical care, and design and implement workplace interventions (as in Herbert et al., 1997).

For the prevention and management of chronic diseases, such as CVD and hypertension related to a stressful work organization, NIOSH recommends that an additional health professional be an integral part of the team—the occupational health psychologist (OHP) (Landsbergis et al., 2002). The OHP requires multidisciplinary training combining methods and content from the fields of occupational health, epidemiology, psychology, management, industrial relations, and other relevant disciplines (National Institute for Occupational Safety and Health, 2002b). Therefore, NIOSH has funded graduate training programs in this field (Sauter and Hurrell, 1999).

A key step in the process of disease prevention, identification, and management is worksite surveillance and monitoring at national and regional levels to identify high-risk occupations, the extent of workplace stressors, health outcomes resulting from such exposures, and baselines against which to evaluate amelioration efforts (Belkic, Schnall, and Ugljesic, 2000; "The Tokyo Declaration," 1998). Such interventions may prevent or slow the development of hypertension and cardiovascular disease in middle-aged workers, and thus help to prevent these diseases among older workers. Standard questionnaires can help assess job characteristics and job stressors (Belkic et al., 1995; Karasek et al., 1985; Siegrist and Peter, 1996). Measurements of blood pressure (BP) at work can help to identify occult (hidden) work-related hypertension, sometimes missed by readings taken in a clinic setting (Schnall and Belkic, 2000). An additional key modality of risk assessment is an occupational history of individual workers.

Both individual health promotion and workplace protection/prevention programs are needed to combat the epidemic of CVD and the toll of disability in older workers. However, due to the limitations of health promotion programs, primary prevention strategies—such as job redesign to promote education, screening for risk factors, and prevention of worker stress—are fundamental.

The effectiveness of a limited number of interventions to improve work organization and job design, reduce job stressors, and create a more healthy work organization have been discussed above. In addition, older workers with CVD or at risk for CVD need to be counseled to reduce their levels of unhealthy behaviors, such as smoking. However, such counseling in isolation may have poor efficacy, particularly among occupational groups with a heavy burden of exposure to occupational stressors: "despite devotion of substantial time and the use of state-of-the-art methods . . . our efforts applied systematically among professional drivers were, at best, only minimally effective, unless there was a concomitant amelioration in stressful working conditions" (Fisher and Belkic, 2000: 247).

Judgments of the cardiovascular work fitness of older workers who have suffered cardiac events are complicated by the issue that jobs in which public safety could be compromised with the occurrence of an acute cardiac event (deGaudemaris, 2000) are often those with high exposure to potentially cardio-deleterious factors (e.g., urban transit operators, air traffic controllers) (Fisher and Belkic, 2000). Fifty-four percent of all U.S. bus drivers are 45 years of age or older (Dohm, 2000). On the other hand, advances in cardiovascular therapy permit the restoration of cardiovascular function of many patients, and this can make returning to work possible (deGaudemaris, 2000). In a Swedish study, men who had suffered a first MI below age 45 were at high risk of five-year CHD mortality if returning to a high-strain job (Theorell et al., 1991). Occupational health professionals with appropriate training need to identify potentially modifiable cardiac stressors in the older workers' job environment and, together with a clinician, need to formulate and implement a plan to provide a safer return to work.

EMPLOYEE ASSISTANCE PROGRAMS

Employee Assistance Programs (EAPs) are employer-provided service programs that aid troubled workers, usually through counseling, support groups, and service referral. While most of these programs have not yet emphasized employee needs specifically related to aging, they have strong potential as a support for older workers in relation to occupational health and safety concerns. EAPs may be of help both in a direct sense and also indirectly by maintaining a person's ability to work, promoting physical and mental health, and relieving stress that can cause accidents and illness or disorder.

In the United States and Canada, EAPs emerged in the post-World War II era primarily as a mechanism for rehabilitating alcohol addicted workers (Trice and Schonbrunn, 1981). Employers saw them as a constructive alternative to disciplinary dismissal, particularly for highly skilled workers who would be expensive to replace. Early EAPs were usually staffed by nonprofessionals, often who were themselves former addicts and were philosophically linked to 12-step programs such as Alcoholics Anonymous (McKibbon, 1993). Around the same period, some unions began to offer Membership Assistance Programs (MAPs) to assist their members (Johnson, 1981). While similar to EAPs in their focus on addiction, these early MAPs tended to put more emphasis on peer counseling by coworkers and to address working conditions that might contribute to workers' personal problems.

Over the next half century, both EAPs and MAPs gradually evolved into more comprehensive broad-brush service resources, able to offer help to workers with a wider array of personal needs (Walsh, 1982). In addition to drug and alcohol abuse treatment, many began to offer mental health counseling for individual workers and their families. Some also offered services such as credit counseling, bereavement counseling, stress management, marital counseling, help with work and family dilemmas and dependent care choices, and career planning. Particularly during the 1990s, many EAPs became integrated with more general worksite health promotion, wellness, and work and family programs offered by employers (Lubin, Shanklin, and Polk, 1996), although the linkage among the different programs was not always close or comfortable (Herlihy, 1996). Despite continuing tensions over these programs' proper scope and emphasis, comprehensive EAPs staffed at least in part by trained mental health professionals have by now become the norm in large corporations (Sciegaj et al., 2001).

A number of evaluation studies have documented that EAP-referred workers do show reductions in absenteeism and illness (Macdonald et al., 2000; Gaton, 1986), and that these programs can be quite cost-effective for the employer (French et al., 1999; Bray et al., 1996; Every and Leong,

1994; Decker, Starrett, and Redhouse, 1986). Some EAP-based interventions have the potential to raise issues of discrimination and employer liability (Starkman, 2000; Capron and Creighton, 1998), but such problems do not appear to be widespread.

In 1989, a national Employee Benefits Survey conducted by the U.S. Bureau of Labor Statistics found that among full-time workers in private-sector establishments with 100 or more employees, 49 percent had access to EAPs, and 23 percent were served by wellness programs (Cooley, 1990). A Canadian study at about the same time underscored the rapid growth of EAPs. During the period from 1988 to 1993, among 647 companies in Ontario with over 50 employees, the percentage with EAPs doubled from 16.1 to 32 percent (Macdonald and Wells, 1994). However, the coverage was very uneven. The same Canadian study also confirmed the existence of wide variations among major work sectors, ranging from highs of 51 percent with EAPs in government and 46 percent in health and education, to lows of 13 percent in retail trade and 3 percent in construction. Small to medium-sized workplaces are much less likely to have such supports, an important fact because the majority of the U.S. workforce is employed in work sites with fewer than 50 employees. Donaldson and Klien (1997: 17) reported that "one of the main findings of the 1992 National Survey of Workplace Health Activities [in the United States] was the identification of a pressing need to understand how to formulate effective strategies for providing comprehensive health promotion [and EAP] services to . . . traditionally underserved employee populations; particularly ethnically diverse operating-level employees working in small, medium-sized, and women and/or minority-owned businesses."

In contrast to the early EAPs, in which at least some direct treatment was usually offered onsite in the workplace, the actual services of EAPs and MAPs are now often delivered by offsite service providers with the program's in-house aspects being limited to assessment and referral; both models have advantages (Brummett, 2000; Csiernik, 1999; Straussner, 1988). Along with these organizational changes, the orientation of EAPs and MAPs has gradually been shifting from rehabilitation to prevention. Instead of a quasidisciplinary intervention aimed at workers whose performance has already suffered because of personal problems, these programs are increasingly seen as a way to keep workers productive and healthy by helping them avoid problems in the first place. Current EAPs tend to encourage self-referrals and promote their services as a positive employee benefit. In addition, there is growing awareness that the work climate itself can contribute to the personal troubles and unhealthy behavior of individual employees. For example, management policies and enabling behavior by peers and supervisors can create a prodrinking, prosmoking, workaholic, or reckless work environment that endangers employee health and safety (Bennet and Lehman, 1997). Some EAP specialists have urged that in such situations the EAP client should be defined as the organization itself (Googins and Davidson, 1993).

To understand the kinds of support that EAPs might offer for older workers, two different sets of concerns are involved:

1. What kinds of EAP support will assist aging employees to continue working safely and productively in their career jobs? Some aging workers find it difficult to balance their work with medical management of emerging health problems, the time demands of caregiving at home, increased difficulty with activities such as driving to work, a changing sense of what matters in life, and stressful work relationships related to age discrimination and stigma. Age-related physical changes such as hearing loss and arthritis may call for job redesign, and they may need retraining for new kinds of work assignment. If the choice to remain working is driven by income insecurity, workers may find themselves between a rock and a hard place as their work ability declines but their need for earning continues.

2. What kinds of EAP support will help aging workers prepare adequately for retirement? Most aging workers expect eventually to be leaving their career jobs, either exiting the workforce entirely or moving into a phased retirement period involving some combination of reduced work hours, periodic leaves of absence while still employed, and alternative paid or unpaid work. At least some may be making unrealistic choices due to lack of information and feeling great distress if their retirement plans are being undermined by economic downturns. If they plan to phase out of the workforce gradually through alternative work, they may be uninformed about their options and legal rights, and unprepared to find the bridge jobs they will need. Even those eager to leave the workforce may be experiencing uncertainty and anxiety about what their financial and social circumstances will be in retirement. Those facing the prospect of being unwillingly forced out through layoffs or pressure to retire at a certain age may be very angry with supervisors and coworkers.

Particularly as workers approach the traditional retirement age, these concerns can overlap. Separately or together, by creating unmanageable levels of stress, they put the older worker at increased risk for workplace accidents, depression, physical illness or disorder, health-damaging personal behavior, and even workplace violence.

There are already at least three ways in which EAPs have begun to offer supports of special relevance to aging workers: eldercare support, preretirement planning, and customized versions of traditional services such as drug and alcohol treatment and outplacement.

Eldercare Support

Also known as support to working caregivers, eldercare support is meant to help employees who are struggling to balance their jobs with their commitments to care for elderly parents, care for an older spouse who is ill, or deal with the responsibilities of caring for elderly parents on top of having dependent children still at home (Eubanks, 1991). These workers, typically women in their 40s and 50s, are in effect working a permanent double shift without relief, at a point in life when they are aging themselves and their career demands may be peaking after delays for childrearing (Winfield, 1987). The result can be extreme stress, fatigue, and isolation for the individual worker, potentially leading to physical illness or disorder, depression, accidents on and off the job, breakdown of work relationships, and alcohol or drug addiction.

Having workers experience this high level of strain is costly to employers as well. Employers' measurable costs associated with eldercare giving have been estimated at $2,500 to $3,100 per year per caregiver from losses in employee productivity, management/administration, and health/mental health care (Marosy, 1998).

A substantial proportion of eldercare givers hold jobs. In 1987, of the approximately 2.2 million persons providing unpaid informal assistance for older adults in the United States, 31 percent were at the same time employed outside the home (Seccombe, 1992). By 1997 that had risen to 55 percent, according to a national survey conducted by the National Alliance for Caregiving and the American Association of Retired Persons (AARP) (Wagner, 1997). Looking at it from the other side, eldercare givers make up a substantial proportion of the workforce. In a survey of 3,658 employees of a major company in southern California, Scharlach and Boyd (1989) found that 23 percent of respondents reported that they were assisting an older person. Of these working caregivers, 80 percent reported emotional strain and 73.7 percent (as compared to 49.1 of other employees) reported interference between work and family responsibilities. About 20 percent said it was likely they would eventually have to quit their jobs to provide care. The sheer amount of time demanded by caregiving activities is quite considerable. Wagner (1990) notes that the employed caregivers in one study reported spending an average of 12.8 hours weekly on caregiving and had been doing so for an average of 6.5 years.

During the 1990s EAPs began to respond to this increasing need by exploring ways to help working caregivers get information, negotiate flextime and leaves, manage financial pressures, and find appropriate counseling. Eldercare support is, in fact, one of the fastest growing new EAP services (Earhart, Middlemist, and Hopkins, 1993). A 1996 survey of 1,050 major U.S. employers found that eldercare programs were offered by nearly one-third of these employers, an increase of 17 percent from 1991 (Hewitt Associates, 1997). As one example, in the mid-1990s, Control Data Corporation expanded its longstanding EAP to include comprehensive eldercare services to more than 1,100 employers with 1.2 million employees (Ensign, 1996). Unfortunately, however, eldercare is not yet offered in the majority of workplaces with EAPs. The need for it is sometimes not recognized by employers and EAP practitioners (Kola and Dunkle, 1988). Even when recognized, awareness of the need does not necessarily translate into an actual program. In a survey of 371 chief executive officers of U.S. corporations, 60 percent of respondents were aware of work-related problems experienced by employees who give care, but less than 20 percent were actively considering offering a specific caregiving program at the worksite.

The 1996 Hewitt survey and other similar ones (Lefkovich, 1992) found the most common approach in EAP-based eldercare support to be a resource information and referral service, sometimes accompanied by related policy changes within the company such as work scheduling that included flex-time, flex-place, compressed work weeks, temporary part-time status, and personal leaves. Other related policy changes include dependent-care spending accounts that set aside up to $5,000 in pretax dollars to pay for eldercare expenses, and management training policies that sensitize managers to employees' caregiving responsibilities. In addition, some EAPs are partnering actively with community-based service resources such as home care agencies, which are already equipped to provide eldercare supports such as emergency backup for in-home adult companion care and child care on short notice; financial planning with a nurse geriatric care manager to develop an affordable care plan; senior day care; respite services; and emotional support for caregivers through support groups, hospice, and certified eldercare counselors (Marosy, 1998; Tober, 1987).

A wealth of information on resources for developing workplace eldercare assistance programs, including case examples and guidance materials such as the AARPs' Caregivers in the Workplace kit, can be found in Dellman-Jenkins, Bennett, and Brahcae (1994). The Washington Business Group on Health has prepared a guidebook intended to help human resources professionals, benefits managers, and other corporate decision makers become more knowledgeable about eldercare issues in the workplace (Coberly, 1991). Additional resources and a good example of union involvement in eldercare support appear in symposium proceedings from a conference sponsored by the Federal Council on the Aging (1984), which includes a description of a New York City service delivery program of the United Auto Workers.

Preretirement Planning

Preretirement planning (PRP) is recognized as a need in the field of employment assistance, but relatively few U.S. firms offer these services to date, and where they do exist, older workers reportedly tend not to use them (Perkins, 1994). However, they could be of enormous benefit to both employees and employers as workers move toward exiting the workforce. By making the transition from work to retirement smoother and less stressful, such planning may increase the chances that retiring workers' final few years in the workforce will be safe and productive ones.

There is a clear need for planning, particularly financial advice to help the worker make realistic choices about retirement timing and budgeting. Numerous studies document that the current generation of aging workers are woefully uninformed about the options and decisions that they will confront on retirement and very unprepared for the realities that await them (Marshall and Mueller, 2002). The economic downturn that started in 2000 has greatly worsened the situation by eroding the value of many workers' retirement savings and pensions. Workers now have diminished resources for their anticipated golden years, but they may not yet fully recognize the need to adapt their previous plans.

LaRock (1998) describes some of the varied approaches that are currently being offered by large employers, often channeled through EAPs. Boeing conducts focus groups to identify life-planning topics of greatest interest to its employees and then offers individualized classes. Weyerhauser holds one-day seminars on retirement planning with separate sessions for those over 30 and those under 30, as well as an enhanced version for employees over 60, consisting of a two-and-a-half day seminar led by outside financial planners and estate attorneys. Dow Agro holds retirement planning sessions during lunch at the company's cafeteria and fitness center. The Washington State Department of Retirement Systems offers one-day seminars at various locations throughout the state, with 300 to 400 people attending each seminar. Good resources for employers interested in developing such planning sessions are readily available (Sherman, 1997).

Preretirement planning involves more than financial information. Exiting the workforce requires developing new ways to use time and find meaning in life, tasks for which many workers are unprepared—particularly men (Moen, 1996, 1998) and those who have left the labor force involuntarily or reluctantly (Sijuwade, 1996). Retirement can also provide enhanced opportunity for enjoying family and other relationships. Perkins (2000) presents a case example of a pre-retirement planning program in which an EAP facilitated a series of lunchtime workshops for older workers to address such issues. The workshops were led by former employees who were leading meaningful and zestful lives after leaving the company—some as retirees, some having reentered the labor market. Subsequent evaluation of the program through focus groups showed that "one of the more prominent issues to emerge from the workshop was the need for older adults to move beyond the 'work ethic' values of the middle years. It was determined that new 'yardsticks' were needed for measuring what makes life worth living" (p. 69).

To date, employer-supported retirement planning support appears to be available mainly to employees of large companies. Encouraging the spread of similar services in smaller firms, perhaps through consortium arrangements, would be desirable since an even greater need for retirement planning exists for many workers employed in small firms and/or intermittent jobs, particularly women and minorities (Angel and Angel, 1998; Mitchell, Levine, and Phillips, 1999; O'Rand and Henretta, 1999; Dancy and Ralston, 2002).

Traditional EAP Services Customized for Older Workers

While substance abuse interventions have long been the backbone of EAP services, these interventions may require modification to meet the needs of older employees with drug or alcohol problems. As Goldmeier (1994: 624) points out, "Substance abuse among the elderly may be masked by physical problems and therefore escape detection; in addition, the elderly tend to underreport physical illnesses or disorders because they fear discrimination, and they may be more vulnerable to the effects of alcohol or illicit drugs because of age-related physical changes." The picture may be further complicated by interactions of alcohol or illicit drugs with prescription drugs that the older worker may be taking. The potential for unrecognized alcoholism is of particular concern, because heavy alcohol consumption is related to occupational injury among older workers. In a nationally representative sample of 6,857 nonfarm workers aged 51–61, alcoholism was positively associated with occupational injury, even after controlling for age, sex, education, occupation, and strenuous job activity (Zwerling et al., 1996). In this study, the injury rate among the older workers who consumed five or more drinks a day was five times greater than for the category showing the lowest injury rate (who consumed one to two drinks per day). Potentially, EAPs can play a useful roles on several levels: (1) primary and secondary prevention of substance abuse among older workers through worksite wellness programs of medical screening, drug screening, education, review of work attendance and accident records, and maintenance of a positive work environment; and (2) tertiary prevention—after a substance abuse problem has been identified—through referral to community resources, counseling, mediation, advocacy, and case management (Goldmeier, 1994; Brummett, 1999).

Another traditional service offered by some EAPs is outplacement, in which employees who are leaving the company but remaining in the labor force are assisted with job-search counseling and skills assessment, help with resume writing, use of company telephones and copiers during the job search, and use of the company mailing address for a period following termination. This kind of service has generally been aimed at younger workers who are leaving the company because of layoffs. However, it could be adapted to serve older workers who expect to seek other work (bridge employment) after leaving their career jobs. Outplacement could also assist the older worker with customized searches for alternative jobs and/or volunteer positions, opportunities for retraining, and information on using legal protections against age discrimination. A 1989 telephone survey of 3,509 adults aged 50–64 found that longest-held positions typically ended long before normal retirement ages, creating a large pool of older individuals seeking bridge jobs in an employment climate rife with age discrimination (Ruhm, 1994).

The bridge employment choices facing older workers are quite complex, and outcomes differ considerably depending on how voluntary the career job exit is (Weckerle and Schultz, 1999). Ruhm (1994: 73) notes: "Of particular concern is the limited ability of some groups of workers (nonwhites, females, the less educated, and those in poorly compensated occupations) to either retain longest jobs or to obtain acceptable bridge employment." These older workers are less likely to be employed in large companies that have EAPs. Reaching them with outplacement support (and other EAP services) would require new strategies for encouraging small firms to make such services available to their workers—for example, tax incentives, technical assistance, and consortium arrangements (Donaldson and Klein, 1997).

ACCOMMODATIONS FOR WORKERS WITH IMPAIRMENTS AND RETURN-TO-WORK PROGRAMS

Accommodations for workers with impairments and return-to-work programs are both important interventions that may play an important role in maintaining older workers productively in the workforce because these workers are more likely to bring impairments into the workplace and because they are likely to be out of work longer than their younger colleagues after an injury.

Workplace Accommodations

Over the last 25 years, there have been changes both in the prevalent conceptual model of disability and in the public policy approach to people with disabilities. Two reports from the National Academies Institute of Medicine (IOM, 1991, 1997) played a major role in the refinement of the conceptual model. This emerging model distinguished between *impairment*, a loss of function at the organ system level; *functional limitation*, the inability to perform a specific task, such as lifting a 20-pound package; and *disability*, a limitation in performing socially expected roles. Impairment and functional limitation are characteristics of an individual; disability denotes a mismatch between an individual's functional capacity and the individual's environment. In the workplace, this translates into a mismatch between an individual's functional capacity and the essential requirements of his or her job. For example, a worker who could not lift a 20-pound package might be totally disabled as a construction laborer, but that same person might be able to carry out all of the job requirements of a secretary. This concept of disability as a mismatch between the worker's functional capacity and the demands of their job leads easily to the concept of workplace accommodations—modifications of the job or workplace that allow the worker to carry out the essential functions of his or her job in spite of functional limitations.

Parallel to this change in the conceptual model of disability, there has emerged a new public policy approach as well (Miller, 2000). As discussed earlier in this report, the Americans with Disabilities Act of 1990 marked the ascendance of a new approach to persons with disabilities, a civil rights approach that aimed to help them overcome the barriers to full participation in American society. Specifically, Title 1 of the ADA was aimed at integrating workers with disabilities more fully into the workforce. It prohibited discrimination against qualified employees (or job applicants) with disabilities. A qualified person with a disability is an individual who, with or without reasonable accommodation, can perform the essential functions of the job. Reasonable accommodation may include, but is not limited to:

(1) making existing facilities readily accessible to persons with disabilities;
(2) restructuring jobs, modifying work schedules, and reassigning employees to vacant positions;
(3) modifying equipment, examinations, training materials, or policies; and
(4) providing qualified readers and interpreters.

As noted above, older workers are more likely to have a wide variety of impairments and may require accommodations to remain in or reenter the workplace. Although a dozen years have passed since ADA became law, we still know relatively little about key aspects of these workplace accommodations.

First, how much do workplace accommodations cost? The President's Committee on Employment of People with Disabilities (1995) suggested that the cost of accommodating an employee with a disability is low, averaging about $200. Blanck (1996) found similar results when examining the costs of accommodations at the Sears Roebuck Company. However, these early estimates may well be significantly lower than the true costs because they were prepared by advocates of the ADA who construed the costs very narrowly. Instead, for example, of just accounting for the cost to buy special equipment, it would be useful to give an accounting of the full opportunity cost of accommodating an average person with a disability. These costs would need to include the time of other employees and managers involved in the accommodation, as well as the time of the disabled person (Chirikos, 2000). It is also likely that the accommodations sampled are not representative of the range of accommodations that may be implemented in the future. One could argue that the least expensive accommodations are likely to be implemented first. Subsequent accommodations might be more expensive (Chirikos, 2000).

Second, how frequent are workplace accommodations? Which accommodations are most frequently provided and who gets them? Daly and Bound (1996) used data from the Health and Retirement Study, a longitudinal panel study of older Americans, to examine the experience of older workers (51–61 years of age) when they had the onset of a medical condition that limited the work they could do. They found that about half of the workers stayed at their current jobs; just less than a quarter changed jobs; just over a quarter stopped working. Of those who remained with their employer, 29 percent of the men and 37 percent of the women received accommodations. Those who changed employers were less likely to receive accommodations: 14 percent of the men and 29 percent of the women. The most commonly provided accommodations included the alteration of job duties, assistance with the job, a change in schedule or a shorter work day, and more breaks. These results are consistent with previous work that suggested that up to one-third of workers experiencing a disability report some type of employer accommodation (Lando, Cutler, and Gamber, 1982; Schechter, 1981; Chirikos, 1991).

Third, how effective are workplace accommodations in allowing workers to remain safely and productively in the workforce? The goal of workplace accommodations is to allow workers with a range of impairments to enter or remain in the workplace. There have been very few studies exploring the effectiveness of these accommodations. In two studies, Burkhauser and colleagues (Burkhauser, Butler, and Kim, 1995; Burkhauser et al., 1999) has addressed this issue. Applying a proportional hazards analysis to the HIS component of the 1978 Survey of Disability and Work, Burkhauser et al. (1995) found that the provision of an accommodation significantly slowed a worker's withdrawal from the workforce after the onset of an impairment. In a subsequent study employing additional data from the Health and Retirement Study and using a proportional hazards model, Burkhauser et al. (1999) found that the time to the beginning of SSDI payments was significantly delayed by the provision of workplace accommodations. However, both of these studies relied on retrospective data on the provision of accommodations. Thus, they are both vulnerable to potential recall bias—those who withdrew from the workforce may be less likely to remember accommodations their employers made than those who remained in the workforce. The longitudinal data now available in the Health and Retirement Study would permit a prospective examination of this issue.

Data summarized above (Zwerling et al., 1998a,b) suggest that older workers with impairments have an increased risk of occupational injuries. Appropriate workplace accommodations might be expected to lower this risk, but we know of no empirical studies addressing that issue. Likewise, it might be expected that appropriate workplace accommodations would increase the productivity of workers with a variety of impairments, but we were only able to find anecdotal evidence on this issue.

Return-to-Work Programs

As noted above, national databases show that older workers are less likely to be injured at work than their younger colleagues, but they are likely to require a longer period of recuperation before they are ready to resume their normal duties. This prolonged period of work disability has been extensively documented among older workers with low back pain (Bigos et al., 1986; Dasinger Krause et al., 2000; Infante-Rivard and Lortie, 1996; Krause et al., 2001a; McIntosh et al., 2000), but it has also been documented among cardiac patients (Karoff et al., 2000) and trauma patients (MacKenzie et al., 1998). Given the prolonged period of recuperation among older workers, the design, implementation, and evaluation of return-to-work programs among older workers merits special attention.

Leigh and colleagues (1997) estimated that occupational injuries cost Americans about $145 billion in 1992. The overwhelming majority of these costs derived from the disability costs of injured workers. These significant costs have been associated with many efforts to find the risk factors that predict prolonged disability after work-related injuries. In a recent review of the literature, Krause and colleagues (2001b) identified about 100 different determinants of return-to-work outcomes. Krause categorized the risk factors for disability in seven broad groups ranging from the most individual level factors to the most societal level factors: the individual level worker characteristics associated with return-to-work outcomes (useful in predicting prolonged disabilities, but generally not amenable to change); the individual-level worker factors that describe the injury; medical and vocational rehabilitation programs; the physical and psychosocial job characteristics; the organizational level employer factors; the employer- or insurer-based disability prevention programs; and the societal level legislative and policy related factors. The factors that most consistently resulted in a shortening of the duration of disability included medical and vocational rehabilitation interventions, organizational level employer factors, and employer- and insurer-based disability prevention and disability management interventions. Each of these three areas provides many opportunities for implementing and evaluating interventions.

However, several challenges must be overcome before researchers can establish which interventions are most effective (Krause et al., 2001b). Researchers need to agree on the best outcome variables to use in return-to-work studies. We need to bring together multidisciplinary teams that can address the social/behavioral, biomedical, and analytic issues in the research. These multidisciplinary teams will need to create new, interdisciplinary conceptual models for the process of returning to work. We need to prioritize among the diverse group of risk factors related to return-to-work outcomes, focusing on those that are amenable to change and relevant to workers and employers. We also need to raise the methodological level of our research, making use of survival models to account for censoring of data and to maximize the efficiency of our modeling (Collett, 1994). That of hierarchical models to simultaneously assess risk factors from several levels, ranging from the individual to the societal (Diez-Roux, 1998).

Of the almost 100 predictors of return-to-work identified in Krause's (2001a) extensive review of the literature, most were only measured in a handful of studies, but one was repeatedly identified in a variety of different studies. In a detailed review of the literature, Krause and colleagues (1998) found that in 13 high-quality studies, modified work programs facilitated the return-to-work of workers with temporary or permanent impairments. Injured workers who were offered modified work were about twice as likely to return to work as those who were not offered modified work, and they returned to work about twice as quickly. Almost all of these work-modification programs centered on making light duty assignments available to impaired workers. One of these studies presented data suggesting that the light-duty program was cost-effective, but most presented no economic data.

9

Conclusions and Recommendations

KEY CONCLUSIONS AND RECOMMENDATIONS

To permit effective examination of the relationship between health and employment and work-related factors among older workers it is necessary to create new, longitudinal data sets containing detailed information on workers' employment histories and the specific demands of the job, as well as objective information on the health and safety risks to workers in the job. Such data sets do not currently exist because they are costly to create.

An ideal longitudinal data set would contain baseline information on the health status and previous work histories of a representative sample of older Americans, with overrepresentation of minority and other high-risk groups. The survey that collects these data would periodically gather from respondents and their employers data that provide researchers with consistent, reliable, and continuous information on respondents' employment and earnings, the risk factors associated with employment, including work organization and job demands on physical and mental capacity, and exposure to risk factors such as harmful chemicals. These data are needed to follow work and retirement patterns in aging cohorts of workers and to assess the effects of work on health. These data are also needed to assess the effects of health, workplace health risks, family obligations, and other causal factors on employment in later life. The old Retirement History Survey and newer Health and Retirement Study, as well as other longitudinal surveys now available, do not contain reliable or continuous information on the risk factors to which workers are exposed in their jobs.

Creating an ideal data set would be very costly, but it may represent the only strategy likely to produce sufficient data to elucidate completely the relationship between workplace risk factors and workers' health and employment patterns in later life. A more limited and less expensive alternative is to modify existing longitudinal and nonlongitudinal surveys so they contain crucial information about workplace health risks. Another alternative is to collect information on a convenience sample for which longitudinal record gathering is less costly in contrast to a nationally representative, random sample with periodic in-person or telephone survey updates. One possibility is to conduct thorough baseline interviews in a cohort of workers and recent retirees from a large national employer, such as the U.S. government. Personnel and other administrative records and less frequent in-person interviews would be used to construct lifetime work histories and measure subsequent employment and retirement patterns in the cohort. The size of the government workforce would also permit targeted sampling for better assessment of demographic subgroups. It would likely, however, exclude the possibility of assessing a full range of occupations.

> **Recommendation 1: New longitudinal data sets should be developed that contain detailed information on workers' employment histories and the specific demands of their jobs, as well as objective information on the health and safety risks to workers in the job. If cost makes it impossible to create a nationally representative, longitudinal survey focused on workplace health and safety, a less expensive alternative is to create a new longitudinal data set using a convenience sample in which information gathering is less costly, for example, a representative sample of workers at a large national employer, such as the U.S. government.**

The risk of workplace injury or illness or disorder varies both across and within occupation and industry, and workers' exposure to such risks varies across the course of their lives. Therefore, analyses that attempt to explain life course health outcomes or that use health characteristics as variables to help explain major life course transitions such as retirement should have good information on these health and safety risks.

However, otherwise richly detailed socioeconomic surveys such as the Health and Retirement Study or the Panel Study of Income Dynamics, which contain detailed information on the health characteristics of their respondents, lack information on the health and safety risks that workers face in their current or past jobs. A National Research Council (2001) report has strongly encouraged longitudinal research to disentangle and illuminate the complex interrelationship among work, health, economic status, and family structure. Without capturing the independent effects of the work environment on these factors, however, it will be difficult to fully achieve this goal.

Regular population-based information on the distribution of common workplace exposures that can be assessed by interview is essential to our understanding of their relationship to the detailed health information in the Health and Retirement Study and the Panel Study of Income Dynamics, and also of the ways these exposures affect labor force exits.

Recommendation 2: Ongoing longitudinal surveys (for example, the Health and Retirement Study and the Panel Study of Income Dynamics) should either increase the information they gather on health and safety risk factors of the workplace or develop periodic modules to do so.

Accurate occupational injury and illness or disorder data are important to the development of public policy concerning older workers. However, there is evidence-based concern that occupational illnesses or disorders and occupational injuries may be underreported; a number of studies have raised concern about how well these data represent the full complement of work-related illness or disorder and injury experiences of older workers. There is insufficient knowledge of trends in under-ascertainment of both work-related injuries and illnesses or disorders, generally and with regard to older workers, and of the contribution of various factors to under-ascertainment (e.g., decline in unionization, increase in immigrant workforce, growth in precarious employment, incentive systems affecting reporting, and the features of workers' compensation systems).

The primary assessment of trends has been directed at how well industries are reporting those injuries and illnesses or disorders of which they are aware. Inadequate attention, however, has been given to the barriers that may interfere with individual workers' documenting of work-related injuries and the even greater barriers to recognizing that their illness or disorder episodes may be work related. The Bureau of Labor Statistics (BLS) has undertaken and needs to continue efforts to evaluate and improve the Occupational Safety and Health Administration (OSHA) based reporting of occupational injury and illnesses or disorders. In addition, new approaches are necessary to cast a broader net in order to describe the full extent of work-related injury and illness or disorder burden among older workers. Approaches should include new initiatives in several areas. Community-based studies that focus on older workers, with particular attention to immigrant and minority workers, should be undertaken to add important new information to that provided solely from current workplace audits. Surveys of workers should be used to complement audits of employer records, with particular attention to small and medium-sized firms where the audits have suggested problems may exist. Research collaborations should be developed with a variety of nongovernmental groups such as workers' compensation insurance carriers, industry associations, labor/management health and welfare funds, and other private groups with direct or indirect access to sources of work-related injury and illness or disorder data.

> Recommendation 3: The National Institute for Occupational Safety and Health should collaborate with the Bureau of Labor Statistics in conducting a comprehensive review and evaluation of occupational injury and illness or disorder reporting systems, examining the extent of and trends in underreporting and underascertainment. This effort should include filling in important knowledge gaps through innovative research approaches and should be complemented by research directed at understanding trends and barriers to reporting, especially for older workers. Studies of incentives/disincentives to injury and illness or disorder reporting should be conducted with the end in mind of surveillance system reform.

To monitor the importance of the job environment on morbidity and mortality in nationally available data sets such as the National Health Interview Survey and National Health and Nutrition Examination Survey, it is necessary to have consistent, reliable, and continuous information on the risk factors associated with jobs. This information must be available at a sufficiently detailed level of industry and occupation (for example, at least as detailed as the three-digit categories defined by the Standard Industrial Classification and the Standard Occupational Classification systems). Currently, when work risk factors are assessed it is most common to consider them in a very limited fashion using job title or industry group only.

Little detail on the nature of work exposures over a broad range of occupations is currently available for linkage to health-based national or representative data sets. Data that characterize the full range of all types of work exposures are needed to permit assessment and tracking of relationships between these exposures and the prevalence or incidence of health conditions.

These exposure data should be structured in a way that allows easy linkage to data sets (both administrative records and surveys) that provide individual information on health and socioeconomic characteristics. Previously the National Institute of Occupational Safety and Health (NIOSH) has carried out surveys focusing only on chemical and a limited set of physical hazards (National Occupational Hazards Survey, National Occupational Exposure Survey). A more comprehensive assessment of work exposures is required associated with regular revisions to accommodate the evolution of existing occupations and the development of new ones.

Recent organizational developments related to stressful systems or features of work organization (e.g., job strain, effort-reward imbalance, and extended work hours) have been associated with increased risk of cardio-vascular disease, already a major cause of disability among older workers. Although tools exist to assess organizational factors in etiologic research, they are not necessarily easily adapted to population surveys. In order to characterize exposures associated with work organization for use in such surveys, research will be needed to identify components or factors related to work organization that provide adequate sensitivity, specificity, and ease of use.

Recommendation 4: NIOSH should be provided sufficient funds to develop a database that characterizes types and levels of exposures associated with work. Exposures considered should include chemical, physical, biomechanical, and psychosocial factors. The database should be organized in a manner that permits the assignment of a full range of exposures to detailed occupation and industry groups and in a form that permits linkage to population health data sets. The database should be revised and updated periodically, at least every decade.

As first cataloged by Shock and others decades ago, populations undergo age-related decrements in the functioning of organs and of the human as a whole. While occupational health research has documented many adverse health effects of specific worksite environmental exposures, there is almost no research on the impact of these and other exposures on the trajectory of normal aging throughout the life span. Similarly, there is little research on how later-life workplace exposures affect age-related processes that are already altered by a variety of earlier occupational exposures. Approaches are needed to these issues at the general population level, as well as for cohorts with specific workplace exposures. Additional issues requiring investigation include how these cumulative and age-dependent exposures affect later-life physical, cognitive, and social function, and the occurrence and natural history of the major disabling diseases of older persons, such as heart disease, stroke, cancer, and degenerative arthritis. An emphasis on the effect of workplace exposures on mental health and function is also needed, particularly those related to workplace social stresses and changing work demands and organization.

Recommendation 5: Substantial research is needed on the physiological, pathological, and functional effects of common and potentially harmful worksite exposures—physiochemical, biological, biomechanical, and psychosocial—on older workers. This research should include determining how these environmental exposures may affect the trajectory of normal age-related human and organ function, including the cumulative effects of various prior workplace exposures, and the net impact on the pathogenesis of age-related chronic illnesses or disorders.

Many older workers have existing chronic illness or disorder and disease risk factors that are under various levels of personal and clinical management and control, including mental illnesses or disorders. Research is needed on how potentially adverse workplace exposures—physiochemical, biological, biomechanical, and psychosocial—affect the status, control, and outcomes of these chronic conditions. For example, these exposures may have direct, toxic effects on already diseased organs, interact pharmacologically with medications used to treat existing conditions, or distract and impede older workers from timely disease management interventions. Outcomes that might be studied include longevity and mortality, changes in disease and illness or disorder severity, changes in physical functional status, social effects on the individual and families, interactions with the health care system, and overall quality of life. Chronic conditions that are high priority for consideration in such investigations include cardiovascular disease and musculoskeletal disorders.

Recommendation 6: A research program should be conducted to provide systematic and substantial understanding of the effects of potentially harmful workplace exposures on individual and population outcomes among older workers with existing chronic conditions, both during periods of employment and after retirement.

A variety of public policy interventions have been designed to enable workers to remain in the labor market while minimizing or preventing occupationally caused morbidity. These include polices that operate directly through regulation of workplace hazards (Occupational Safety and Health Act, Mine Safety and Health Act) or indirectly through intervention in more general employment practices that impact older or disabled workers (Americans with Disabilities Act, Age Discrimination in Employment Act, Family and Medical Leave Act). Little is known about the effectiveness of these laws in achieving their goals for older workers. For example, there are insufficient data regarding whether the Americans with Disabilities Act has resulted in increased job accommodation, and therefore greater work longevity, for aging workers with qualifying disabilities. There has been no systematic evaluation of the combined and independent effectiveness of the Age Discrimination in Employment Act, the Americans with Disabilities Act, or the Family and Medical Leave Act in assisting aging workers to remain in the workforce and to obtain new employment when they are dislocated. Further study is also needed to assess whether these laws create barriers for continued and safe employment or reemployment of aging workers.

Recommendation 7: Evaluation research is needed to determine the degree to which public policies intended to enable workers to remain at

work safely and productively have met these objectives specifically with regard to older workers. Policies that should be the subject of such evaluation research include the Occupational Safety and Health Act and other health and safety laws; the Americans with Disabilities Act; the Age Discrimination in Employment Act; the Family and Medical Leave Act; and related state laws.

Many existing intervention programs have demonstrated at least some efficacy for workers generally, and some for older workers, specifically. In principle, effective workplace interventions address hazards as close to the source as possible. Therefore, job design, including redesign and engineering to improve the exposures and accommodations for older workers, deserves the highest level of attention. There are design approaches to address a variety of age-related changes in vision, hearing, and physical strength and capacity and approaches that address work-related musculoskeletal disorders that are anticipated to be an important problem for aging workers. There is evidence for the effectiveness of a limited number of interventions to address cardiovascular disease by improving work organization and job design and by reducing job stressors. Many effective interventions also involve changing the social climate in the workplace (e.g., empowering workers), introducing better work practices (e.g., ergonomic interventions to improve body posture for bending and lifting), improving physical fitness with exercise, and substituting machine work for human exertion. Training is an intervention that seems particularly relevant for older workers, who are likely to be the most distant from initial professional training and from initial job training. Access to training, however, is often too limited.

Accommodations for workers with impairments and return-to-work programs are important interventions for older workers, who are more likely to bring impairments into the workplace and to be out of work longer than their younger colleagues after an injury at work. Modified work programs have been clearly shown to facilitate the return to work of workers with temporary or permanent impairments.

Attention to general health promotion programs is relevant for older workers, in part because chronic illness or disorder rates are higher at older ages. It is important to add, however, that general health promotion programs directed at workers appear to be more effective when tied to environmental controls in the workplace. Factors known to result in shortening the duration of disability consistently include medical and vocational rehabilitation interventions, organizational level employer factors, and employer- and insurer-based disability prevention and disability management interventions. Although most employee assistance programs (EAPs) have not emphasized employee needs related to aging, they have strong potential as a support for older workers in relation to occupational health and safety concerns. EAPs can also assist workers challenged by the need to provide eldercare support, plan for retirement or outplacement, and address substance abuse and emotional distress.

For each of these interventions there is need for research on the prevalence of the intervention (which firms and older workers use them), on the effectiveness of the intervention (the degree to which it protects older workers' health and safety), and on the costs of the intervention (how it compares with the benefits obtained).

For instance, ergonomic job designs have the potential to create workplaces that are suitable for the widest range of worker abilities. Workplace accommodations may permit older adults with a variety of impairments to work safely and productively. It is important to assess prevalence in part to determine whether an efficacious practice is not being employed as well as to assess the extent to which interventions not determined to be efficacious or ones known to be ineffective are being employed.

Although many intervention programs have at least some demonstrated efficacy, nearly all have been incompletely evaluated. For instance, weaknesses in existing evaluations of job design and training interventions include the use of small and unrepresentative samples in a small set of occupations. In addition, intermediate outcome measures such as changes in posture or self-ratings of work ability need to be complemented by direct measures of illness or disorder, injury, and symptom syndromes.

Few of the interventions and even fewer of the evaluations of those programs have tested their effectiveness specifically for older workers. Moreover, studies have not routinely included samples representative of the workforce of the future that will include increasing proportions of women and minority workers. Past research has focused on a limited set of occupations and workplace environments, and little is currently known about those that will in the future be employing increasing proportions of older workers. For instance, computer workstations have been introduced in many job settings, and yet there has been little evaluation of the adequacy of their design for older users. Such research can lead to the creation of guidelines and best practices that will lead to safer, healthier, and more productive workplaces.

> **Recommendation 8: For promising job design, training, and workplace accommodation interventions, research should be conducted to determine the prevalence, effectiveness, and associated costs of intervention. The resulting data should be used to perform evaluations and benefit-cost analyses to guide the implementation of future interventions.**

There are gaps in our knowledge about how socioeconomic and demographic variables (e.g., minority or immigration status, low literacy, low-education level, lack of fluency in English, lack of continuous connection to the formal labor market) might increase health and safety risks for sub-populations of older workers, and about the degree to which these variables predict employment in hazardous occupations and industries. There are also gaps in our knowledge about variables that may lead some older workers to stay in the workforce despite declining health (e.g., income insecurity, low-income levels, gaps in health insurance coverage, barriers to access to other public and private benefit programs).

A separate research effort is needed to collect data about these high-risk older workers, given that this population may be less readily identified through standard sampling procedures. To assure comparability with findings from other studies, it is important that standard instruments be used when feasible.

> **Recommendation 9: Targeted research should be undertaken to identify the extent to which, and mechanisms whereby, socioeconomic and demographic variables are related to health and safety risks of older workers; the degree to which these variables predict employment in hazardous occupations and industries; and how they may be associated with retirement decisions and barriers.**

ADDITIONAL CONCLUSIONS AND RECOMMENDATIONS

According to an agreement with OSHA, the BLS annually collects and analyzes workplace injury and illness or disorder statistics. The employer survey instrument required by OSHA, however, does not seek demographic information on employees at risk of injury or illness or disorder. Consequently, much of the data on workplace injury and illness or disorder are presented only as counts or proportions. Denominator data can be developed using occupation and injury data available in the Current Population Survey. The necessary compromises needed to apply Current Population Survey data to this purpose are minor compared with the benefits that result from detailed rate-based data reporting. It has already been determined that it is feasible to determine quite accurate death rates by this method.

> **Recommendation 10: The Bureau of Labor Statistics should initiate reporting of workplace injury and illness or disorder rates according to demographic characteristics (for age, gender, and ethnicity at a minimum) based on Current Population Survey reports of total number of hours worked by people in subpopulations defined by age, gender, industry, and occupation.**

Worksite health promotion programs and employee assistance programs have demonstrated benefits for workers' health, but their effectiveness, specifically for older workers, has not been studied. Worksites can promote the health of older workers through health promotion programs that aim to reduce risk-related behaviors (e.g., tobacco use, physical inactivity) and promote screening for early detection and treatment of illness or disorder and disease (e.g., ambulatory blood pressure monitoring at work to detect hidden workplace hypertension). While there is evidence that the integration of health promotion programs with work risk reductions is successful in reducing risky behaviors, little research has been conducted to identify effective ways to tailor these programs to older workers' needs or strategies to maximize worker participation in programs. In addition, there is need for research to assess the efficacy of these interventions, specifically for older workers.

Employee assistance programs can also play a useful role in protecting and promoting the health and safety of older workers, and they may offer support services specifically tailored for older workers, such as preretirement planning, substance abuse interventions customized for older workers, or family care programs. Research is needed to develop and assess the effectiveness of such services as well.

Another domain of prevention and health promotion programs at the worksite is the possibility of disease management programs for older workers. These programs help manage disease risk factors or physiological domains that can prevent disease progression. Examples include diabetes, hypertension, and asthma management. Evaluation is needed to assess the feasibility, cost, and maintenance of these worker health programs. Simultaneously, the overarching problem of maintaining confidentiality or worker medical conditions needs to be considered.

In addition, particular attention is needed to develop strategies for extending these interventions to small business settings, where they are often lacking.

Recommendation 11: Research should be conducted to assess the effectiveness, benefits, and costs of worksite health promotion programs and employee assistance interventions tailored to older workers in both small and large worksites.

The Department of Labor has been developing and validating a system called O*NET™ intended to advance information useful in describing the nature and scope of job characteristics that can be collected for use in a number of settings, most particularly in the BLS statistical systems. The O*NET database, when complete, will provide a valuable description of the knowledge, skills, and abilities required for various jobs; that information will permit detailed comparison of job requirements with the developing knowledge of the capacities of older workers. The O*NET is a large undertaking, and progress on this valuable resource has been slow.

Recommendation 12: This committee endorses the recommendation, defined in the 1999 National Research Council report *The Changing Nature of Work*, that the O*NET system be developed as a fully operational system. A sense of urgency should be applied: efforts should be devoted to achieving a comprehensive, interactive O*NET database as quickly as possible.

Development of information on the individual, family, and societal costs of occupational injuries and illnesses or disorders is necessary to allow policy makers to place a proper priority on the problem and determine the necessary level of effort for prevention efforts focused on this older worker population. Much of the necessary data to carry out such studies is available from the Health Care Financing Administration, the National Hospital Discharge Survey, the Healthcare Cost and Utilization Project, the Health and Retirement Study, and the Ambulatory Care Visits Study, along with data from the BLS that provides age-specific rates on all categories of occupational injuries and illnesses or disorders, including days away from work, restricted workdays, and events with no lost or restricted time.

Recommendation 13: Research should be undertaken to assess the full (direct and indirect) costs of older workers' occupational injuries and illnesses or disorders to individuals, families, and society.

The National Health Interview Survey (NHIS) is the principal source of information on the health of the civilian noninstitutionalized population of the United States. The main objective of the NHIS is to monitor the health of the U.S. population through the collection and analysis of data on a broad range of health topics. A major strength of this survey lies in its ability to display these health characteristics by many demographic and socioeconomic characteristics. To date, only the 1988 survey included substantial information about population exposure to work-related risk factors and detailed assessment of the occupational nature of selected conditions. Regular population-based information on the distribution of common workplace exposures that can be assessed by interview is essential to understanding the relationship of these risk factors to health data contained within NHIS.

Recommendation 14: The National Center for Health Statistics and the National Institute for Occupational Safety and Health should develop a survey supplement on work risk factors and occupational disorders for periodic inclusion in the National Health Interview Surveys. Additional funds should be devoted to support this effort.

The National Health and Nutrition Examination Survey (NHANES) is a continuous annual survey designed to examine public health issues that can best be addressed through physical and laboratory examinations of the U.S. population. Currently over 100 environmental chemicals are measured in either blood or urine specimens for various subpopulations.

> Recommendation 15: The National Center for Health Statistics and the National Institute for Occupational Safety and Health should collaborate in an effort to identify, using the National Health and Nutrition Examination Survey, subpopulations of older workers where chemical exposure is likely to be an important work risk factor and to develop a list of chemicals to be included in surveys of such populations in the future. Additional funds should be devoted to support this effort.

In the 1970s, the BLS carried out national Quality of Employment Surveys to describe the prevalence of and trends in job characteristics and other workplace risk factors. These nationally representative databases proved a valuable resource for assessing prevalence and trends for work risk factors. For example, the surveys were central to the development of the Job Content Questionnaire.

> Recommendation 16: The National Institute for Occupational Safety and Health and the Department of Labor should collaborate and be funded to develop a survey instrument and periodically conduct surveys to describe the prevalence of and trends in job characteristics and other workplace risk factors in a manner similar to the Quality of Employment Surveys.

References

CHAPTER 1

Barker, K., and Christensen, K. (1998). *Contingent work: American employment relations in transition*. Ithaca, NY: Cornell University Press.

Best, F. (1980). *Flexible life scheduling: Breaking the education-work-retirement lockstep*. New York: Praeger.

Blau, D.M. (1998). Labor force dynamics of older married couples. *Journal of Labor Economics, 16*, 595-629.

Brandt, E.N., Jr., and Pope, A.M. (eds.), (1997). Enabling America: Assessing the role of rehabilitation science and engineering (pp. 67-73), Report of the Committee on Assessing Rehabilitation Science and Engineering, Institute of Medicine. Washington, DC: National Academy Press.

Cain, L.D., Jr. (1964). Life course and social structure. In R.E.L. Faris (ed.), *Handbook of modern sociology*. Chicago: Rand McNally Co.

Capelli, P., Laurie, B., Katz, H., Knoke, D., Osterman, P., and Useem, M. (1997). *Change at work*. Oxford: Oxford University Press.

Dannefer, D., and Uhlenberg, P. (1999). Paths of the life course: A typology. In V.L. Bengtson and K.W. Schaie (eds.), *Handbook of theories of aging* (pp. 306-326). New York: Springer Publishing Co.

Dressel, P.L. (1988). Gender, race, and class: Beyond the feminization of poverty in later life. *Gerontologist, 28*(2), 177-180.

Elder, G.H., Jr. (1994). Time, human agency, and social change: Perspectives on the life course. *Social Psychology Quarterly, 57*(1), 4-15.

Elder, G.H., Jr. (1997). The life course and human development. In R.M. Lerner (ed.), *Handbook of child psychology: Theortetical models of human development* (Vol. 1, pp. 939-991). New York: Wiley.

Elder, G.H., Jr., and Johnson, M.K. (in press). Life course and aging: Challenges, lessons, and new directions. In R.A. Settersten, Jr. (ed.), *Invitation to the life course: Toward new understandings of later life*. New York: Baywood.

231

Elder, G.H., Jr., and O'Rand, A.M. (1995). Adult lives in a changing society. In K.S. Cook, G.A. Fine, and J.S. House (eds.), *Sociological perspectives on social psychology* (pp. 452-475). Needham Heights, MA: Allyn and Bacon.

Estes, C.L. (2001). *Social policy and aging: A critical perspective.* Thousand Oaks, CA: Sage.

Estes, C.L., Gerard, L., and Clarke, A. (1984). Women and the economics of aging. *International Journal of Health Services, 14*(1), 55-68.

Gustman, A.L., and Steinmeier, T.L. (2001). *Imperfect knowledge, retirement, and saving* (Report No. NBER Working paper 8406). Cambridge, MA: National Bureau of Economics Research.

Harootyan, R.A., and Feldman, N.S. (1990). Lifelong education, lifelong needs: Future roles in an aging society. *Educational Gerontology, 16*(4), 347-358.

Henretta, J.C., and Campbell, R.T. (1976). Status attainment and status maintenance: A study of stratification in old age. *American Sociological Review, 41*(6), 981-992.

Henretta, J.C., O'Rand, A.M., and Chan, C.G. (1993). Gender differences in employment after spouse's retirement. *Research on Aging, 15*(2), 148-169.

Hondagneu-Sotelo, P. (2001). *Domestica: Immigrant workers cleaning and caring in the shadows of affluence.* Berkeley: University of California Press.

Houseman, S., and Nakamura, A.E. (2001). *Working time in comparative perspective. Volume 2. Life-cycle working time and nonstandard work* (p. 371). Kalamazoo, MI: W.E. Upjohn Institute for Employment Research.

Hurd, M.D. (1998). *The joint retirement decisions of husbands and wives.* (Report No. NBER working paper 2803). Cambridge, MA: National Bureau of Economic Research.

Institute of Medicine. (1997). *Enabling America.* In E.N. Brandt and A.M. Pope (eds.), Committee on Assessing Rehabilitation Science and Engineering (pp. 67-73). Washington, DC: National Academy Press.

Johnson, R.W., and Favreault, M.M. (2001, March). *Retiring together or retiring alone: The impact of spousal employment and disability on retirement decisions.* (Working paper 2001-01). Boston: Center for Retirement Research at Boston College.

Kohli, M. (1986). The world we forgot: A historical review of the life course. In V.W. Marshall (ed.), *Later life: The social psychology of aging* (pp. 271-303). Beverly Hills, CA: Sage.

Markson, E.W., and Hollis-Sawyer, L.A. (2000). *Intersections of Aging: Readings in social gerontology.* Los Angeles: Roxbury.

Marshall, V.W. (1995). Rethinking retirement: Issues for the twenty-first century. In E.M. Gee and G.M. Gutman (eds.), *Rethinking retirement* (pp. 31-50). Vancouver: Gerontology Research Centre, Simon Fraser University.

Marshall, V.W., and Clarke, P.J. (1998). *Facilitating the transition from employment to retirement.* (Report No. 171-207). Ste Foy, Quebec: Editions MutiModes.

Marshall, V.W., and Mueller, M.M. (2002). Rethinking Social Policy for an Aging Workforce and Society: Insights from the Life Course Perspective. (Discussion Paper 57). Ottawa: Canadian Policy Research Network.

Moen, P., Robison, J., and Dempster-McClain, D. (1995). Caregiving and women's well-being: A life course approach. *Journal of Health and Social Behavior, 36*(3), 259-273.

Moody, H.R. (2002). *Aging: concepts and controversies* (4ed.). Thousand Oaks, CA: Sage.

Mutchler, J.E., Burr, J.A., Pienta, A.M., and Massagli, M.P. (1997). Pathways to labor force exit: work transitions and work instability. *Journals of Gerontology Series B-Psychological Sciences and Social Sciences, 52*(1), S4-S12.

Myles, J. (1989). *Old age in the welfare state: The political economy of public pensions.* Lawrence, KS: University of Kansas Press.

Myles, J., and Street, D. (1995). Should the economic life course be redesigned? Old age security in a time of transition. *Canadian Journal on Aging/La Revue Canadienne Du Vieillissement*, *14*(2), 335-359.

National Research Council. (2001). *Preparing for an Aging World: The case for cross-national research*. Panel on a Research Agenda and New Data for an Aging World, Committee on Population, Committee on National Statistics, Division of Behavioral of Social Sciencs and Education. Washington, DC: National Academy Press.

Occupational Safety and Health Act of 1970, Pub. L. 91-596, 91st Congress, Stat. 2193 (1970).

Redburn, D.E. (1998). "Graying of the world's population." In D.E. Redburn and R.P. NcNamara (eds.), *Social Gerontology* (pp. 1-16). Westport, CT: Auburn House.

Regan, J. (1981). Protecting the elderly: The new paternalism. *Hastings Law Journal*, *32*(5), 1111-1132.

Riley, M.W. (1979). Introduction: Life course perspectives. In M.W. Riley (ed.), *Aging from Birth to Death* (pp. 3-13). Boulder, CO: Westview Press.

Riley, M.W., and Riley, J.W., Jr. (1994). Age integration and the lives of older people. *Gerontologist*, *34*(1), 110-115.

Riley, M.W., Foner, A., and Riley, J.W., Jr. (1999). The "aging and society" paradigm. In V.L. Bengtson and K.W. Schaie (eds.), *Handbook of Theories of Aging* (pp. 327-343).

Rindfuss, R.R., Swicegood, C.G., and Rosenfeld, R.A. (1987). Disorder in the life course: How common and does it matter? *American Sociological Review*, *52*(6), 785-801.

Robinson, V.E. (1999). Women and retirement. *Journal of Women and Aging*, *11*(2/3), 49-66.

Schulz, J.H. (2000). "The Full Monty" and life-long learning in the 21st century. *Journal of Aging and Social Policy*, *11*(2-3), 71-82.

U.S. Bureau of the Census. (2001). *Current Population Survey*. Washington, DC: U.S. Government Printing Office.

U.S. General Accounting Office. (1988). *"Sweatshops" in the U.S.: Opinions on their extent and possible enforcement options*. (Report No. GAO/HRD-88-130BR). Washington, DC: U.S. General Accounting Office.

U.S. General Accounting Office. (2001). *Older Workers: Demographic trends pose challenges for employers and workers*. (Report No. GAO-02-85). Washington, DC: U.S. General Accounting Office.

Warr, P. (1998). Age, work, and mental health. K.W. Schaie and C. Schooler (eds.), *Impact of Work on Older Adults. Societal Impact on Aging Series* (pp. 252-303). New York: Springer.

Weaver, D.A. (1994). The work and retirement decisions of older women: A literature review. *Social Security Bulletin*, *57*(1), 3-24.

Wiatrowski, W.J. (2001). Changing retirement age: Ups and downs. *Monthly Labor Review*, *124*(4), 3-12.

Wong, G.E., and Picot, G.E. (2001). *Working time in comparative perspective: Patterns, trends, and the policy implications for earnings inequality and unemployment* (p. 424). Kalamazoo, MI: Upjohn Institute.

CHAPTER 2

Bass, S.A., Quinn, J.F., and Burkhauser, R.V. (1995). "Toward pro-work policies and programs for older americans." In S.A. Bass (ed.), *Older and active: How Americans over 55 are contributing to society* (pp. 263-294). New Haven: Yale University Press.

Berman, J.M. (2001). Industry output and employment projections to 2010. *Monthly Labor Review*, *124*(11), 39-56.

Bregger, J.E. (1996). Measuring self-employment in the United States. *Monthly Labor Review, 119*(1-2), 3-9.

Burkhauser, R.B., Clark, R., Moon, M., Quinn, J., and Smeeding, T. (in press). *Causes and consequences of aging: Economic, demographic, and policy issues.* Malden, MA: Blackwell Publishing Co.

Burtless, G., and Moffitt, R.A. (1984). The effect of social security benefits on the labor supply of the aged. Retirement and Economic Behavior. A. Henry and G. Burtless (eds.), *Studies in Social Economics Series* (pp. 135-71). Washington, DC: Brookings Institution.

Burtless, G., and Moffit, R. (2001). Retirement trends and policies to encourage work among older americans. In P.P. Budetti, R.V. Burkhauser, J.M. Gregory, and H.A. Hunt (eds.), *Insuring Health and Income Security for an Aging Workforce* (pp. 375-415). Kalamazoo, MI: W.E. Upjohn Institute for Employment Research.

Clark, R.L., York, E.A., and Anker, R. (1999). Economic development and labor force participation of older persons. *Population Research and Policy Review, 18*(5), 411-432.

Costa, D.L. (1998). The evolution of retirement: An American Economic history, 1880-1990. *NBER Series on Long-Term Factors in Economic Development.* Chicago and London: University of Chicago Press.

Crimmins, E.M., Reynolds, S.L., and Saito, Y. (1999). Trends in health and ability to work among the older working-age population. *Journals of Gerontology Series B-Psychological Sciences and Social Sciences, 54*(1), S31-S40.

Fullerton, H.N., Jr., and Toossi, M. (2001). Labor force projections to 2010: Steady growth and changing composition. *Monthly Labor Review, 124*(11), 21-38.

Ghent, L., Allen, S., and Clark, R. (2002). "The impact of a new phased retirement option on faculty retirement decisions." *Research on Aging, 23*(6), 671-693.

Gruber, J., and Wise, D. (1999). *An international comparison of social security systems.* Chicago: The University Chicago Press.

Health and Retirement Study (HRS). (2004). The Health and Retirement Study: A longitudinal Study of Health, Retirement and Aging. Available: http://hrsonline.isr.umich.edu/ [accessed February 6, 2004].

Hecker, D.E. (2001). Occupational employment projections to 2010. *Monthly Labor Review, 124*(11), 57-84.

Kinsella, K., and Gist, Y.J. (1995). *Older workers, retirement, and pensions: A comparative international chartbook.* Washington, DC: U.S. Bureau of the Census (P95/92-3).

Manton, K.G., Corder, L., and Stallard, E. (1997). Chronic disability trends in elderly United States populations: 1982-1994. *Proceedings of the National Academy of Sciences of the United States of America, 94*(6), 2593-2598.

Moody, H.R. (2002). *Aging: Concepts and controversies* (4th ed.). Thousand Oaks, CA: Sage.

National Research Council. (2001). *Preparing for an aging world: The case for cross-national research.* Panel on a Research Agenda and New Data for an Aging World, Committee on Population, Committee on National Statistics, Division of Behavioral and Social Sciences and Education, National Research Council. Washington, DC: National Academy Press.

Quinn, J. (2002). Retirement trends and patterns among older Amercian workers. In S. Altman and D. Shactman (eds.), *Policies for an Aging Society.* Baltimore, MD: Johns Hopkins University Press.

Quinn, J.F., Burkhauser, R.V., and Myers, D.A. (1990). *Passing the torch: The influence of economic incentives on work and retirement* (p. 269). Kalamazoo, MI: W.E. Upjohn Institute for Employment Research.

Redburn, D.E. (1998). "'Graying of the world's population." In D.E. Redburn and R.P. NcNamara (eds.), *Social Gerontology* (pp. 1-16). Westport, CT: Auburn House.

Social Security Advisory Council Technical Committee. (1997). Washington, DC: U.S. Government Printing Office.

U.S. Bureau of the Census. (1993). *We the American elderly.* U.S. Department of Commerce. Economics and Statistics Administration. Washington, DC: U.S. Government Printing Office.

U.S. Bureau of the Census. (1999). *Current population reports, Series P60-207, Poverty in the United States: 1998.* Washington, DC: U.S. Government Printing Office.

U.S. Bureau of the Census. (2000). *Projection of the total resident population by 5-year age groups, and sex with special age categories: Middle series.* Washington, DC: U.S. Government Printing Office.

U.S. Department of Health and Human Services. (1994). National Health Interview Survey (NHIS) 1993, U.S. Department of Health and Human Services, National Center for Health Statistics. Ann Arbor, MI: Inter-university Consortium for Political and Social Research.

U.S. Department of Health and Human Services. (2000). 1998 National Health Interview Survey (NHIS), U.S. Department of Health and Human Services, National Center for Health Statistics. Hyattsville, MD.

Wagener, D.K., Walstedt, J., Jenkins, L., and Burnett, C. (1997). Women: Work and health. *Vital Health Statistics, 3*(31).

CHAPTER 3

Adler, P.S., Goldoftas, B., and Levine, D.I. (1997). Ergonomics, employee involvement and the toyota production system: A case study of nummi's 1993 model introduction. *Industrial and Labor Relations Review, 50*(3), 416-437.

Aiken, L.H., Sloane, D.M., and Klocinski, J.L. (1997). Hospital nurses' occupational exposure to blood: Prospective, retrospective, and institutional reports. *American Journal of Public Health, 87*(1), 103-107.

Appelbaum, E., and Batt R. (1994). The new American workplace: Transforming work systems in the United States. Ithaca: ILR Press.

Azaroff, L., and Levenstein, C. (2002). Innovations in monitoring work security: A case study of Sourtheast Asian Refugees in Lowell, Massachusetts. Geneva: International Labor Organization.

Babson, S. (1993). Lean or mean: The MIT model and lean production at Mazda. *Labor Studies Journal, 18*, 3-24.

Babson, S. (1995). Lean production and labor: Empowerment and exploitation. In S. Babson (ed.), *Lean work: Empowerment and exploitation in the global auto industry* (pp. 1-37). Detroit, MI: Wayne State University Press.

Bailey, T. (1993). Organizational innovation in the apparel industry. *Industrial Relations, 32*(1), 30-48.

Batt, R., and Appelbaum, E. (1995). Worker participation in diverse settings: Does the form affect the outcome, and if so, who benefits? *British Journal of Industrial Relations, 33*, 353-378.

Berg, P., Appelbaum, E., Bailey, T., and Kalleberg, A.L. (1996). The performance effects of modular production in the apparel industry. *Industrial Relations, 35*(3), 356-373.

Berggren, C., Bjorkman, T., and Hollander, E. (1991). *Are they unbeatable? Report from a field trip to study transplants, the Japanese owned auto plants in North America.* Stockholm: Royal Institute of Technology.

Biddle, J., Roberts, K., Rosenman, K.D., and Welch, E.M. (1998). What percentage of workers with work-related illnesses receive workers' compensation benefits? *Journal of Occupational & Environmental Medicine, 40*(4), 325-331.

Bjorkman, T. (1996). The Rationalisation Movement in perspective and some ergonomic implications. *Applied Ergonomics*, 27(2), 111-117.

Bond, J.T., Galinsky, E., and Swanberg, J.E. (1997). The national study of the changing workforce, Vol. 2. 175 pp.

Brannon, R.L. (1996). Restructuring hospital nursing: Reversing the trend toward a professional work force. *International Journal of Health Services*, 26(4), 643-654.

Brisson, C., Vinet, A., Vezina, M., and Gingras, S. (1989). Effect of duration of employment in piecework on severe disability among female garment workers. *Scandinavian Journal of Work, Environment and Health*, 15(5), 329-334.

Conway, H., and Svenson, J. (1998). Occupational injury and illness rates, 1992-96: Why they fell. *Monthly Labor Review*, 121(11), 36-58.

Council of Economic Advisors. (2002). *Economic report of the President*. Washington, DC: Executive Office of the President.

Crimmins, E.M., Reynolds, S.L., and Saito, Y. (1999). Trends in health and ability to work among the older working-age population. *Journals of Gerontology Series B-Psychological Sciences & Social Sciences*, 54(1), S31-S40.

Deaton, A. (2003). Health, inequality, and economic development. *Journal of Economic Literature*, 41(1), 113-158.

Delbridge, R.T.P., and Turnbull, P. (1992). Human resource maximization: The management of labour under just-in-time manufacturing systems. In P. Blyton and P. Turnbull (eds.), *Reassessing Human Resource Management*. London: Sage Publications.

Delbridge, R., Turnbull, P., and Wilkinson, B. (1993). Pushing back the frontiers: Management control and work intensification under JIT/TQM factory regimes. *New Technology, Work and Employment*, 7, 97-106.

Dohm, A. (2000). Gauging the labor force effects of retiring baby-boomers. *Monthly Labor Review*, 123(7), 17-25.

European Foundation. (1997). *Time constraints and autonomy at work in the European Union*. Dublin: European Foundation for the Improvement of Living and Working Conditions.

European Foundation. (2000). *Ten years of working conditions in the European Union*. Dublin: European Foundation for the Improvement of Living and Working Conditions.

Gabriel, P., and Liimatainen, M.R. (2000). *Mental health in the workplace*. Geneva: International Labour Office.

Gibson, C.J., and Lennon, E. (1999). Historical Census Statistics on the Foreign-born Population of the United States: 1850-1990. Washington, DC: U.S. Government Printing Office.

Greiner, A. (1995). Cost and quality matters: Workplace innovations in the health care industry. Washington, DC: Economic Policy Institute.

Hecker, D. (2001). Occupation employment projections to 2010. *Monthly Labor Review*, 124(11), 57-84.

Hirsch, B.T., Macpherson, D.A., Vroman, W.G. (2001). "Estimates of Union Density by State." *Monthly Labor Review*, 124(7), 51-55.

Houseman, S.N. (2001). *The Benefits Implication of Recent Trends in Flexible Staffing Arrangements*. Philadelphia, PA: The Wharton School, University of Pennsylvania.

Ilmarinen, J. (1997). *Aging and work: Problems and solutions for promoting the work ability*. Helsinki: Finnish Institute of Occupational Health.

International Labour Office (ILO). (2001). *Key Indicators of the Labour Market 2001-2002*. Geneva: International Labour Office.

Johnson, J.V. (1997). Empowerment in future worklife. *Scandinavian Journal of Work, Environment and Health*, 23(Suppl 4):23-27.

Joint Commission on Accreditation of Healthcare Organizations. (2002). *Health care at the crossroads*. Oakbrook Terrace, IL: Joint Commission on Accreditation of Healthcare Organizations.

Kalleberg, A.L., Rasell, E., Cassirer, N., Reskin, B.F., Hudson, K., Webster, D., Appelbaum, E., and Spalter-Roth, R.M. (1997). *Nonstandard work, substandard jobs: Flexible work arrangements in the U.S.* Washington, DC: Economic Policy Institute. Pp. 119.

Kaminski, M. (1996). Wayne integrated stamping and assembly plant, Ford Motor Co/UAW local 900. In M. Kaminski, D. Bertell, M. Moye, and J. Yudken (eds.), *Making change happen: Six cases of unions and companies transforming their workplaces*. Washington, DC: Work and Technology Institute.

Kaplan, G.A., Pamuk, E.R., Lynch, J.W., Cohen, R.D., and Balfour, J.L. (1996). Inequality in income and mortality in the United States: Analysis of mortality and potential pathways erratum appears in British Medical Journal, *18*(312), 7041.

Karasek, R., Brisson, C., Kawakami, N., Houtman, I., Bongers, P., and Amick, B. (1998). The job content questionnaire (JCQ): An instrument for internationally comparative assessments of psychosocial job characteristics. *Journal of Occupational Health Psychology, 3*(4), 322-355.

Klein, J.A. (1991). A reexamination of autonomy in light of new manufacturing practices. *Human Relations, 44*(1), 1921-1938.

Kramer, M., and Schmalenberg, C. (1988). Magnet hospitals: Part II. Institutions of excellence. *Journal of Nursing Administration, 18*(2), 11-19.

Landrigan, P.J., and Baker, D.B. (1991). The recognition and control of occupational disease. *Journal of the American Medical Association, 266*(5), 676-680.

Landsbergis, P.A. (2003). The changing organization of work and the health and safety of working people: A commentary. *Journal of Occupational and Environmental Medicine, 45*(1), 61-72.

Landsbergis, P.A., Cahill, J., and Schnall, P. (1999). The impact of lean production and related new systems of work organization on worker health. *Journal of Occupational Health Psychology, 4*(2), 108-130.

Levenstein, C., and Wooding, J. (1997). *Work, health, and environment: Old problems, new solutions*. Foreword by A. Mazzocchi, Democracy and Ecology Series. New York: Guilford Press.

Lewchuk, W., and Robertson D. (1996). Working conditions under lean production: A worker-based benchmarking study. *Asia Pacific Business Review, 2*(4), 60-81.

Manton, K.G., Corder, L.S., and Stallard, E. (1993). Estimates of change in chronic disability and institutional incidence and prevalence rates in the U.S. elderly population from the 1982, 1984, and 1989 National Long Term Care Survey. *Journal of Gerontology, 48*(4), S153-S166.

Manton, K.G., Corder, L., and Stallard, E. (1997). Chronic disability trends in elderly United States populations: 1982-1994. *Proceedings of the National Academy of Sciences of the United States of America, 94*(6), 2593-2598.

McClure, M.L., Poulin, M.A., Sovie, M.D., and Wandelt, M.A. (1983). Magnet hospitals: Attraction and retention of professional nurses. Kansas City, MO: American Academy of Nurses.

Mishel, L., Bernstein, J., and Boushey, H. (2003). *The state of working America 2002/2003*. New York: Cornell University Press.

Murphy, L.R. (2002). Job stress research at NIOSH: 1972-2002. In P.L. Perrewe and D.C. Ganster (eds.), *Historical and current perspectives on stress and health* (Vol. 2, pp. 1-55). New York: JAI Elsevier.

National Institute for Occupational Safety and Health. (2002). *The changing organization of work and the safety and health of working people*. Cincinnati, OH: NIOSH.

National Research Council. (1987). *Counting Injuries and Illnesses in the Workplace: Proposals for a Better System.* Committee on National Statistics. Washington, DC: National Academy Press.

National Research Council. (1999). *The Changing Nature of Work: Implications for Occupational Analysis.* Committee on Techniques for the Enhancement of Human Performance, Commission on Behavioral and Social Sciences and Education, National Research Council. Washington, DC: National Academy Press.

Organization for Economic Co-operation and Development. (2002). *Employment Outlook.* Paris: Organization for Economic Co-operation and Development.

Osterman, P. (1994). How common is workplace transformation and who adopts it? *Industrial and Labor Relations Review, 47*(2), 173-188.

Paoli, P. (1997). *Working conditions in the European Union.* Dublin: European Foundation.

Paoli, P., and Merllie, D. (2001). *Third European Survey on Working Conditions.* Dublin: European Foundation for the Improvement of Living and Working Conditions.

Parker, S.K., and Sprigg, C.A. (1998). *A move backwards? The introduction of a moving assembly line.* Paper presented at the British Psychological Society Annual Occupational Psychology Conference, United Kingdom.

Parker, S.K., Myers, C., and Wall, T.D. (1995). The effects of a manufacturing initiative on employee jobs and strain. In S.A. Robertson (ed.), *Contemporary Economics 1995.* London: Taylor and Francis.

Punnett, L., Robins, J.M., Wegman, D.H., and Keyserling, W.M. (1985). Soft tissue disorders in the upper limbs of female garment workers. *Scandinavian Journal of Work, Environment and Health, 11*(6), 417-425.

Quinlan, M., and Mayhew, C. (2000). Precarious employment, work reorganisation and the fracturing of OHS management. In K. Frick, P.L. Jensen, M. Quinlan, and T. Wilthagen (eds.), *Systematic occupational health and safety management: Perspectives on an International Development* (pp. 175-198). New York: Pergamon.

Quinn, R.P., and Staines, G.L. (1979). *The 1977 Quality of Employment Survey.* Ann Arbor, MI: Institute of Social Research, University of Michigan.

Richardson, T. (1994). Reengineering the hospital: Patient-focused care. In M. Parker and J. Slaughter (eds.), *Working Smart* (pp. 113-120). Detroit: Labor Education and Research Project.

Robertson, D., Rinehart, J., Huxley, C., Wareham, J., Rosenfeld, H., McGough, A., and Benedict, S. (1993). *The CAMI report: Lean production in a unionized auto plant.* Ontario: Canadian Auto Workers.

Rones, P.L., Ilg, R.E., and Gardner J.M. (1997). Trends in hours of work since the mid-1970s. *Monthly Labor Review, 120*(4), 3-14.

Rosenman, K.D., Gardiner, J.C., Wang, J., Biddle, J., Hogan, A., Reilly, M.J., Roberts, K., and Welch, E. (2000). Why most workers with occupational repetitive trauma do not file for workers' compensation. *Journal of Occupational & Environmental Medicine, 42*(1), 25-34.

Schibye, B., Skov, T., Ekner, D., Christiansen, J.U., and Sjogaard, G. (1995). Musculoskeletal symptoms among sewing machine operators. *Scandinavian Journal of Work, Environment and Health, 21*(6), 427-434.

Schnall, P., Belkic, K., Landsbergis, P., and Baker, D. (2000). Why the workplace and cardiovascular disease? *Occupational Medicine, 15*(1), 1-6.

Singh, G.K., and Siahpush, M. (2002). Increasing inequalities in all-cause and cardiovascular mortality among US adults aged 25-64 years by area socioeconomic status, 1969-1998. *International Journal of Epidemiology, 31*(3), 600-613.

Sochalski, J., Aiken, L.H., and Fagin, C.M. (1997). Hospital restructuring in the United States, Canada, and Western Europe: An outcomes research agenda. *Medical Care, 35*(10 Suppl), S13-S25.

Standing, G. (1999). Global labour flexibility: Seeking distributive justice. London: Macmillan Press.

Subramanian, S.V., Blakely, T., and Kawachi, I. (2003). Income inequality as a public health concern: Where do we stand? Commentary on "Is exposure to income inequality a public health concern?" *Health Services Research, 38*(1 Pt 1), 153-167.

The Tokyo Declaration. (1998). The Tokyo Declaration. *Journal of the Tokyo Medical University, 56*(6), 760-767.

Tuchsen, F., and Endahl, L.A. (1999). Increasing inequality in ischaemic heart disease morbidity among employed men in Denmark 1981-1993: The need for a new preventive policy. *International Journal of Epidemiology, 28*(4), 640-644.

U.S. Bureau of Labor Statistics. (2000). Industry at a glance. Available: http://www.bls.gov/iag [accessed January 2004].

U.S. Bureau of Labor Statistics. (2003). Industry at a glance. Available: http://www.bls.gov/iag [accessed June 2004].

Vogel, J. (2002). Swedish level of living survey data. In P. Landsbergis (ed.), *Swedish level of living survey data*. Stockholm: Statistics Sweden.

Walters, D. (1998). Health and safety strategies in a changing Europe. *International Journal of Health Services, 28*(2), 305-331.

Weil, D. (1991). "Enforcing OSHA: The role of labor unions". *Industrial Relations, 30*(1), 20-36.

Wells, J., Kochan, T., and Smith, M. (1991). Managing workplace safety and health: The case of contract labor in the U.S. petrochemical industry. Beaumont, TX: John Gray Institute.

Womack, J., Jones, D., and Roos, D. (1990). *The machine that changed the world*. New York: Rawson.

CHAPTER 4

American Association of Retired Persons (AARP). (2002). AARP survey outlines what 45+ workers seek from employers. Available: http://www.aarp.org/research/press/presscurrentnews/cn-2002/Articles/a2003-06-03-nr092302.html [accessed April 20, 2004].

Anastas, J.W., Gibeau, J.L., and Larson, P.J. (1990). Working families and eldercare: A national perspective in an aging America. *Social Work, 35*(5), 405-411.

Arber, S. (1991). Class, paid employment and family roles: Making sense of structural disadvantage, gender and health status. *Social Science & Medicine, 32*(4), 425-436.

Archibold, P.G. (1983). An impact of parent-caring on women. *Family Relations, 32,* 39-45.

Barnett, R.C., and Baruch, G.K. (1987). Social roles, gender, and psychological distress. In R.C. Barnett and L. Biener (eds.), *Gender and stress* (pp. 122-143). Wellesley, MA: Wellesley Coll, Center for Research on Women, Research Associate.

Barnett, R.C., and Shen, Y.-C. (1997). Gender, high- and low-schedule-control housework tasks, and psychological distress: A study of dual-earner couples. *Journal of Family Issues, 18*(4), 403-428.

Bird, C.E. (1997). Gender differences in the social and economic burdens of parenting and psychological distress. *Journal of Marriage & the Family, 59*(4), 809-823.

Black, D., Morris, J.N., Smith, C., Townsend, P., and Whitehead, M. (1988). *Inequalities in Health: The Black Report—The Health Divide*. London: Penguin.

Bobak, M., Hertzman, C., Skodova, Z., and Marmot, M. (1998). Association between psychosocial factors at work and nonfatal myocardial infarction in a population-based case-control study in Czech men. *Epidemiology, 9*(1), 43-47.

Bosma, H., Marmot, M.G., Hemingway, H., Nicholson, A.C., Brunner, E., and Stansfeld, S.A. (1997). Low job control and risk of coronary heart disease in Whitehall II (prospective cohort) study. *British Medical Journal, 314*(7080), 558-565.

Bosma, H., Peter, R., Siegrist, J., and Marmot, M. (1998). Two alternative job stress models and the risk of coronary heart disease. *American Journal of Public Health, 88*(1), 68-74.

Bound, J., Duncan, G.J., Laren, D.S., and Oleinick, L. (1991). Poverty dynamics in widowhood. *Journal of Gerontology, 46*(3), S115-S124.

Braithwaite, R.L., and Taylor, S.E. (1992). *Health Issues in the Black Community*. San Francisco: Jossey-Bass.

Breeze, E., Fletcher, A.E., Leon, D.A., Marmot, M.G., Clarke, R.J., and Shipley, M.J. (2001). Do socioeconomic disadvantages persist into old age? Self-reported morbidity in a 29-year follow-up of the Whitehall Study. *American Journal of Public Health, 91*(2), 277-283.

Bryant, B., and Mohai, P. (1992). *Race and the Incidence of Environmental Hazards*. Boulder, CO: Westview Press.

Bulan, H.F., Erickson, R.J., and Wharton, A.S. (1997). Doing for others on the job: The affective requirements of service work, gender, and emotional well-being. *Social Problems, 44*(2), 235-256.

Bullard, R.D. (1990). *Dumping in Dixie: Race, Class, and Environmental Quality*. Boulder, CO: Westview Press.

Bullard, R.D. (1996). *Unequal Protection: Environmental Justice and Communities of Color*. San Francisco: Sierra Club Books.

Bunker, J.P., Gomby, D.S., and Kehrer, B.H. (1989). *Pathways to Health: The Role of Social Factors*. Menlo Park, CA: Henry J. Kaiser Family Foundation.

Burnett, C.A., and Lalich, N.R. (1993). Measuring work-related health disparities for minority populations. In *Toward the Year 2000: Refining the Measures*. Proceedings of the 1993 Public Health Conference on Records and Statistics, July 19-21, 1993. (DHHS Publication PHS 94-1214). Hyattsville, MD: National Center for Health Statistics.

Bury, M. (1995). Aging, gender and sociological theory. In S. Arber and J.E. Ginn (eds.), *Connecting gender and aging: A sociological approach*. Buckingham, UK: Open University Press.

Canadian Advisory Council on the Status of Women. (1994). *110 Canadian statistics on work and family*. Ottawa: Canadian Advisory Council on the Status of Women.

Carr-Hill, R. (1987). The inequalities in health debate: A critical review of the issues. *Social Policy, 16*, 509-542.

Centers for Disease Control and Prevention (1997, December). *Women: Work and Health*. (NCHS Series 3, No. 31). National Center for Health Statistics, Vital and Health Statistics. Washington, DC: U.S. Department of Health and Human Services.

Chen, Y.-P. (1995). Improving the economic security of minority persons as they enter old age. In J.S. Jackson, J. Albright, T.P. Miles, M.R. Miranda, C. Nunez, E.P. Stanford, B.W.K. Yee, D.L. Yee, and G. Yeo (eds.), *Minority elders* (pp. 22-31). Washington, DC: The Gerontological Society of America.

Cohen, S. (1988). Psychosocial models of the role of social support in the etiology of physical disease. *Health Psychology, 7*(3), 269-297.

Dressel, P.L. (1988). Gender, race, and class: Beyond the feminization of poverty in later life. *Gerontologist, 28*(2), 177-180.

Dressel, P.L., and Barnhill, S.K. (1994). Reframing gerontological thought and practice: The case of grandmothers with daughters in prison. *Gerontologist, 34*(5), 685-689.

Dressel, P.L., Minkler, M., and Yen, I. (1997). Gender, race, class, and aging: Advances and opportunities. *International Journal of Health Services, 27*(4), 579-600.

Duncan G.J. (1996). Income dynamics and health. *International Journal of Health Services*, 26(3), 419-444.

Estes, C.L. (1999). The Political Economy of Aging. In G. Maddox (ed.), *Encyclopedia of Aging*. NY: Springer.

Evans, R.G., Barer, M.L., and Marmor, T.R. (1994). Why are Some People Healthy and Others Not? *The Determinants of Health of Populations*. New York: Aldine de Gruyter.

Federal Interagency Forum on Aging-Related Statistics. (2000). *Older Americans 2000: Key Indicators of Well-Being*. Federal Interagency Forum on Aging-Related Statistics. Washington, DC: U.S. Government Printing Office.

Fogel, R.W. (2000). The Fourth Great Awakening and the Future of Egalitarianism. Chicago: University of Chicago Press.

Friedman-Jimenez, G., and Claudio, L. (1998). Environmental justice. In W.N. Rom (ed.), *Environmental and Occupational Medicine* (3rd ed). Philadelphia: Lippincott-Raven Publishers.

Frumkin, H., and Pransky, G. (1999). Special populations in occupational health. *Occupational Medicine, State of the Art Reviews*, 14(3), 479-484.

Fullerton, H.N., Jr. (1999). Labor force projections to 2008: Steady growth and changing composition. *Monthly Labor Review*, 122(11), 19-32.

Gibson, R.C. (1991). Race and the self-reported health of elderly persons. *Journal of Gerontology*, 46(5), S235-S242.

Gruber, J., and Wise, D. (1999). In *International Comparison of Social Security Systems*. Chicago: The University Chicago Press.

Haider, S.J., and Loughran, D.S. (2001). *"Elderly Labor Supply: Work or Play?"* DRU-2582, Santa Monica, CA: RAND.

Han, S.-K., and Moen, P. (1998). Interlocking Careers: Pathways through Work and Family for Men and Women. In P.B. Voos (ed.), *Proceedings of the Fiftieth Annual Meeting, Vol. 1*. Madison, WI: Industrial Relations Research Association.

Hendley, A.A., and Bilimoria, N.F. (1999). Minorities and Social Security: An analysis of racial and ethnic differences in the current program. *Social Security Bulletin*, 62(2), 59-64.

Hill, E.T. (2002). The labor force participation of older women: Retired? Working? Both? *Monthly Labor Review*, 125(9), 39-48.

Himes, C.L. (1994). Parental caregiving by adult women: A demographic perspective. *Research on Aging*, 16(2), 191-211.

Honig, M. (1985). Partial retirement among women [Partial Retirement as a Separate Mode of Retirement Behavior]. *Journal of Human Resources*, 20(4), 613-621.

Hopflinger, F. (1999). *Elderly women: Social context, health and development*. Switzerland: Instiut fur Sozial- und Praventivmedizin.

Institute of Medicine. (1999). Toward Environmental Justice: Research, Education, and Health Policy Needs. Committee on Environmental Justice. Washington, DC: National Academy Press.

John R. (1996). Demography of American Indian elders: Social, economic, and health status. In G.D. Sandefur, R.R. Rindfuss, and B. Cohen (eds.), *Changing numbers, changing needs: American Indian demography and public health*. Washington, DC: National Academy Press.

Kirkpatrick, P. (1994). Triple jeopardy: Disability, race and poverty in America. *Poverty and Race*, 3, 1-8.

Krieger, N. (2000). Counting accountably: Implications of the new approaches to classifying race/ethnicity in the 2000 census. *American Journal of Public Health*, 90(11):1687-1689.

Krieger, N., Rowley, D.L., Herman, A.A., Avery, B., and Phillips, M.T. (1993). Racism, sexism, and social class: Implications for studies of health, disease, and well-being. *American Journal of Preventive Medicine, 9*(6 Supp), 82-122.

Lieberson, S. (1980). *A piece of the pie: Black and white immigrants since 1880*. Berkeley, CA: University of California Press.

Logue, B.J. (1990). Women in female-dominated occupations: Correlates of well-being in retirement. *American Sociological Association*.

Marini, M.M. (1980). Sex differences in the process of occupational attainment: A closer look. *Social Science Research, 9*(4), 307-361.

Marmot, M.G. (1985). Psychosocial factors and blood pressure. *Preventive Medicine, 14*(4), 451-465.

Marmot, M.G., and Shipley, M.J. (1996). Do socioeconomic differences in mortality persist after retirement? 25 year follow up of civil servants from the first Whitehall study. *British Medical Journal, 313*(7066), 1177-1180.

Marmot, M.G., Smith, G.D., Stansfeld, S., Patel, C., North, F., Head, J., White, I., Brunner, E., and Feeney, A. (1991). Health inequalities among British civil servants: The Whitehall II study. *Lancet, 337*(8754), 1387-1393.

Marmot, M.G., Bosma, H., Hemingway, H., Brunner, E., and Stansfeld, S. (1997). Contribution of job control and other risk factors to social variations in coronary heart disease incidence. *Lancet, 350*(9073), 235-239.

Marmot M.G., Fuhrer R., Ettner S.L., Marks N., Bumpass L.L., and Ryff C.D. (1998). Contribution of psychosocial factors to socio-economic differences in health. *Millbank Memorial Fund Quarterly, 76,* 403-448.

Marshall, N.L. (1997). Combining work and family. In S. Gallant, G.P. Keita, and R. Royak-Schaler (eds.), *Health Care for Women: Psychosocial, Social and Behavioral Influences* (pp. 163-174). Washington, DC: APA Books.

Marshall, N.L. (2001). Health and illness issues facing an aging workforce in the new millennium. *Sociological Spectrum, 21*(3), 431-439.

Marshall, V., and Clarke, P.J. (1998). *Facilitating the transition from employment to retirement*. (Report No. 171-207). Ste Foy, Quebec: Editions MutiModes.

Massey, D.S., and Denton, N.A. (1993). *American apartheid: Segregation and the making of the underclass*. Cambridge, MA: Harvard University Press.

McDonough, P., Duncan, G.J., Williams D., and House, J. (1997). Income dynamics and adult mortality in the United States, 1972 through 1989. *American Journal of Public Health, 87,* 1476-1483.

McGuire, G.M., and Reskin, B.F. (1993). Authority hierarchies at work: The impacts of race and sex. *Gender and Society, 7*(4), 487-506.

Mein, G., Martikainen, P., Stansfeld, S.A., Brunner, E.J., Fuhrer, R., and Marmot, M.G. (2000). Predictors of early retirement in British civil servants. *Age and Ageing, 29*(6), 529-536.

Messing, K. (2000). Ergonomic studies provide information about occupational exposure differences between women and men. *Journal of the American Medical Womens Association, 55*(2), 72-75.

Messing, K., Lippel, K., Demers, D., and Mergler, D. (2000). Equality and difference in the workplace: Physical job demands, occupational illnesses, and sex differences. *National Women's Studies Association Journal, 12*(3), 21-49.

Minkler, M. and Estes, C. (1999). *Critical Gerontolgy: Perspectives from Political and Moral Economy*. Amityville, NY: Baywood Publishing Co.

Moen, P. (1996). A life course perspective on retirement, gender, and well-being. *Journal of Occupational Health Psychology, 1*(2), 131-144.

Moen, P. (2001). The Career Quandary. *Population Reference Bureau Reports on America*. Washington, DC: Population Reference Bureau.

Moen, P., Dempster-McClain, D., and Williams, R.M. (1989). Social integration and longevity: An event history analysis of women's roles and resilience. *American Sociological Review*, 54(4), 635-647.

Moen, P., Dempster-McClain, D., and Williams, R.M. (1992). Successful aging: A life-course perspective on women's multiple roles and health. *American Journal of Sociology*, 97(6), 1612-1638.

Moen, P., Robison, J., and Dempster-McClain, D. (1995). Caregiving and women's well-being: A life course approach. *Journal of Health & Social Behavior*, 36(3), 259-273.

Molina, C.W., and Aguirre-Molina, M. (1994). *Latino Health in the US: A Growing Challenge*. Washington, DC: American Public Health Association.

Montgomery, S.M., Cook, D.G., Bartley, M.J., and Wadsworth, M.E. (1999). Unemployment pre-dates symptoms of depression and anxiety resulting in medical consultation in young men. *International Journal of Epidemiology*, 28(1), 95-100.

Moss, N. (2000). Socioeconomic inequalities in women's health. In M.B. Goldman and M.C. Hatch (eds.), *Women and Health* (pp. 541-552). San Diego, CA: Academic Press.

National Center for Health Statistics. (1986). National Mortality Followback Survey. Hyattsville, MD: Centers for Disease Control and Prevention.

National Center for Health Statistics. (1998). Health, United States, 1998, with Socioeconomic Status and Health Chartbook. Hyattsville, MD: NCHS/CDC.

National Health Interview Survey. (1986). Multiple cause of death, dates of death, 1986-1991(ICPSR 6475). U.S. Department of Health and Human Services, National Center for Health Statistics.

National Research Council. (1999). *The Changing Nature of Work: Implications for Occupational Analysis*. Committee on Techniques for the Enhancement of Human Performance, Commission on Behavioral and Social Sciences and Education, National Research Council. Washington, DC: National Academy Press.

Needleman, C. (1997). Applied epidemiology and environmental health: Emerging controversies. *American Journal of Infection Control and Applied Epidemiology*, 25(3), 262-274.

Newman K.S., and Attewell P. (1999). The downsizing epidemic in the United States: Towards a cultural analysis of economic dislocation. In J.E. Ferrie, M.G. Marmot, J. Griffiths, E. Ziglio, (eds.), *Labour Market Changes and Job Insecurity: A Challenge for Social Welfare and Health Promotion* (pp. 101-125). Denmark: WHO Regional Publications.

North, F.M., Syme, S.L., Feeney, A., Shipley, M., and Marmot, M. (1996). Psychosocial work environment and sickness absence among British civil servants: The Whitehall II study. *American Journal of Public Health*, 86(3), 332-340.

Pappas, G., Queen, S., Hadden, W., and Fisher, G. (1993). The increasing disparity in mortality between socioeconomic groups in the United States, 1960 and 1986. *New England Journal of Medicine*, 329(2):103-109.

Parsons, D.O. (1995). Review of: Profit sharing: Does it make a difference? The productivity and stability effects of employee profit-sharing plans. *Journal of Economic Literature*, 33(3), 1373-1374.

Pienta, A., Burr, J.A., and Mutchler, J.E. (1994). Women's labor force participation in later life: The effects of early work and family experience. *Journal of Gerontology: Social Sciences*, 49, S231-S239.

Polednak, A.P. (1989). *Racial and Ethnic Differences in Disease*. New York: Oxford University Press.

Pugliesi, K. (1995). Work and well-being: Gender differences in the psychological consequences of employment. *Journal of Health and Social Behavior*, 36(1), 57-71.

Punnett L., and Herbert R. (1999).Work-related Musculoskeletal Disorders: Is there a Gender Differential, and if so, what does it mean? In M.B. Goldman and M. Hatch (eds.), *Women and Health* (pp. 474-492). San Diego, CA: Academic Press.

Richardson, V.E. (1999). Women and retirement. *Journal of Women & Aging, 11*(2-3), 49-66.

Robinson, J.C. (1984). Racial inequality and the probability of occupation-related injury or illness. *Milbank Memorial Fund Quarterly, 62*, 567-590.

Robinson, J.C. (1989). Trends in racial inequality and exposure to work-related hazards, 1968-86. *American Association Occupational Health Nurses Journal, 37*, 56-63.

Ross, C.E., and Mirowsky, J. (1992). Households, employment, and the sense of control. *Social Psychology Quarterly, 55*(3), 217-235.

Santiago, A.M. and Muschkin, C.G. (1996). Disentangling the effects of disability status and gender on the labor supply of Anglo, black, and Latino older workers. *Gerontologist, 36*, 299-310.

Schulz, R., Visintainer, P., and Williamson, G.M. (1990). Psychiatric and physical morbidity effects of caregiving. *Journal of Gerontology. 45*(5), P181-P191.

Schwartz, S. (1994). The fallacy of the ecological fallacy: The potential misuse of a concept and the consequences. *American Journal Public Health, 84*, 819-824.

Seifert, A.M., Messing, K., and Dumais, L. (1997). Star wars and strategic defense initiatives: Work activity and health symptoms of unionized bank tellers during work reorganization. *International Journal of Health Services, 27*(3), 455-477.

Sidel, R. (1996). Workfare or fair work: Women, welfare, and government work programs. *Journal of American History, 83*(2), 665-666.

Siegel, J. (1996). *Aging into the 21st Century.* Washington, DC: Administration on Aging.

Singh, G.K., and Siahpush, M. (2002). Increasing inequalities in all-cause and cardiovascular mortality among US adults aged 25-64 years by area socioeconomic status, 1969-1998. *International Journal of Epidemiology, 31*(3), 600-613.

Social Security Administration (SSA). (2000, March). *Income of the Population 55 or Older, 1998.* Social Security Administration Office of Policy, Office of Research, Evaulation, and Statisitics. Washington, DC: U.S. Government Printing Office.

Stansfeld, S.A., Fuhrer, R., Shipley, M.J., and Marmot, M.G. (1999). Work characteristics predict psychiatric disorder: prospective results from the Whitehall II Study. *Occupational and Environmental Medicine, 56*(5), 302-307.

Starrels, M.E. (1994). Husbands' involvement in female gender-typed household chores. *Sex Roles, 31*(7-8), 473-491.

Starrels, M.E., Ingersoll-Dayton, B., Dowler, D.W., and Neal, M.B. (1997). The stress of caring for a parent: Effects of the elder's impairment on an employed, adult child. *Journal of Marriage & the Family, 59*(4), 860-872.

Steenland, K., Henley, J., and Thun, M. (2002). All-cause and cause-specific death rates by educational status for two million people in two American Cancer Society cohorts, 1959-1996. *American Journal of Epidemiology, 156*(1), 11-21.

Stone, R.I., and Short, P.F. (1990). The competing demands of employment and informal caregiving to disabled elders. *Medical Care, 28*(6), 513-526.

Stuck, A.E., Aronow, H.U., Steiner, A., Alessi, C.A., Bula, C.J., Gold, M.N., Yuhas, K.E., Nisenbaum, R., Rubenstein, L.Z., and Beck, J.C. (1995). A trial of annual in-home comprehensive geriatric assessments for elderly people living in the community. *New England Journal of Medicine, 333*(18), 1184-1189.

Thoits, P.A. (1995). Stress, coping, and social support processes: Where are we? What next? *Journal of Health & Social Behavior.* Extra Issue, 53-79.

Turner, R.J., and Marino, F. (1994). Social support and social structure: A descriptive epidemiology. *Journal of Health & Social Behavior, 35*(3), 193-212.

Umberson, D., Wortman, C.B., and Kessler, R.C. (1992). Widowhood and depression: Explaining long-term gender differences in vulnerability. *Journal of Health and Social Behavior, 33*(1), 10-24.

Umberson, D., Chen, M.D., House, J.S., and Hopkins, K. (1996). The effect of social relationships on psychological well-being: Are men and women really so different? *American Sociological Review, 61*(5), 837-857.

U.S. Bureau of the Census. (1991). Poverty in the United States: 1990. Washington, DC: U.S. Government Printing Office.

U.S. Bureau of the Census. (1996). *65+ in the United States. Current Population Reports, Special Studies, P-23-190.* Washington, DC: U.S. Government Printing Office.

U.S. Bureau of the Census. (1999). *Current Population Reports, Series P60-207, Poverty in the United States: 1998.* Washington, DC: U.S. Government Printing Office.

U.S. Bureau of the Census. (2000). *Projection of the total resident population by 5-year age groups, and sex with special age categories: Middle Series.* Washington, DC: U.S. Government Printing Office.

U.S. Bureau of the Census. (2001). *Current Population Survey.* Washington, DC: U.S. Government Printing Office.

U.S. Department of Labor. (2001). Occupational Employment and Wages, 2000. Washington, DC: U.S. Department of Labor: No. 01-415.

U.S. General Accounting Office. (2001). *Older Workers: Demographic trends pose challenges for employers and workers.* (Report No. GAO-02-85). Washington, DC: U.S. General Accounting Office.

van Rossum, C.T., Shipley, M.J., van de Mheen, H., Grobbee, D.E., and Marmot, M.G. (2000). Employment grade differences in cause specific mortality. A 25 year follow up of civil servants from the first Whitehall study. *Journal of Epidemiology & Community Health, 54*(3), 178-184.

Vega, W.A., and Amaro, H. (1994). Latino outlook: Good health, uncertain prognosis. *Annual Review of Public Health, 15,* 39-67.

Walker, A.J., Pratt, C.C., and Eddy, L. (1995). Informal caregiving to aging family members: A critical review. *Family Relations: Journal of Applied Family & Child Studies, 44*(4), 402-411.

Walsh, D.C., Sorensen, G., and Leonard, L. (1995). Gender, health, and cigarette smoking. In B.C.I. Amick, S. Levine, A.R. Tarlov, and D.C. Walsh (eds.), *Society and health* (pp. 131-171). New York: Oxford University Press.

Walstedt, J. (2000). Employment patterns and health among U.S. working women. In M.B. Goldman and M.C. Hatch (eds.), *Women and health* (pp. 447-454). San Diego, CA: Academic Press.

Wilkinson, R.G. (1986). *Class and Health: Research and Longitudinal Data.* London: Tavistock.

Williams, D.R., and Collins, C. (1995). U.S. Socioeconomic and racial differences in health. *Annual Review of Sociology, 21,* 349-386.

Williams, D.R., and Wilson, C.M. (2001). Race, ethnicity, and ageing. In *Handbook of ageing and the social sciences.*

Wright, P., Ferris, S.P., Hiller, J.S., and Kroll, M. (1995). Competitiveness through management of diversity: Effects on stock price valuation. *Academy of Management Journal, 38,* 272-287.

Zahm, S.H. (2000). Women at work. In M.B. Goldman and M.C. Hatch (eds.), *Women and health* (pp. 441-445). San Diego, CA: Academic Press.

CHAPTER 5

Adler N.E., and Newman K. (2002). Socioeconomic disparities in health: Pathways and policies. Inequality in education, income, and occupation exacerbates the gaps between the health "haves" and "have-nots." *Health Affairs, 21*(2), 60-76

Arking, R. (1998). *Biology of aging: Observations and principles.* Sunderland, MA: Sinauer Associates.

Atchley, R.C. (1974). The meaning of retirement. *Journal of Communication, 24*(4), 97-100.

Avolio, B.J., Waldman, D.A., and McDaniel, M.A. (1990). Age and work performance in nonmanagerial jobs: The effects of experience and occupational type. *Academy of Management Journal, 33*, 407-422.

Babb, T.G., and Rodarte, J.R. (2000). Mechanism of reduced maximal expiratory flow with aging. *Journal of Applied Physiology, 89*(2), 505-511.

Baltes, P.B. (1997). On the incomplete architecture of human ontogeny. Selection, optimization, and compensation as foundation of developmental theory. *American Psychologist, 52*(4), 366-380.

Bazylewicz-Walczak, B., Majczakowa, W., and Szymczak, M. (1999) Behavioral effects of occupational exposure to organophosphorous pesticides in female greenhouse planting workers. *Neurotoxicity, 20*, 819-826.

Becker, J.T., and Milke, R.M. (1998). Cognition and aging in a complex work environment: Relationships with performance among air traffic control specialists. *Aviation, Space, and Environmental Medicine, 69*, 944-951.

Bosman, E.A. (1993). Age-related differences in the motoric aspects of transcription typing skill. *Psychology & Aging, 8*(1), 87-102.

Bosman, E.A. (1994). Age and skill differences in typing related and unrelated reaction time tasks. *Aging Neuropsychology & Cognition, 1*(4), 310-322.

Bosman, E.A., and Charness, N. (1996). Age differences in skilled performance and skill acquisition. In T. Hess and F. Blanchard-Fields (eds.), *Perspectives on cognitive change in adulthood and aging* (pp. 428-453). New York: McGraw-Hill.

Brody, J.A., and Grant, M.D. (2001). Age-associated diseases and conditions: Implications for decreasing late life morbidity. *Aging, 13*, 64-67.

Brouwer, W.H., and Withaar, F.K. (1997). Fitness to drive after traumatic brain injury. *Neuropsychological Rehabilitation, 7*, 177-193.

Bryant, S.R., and Zarb, G.A (2002). Oucomes of implant prosthodontic treatment in older adults. *Journal Canadian Dental Association, 68*, 97-102.

Cattell, R.B. (1972). *Abilities: Their Structure, Growth and Action.* Boston: Houghton-Mifflin.

Charness, N. (1981a). Aging and skilled problem solving. *Journal of Experimental Psychology: General, 110*, 21-38.

Charness, N. (1981b). Search in chess: Age and skill differences. *Journal of Experimental Psychology: Human Perception and Performance, 7*, 467-476.

Charness, N. (1983). Age, skill, and bridge bidding: A chronometric analysis. *Journal of Verbal Learning and Verbal Behavior, 22*, 406-416.

Charness, N. (1987). Component processes in bridge bidding and novel problem-solving tasks. *Canadian Journal of Psychology, 41*, 223-243.

Charness, N., Krampe, R., and Mayr, U. (1996). The role of practice and coaching in entrepreneurial skill domains: An international comparison of life-span chess skill acquisition. In K.A. Ericsson (ed.), *The road to excellence: The acquisition of expert performance in the Arts and Sciences, Sports and Games* (pp. 51-80). Mahwah, NJ: Erlbaum.

Christensen, H., Jorm, A.F., Mackinnon, A.J., Korten, A.E., Jacomb, P.A., Henderson, A.S., and Rodgers, B. (1999). Age differences in depression and anxiety symptoms: A structural equation modeling analysis of data from a general population sample. *Psychological Medicine, 29*, 325-329.

Compston, J.E. (2002). Bone marrow and bone: A functional unit. *Journal of Endocrinology*, *173*, 387-394.

de Zwart, B.C., Frings-Dresen, M.H., and van Dijk, F.J. (1995) Physical workload and the aging worker: A review of the literature. *International Archives of Occupational and Environmental Health*, *68*(1), 1-12.

Dobie, R.A. (1996). Compensation for hearing loss. *Audiology*, *35*, 1-7.

Doherty, T.J. (2001). The influence of aging and sex on skeletal muscle mass and strength. *Current Opinion in Clinical Nutrition and Metabolic Care*, *4*, 503-508.

Druss, B.G., Rosenheck, R.A., and Sledge, W.H. (2000). Health and disability costs of depressive illness in a major U.S. corporation. *American Journal of Psychiatry*, *157*(8), 1274-1278.

Edwards, A.B., Zarit, S.H., Stephens, M.A., and Townsend A. (2002). Employed family caregivers of cognitively impaired elderly: An examination of role strain and depressive symptoms. *Aging and Mental Health*, *6*, 55-61.

Eke, B.C., Vural, N., and Iscan, M. (1997). Age dependent differential effects of cigarette smoking on hepatic and pulmonary xenobiotic enzymes in rats. *Archives of Toxicology*, *71*, 696-702.

Elias, P.M., and Ghadially, R. (2002). The age epidermis permeability barrier: Basis for functional abnormalities. *Clinics in Geriatric Medicine*, *18*, 103-120.

Elo, A.E. (1965). Age changes in master chess performances. *Journal of Gerontology*, *20*, 289-299.

Enoch, J.M., Werner, J.S., Haegerstron-Portnoy, G., Lakshminarayanan, V., and Rynders, M. (1999). Forever young: Visual functions not affected or minimally affected by aging: A review. *Journal of Gerontology Series A-Biological Sciences and Medical Sciences*, *54*, B336-B351.

Ericsson, K.A., and Charness, N. (1994). Expert Performance: Its structure and acquisition. *American Psychologist*, *49*, 725-747.

Estryn-Behar, M., Kaminski, M., Peigne, E., Maillard, M.F., Pelletier, A., Berthier, C., Delaporte, M.F., Paoli, M.C., and Leroux, J.M. (1990). Strenuous working conditions and musculo-skeletal disorders among female hospital workers. *International Archives of Occupational and Environmental Health*, *62*(1), 47-57.

Ferrucci, L., Guralnik, J.M., Simonsick, E., Salive, M.E., Corti, C., and Langlois, J. (1996). Progressive versus catastrophic disability: A longitudinal view of the disablement process. *Journals of Gerontology Series A-Biological Sciences and Medical Sciences*, *51*(3), M123-M130.

Feskanich, D., Hastrup, J.L., Marshall, J.R., Colditz, G.A., Stampfer, M.J., Willett, W.C., and Kawachi, I. (2002). Stress and suicide in the Nurses' Health Study. *Journal of Epidemiology and Community Health*, *56*(2), 95-98.

Fielding, R.A., and Meydani, M. (1997) Exercise, free radical generation, and aging. *Aging*, *9*(1-2), 12-18.

Florez-Duquet, M., and McDonald, R.B. (1998). Cold-induced thermoregulation and biological aging. *Physiological Reviews*, *78*(2), 339-358.

Foley, D.J., Monjan, A.A., Masaki, K.H., Enright, P.L., Quan, S.F., and White, L.R. (1999). Associations of symptoms of sleep apnea with cardiovascular disease, cognitive impairment, and mortality among older Japanese-American men. *Journal of the American Geriatrics Society*, *47*(5), 524-528.

Franssen, F.M., Wouters, E.F., and Schols, A.M. (2002). The contribution of starvation, deconditioning and ageing to observed alterations in skeletal muscle in chronic organ diseases. *Clinical Nutrition*, *21*, 1-14.

Freedman, V.A., Aykan, H., and Martin, L.G. (2001). Aggregate changes in severe cognitive impairment among older Americans: 1993 and 1998. *Journals of Gerontology Series B-Psychological Sciences and Social Sciences, 56*(2), S100-S111.

Gijsen, R., Hoeymans, N., Schellevis, F.G., Ruwaard, D., Satariano, W.A., and van den Bos, G.A. (2001). Causes and consequences of comorbidity: A review. *Journal of Clinical Epidemiology, 54*(7), 661-674.

Ginaldi, L., Loreto, M.F., Corsi, M.P., Modesti, M., and DeMartinis M. (2001). Immuno-senescence and infectious disease. *Microbes and Infection, 3*, 851-857.

Goetzel, R.Z., Ozminkowski, R.J., Sederer, L.I., and Mark, T.L. (2002). The business case for quality mental health services: Why employers should care about the mental health and well-being of their employees. *Journal of Occupational and Environmental Medicine, 4*, 320-330.

Goldberg, R.J., and Steury, S. (2001). Depression in the workplace: Costs and barriers to treatment. *Psychiatric Services, 52*(12), 1639-1643.

Gomberg, E.S. (1995). Older women and alcohol. Use and abuse. *Recent Developments in Alcoholism, 12*, 61-79.

Griffiths, A. (2000). Designing and managing healthy work for older workers. *Occupational Medicine, 50*(7), 473-477.

Hambrick, D.Z., Salthouse, T.A., and Meinz, E.J. (1999). Predictors of crossword puzzle proficiency and moderators of age-cognition relations. *Journal of Experimental Psychology: General, 128*, 131-164.

Holowatz, L.A., Houghton, B.L., Wong, B.J., Wilkins, B.W., Harding, A.W., Kenney, W.L., and Minson, C.T. (2003). Nitric oxide and attenuated reflex cutaneous vasodilation in aged skin. *American Journal of Physiology—Heart and Circulatory Physiology, 284*(5), 662-667.

Horner, K.L., Rushton, J.P., and Vernon, P.A. (1986). Relation between aging and research productivity of academic psychologists. *Psychology and Aging, 4*, 319-324.

Hotopf, M., and Wessely, S. (1997). Stress in the workplace: Unfinished business. *Journal of Psychosomatic Research, 43*(1), 1-6.

Hunt, E.B. (1995). *Will we be smart enough? A cognitive analysis of the coming workforce.* New York: Russell Sage Foundation.

Irwin, J. (2000). What are the causes, prevention and treatment of hearing loss in the ageing worker? *Occupational Medicine, 50*, 492-495.

Jansen, P.L. (2002). Liver disease in the elderly. *Best Practice and Research in Clinical Gastroenterology, 16*, 149-158.

Janssens, J.P., Pache, J.P., and Nicod, L.P. (1999). Physiological changes in respiratory function with ageing. *European Respiratory Journal, 13*, 197-205.

Jenkins, G. (2002). Molecular mechanisms of skin aging. *Mechanisms of Ageing and Development, 123*, 801-810.

Jorm, A.F. (2000). Does old age reduce the risk of anxiety and depression? A review of epidemiological studies across the adult life span. *Psychological Medicine, 30*, 11-22.

Kenney, W.L. (1997). Thermoregulation at rest and during exercise in healthy older adults. *Exercise and Sport Sciences Reviews, 25*, 41-76.

Keogh, J.P., Nuwayhid, I., Gordon, J.L., and Gucer, P.W. (2000). The impact of occupational injury on injured worker and family: Outcomes of upper extremity cumulative trauma disorders in Maryland workers. *American Journal of Industrial Medicine, 38*, 498-506.

Khalil, Z., and Merhi, M. (2000). Effects of aging on neurogenic vasodilator responses evoked by transcutaneous electrical nerve stimulation: Relevance to wound healing. *Journals of Gerontology Series A-Biological Sciences and Medical Sciences, 55*(6), B257-B263.

Kiecolt-Glaser, J.K., McGuire, L., Robles, T.F., and Glaser, R. (2002) Psychoneuroimmunology and psychosomatic medicine: Back to the future. *Psychosomatic Medicine, 64*(1), 15-28.

Klotz, U. (1998). Effect of age on pharmacokinetics and pharmacodynamics in man. *International Journal of Clinical Pharmacology and Therapeutics, 36,* 581-585.

Krampe, R.T., and Ericsson, K.A. (1996). Maintaining excellence: Deliberate practice and elite performance in young and older pianists. *Journal of Experimental Psychology, 125,* 331-359.

Kubeck, J.E., Delp, N.D., Haslett, T.K., and McDaniel, M.A. (1996). Does job-related training performance decline with age? *Psychology and Aging, 11,* 92-107.

Larrsson, L., Yu, F., Hook, P., Ramamurthy, B., Marx, J.O., and Pircher, P. (2001). Effects of aging on regulation of muscle contraction at the motor unit, muscle cell, and molecular levels. *International Journal of Sport Nutrition and Exercise Metabolism, 11*(Suppl), S28-S43.

Leubke, R.W., Copeland, C.V., and Andrews, D.L. (2000). Aging and resistance to Trichinella spiralis infection following xenobiotic exposure. *Annals of the New York Academy of Sciences, 919,* 221-230.

Liberto, J.G., and Oslin, D.W. (1995). Early versus late onset of alcoholism in the elderly. *International Journal of the Addictions, 30*(13-14), 1799-1818.

Louis, T.A., Robins, J., Dockery, D.W., Spiro, A., and Ware, J.H. (1986). Explaining discrepancies between longitudinal and cross-sectional models. *Journal of Chronic Disorders, 39*(10), 831-839.

Lusk, S.L. (1997). Health complaints of older workers. *American Association of Occupational Health Nurses (AOHN) Journal, 45*(9), 461-464.

Manocchia, M., Keller, S., and Ware, J.E. (2001). Sleep problems, health-related quality of life, work functioning and health care utilization among the chronically ill. *Quality of Life Research, 10*(4), 331-345.

Manton, K.G., Corder, L., and Stallard E. (1997). Chronic disability trends in elderly United States populations: 1982-1994. *Proceedings of the National Academy of Sciences of the United States of America, 94*(6), 2593-2598.

Masuo, K., Kumagai, K., Tanaka, T., Yamagata, K., Shimizu, K., Nishida, Y., and Iimori, T. (1998). "Physiological" age as an outcome predictor for abdominal surgery in elderly patients. *Surgery Today, 28*(10), 997-1000.

McArdle, A., Vasilaki, A., and Jackson, M. (2002). Exercise and skeletal muscle aging: Cellular and molecular mechanisms. *Ageing Research Reviews, 1,* 79-93.

McDaniel, M.A., Schmidt, F.L., and Hunter, J.E. (1988). Job experience correlates of job performance. *Journal of Applied Psychology, 73,* 327-330.

McEvoy, G.M., and Cascio, W.F. (1989). Cumulative evidence of the relationship between employee age and job performance. *Journal of Applied Psychology, 74,* 11-17.

Meinz, E.J. (2000). Experience-based attenuation of age-related differences in music cognition tasks. *Psychology and Aging, 15,* 297-312.

Meinz, E.J., and Salthouse, T.A. (1998). The effects of age and experience on memory for visually presented music. *Journal of Gerontology: Psychological Science, 53B,* P60-P69.

Meyer, K.C. (2001). The role of immunity in susceptibility to respiratory infection in the aging lung. *Respiration Physiology, 128,* 23-31.

Mittendorfer, B., and Klein, S. (2001). Effect of aging on glucose and lipid metabolism during endurance exercise. *International Journal of Sport Nutrition and Exercise Metabolism.* (Suppl), S86-S91.

Morrow, D. (in press). Technology as environmental support for older adults' daily activities. In K.W. Schaie and N. Charness (eds.), *The Impact of technological change on successful aging.* New York: Springer.

Morrow, D., Yesavage, J., Leirer, V., and Tinklenberg, J. (1993). Influence of aging and practice on piloting task. *Experimental Aging Research, 19,* 53-70.

Morrow, D., Leirer, V., Altieri, P., and Fitzsimmons, C. (1994). When expertise reduces age differences in performance. *Psychology and Aging, 9,* 134-148.

Morrow, D., Menard, W.E., Stine-Morrow, E.A.L., Teller, T., and Bryant, D. (2001). The influence of expertise and task factors on age differences in pilot communication. *Psychology and Aging, 16,* 31-46.

Mroczek, D.K., and Kolarz, C.M. (1998). The effect of age on positive and negative affect: A developmental perspective on happiness. *Journal of Personality and Social Psychology, 75,* 1333-1349.

Mullan, E., Katona, C., and Bellew, M. (1994). Patterns of sleep disorders and sedative hypnotic use in seniors. *Drugs and Aging, 5*(1), 49-58.

Murasko, D.M., Bernstein, E.D., Gardner, E.M., Gross, P., Munk, G., Dran, S., and Abrutyn, E. (2002). Role of humoral and cell-mediated immunity in protection from influenza disease after immunization of healthy elderly. *Experimental Gerontology, 37*(2-3), 427-439.

Ohayon, M., Caulet, M., and Lemoine, P. (1996). The elderly, sleep habits and use of psychotropic drugs by the French population. *Encephale, 22*(5), 337-350.

Palmer, K.T., Poole, J., Ayres, J.G., Mann, J., Burge, P.S. and Coggon D. (2003). Exposure to metal fume and infectious pneumonia. *American Journal of Epidemiology, 157*(3), 227-233.

Park, D.C., Lautenschlager, G., Hedden, T., Davidson, N.S., Smith, A.D., and Smith, P.K. (2002). Models of visuospatial and verbal memory across the adult life span. *Psychology and Aging, 17,* 299-320.

Peate, W.E. (2002). Occupational skin disease. *American Family Physician, 66*(6), 1025-1032.

Pedersen, W.A., Wan, R., and Mattson, M.P. (2001). Impact of aging on stress-responsive neuroendocrine systems. *Mechanisms of Ageing and Development, 122*(9), 963-983.

Petty, T.L. (1998). Can "old" lungs be restored? Strategies for preserving lung health and preventing and treating COPD. *Postgraduate Medicine, 104,* 173-178.

Pillitteri, J.L., Kozlowski, L.T., Person, D.C., and Spear, M.E. (1994). Over-the-counter sleep aids: Widely used but rarely studied. *Journal of Substance Abuse, 6*(3), 315-323.

Prince, M.M. (2002). Distribution of risk factors for hearing loss: Implications for evaluating risk of occupational noise-induced hearing loss. *Journal of the Acoustical Society of America, 112*(2), 557-567.

Regestein, Q.R., and Monk, T.H. (1991). Is the poor sleep of shift workers a disorder? *American Journal of Psychiatry, 148*(11), 1487-1493.

Reitzes, D.C., Mutran, E.J., and Fernandez, M.E. (1996). Preretirement influences on postretirement self-esteem. *Journals of Gerontology Series B-Psychological Sciences and Social Sciences, 51*(5), S242-S249.

Riggs, B.L. (2002). Endocrine causes of age-related bone loss and osteoporosis. *Novartis Research Symposium, 242,* 247-259.

Rigler, S.K. (1996). Instability in the older adult. *Comprehensive Therapy, 22*(5), 297-303.

Rigler, S.K. (2000). Alcoholism in the elderly. *American Family Physician, 61*(6), 1710-1716.

Roberts, S., and Fallon, L.F., Jr. (2001). Administrative issues related to addiction in the workplace. *Occupational Medicine, 16*(3), 509-515.

Ruchlin, H.S. (1997). Prevalence and correlates of alcohol use among older adults. *Preventive Medicine, 26*(5 Pt 1), 651-657.

Ryff, C.D., Kwan, C.M.L., and Singer, B.H. (2001). Personality and aging: Flourishing agendas and future challenges. In J.E. Birren and K.W. Schaie (eds.), *Handbook of the Psychology of Aging* (5th ed., pp. 477-499). San Diego: Academic Press.

Salthouse, T.A. (1984). Effects of age and skill in typing. *Journal of Experimental Psychology: General, 13,* 345-371.

Salthouse, T.A. (1990). Cognitive competence and expertise in aging. In J.E. Birren and K.W. Schaie (eds.), *Handbook of the psychology of aging* (3rd ed., pp. 310-319). San Diego: Academic Press.

Salthouse, T.A. (1991). Age and experience effects on the interpretation of orthographic drawings of three-dimensional objects. *Psychology and Aging, 6,* 426-433.

Salthouse, T.A. (2001). Structural models of the relations between age and measures of cognitive functioning. *Intelligence, 29,* 93-115.

Salthouse, T.A., and Maurer, T.J. (1996). Aging, job performance, and career development. In J.E. Birren, K.W. Schaie, R.P. Abeles, M. Gatz, and T.A. Salthouse (eds.), *Handbook of the psychology of aging* (4th ed., pp. 353-364). New York: Kluwer Academic Publishers.

Salthouse, T.A., Berish, D.E., and Miles, J.D. (2002). The role of cognitive stimulation on the relations between age and cognitive functioning. *Psychology and Aging 17*(4), 548-557.

Schmidt, F.L., and Hunter, J.E. (1998). The validity and utility of selection methods in personnel psychology: Practical and theoretical implications of 85 years of research findings. *Psychological Bulletin, 124,* 262-274.

Schober-Flores, C. (2001). The sun's damaging effects. *Dermatology Nursing, 13,* 279-286.

Schoeni, R.F., Freedman, V.A., and Wallace, R.B. (2001). Persistent, consistent, widespread, and robust? Another look at recent trends in old-age disability. *Journals of Gerontology Series B-Psychological Sciences and Social Sciences, 56*(4), S206-S218.

Schooler, C., Mulatu, M.S., Oates, G. (1999). The continuing effects of substantively complex work on the intellectual functioning of older workers. *Psychology and Aging, 14,* 483-506.

Schwartz, B.S., Stewart, W.F., Bolla, K.I., Simon, D., Bandeen-Roche, K., Gordon, B., Links, J.M., and Todd, A.C. (2000). Past adult lead exposure is associated with longitudinal decline in cognitive function. *Neurology, 55,* 1144-1150.

Seeman, E. (2002). Pathogenesis of bone fragility in men and women. *Lancet, 359,* 1841-1850.

Seidman, M.D., Ahmad, N., and Bai, U. (2002). Molecular mechanisms of age-related hearing loss. *Ageing Research Reviews, 1,* 331-343.

Sharpe, M., Chalder, T., Palmer, I., and Wessely, S. (1997). Chronic fatigue syndrome. A practical guide to assessment and management. *General Hospital Psychiatry, 19*(3), 185-199.

Shigemi, J., Mino, Y., Ohtsu, T., and Tsuda, T. (2000). Effects of perceived job stress on mental health. A longitudinal survey in a Japanese electronics company. *European Journal of Epidemiology, 16*(4), 371-376.

Simonton, D.K. (1988). Age and outstanding achievement: What do we know after a century of research? *Psychological Bulletin, 104,* 251-267.

Simonton, D.K. (1997). Creative productivity: A predictive and explanatory model of career trajectories and landmarks. *Psychological Review, 104,* 66-89.

Smolander, J. (2002). Effect of cold exposure on older humans. *International Journal of Sports Medicine, 23*(2), 86-92.

Sowers, M.F. (2001). Epidemiology of risk factors for osteoarthritis: systemic factors. *Current Opinion in Rheumatology, 13,* 447-451.

Stoohs, R.A., Bingham, L.A., Itoi, A., Guilleminault, C., and Dement, W.C. (1995). Sleep and sleep-disordered breathing in commercial long-haul truck drivers. *Chest, 107*(5), 1275-1282.

Sukhodub, A.L., and Padalko, V.I. (1999). Age-dependent changes in rat liver microsomal membrane structure and functions under benzene treatment. *Mechanisms of Ageing and Development*, *106*, 273-282.

Sutherland, V.J., and Cooper, C.L. (1992). Job stress, satisfaction, and mental health among general practitioners before and after introduction of new contract. *British Medical Journal*, *304*(6841), 1545-1548.

Sward, K. (1945). Age and mental ability in superior men. *American Journal of Psychology*, *58*, 443-479.

Taylor, J.L., O'Hara, R., Mumenthaler, M.S., and Yesavage, J.A. (2000). Relationship of CogScreen-AE to Flight Simulator Performance and Pilot Age. *Aviation, Space, and Environmental Medicine*, *71*, 373-380.

Tennant, C. (2001). Work-related stress and depressive disorders. *Journal of Psychosomatic Research*, *51*(5), 697-704.

Thomas, D.R. (2001). Age-related changes in wound healing. *Drugs and Aging*, *18*, 607-620.

van Wijngaarden, E., Savitz, D.A., Kleckner, R.C., Cai, J., and Loomis, D. (2000). Exposure to electromagnetic fields and suicide among electric utility workers: A nested case-control study. *Western Journal of Medicine*, *173*, 94-100.

Waldman, D.A., and Avolio, B.J. (1986). A meta-analysis of age differences in job performance. *Journal of Applied Psychology*, *71*, 33-38.

Warr, P.B. (1992). Age and occupational well-being. *Psychology and Aging*, *7*, 37-45.

Warr, P.B. (1994). Age and employment. In H.C. Triandis, M.D. Dunnette, and L.M. Hough (eds.), *Handbook of Industrial and Organizational Psychology* (Vol. 4., pp. 485-550). Palo Alto, CA: Consulting Psychologists Press.

Wechsler, D. (1997a). Wechsler Adult Intelligence Scale—Third Edition. San Antonio, TX: The Psychological Corporation.

Wechsler, D. (1997b). Wechsler Memory Scale—Third Edition. San Antonio, TX: The Psychological Corporation.

Wei, Y.H., and Lee, H.C. (2002). Oxidative stress, mitochondrial DNA mutation, an impairment of antioxidant enzymes in aging. *Experimental Biology and Medicine*, *227*, 671-682.

Welford, A.T. (1958). *Ageing and Human Skill*. London: Greenwood Publishing Group.

West, S., and Sommer, A. (2001). Prevention of blindness and priorities for the future. *Bulletin of the World Health Organization*, *79*(3), 244-248.

Whetstone, L.M., Fozard, J.L., Metter, E.J., Hiscock, B.S., Burke, R., Gittings, N., and Fried, L.P. (2001). The physical functioning inventory: A procedure for assessing physical function in adults. *Journal of Aging and Health*, *13*(4), 467-493.

Williams, D., and Woodhouse, K. (1996). Age-related changes in O-deethylase and aldrin epoxidase activity in mouse skin and liver microsomes. *Age and ageing*, *25*, 377-380.

Wilson, R.S., Mendes de Leon, C.F., Barnes, L.L., Schneider, J.A., Bienias, J.L., Evans, D.A., and Bennett, D.A. (2002). Participation in cognitively stimulating activities and risk of incident Alzheimer Disease. *Journal of the American Medical Association*, *287*(6), 742-748.

Withaar, F.K., Brouwer, W.H., and van Zomeren, A.H. (2000). Fitness to drive in older drivers with cognitive impairment. *Journal of the International Neuropsychological Society*, *6*, 409-490.

Woodcock, R.W., McGrew, K.S., and Mather, N. (2001). *Woodcock-Johnson III*. Itasca, IL: Riverside Publishing.

Zwerling, C., Whitten, P.S., Davis, C.S., and Sprince, N.L. (1998). Occupational injuries among older workers with visual, auditory, and other impairments. A validation study. *Journal of Occupational and Environmental Medicine*, *40*(8), 720-723.

CHAPTER 6

Agnew, J., and Suruda, A.J. (1993). Age and fatal work-related falls. *Human Factors*, 35(4), 731-736.

Ahlberg-Hulten, G.K., Theorell, T., and Sigala, F. (1995). Social support, job strain and musculoskeletal pain among female health care personnel. *Scandinavian Journal of Work, Environment and Health*, 21(6), 435-439.

Aiken, L.H., and Fagin, C.M. (1997). Evaluating the consequences of hospital restructuring. *Medical Care*, 35(10 Suppl), OS1-OS4.

Alfredsson, L., Karasek, R., and Theorell, T. (1982). Myocardial infarction risk and psychosocial work environment: An analysis of the male Swedish working force. *Social Science and Medicine*, 16(4), 463-467.

Alfredsson, L., Spetz, C.L., and Theorell, T. (1985). Type of occupation and near-future hospitalization for myocardial infarction and some other diagnoses. *International Journal of Epidemiology*, 14(3), 378-388.

American Heart Association. (1998). *1999 Heart and Stroke Statistical Update*. Dallas, TX: American Heart Association.

American Nurses Association. (1995). *The report of survey results: The 1994 ANA layoffs Survey*. Washington, DC: ANA.

Anan, K.A. (1997). Occupational health and safety: A high priority on the global, international and national agenda. *Asian-Pacific Newsletter on Occupational Health and Safety, 4*, 59.

Avolio, B.J., and Waldman, D.A. (1987). Personnel aptitude test scores as a function of age, education and job type. *Experimental Aging Research*, 13(1-2), 109-113.

Azaroff, L., and Levenstein, C. (2002). *Innovations in monitoring work security: A case study of Southeast Asian Refugees in Lowell, Massachusetts*. Geneva: International Labor Organization.

Bailer J.A., Bena, J.F., Stayner, L.T., Halperin, W.E., and Park, R.M. (2003). External cause-specific summaries of occupational fatal injuries. Part I: An analysis of rates. *American Journal of Industrial Medicine*, 43(3), 237-250.

Beilin, L.J., and Puddey, I.B. (1993). Alcohol, hypertension and cardiovascular disease—implications for management. *Clinical and Experimental Hypertension*, 15(6), 1157-1170.

Belkic, K., Savic, C., Djordjevic, M., Ugljesic, M., and Mickovic, L. (1992). Event-related potentials in professional city drivers: Heightened sensitivity to cognitively relevant visual signals. *Physiology & Behavior*, 52(3), 423-427.

Belkic, K., Emdad, R., and Theorell, T. (1998). Occupational profile and cardiac risk: Possible mechanisms and implications for professional drivers. *International Journal of Occupational Medicine and Environmental Health*, 11(1), 37-57.

Belkic, K., Landsbergis, P.A., Schnall, P., Baker, D., Theorell, T., Seigrist, J., Peter, R., and Darasek, R. (2000). Psychlsocial factors: Review of the empirical data among men. In P. Schnall, K. Belkic, P.A. Landsbergis, and D.E. Baker (eds.), *The workplace and cardiovasuclar disease. Occupational Medicine: State of the Art Reviews* (Vol. 15, pp. 24-46). Philadelphia, PA: Hanley and Belfus.

Belkic, K., Schnall, P., and Ugljesic, M. (2000). Cardiovascular evaluation of the worker and workplace: A practical guide for clinicians. *Occupational Medicine*, 15(1), 213-222.

Belkic, K.L., Schnall, P.L., Landsbergis, P.A., Schwartz, J.E., Gerber, L.M., Baker, D., and Pickering, T.G. (2001). Hypertension at the workplace—an occult disease? The need for work site surveillance. *Advances in Psychosomatic Medicine*, 22, 116-138.

Bergqvist, U., Wolgast, E., Nilsson, B., and Voss, M. (1995). Musculoskeletal disorders among visual display terminal workers: Individual, ergonomic, and work organizational factors. *Ergonomics*, 38(4), 763-776.

Bernard, B., Sauter, S., Fine, L., Petersen, M., and Hales, T. (1994). Job task and psychosocial risk factors for work-related musculoskeletal disorders among newspaper employees. *Scandinavian Journal of Work, Environment and Health*, 20(6), 417-426.

Biddle, J., Roberts, K., Rosenman, K.D., and Welch, E.M. (1998). What percentage of workers with work-related illnesses receive workers' compensation benefits? *Journal of Occupational and Environmental Medicine*, 40(4), 325-331.

Blanck, P.D., Sandler, L.A., Schmeling, J.L., and Schartz, H.A. (2000). The emerging workforce of entrepreneurs with disabilities: Preliminary study of entrepreneurship in Iowa. *Iowa Law Review*, 85, 1583-1661.

Bongers, P.M., de Winter, C.R., Kompier, M.A., and Hildebrandt, V.H. (1993). Psychosocial factors at work and musculoskeletal disease. *Scandinavian Journal of Work, Environment and Health*, 19(5), 297-312.

Borg, V., Burr, H., and Christensen, H. (1997). *Work environment, global self-rated health, and early retirement*. Helsinki: Finnish Institute of Occupational Health.

Bosma, H., Peter, R., Siegrist, J., and Marmot, M. (1998). Two alternative job stress models and the risk of coronary heart disease. *American Journal of Public Health*, 88(1), 68-74.

Brisson, C. (2000). Women, work and cardiovascular disease. In P. Schnall, K. Belkic, P.A. Landsbergis, and D.E. Baker (eds.), *The workplace and cardiovascular diease. Occupational Medicine: State of the Art Reviews* (Vol. 15, pp. 49-57). Philadelphia, PA: Hanley and Belfus.

Brisson, C., Vinet, A., Vezina, M., and Gingras, S. (1989). Effect of duration of employment in piecework on severe disability among female garment workers. *Scandinavian Journal of Work, Environment and Health*, 15(5), 329-334.

Brisson, C., Vezina, M., and Vinet, A. (1992). Health problems of women employed in jobs involving psychological and ergonomic stressors: The case of garment workers in Quebec. *Women and Health*, 18(3), 49-65.

Brody, J.E. (1994). *Heart diseases are persisting in study's second generation*. New York Times, January 5, p. C12.

Burt, V.L., Cutler, J.A., Higgins, M., Horan, M.J., Labarthe, D., Whelton, P., Brown, C., and Roccella, E.J. (1995). Trends in the prevalence, awareness, treatment, and control of hypertension in the adult US population. Data from the health examination surveys, 1960 to 1991. *Hypertension*, 26(1), 60-69.

Carvalho, J.J., Baruzzi, R.G., Howard, P.F., Poulter, N., Alpers, M.P., Franco, L.J., Marcopito, L.F., Spooner, V.J., Dyer, A.R., Elliott, P. et al. (1989). Blood pressure in four remote populations in the INTERSALT Study. *Hypertension*, 14(3), 238-246.

Chi, C.F., Chen, C.L., and Lin, T.U. (2001). Risk for occupational injury of handicapped workers in Taiwan. *Perceptual & Motor Skills*, 93(1), 89-94.

Clarke, S.P., Sloane, D.M., and Aiken, L.H. (2002). Effects of hospital staffing and organizational climate on needlestick injuries to nurses. *American Journal of Public Health*, 92(7), 1115-1119.

Conway, H., and Svenson, J. (1998). Occupational injury and illness rates, 1992-96: Why they fell. *Monthly Labor Review*, 121(11), 36-58.

Cooper, R.S., Rotimi, C.N., and Ward, R. (1999). The puzzle of hypertension in African-Americans. *Scientific American*, 280(2), 56-63.

Czaja, S.J., and Sharit, J. (1993). Age differences in the performance of computer-based work. *Psychology and Aging*, 8(1), 59-67.

Daltroy, L.H., Larson, M.G., Wright, E.A., Malspeis, S., Fossel, A.H., Ryan, J., Zwerling, C., and Liang, M.H. (1991). A case-control study of risk factors for industrial low back injury: implications for primary and secondary prevention programs. *American Journal of Industrial Medicine*, 20(4), 505-515.

Derby, C.A., Lapane, K.L., Feldman, H.A., and Carleton, R.A. (2000). Sex-specific trends in validated coronary heart disease rates in southeastern New England, 1980-1991. *American Journal of Epidemiology, 151*(4), 417-429.

Dohm, A. (2000). Gauging the labor force effects of retiring baby-boomers. *Monthly Labor Review, 123*(7), 17-25.

Dunlop, J.T. (1994). Organizations and Human Resources: Internal and External Markets. In C. Kerr and P.D. Staudohar (eds.), *Labor economics and industrial relations: Markets and institutions* (pp. 375-400). Cambridge, MA: Harvard University Press.

Eaker, E.D., Packard, B., and Thom, T.J. (1989). Epidemiology and risk factors for coronary heart disease in women. *Cardiovascular Clinics, 19*(3), 129-145.

Eaker, E.D., Pinsky, J., and Castelli, W.P. (1992). Myocardial infarction and coronary death among women: Psychosocial predictors from a 20-year follow-up of women in the Framingham Study. *American Journal of Epidemiology, 135*(8), 854-864.

Elveback, L.R., Connolly, D.C., and Melton, L.J. (1986). Coronary heart disease in residents of Rochester, Minnesota. VII. Incidence, 1950 through 1982. *Mayo Clinic Proceedings, 61*(11), 896-900.

European Agency for Safety and Health at Work. (2002). *The changing world of work.* Bilbao, Spain: European Agency for Safety and Health at Work.

European Foundation. (1997). *Time constraints and autonomy at work in the European Union.* Dublin: European Foundation for the Improvement of Living and Working Conditions.

Falger, P.R.J., and Schouten, E.G.W. (1992). Exhaustion, psychologic stress in the work environment and acute myocardial infarction in adult men. *Journal of Psychosomatic Research, 36*, 777-786.

Ferrie, J.E., Shipley, M.J., Marmot, M.G., Stansfeld, S., and Smith, G.D. (1998). The health effects of major organisational change and job insecurity. *Social Science and Medicine, 46*(2), 243-254.

Finnish Institute of Occupational Health. (1994). Occupational diseases in Finland in 1993. Helsinki: Finnish Institute of Occupational Health. Available: http://www.occuphealth.fi/internet/english/ [accessed April 2004].

Gabriel, P., and Liimatainen, M.R. (2000). *Mental health in the workplace.* Geneva: International Labour Office.

Gillum, R.F., Folsom, A.R., and Blackburn, H. (1984). Decline in coronary heart disease mortality. Old questions and new facts. *American Journal of Medicine, 76*(6), 1055-1065.

Goldberg, R.J., Yarzebski, J., Lessard, D., and Gore, J.M. (1999). A two-decades (1975 to 1995) long experience in the incidence, in-hospital and long-term case-fatality rates of acute myocardial infarction: A community-wide perspective. *Journal of the American College of Cardiology, 33*(6), 1533-1539.

Gornel, D.L. (1999). Rates of death from coronary heart disease. *New England Journal of Medicine, 340*(9), 730.

Griffiths, A. (1997). Ageing, health and productivity: A challenge for the new millennium. *Work and Stress, 11*(3), 197-214.

Haermae, M. (1996). Ageing, physical fitness and shiftwork tolerance. *Applied Ergonomics, 27*(1), 25-29.

Hale, A., and Hovden, J. (1998). Management and culture: The third age of safety. A review of approaches to organizational aspects of safety, health and environment. In A.M. Feyer and A. Williamson (eds.), *Occupational injury: Risk, prevention and intervention.* London: Taylor and Francis.

Hallqvist, J., Lundberg, M., Diderichsen, F., and Ahlbom, A. (1998). Socioeconomic differences in risk of myocardial infarction 1971-1994 in Sweden: Time trends, relative risks and population attributable risks. *International Journal of Epidemiology, 27*(3), 410-415.

Hanecke, K., Tiedemann, S., Nachreiner, F., and Grzech-Sukalo, H. (1998). Accident risk as a function of hour at work and time of day as determined from accident data and exposure models for the German working population. *Scandinavian Journal of Work, Environment and Health, 24*(Suppl 3), 43-48.

Harris, M.I., Flegal, K.M., Cowie, C.C., Eberhardt, M.S., Goldstein, D.E., Little, R.R., Wiedmeyer, H.M., and Byrd-Holt, D.D. (1998). Prevalence of diabetes, impaired fasting glucose, and impaired glucose tolerance in U.S. adults. The Third National Health and Nutrition Examination Survey, 1988-1994. *Diabetes Care, 21*(4), 518-524.

Hayashi, T., Kobayashi, Y., Yamaoka, K., and Yano, E. (1996). Effect of overtime work on 24-hour ambulatory blood pressure. *Journal of Occupational and Environmental Medicine, 38*(10), 1007-1011.

Haynes, S.G., and Feinleib, M. (1980). Women, work and coronary heart disease: Prospective findings from the Framingham heart study. *American Journal of Public Health, 70*(2), 133-141.

Hirsch, B.T., Macpherson, D.A., and Vroman, W.G. (2001). Estimates of union density by state. *Monthly Labor Review, 124*(7), 51-55.

Hoffman, C., and Schlobohm, A. (2000). *Uninsured in America: A Chart Book.* Report for the Kaiser Commission, Washington, DC.

Holahan, J., and Kim, J. (2000). Why does the number of uninsured Americans continue to grow? *Health Affairs, 19*(4), 188-196.

Ilmarinen, J. (1994). Aging, work and health. In J. Snel and R. Cremer (eds.), *Work and aging: A European perspective* (pp. 47-63). London: Taylor and Francis.

Ilmarinen, J. (1997). *Aging and work: Problems and solutions for promoting the work ability.* Helsinki: Finnish Institute of Occupational Health.

Institute of Medicine. (1996). *Nursing staff in hospitals and nursing homes: Is it adequate?* In G.S. Wunderlich, F. Sloan, and C.K. Davis, (eds.), Committee on the Adequacy of Nursing Staff in Hospitals and Nursing Homes. Washington, DC: National Academy Press.

International Labor Organization. (2004). ILC91 Annual ILO Conference tackles new social agenda. Available: http://www.ilo.org/public/english/bureau/inf/magazine/48/ilc91.htm [accessed April 28, 2004].

Iwasaki, K., Sasaki, T., Oka, T., and Hisanaga, N. (1998). Effect of working hours on biological functions related to cardiovascular system among salesmen in a machinery manufacturing company. *Industrial Health, 36*(4), 361-367.

Jensen, R., and Sinkule, E. (1988). Press operator amputations: Is risk associated with age and gender? *Journal of Safety Research, 19*(3), 125-133.

Johnson, C.L., Rifkind, B.M., Sempos, C.T., Carroll, M.D., Bachorik, P.S., Briefel, R.R., Gordon, D.J., Burt, V.L., Brown, C.D., and Lippel, K. (1993). Declining serum total cholesterol levels among US adults. The National Health and Nutrition Examination Surveys. *Journal of the American Medical Association, 269*(23), 3002-3008.

Johnson, J.V., Hall, E.M., and Theorell, T. (1989). Combined effects of job strain and social isolation on cardiovascular disease morbidity and mortality in a random sample of the Swedish male working population. *Scandinavian Journal of Work, Environment and Health, 15*(4), 271-279.

Kannel, W.B., Garrison, R.J., and Dannenberg, A.L. (1993). Secular blood pressure trends in normotensive persons: The Framingham Study. *American Heart Journal, 125*(4), 1154-1158.

Karasek, R. (1979). Job demands, job decision latitude, and mental strain: Implications for job redesign. *Administrative Science Quarterly, 24*(2), 285-308.

Karasek, R. (1990). Lower health risk with increased job control among white collar workers. *Journal of Organizational Behavior, 11*(3), 171-185.

Karasek, R., and Theorell, T. (1990). *Healthy work: Stress, productivity, and the reconstruction of working life.* New York: Basic Books.

Kerr, M.S., Frank, J.W., Shannon, H.S., Norman, R.W., Wells, R.P., Neumann, W.P., Bombardier, C., and Ontario Universities Back Pain Study Group. (2001). Biomechanical and psychosocial risk factors for low back pain at work. *American Journal of Public Health, 91*(7), 1069-1075.

Kisner, S.M., and Pratt, S.G. (1997). Occupational fatalities among older workers in the United States: 1980-1991. *Journal of Occupational and Environmental Medicine, 39*(8), 715-721.

Kisner, S.M, and Pratt, S.G. (1999). Occupational injury fatalities among older workers in the United States, 1980-1994. *American Journal of Industrial Medicine Supplement 1,* 24-25.

Kivimäki, M., Vahtera, J., Virtanen, M., Elovainio, M., Pentti, J., and Ferrie, J.E. (2003). Temporary employment and risk of overall and cause-specific mortality. *American Journal of Epidemiology, 158*(7), 663-668.

Kohn, M.L., and Schooler, C. (1982). Job conditions and personality: A longitudinal assessment of their reciprocal effects. *American Journal of Sociology, 87*(6), 1257-1286.

Kossoris, M.D. (1940). Relation of age to industrial injuries. *Monthly Labor Review,* 789-805.

Kostis, J.B., Wilson, A.C., Lacy, C.R., Cosgrove, N.M., Ranjan, R., Lawrence-Nelson, J., and The Myocardial Infarction Data Acquistion System (MIDAS #7) Study Group. (2001). Time trends in the occurrence and outcome of acute myocardial infarction and coronary heart disease death between 1986 and 1996 (a New Jersey statewide study). *American Journal of Cardiology, 88*(8), 837-841.

Kraus, L.E., and Stoddard, S. (1991). *Chartbook on Work Disability in the United States.* Washington, DC: U.S. Government Printing Office. P. 67.

Krause, N., Ragland, D.R., Greiner, B.A., Syme, S.L., and Fisher, J.M. (1997). Psychosocial job factors associated with back and neck pain in public transit operators. *Scandinavian Journal of Work, Environment and Health, 23*(3), 179-186.

Kristensen, T.S., Kronitzer, M., and Alfredsson, L. (1998). *Social factors, work, stress and cardiovascular disease prevention.* Brussels: The European Heart Network.

Kuczmarski, R.J., Flegal, K.M., Campbell, S.M., and Johnson, C.L. (1994). Increasing prevalence of overweight among US adults. The National Health and Nutrition Examination Surveys, 1960 to 1991. *Journal of the America Medical Association, 272*(3), 205-211.

LaCroix, A.Z. (1984). *High demands/low control work and the incidence of CHD in the Framingham cohort.* Unpublished doctoral dissertation, University of North Carolina, Chapel Hill, NC.

Laflamme, L., and Menckel, E. (1995). Aging and occupational accidents: A review of the literature of the last three decades. *Safety Science 21,* 145-161.

Landen, D.D., and Hendricks, S.A. (1992). Estimates from the National Health Interview Survey on occupational injury among older workers in the United States. *Scandinavian Journal of Work, Environment, and Health, 18*(2), 18-20.

Landrigan, P.J., and Baker, D.B. (1991). The recognition and control of occupational disease. *Journal of the American Medical Association, 266*(5), 676-680.

Landsbergis, P., Schnall, P., Pickering, T., Warren, K., and Schwartz, J. (2003). Lower socioeconomic status among men in relation to the association between job strain and blood pressure. *Scandinavian Journal of Work, Environment and Health, 29*(3), 206-215.

Landsbergis, P.A., Schnall, P.L., Warren, K., Pickering, T.G., and Schwartz, J.E. (1994). Association between ambulatory blood pressure and alternative formulations of job strain. *Scandinavian Journal of Work, Environment and Health*, 20(5), 349-363.

Landsbergis, P.A., Schnall, P.L., Deitz, D.K., Warren, K., Pickering, T.G., and Schwartz, J.E. (1998). Job strain and health behaviors: Results of a prospective study. *American Journal of Health Promotion*, 12(4), 237-245.

Landsbergis, P.A., Cahill, J., and Schnall, P. (1999). The impact of lean production and related new systems of work organization on worker health. *Journal of Occupational Health Psychology*, 4(2), 108-130.

Larese, F., and Fiorito, A. (1994). Musculoskeletal disorders in hospital nurses: A comparison between two hospitals. *Ergonomics*, 37(7), 1205-1211.

Leigh, J.P. (1986). Individual and job characteristics as predictors of industrial accidents. *Accident Analysis and Prevention*, 18(3), 209-216.

Leigh, J.P., and Schnall, P. (2000). Costs of occupational circulatory disease. *Occupational Medicine*, 15(1), 257-267.

Leigh, J., Macaskill, P., Kuosma, E., and Mandryk, J. (1999). Global Burden of Disease and Injury Due to Occupational Factors. *Epidemiology, 10,* 626-631.

Leino, P.I., and Hanninen, V. (1995). Psychosocial factors at work in relation to back and limb disorders. *Scandinavian Journal of Work, Environment and Health*, 21(2), 134-142.

The Lexington Group and Eastern Research Group, Inc. (2002, March 15). An estimate of OSHA's progress from FY 1995 to FY 2001 in attaining its performance goal of reducing injuries and illnesses in 100,000 workplaces. Prepared for the Office of Statistics, Occupational Safety and Health Administration, Washington, DC, Contract No. J-9-F-7-0043.

Liao, Y., and Cooper, R.S. (1995). Continued adverse trends in coronary heart disease mortality among blacks, 1980-91. *Public Health Reports*, 110(5), 572-579.

Liu, Y., Tanaka, H., and The Fukuoka Heart Study Group. (2002). Overtime work, insufficient sleep, and risk of non-fatal acute myocardial infarction in Japanese men. *Occupational and Environmental Medicine*, 59(7), 447-451.

Lowery, J.T., Borgerding, J.A., Zhen, B., Glazner, J.E., Bondy, J., and Kreiss, K. (1998). Risk factors for injury among construction workers at Denver International Airport. *American Journal of Industrial Medicine*, 34(2), 113-120.

McGovern, P.G., Jacobs, D.R. Jr., Shahar, E., Arnett, D.K., Folsom, A.R., Blackburn, H., and Luepker, R.V. (2001). Trends in acute coronary heart disease mortality, morbidity, and medical care from 1985 through 1997: The Minnesota heart survey. *Circulation*, 104(1), 19-24.

Minter, S.G. (1996). Putting incentives to work. *Occupational Hazards, 58*(6), S7-S9.

Mitchell, O.S. (1988). The relation of age to workplace injuries. *Monthly Labor Review*, 111(7), 8-13.

Molinie, A.F., and Volkoff, S. (1994). Working conditions: Problems ahead for workers over the age of 40. In J. Snel and R. Cremer (eds.), *Work and Aging: A European Perspective* (pp. 214-223). London: Taylor and Francis.

Moon, S.D., and Sauter, S.L. (1996). *Beyond Biomechanics: Psychosocial aspects of musculoskeletal disorders in office work*. London: Taylor and Francis.

Mueller, B.A, Mohr, D.L., Rice, J.C., and Clemmer, D.I. (1987). Factors affecting individual injury experience among petroleum drilling workers. *Journal of Occupational Medicine*, 29(2), 126-131.

Myers, J.R., Hard, D.L., Snyder, K.A., Casini, V.J., Cianfrocco, R., Fields, J., and Morton, L. (1999). Risks of fatal injuries to farm workers 55-years of age and older. *American Journal of Industrial Medicine, Supplement 1,* 29-30.

National Health Interview Survey. (1994). National Health Interview Survey on Disability (NHIS-D). National Center for Health Statistics, Centers for Disease Control and Prevention. Hyattsville, MD: NCHS/CDC.

National Institute for Occupational Safety and Health. (1994). *Participatory ergonomics interventions in meatpacking plants.* (Report No. Publication no. 94-124). Cincinnati, OH: NIOSH.

National Institute for Occupational Safety and Health. (2001). National Occupational Research Agenda for Musculoskeletal Disorders. Cincinnati, OH: NIOSH.

National Research Council. (1987). *Counting Injuries and Illnesses in the Workplace: Proposals for a Better System.* Committee on National Statistics. Washington, DC: National Academy Press.

National Research Council and the Institute of Medicine. (2001). *Musculoskeletal Disorders and the Workplace: Low Back and Upper Extremities.* Panel on Musculoskeletal Disorders and the Workplace, Commission on Behavioral and Social Sciences and Education. Washington, DC: National Academy Press.

Netterstrom, B., and Hansen, A.M. (2000). Outsourcing and stress: Physiological effects on bus drivers. *Stress Medicine, 16*(3), 149-160.

Nicholson, P.J. (1995). The ageing labour force. *Occupational Medicine (Oxford), 45*(5), 229-230.

North, F.M., Syme, S.L., Feeney, A., Shipley, M., and Marmot, M. (1996). Psychosocial work environment and sickness absence among British civil servants: The Whitehall II study. *American Journal of Public Health, 86*(3), 332-340.

Novek, J., Yassi, A., and Spiegel, J. (1990). Mechanization, the labor process, and injury risks in the Canadian meat packing industry. *International Journal of Health Services, 20*(2), 281-296.

Oleske, D.M., Brewer, R.D., Doan, P., and Hahn, J. (1989). An epidemiologic evaluation of the injury experience of a cohort of automotive parts workers: A model for surveillance in small industries. *Journal of Occupational Accidents 10,* 239-253.

Pell, S., and Fayerweather, W.E. (1985). Trends in the incidence of myocardial infarction and in associated mortality and morbidity in a large employed population, 1957-1983. *New England Journal of Medicine, 312*(16), 1005-1011.

Personick, M.E., and Windau, J.A. (1995). Self-employed individuals fatally injured at work. *Monthly Labor Review, 118*(8), 24-30.

Peter, R., Siegrist, J., Hallqvist, J., Reuterwall, C., and Theorell, T. (2002). SHEEP Study Group. Psychosocial work environment and myocardial infarction: Improving risk estimation by combining two complementary job stress models in the SHEEP Study. *Journal of Epidemiology & Community Health, 56*(4), 294-300.

Pollard, T.M. (2001). Changes in mental well-being, blood pressure and total cholesterol levels during workplace reorganization: The impact of uncertainty. *Work and Stress, 15*(1), 1914-1928.

Pransky, G., Benjamin, K., Hill-Fotouhi, C., Himmelstein, J., Fletcher, K.E., Katz, J.N., and Johnson, W.G. (2000). Outcomes in work-related upper extremity and low back injuries: Results of a retrospective study. *American Journal of Industrial Medicine 2000, 37*(4), 400-409

Quinlan, M., and Mayhew, C. (2000). Precarious employment, work re-organisation and the fracturing of OHS management. In K. Frick, P.L. Jensen, M. Quinlan, and T. Wilthagen (eds.), *Systematic Occupational Health and Safety Management: Perspectives on an International Development* (pp. 175-198). New York: Pergamon.

Rebitzer, J.B. (1995). Job safety and contract workers in the petrochemical industry. *Industrial Relations, 34*(1), 40-57.

Richardson, D., and Loomis, D. (1997). Trends in fatal occupational injuries and industrial restructuring in North Carolina in the 1980s. *American Journal of Public Health*, *87*(6), 1041-1043.

Robertson, A., and Tracy, C.S. (1998). Health and productivity of older workers. *Scandinavian Journal of Work, Environment and Health*, *24*(2), 85-97.

Root, N. (1981). Injuries at work are fewer among older employees. *Monthly Labor Review*, *104*(3), 30-34.

Roquelaure, Y., Gabignon, Y., Gillant, J.C., Delalieux, P., Ferrari, C., Mea, M., Fanello, S., and Penneau-Fontbonne, D. (2001). Transient hand paresthesias in Champagne vineyard workers. *American Journal of Industrial Medicine*, *40*(6), 639-645.

Rosamond, W.D., Chambless, L.E., Folsom, A.R., Cooper, L.S., Conwill, D.E., Clegg, L., Wang, C.H., and Heiss, G. (1998). Trends in the incidence of myocardial infarction and in mortality due to coronary heart disease, 1987 to 1994. *New England Journal of Medicine*, *339*(13), 861-867.

Rosamond, W.D., Folsom, A.R., Chambless, L.E., Wang, C.H., ARIC Investigators, and Atherosclerosis Risk in Communities. (2001). Coronary heart disease trends in four United States communities. The Atherosclerosis Risk in Communities (ARIC) study 1987-1996. *International Journal of Epidemiology*, *30*(Suppl 1), S17-S22.

Rosenman, K.D., Gardiner, J.C., Wang, J., Biddle, J., Hogan, A., Reilly, M. J., Roberts, K., and Welch, E. (2000). Why most workers with occupational repetitive trauma do not file for workers' compensation. *Journal of Occupational & Environmental Medicine*, *42*(1), 25-34.

Ruser, J.W. (1998). Denominator choice in the calculation of workplace fatality rates. *American Journal of Industrial Medicine*, *33*(2):151-156.

Russek, H.I., and Zohman, B.L. (1958). Relative significance of heredity, diet, and occupational stress in coronary heart disease of young adults. *American Journal of Medical Science*, *235*, 266-275.

Schmitt, E. (2001). Other Immigrants, Envying Mexicans, Demand a Break, Too. New York Times, July 26, p. A1.

Schnall, P., and Belkic, K. (2000). Point estimates of blood pressure at the worksite. *Occupational Medicine: State-of-the-Art Reviews*, *15*(1), 203-208.

Schnall, P.L., Landsbergis, P.A., Pieper, C.F., Schwartz, J., Dietz, D., Gerin, W., Schlussel, Y., Warren, K., and Pickering, T.G. (1992). The impact of anticipation of job loss on psychological distress and worksite blood pressure. *American Journal of Industrial Medicine*, *21*(3), 417-432.

Schnall, P.L., Schwartz, J.E., Landsbergis, P.A., Warren, K., and Pickering, T.G. (1992). Relation between job strain, alcohol, and ambulatory blood pressure. *Hypertension*, *19*, 488-494.

Schnall, P.L., Landsbergis, P.A., and Baker, D. (1994). Job strain and cardiovascular disease. *Annual Review of Public Health*, *15*, 381-411.

Schnall, P.L., Schwartz, J.E., Landsbergis, P.A., Warren, K., and Pickering, T.G. (1998). A longitudinal study of job strain and ambulatory blood pressure: Results from a three-year follow-up. *Psychosomatic Medicine*, *60*(6), 697-706.

Schooler, C., and Mulatu, M.S. (2001). The reciprocal effects of leisure time activities and intellectual functioning in older people: A longitudinal analysis. *Psychology and Aging*, *16*(3), 466-482.

Schooler, C., Mulatu, M.S., and Oates, G. (1999). The continuing effects of substantively complex work on the intellectual functioning of older workers. *Psychology and Aging*, *14*(3), 483-506.

Service Employees International Union. (1995). *Caring till it hurts*. Washington, DC: Service Employees International Union.

Shannon, H., Mayr, J., and Haines, T. (1997). Overview of the relationship between organizational and workplace factors and injury rates. *Safety Science*, 26(3), 201-217.

Shannon, H.S., Woodward, C.A., Cunningham, C.E., McIntosh, J., Lendrum, B., Brown, J., and Rosenbloom, D. (2001). Changes in general health and musculoskeletal outcomes in the workforce of a hospital undergoing rapid change: A longitudinal study. *Journal of Occupational Health Psychology*, 6(1), 3-14.

Shogren, E., and Calkins, A. (1997). *Findings of Minnesota Nurses Association Research Project on Occupational Injury/Illness in Minnesota between 1990-1994*. St. Paul, MN: Minnesota Nurses Association.

Siegrist, J. (1996). Adverse health effects of high-effort/low-reward conditions. *Journal of Occupational Health Psychology*, 1(1), 27-41.

Singh, G.K., and Siahpush, M. (2002). Increasing inequalities in all-cause and cardiovascular mortality among US adults aged 25-64 years by area socioeconomic status, 1969-1998. *International Journal of Epidemiology*, 31(3), 600-613.

Sokejima, S., and Kagamimori, S. (1998). Working hours as a risk factor for acute myocardial infarction in Japan: Case-control study. *British Medical Journal*, 317(7161), 775-780.

Sparks, K., Cooper, C., Fried, Y., and Shirom, A. (1997). The effects of hours of work on health: A meta-analytic review. *Journal of Occupational and Organizational Psychology*, 70(4), 391-408.

Spurgeon, A., Harrington, J.M., and Cooper, C.L. (1997). Health and safety problems associated with long working hours: A review of the current position. *Occupational and Environmental Medicine*, 54(6), 367-375.

Stansfeld, S., Bosma H., Hemingway, H., and Marmot, M. (1998). Psychosocial work characteristics and social support as predictors of SF-36 functioning: The Whitehall II study. *Psychosomatic Medicine*, 60, 247-255.

Stansfeld, S.A., Fuhrer, R., Shipley, M.J., and Marmot, M.G. (1999). Work characteristics predict psychiatric disorder: Prospective results from the Whitehall II Study. *Occupational and Environmental Medicine*, 56(5), 302-307.

Steenland, K., Henley, J., and Thun, M. (2002). All-cause and cause-specific death rates by educational status for two million people in two American Cancer Society cohorts, 1959-1996. *American Journal of Epidemiology*, 156(1), 11-21.

Sytkowski, P.A., D'Agostino, R.B., Belanger, A., and Kannel, W.B. (1996). Sex and time trends in cardiovascular disease incidence and mortality: The Framingham Heart Study, 1950-1989. *American Journal of Epidemiology*, 143(4), 338-350.

Theorell, T., and Rahe, R.H. (1972). Behavior and life satisfactions of Swedish subjects with myocaridal infarction. *Journal of Chronic Disabilities*, 25, 139-147.

Theorell, T., Tsutsumi, A., Hallquist, J., Reuterwall, C., Hogstedt, C., Fredlund, P., Emlund, N., and Johnson, J.V. (1998). Decision latitude, job strain, and myocardial infarction: A study of working men in Stockholm. The SHEEP Study Group. Stockholm Heart epidemiology Program. *American Journal of Public Health*, 88(3), 382-388.

Tuchsen, F., and Endahl, L.A. (1999). Increasing inequality in ischaemic heart disease morbidity among employed men in Denmark 1981-1993: The need for a new preventive policy. *International Journal of Epidemiology*, 28(4), 640-644.

Tuomi, K., Ilmarinen, J., Martikainen, R., Aalto, L., and Klockars, M. (1997). Aging, work, life-style and work ability among Finnish municipal workers in 1981-1992. *Scandinavian Journal of Work, Environment and Health*, 23(Suppl 1), 58-65.

Tuomi, K., Ilmarinen, J., Seitsamo, J., Huuhtanen, P., Martikainen, R., Nygard, C. H., and Klockars, M. (1997). Summary of the Finnish research project (1981-1992) to promote the health and work ability of aging workers. *Scandinavian Journal of Work, Environment and Health*, 23(Suppl 1), 66-71.

U.S. Bureau of Labor Statistics. (1996). *Older workers' injuries entail lengthy absences from work, BLS Issue Summary 96-6.* Washington, DC: U.S. Department of Labor.

U.S. Bureau of Labor Statistics. (2002). *Lost-work time. Injuries and Illnesses: Characteristics and resulting time away from work, 2000.* Washington, DC: U.S. Department of Labor.

U.S. General Accounting Office. (2000). Contingent Workers: Incomes and Benefits Lag Behind Those of Rest of Workforce. Washington, DC: GAO. P. 14. Report No. GAO/HEHS-00-76.

Vahtera, J., Kivimaki, M., and Pentti, J. (1997). Effect of organizational downsizing on health employees. *Lancet, 350,* 1124-1128.

Verdecchia, P., Clement, D., Fagard, R., Palatini, P., and Parati, G. (1999). Blood Pressure Monitoring. Task force III: Target-organ damage, morbidity and mortality. *Blood Pressure Monitoring, 4*(6), 303-317.

Vogel, J. (2002). *Swedish level of living survey data.* Stockholm: Statistics Sweden.

Waldron, I., Nowotarski, M., Freimer, M., Henry, J.P., Post, N., and Witten, C. (1982). Cross-cultural variation in blood pressure: A quantitative analysis of the relationships of blood pressure to cultural characteristics, salt consumption and body weight. *Social Science and Medicine, 16*(4), 419-430.

Warren, N. (2000). U.S. regulations for work organization. *Occupational Medicine: State-of-the-Art Reviews, 15*(1), 275-280.

Warren, N., Dillon, C., Morse, T., Hall, C., and Warren, A. (2000). Biomechanical, psychosocial, and organizational risk factors for WRMSD: Population-based estimates from the Connecticut upper-extremity surveillance project (CUSP). *Journal of Occupational Health Psychology, 5*(1), 164-181.

Washington State Department of Labor and Industries. (2000). Cost Benefit Analysis and Concise Explanatory Statement of the Ergonomics Standard. Olympia, WA: Washington State Department of Labor and Industries.

Washington State Department of Labor and Industries. (2002). *Work-related musculoskeltal disorders of the neck, back and upper extremity in Washington State, 1992-2000.* (Report No. SHARP Technical Report No. 40-6-2002). Olympia, WA: Washington State Department of Labor and Industries.

Westman, M., Eden, D., and Shirom, A. (1985). Job stress, cigarette smoking and cessation: The conditioning effects of peer support. *Social Science and Medicine, 20*(6), 637-644.

Worksafe Australia. (1995). Compendium of workers compensation statistics, Australia, 1992-1993. Canberra, Australia: Australian Government Publishing Service.

World Health Organization. (1993). (Report No. Technical Report No. 835). Geneva: WHO.

Yassi, A., Tate, R., Cooper, J.E., Snow, C., Vallentyne, S., and Khokhar, J.B. (1995). Early intervention for back-injured nurses at a large Canadian tertiary care hospital: An evaluation of the effectiveness and cost benefits of a two-year pilot project. *Occupational Medicine (Oxford), 45*(4), 209-214.

Zwerling, C., Whitten, P.S., Davis, C.S., and Sprince, N.L. (1997). Occupational injuries among workers with disabilities: The National Health Interview Survey, 1985-1994. *Journal of the American Medical Association, 278*(24), 2163-2166.

Zwerling, C., Whitten, P.S., Davis, C.S., and Sprince, N.L. (1998). Occupational injuries among older workers with visual, auditory, and other impairments. A validation study. *Journal of Occupational & Environmental Medicine, 40*(8), 720-723.

Zwerling, C., Sprince, N.L., Davis, C.S., Whitten, P.S., Wallace, R.R., and Heeringa, S.G. (1998). Occupational injuries among older workers with disabilities: A prospective cohort study of the Health and Retirement Survey, 1992 to 1994. *American Journal of Public Health, 88*(11), 1691-1695.

CHAPTER 7

Acemoglu, D., and Angrist, J.D. (2001). Consequences of Employment Protection? The Case of the Americans with Disabilities Act. *Journal of Political Economy*, *109*(5), 915-957.

Biddle, J.E., Boden, L.I., and Reville, R.T. (2001). Permanent partial disability from occupational injuries: Earnings losses and replacement in three stages. In P.P. Budetti, R.V. Burkhauser, J.H. Gregory, and A. Hunt (eds.), *Ensuring health and income security for an aging workforce* (pp. 263-290). Kalamazoo, MI: W.E. Upjohn Institute for Employment Research.

Bound, J., and Waidmann, T. (2000). *Accounting for recent declines in employment rates among the working-age disabled.* (Report No. Research Report 00-460). Michigan: University of Michigan.

Burkhauser, R.V., Butler, J.S, and Kim, Y.W. (1995). The importance of employer accommodation on the job duration of workers with disabilities: A hazard model approach. *Labour Economics*, *2*(2), 109-130.

Burkhauser, R.V., Daly, M.C., and Houtenville, A.J. (2001). How working age people with disabilities fared over the 1990s buisness cycle. In P.P. Budetti, R.V. Burkhauser, J.M. Gregory, and A. Hunt (eds.), *Ensuring health and income security for an aging workforce* (pp. 291-346). Kalamazoo, MI: Upjohn Institute for Employment Research.

Burton, J.F., and Spieler, E.A. (2001). Workers' compensation and older workers. In P.P. Budetti, R.V. Burkhauser, J.M. Gregory, and A. Hunt (eds.), *Ensuring health and income Security for an aging workforce* (pp. 41-83). Kalamazoo, MI: W.E. Upjohn Institute for Employment Research.

Chan, S., and Stevens, A.H. (2001). The effects of job loss on older workers. In P.P. Budetti, R.V. Burkhauser, J.M. Gregory, and A. Hunt (eds.), *Ensuring Health and Income Security for an aging workforce* (pp. 189-211). Kalamazoo, MI: W.E. Upjohn Institute for Employment Research.

Colker, R. (1999). The Americans with Disabilities Act: A windfall for Defendants. *Harvard Civil Right-Civil Liberties Law Review*, *34*, 99-162.

Colker, R. (2001). Winning and losing under the Americans with Disabilities Act. *Ohio State Law Journal*, *62*, 239-279.

Conway, H., and Svenson, J. (1998) Occupational injury and illness rates, 1992-96: Why they fell. *Monthly Labor Review*, *121*(11), 36-58.

Daly, M.C., and Bound, J. (1996). Worker adaptation and employer accommodation following the onset of a health impairment. *Journals of Gerontology Series B-Psychological Sciences & Social Sciences.* *51*(2), S53-S60.

DeLeire, T. (2000). The wage and employment effects of the americans with disabilities act. *Journal of Human Resources*, *35*(4), 693-715.

Eglit, H.C. (1997). The age discrimination in employment act at thirty: Where it's been, where it is today, where it's going. *University of Richmond Law Review*, *31*(3), 579-756.

Fronstin, P. (1997). Employee Benefits, Retirement Patterns, and Implications for Increased Work Life. Employee Benefit Retirement Institute (EBRI) Issue Brief no. 184.

Gross, J.A., and Greenfield, P.A. (1985). Arbitral value judgements in health and safety disputes: Management rights over workers' rights. *Buffalo Law Review*, *34*, 645-691.

Gustman, A.L., Steinmeier, T.L. (1994). Employer-provided health insurance and retirement behavior. *Industrial & Labor Relations Review*, *48*(1), 124-140.

Haider, S., and Stephens, M. (2001). *The Impact of displacement for older workers.* (Report No. Report DRU-2631-NIA). Santa Monica, CA: RAND.

Jolls, C. (1996). Hands-tying and the age discrimination in employment act. *Texas Law Review*, *74*, 1813-1846.

Kruse, D.L., and Mahony, D. (2000). Illegal child labor in the United States: Prevalance and characteristics. *Industrial and Labor Review, 54*(17), 17-37.

Miller, D. (1966). Age discrimination in employment: The problem of the older worker. *New York University Law Review, 41*, 383-424.

Mont, D., Burton, J.F., Reno, V., and Thompson, C. (2002). *Workers' Compensation: Benefits, Coverage, and Costs, 2000 New Estimates.* Washington, DC: National Academy of Social Insurance.

National Academy of Social Insurance. (2002). *Workers' compensation Data Fact Sheet.* Washington, DC: National Academy of Social Insurance.

National Council on Compensation Insurance (NCCI). (2002). *Annual Statistical Bulletin.* Washington, DC: NCCI.

Neumark, D. (2001). *Age Discrimination Legislation in the United States (NBER).* (Report No. Working Paper No. 8152).

Patel, B., and Kleiner, B.H. (1994). New developments in age discrimination. *Labor Law Journal, 45*, 709-712.

Quinn, J.F. (1999). Retirement patterns and bridge jobs in the 1990s. *Employee Benefit Research Institute Issue Brief,* (206), 1-22.

Rabinowitz, R.S. (2002). The Americans with Disabilities Act and the Family and Medical Leave Act: Application of the ADA to Occupational Injuries and Illness. In R.S. Rabinowitz (ed.), *Occupational Safety and Health Law* (2nd ed., pp. 876-887).Washington, DC: Bureau of National Affairs.

Scholz, J.T., and Gray, W.B. (1990). OSHA enforcement and workplace injuries: A behavioral approach to risk assessment. *Journal of Risk & Uncertainty, 3*(3), 283-305.

Shapiro, S., and McGarity, T. (1993). *Workers at risk: The failed promise of the occupational safety and health administration.* Westport, Connecticut: Praeger.

Shapiro, S., and Rabinowitz, R. (2000). Voluntary regulatory compliance in theory and practice: The case of OSHA. *Administrative Law Review, 52*, 97-155.

Spieler, E. (1989). Can Coal Miners Escape Black Lung? An Analysis of the coal Miner Job Transfer Program and Its Implications for Occupational Medical Removal Protection Programs. *West Virginia Law Review, 91*, 775-816.

Summers, C. (1992). Effective remedies for employment rights: Preliminary guidelines and proposals. *University of Pennsylvania Law Review, 141*, 457-546.

U.S. Equal Employment Opportunity Commission (EEOC). (2003). Charge Statistics FY 1992 Through 2002. Available: http://www.eeoc.gov/stats/charges.html [accessed April 2003].

Weil, D. (1991) Enforcing OSHA: The role of labor unions. *Industrial Relations, 30*(1), 20-36.

Wood, H.G. (1877). A Treatise on the Law of Master and Servant. New York: John D. Parsons, Jr.

CHAPTER 8

Aaras, A., Horgen, G., Bjørset, H-H., Ro, O., and Walsøe H. (2001). Musculoskeletal, visual and psychosocial stress in VDU operators before and after multidisciplinary ergonomic interventions. A 6 years prospective study—Part II. *Applied Ergonomics, 32*, 559-571.

Agnew, J., and Suruda, A.J. (1993). Age and fatal work-related falls. *Human Factors, 35*, 731-736.

Angel, J.L., and Angel, R.J. (1998). Aging trends—Mexican Americans in the Southwestern USA. *Journal of Cross Cultural Gerontology, 13*(3), 281-290.

Anonymous (2002). Aspirin for the prevention of heart attacks in people without previous cardiovascular events: Recommendations from the United States Preventive Services Task Force. *Annals of Internal Medicine, 136*(2), 157-160.

Arnetz, B.B., Sjogren, B., Rydehn, B., and Meisel, R. (2003). Early workplace intervention for employees with musculoskeletal-related absenteeism: A prospective controlled intervention study. *Journal of Occupational and Environmental Medicine, 45*, 499-506.

Avison, W.R. (2001). Unemployment and its consequences for mental health. In V.W. Marshall, W.R. Heinz, H. Krüger, and A. Verma (eds.), *Restructuring work and the life course* (pp. 177-200). Toronto: University of Toronto Press.

Bailer J.A., Bena, J.F., Stayner, L.T., Halperin, W.E., Park, R.M. (2003). External cause-specific summaries of occupational fatal injuries. Part II: An analysis of years of potential life lost. *American Journal of Industrial Medicine, 43*(3), 251-261.

Ball, K., Owsley, C., Stalvey, B., Roenker, D.L., Sloane, M.E., and Graves, M. (1998). Driving avoidance and functional impairment in older drivers. *Accident Analysis and Prevention, 30*, 313-322.

Ball, K., Berch, D.B., Helmers, K.F., Jobe, J.B., Leveck, M.D., Marsiske, M., Morris, J.N., Rebok, G.W., Smith, D.M., Tennstedt, S.L., Unverzagt, F.W., and Willis, S.L. (2002). Effects of cognitive training interventions with older adults: A randomized control trial. *Journal of the American Medical Association, 288*, 2271-2281.

Barth, M.C. (2000). An aging workforce in an increasingly global world. *Journal of Aging and Social Policy, 11*, 83-88.

Barth, M.C., McNaught, W., and Rizzi, P. (1996). The costs and benefits of older workers. In W.H. Crown (ed.), *Handbook on employment and the elderly* (pp. 324-348). Westport, CT: Greenport Press.

Belbin, E., and Belbin, R.M. (1972). *Problems in adult retraining*. London: Heineman.

Belbin, R.M. (1965). *Training methods for older workers*. Paris: Organisation for Economic Co-operation and Development.

Belbin, R.M. (1969). *The Discovery Method: An International Experiment in Retraining*. Paris: Organisation for Economic Co-operation and Development.

Belkic, K., Savic, C., Theorell, T., and Cizinsky, S. (1995). *Work Stressors and Cardiovascular Risk: Assessment for Clinical Practice. Part I* (256). Stockholm: National Institute for Psychosocial Factors and Health. Section for Stress Research, Karolinska Institute, WHO Psychosocial Center.

Belkic, K., Schnall, P., and Ugljesic, M. (2000). Cardiovascular evaluation of the worker and workplace: A practical guide for clinicians. *Occupational Medicine: State of the Art Reviews, 15*(1), 213-222.

Bell, C.M., Araki, S.S., and Neumann, P.J. (2001). The association between caregiver burden and caregiver health-related quality of life in Alzheimer disease. *Alzheimer Disease and Associated Disorders, 15*(3), 129-136.

Bennett, J.B., and Lehman, W.E.K. (1997). Employee views of organizational wellness and EAP: influence on substance use, drinking climates, and policy attitudes. *Employee Assistance Quarterly, 13*(1), 55-71.

Berg, G.D., and Wadhwa, S. (2002). Diabetes disease management in a community-based setting. *Managed Care, 11*(6), 42, 45-50.

Bernacki, E., Guidera, J., Schaefer, J., Lavin, R. and Tsai, S. (1999). An ergonomics program designed to reduce the incidence of upper extremity work related musculoskeletal disorders. *Journal of Occupational Environmental Medicine, 41*, 1032-1041.

Bigos, S.J., Spengler, D.M., Martin, N.A., Zeh, J., Fisher, L., and Nachemson, A. (1986). Back injuries in industry: A retrospective study. III. Employee-related factors. *Spine, 11*(3), 252-256.

Blanck, P.D. (1996). *Communicating the Americans with Disabilities Act, Transcending compliance: A case report on Sears, Roebuck and Company*. Washington, DC: Annenberg Washington Program Reports.

Blanck, P.D. (2000). *Employment, disability, and the Americans with Disabilities Act: Issues in law, public policy and research.* Evanston, IL: Northwestern University Press.

Bornstein, S., and Shultz, M.M. (2002). Balancing acts: Support for workers to provide family care. *Journal of Gender-Specific Medicine, 5*(3), 12-16.

Bray, D.W., and Howard, A. (1983). The ATandT longitudinal studies of managers. In K.W. Schaie (ed.), *Longitudinal studies of adult psychological development.* New York: Guilford Press.

Bray, J.W., French, M.T., Bowland, B.J., and Dunlap, L.J. (1996). The cost of employee assistance programs (EAPs): Findings from seven case studies. *Employee Assistance Quarterly, 11*(4), 1-19.

Breitner, J.C., and Zandi, P.P. (2001). Do nonsteroidal antiinflammatory drugs reduce the risk of Alzheimer's disease? *New England Journal of Medicine, 345*(21), 1567-1568.

Brisson, C., Montreuil, S., and Punnett, L. (1999). Effects of an ergonomic training program on workers with video display units. *Scandinavian Journal of Work Environmental Health, 25*(3), 255-263.

Brophy, M.O., Achimore, L., and Moore-Dawson, J. (2001). Reducing incidence of low-back injuries reduces cost. *American Industrial Hygiene Association Journal, 62*, 508-511.

Brummett, P.O. (1999). Successfully matching employee to substance abuse treatment through non-routinized employee assistance program (EAP) referral. *Human Resources Abstracts, 35*(2), 1-20.

Brummett, P.O. (2000). A comparison of employee assistance programs providing internal versus external treatment services: A research note. *Employee Assistance Quarterly, 15*(4), 19-28.

Burkhauser, R.V., Butler, J.S., and Kim, Y-W. (1995). The importance of employer accommodation on job duration of workers with disabilities: A hazard model approach. *Labour Economics, 3*(1), 1-22.

Burkhauser, R.V., Butler J.S., Kim Y-W, and Weathers R.R. (1999). The importance of accommodation on the timing of male disability insurance application: Results from the Survey of Disability and Work and the Health and Retirement Study. *Journal of Human Resources, 34*(3), 589-611.

Bush, D.M., and Autry, J.H. (2002). Substance abuse in the workplace: Epidemiology, effects, and industry response. *Occupational Medicine, 17*(1), 13-25.

Cahill, J., and Feldman, L.H. (1993). Computers in child welfare: Planning for a more serviceable work environment. *Child Welfare, 72*, 3-12.

Capron, J.M., and Creighton, M.K. (1998). No good deed goes unpunished: Employee assistance programs as sources of liability. *Employee Relations Law Journal, 24*, 79-99.

Carrivick, P.J.W., Lee, A.H., and Yau, K.K.W. (2002). Effectiveness of a workplace risk assessment team in reducing the rate, cost, and duration of occupational injury. *Journal of Occupational and Environmental Medicine, 44*(2), 155-159.

Chan, D.C., Marshall, J.G., and Marshall, V.W. (2001). Linking technology, work, and the life course: Findings from the NOVA case study. In V.W. Marshall, W.R. Heinz, H. Krüger, and A. Verma (eds.), *Restructuring work and the life course* (pp. 270-287). Toronto: University of Toronto Press.

Chapanis, A. (1985). *To Err Is Human, To Forgive Design.* Unpublished paper given at the American Society of Safety Engineers.

Charness, N., and Bosman, E.A. (1992). Age and human factors. In F.I.M. Craik and T.A. Salthouse (eds.), *The handbook of aging and cognition* (pp. 495-551). Hillsdale, NJ: Erlbaum.

Charness, N., and Dijkstra, K. (1999). Age, luminance, and print legibility in homes, offices, and public places. *Human Factors, 41*(2), 173-193.

Charness, N., Schumann, C.E., and Boritz, G.M. (1992). Training older adults in word processing: Effects of age, training technique, and computer anxiety. *International Journal of Technology and Aging*, 5, 79-106.

Charness, N., Kelley, C.L., Bosman, E.A., and Mottram, M. (2001). Word processing training and retraining: Effects of adult age, experience, and interface. *Psychology and Aging*, 16, 110-127.

Chase, W.G., and Simon, H.A. (1973). Perception in chess. *Cognitive Psychology*, 4, 55-81.

Chirikos, T.N. (1991). The economics of employment. *Milbank Quarterly*, 69(Suppl 1-2), 150-179.

Chirikos, T.N. (2000). Employer accommodation of older workers with disabilities: some empirical evidence and policy lessons. In P.D. Blanck (ed.), *Employment, disability, and the Americans with Disabilities Act*. Evanston, IL, Northwestern University Press.

Christmansson, M., Fridén, J., and Sollerman, C. (1999). Task design, psycho-social work climate and upper extremity pain disorders—effects of an organisational redesign on manual repetitive assembly jobs. *Applied Ergonomics*, 30, 463-472.

Coberly, S. (1991). Employer's guide to eldercare. Washington, DC: Washington Business Group on Health; Institute on Aging, Work and Health.

Cohen, A., and Colligan, M. (1998). Assessing occupational safety and health training: A literature review. Cincinnati, OH: National Institute for Occupational Safety and Health. Available: http://www.cdc.gov/niosh/98-145-b.html [accessed October 8, 2002].

Cole, B., and Brown, M. (1996). Action on worksite health and safety problems: A follow-up survey of workers participating in a hazardous waste worker training program. *American Journal of Industrial Medicine*, 30, 730-743.

Collett, D. (1994). *Modelling survival data in medical research*. London: Chapman and Hall. P. 347.

Colquitt, J.A., LePine, J.A., and Noe, R.A. (2000). Toward an integrative theory of training motivation: A meta-analytic path analysis of 20 years of research. *Journal of Applied Psychology*, 85, 678-707.

Cooley, C.A. (1990). Employee benefits address family concerns. *Monthly Labor Review*, 113(6), 60-63.

Corso, J.F. (1981). *Aging, sensory systems and perception*. New York: Praeger.

Crocker, M.J. (1997). Noise. In G. Salvendy (ed.), *Handbook of human factors and ergonomics* (pp. 790-827). New York: John Wiley and Sons.

Crook, J., Moldofsky, H., and Shannon, H. (1998). Determinants of disability after a work related musculoskeletal injury. *Journal of Rheumatology*, 25, 1570-1577.

Csiernik, R. (1999). Internal versus external employee assistance programs: What the Canadian data adds to the debate. *Employee Assistance Quarterly*, 15(2), 1-12.

Cumming, R.G. (2002). Intervention strategies and risk-factor modification for falls prevention. A review of recent intervention studies. *Clinics in Geriatric Medicine*, 18(2), 175-189.

Czaja, S.J. (2001). Technological change and the older worker. In J.E. Birren and K.W. Schaie (eds.), *Handbook of the psychology of aging* (5th ed., pp. 547-568). San Diego: Academic Press.

Czaja, S.J., and Drury, C.G. (1981a). Training programs for inspection. *Human Factors*, 23, 473-484.

Czaja, S.J., and Drury, C.G. (1981b). Aging and pretraining in industrial inspection. *Human Factors*, 23, 485-494.

Czaja, S.J., and Sharit, J. (1993). Age differences in the performance of computer-based work. *Psychology and Aging*, 8, 59-67.

Czaja, S.J., and Sharit, J. (1998). Ability-performance relationships as a function of age and task experience for a data entry task. *Journal of Experimental Psychology: Applied, 4*, 332-351.

Daltroy, L.H., Iversen, M.D., Larson, M.G., Lew, R., Wright, E., Ryan, J., Zwerling, C., Fossel, A.H., and Liang, M.H. (1997). A controlled trial of an educational program to prevent low back injuries. *New England Journal of Medicine, 337*(5), 322-328.

Daly, M.C., and Bound, J. (1996). Worker adaptation and employer accommodation following the onset of a health impairment. *Journals of Gerontology Series B-Psychological Sciences and Social Sciences, 51*(2), S53-S60.

Dancy, J., Jr., and Ralston, P.A. (2002). Health promotion and black elders: Subgroups of greatest need. *Research on Aging, 24*(2), 218-242.

Dasinger, L.K., Krause, N., Deegan, L.J., Brand, J.B., and Rudolph, L. (2000). Physical workplace factors and return to work after compensated low back injury: A disability phase-specific analysis. *Journal of Occupational Environmental Medicine, 42*(3), 323-333.

de Zwart, B.C.H., Broersen, J.P.J., Frings-Dresen, M.H.W., and van Dijk, F.J.H. (1997). Musculoskeletal complaints in the Netherlands in relation to age, gender and physically demanding work. *International Archives of Occupational and Environmental Health, 70*, 352-360.

Decker, J.T., Starrett, R., and Redhourse, J. (1986). Evaluating the cost-effectiveness of employee assistance programs. *Social Work, 31*(5), 391-393.

deGaudemaris, R. (2000). Clinical issues: Return to work and public safety. *Occupational Medicine: State of the Art Reviews, 15*(1), 223-230.

Dellman-Jenkins, M., Bennett, J.M., and Brahcae, C.I. (1994). Shaping the corporate response to workers with elder care commitments: Considerations for gerontologists. *Educational Gerontology, 20*(4), 395-405.

Demure, B., Mundt, K., Bigelow, C., Luippold, R., Ali, D., and Liese, B. (2000). Video display terminal workstation improvement program: II. Ergonomic intervention and reduction of musculoskeletal discomfort. *Journal of Occupational and Environmental Medicine, 42*, 792-797.

Deutsch, S. (1996). Building a trainers' community: Innovations in worker health and safety training. *New Solutions, 6*(3), 68-72.

Diez-Roux, A.V. (1998). Bringing context back into epidemiology: Variables and fallacies in multilevel analyses. *American Journal of Public Health, 88*, 216-222.

Dohm, A. (2000). Gauging the labor force effects of retiring baby boomers. *Monthly Labor Review, 123*(7), 17-25.

Donaldson, S.I., and Klein, D. (1997). Creating healthful work environments for ethnically diverse employees working in small and medium-sized businesses: A non-profit industry/community/university collaboration model. *Employee Assistance Quarterly, 13*(1), 17-32.

Drudi, D. (1997). BRIEF: Have disorders associated with repeated trauma stopped increasing? Available: http://stats.bls.gov/opub/cwc/1997/summer/brief4.htm [accessed May 19, 1999].

Earhart, K.M., Middlemist, R.D., and Hopkins, W.E. (1993). Eldercare: An emerging employee assistance issue. *Employee Assistance Quarterly, 8*(3), 1-10.

Ensign, D.A. (1996). Integrated employee assistance program response to aging issues. *Ageing International, 23*(2), 38-52.

Eubanks, P. (1991). Hospitals face the challenges of "sandwich generation" employees. *Hospitals, 65*(7), 60.

Evanoff, B.A., Bohr, F.C., and Wolf, L.D. (1999). Effects of a participatory ergonomics team among hospital orderlies. *American Journal of Industrial Medicine, 35*, 358-365.

Evans, L. (1991). *Traffic safety and the driver.* New York: Van Nostrand Reinhold.

Evans, W.J. (1998). Exercise and nutritional needs of elderly people: Effects on muscle and bone. *Gerontology*, 15(1), 15-24.

Every, D.K., and Leong, D.M. (1994). Exploring EAP cost-effectiveness: Profile of a nuclear power plant internal EAP. *Employee Assistance Quarterly*, 10(1), 1-12.

Federal Council on the Aging. (1984). Working person as caregiver: A symposium on increasing support services for the frail elderly. Washington, DC. 58 pp.

Federal Highway Administration. (2000). Highway design handbook for older drivers and pedestrians: Recommendations and guidelines, FHWA-RD-01-051. Washington, DC.

Fernandez, J., Daltuva, J., and Robins, T. (2000). Industrial emergency response training: An assessment of long-term impact of a union-based program. *American Journal of Industrial Medicine*, 38, 598-605.

Feuerstein, M., Marshall, L., Shaw, W.S., and Burrell, L.M. (2000). Multicomponent intervention for work-related upper extremity disorders. *Journal of Occupational Rehabilitation*, 10(1), 71-83.

Fisher, J., and Belkic, K. (2000). A public health approach in clinical practice. In P. Schnall, K. Belkic, P.A. Landsbergis, and D. Baker (eds.), *The Workplace and Cardiovascular Disease. Occupational Medicine: State of the Art Reviews* (Vol. 15, pp. 245-256). Philadelphia: Hanley and Belfus.

Fisher, R.L. (1993). Optimal performance engineering: Good, better, best. *Human Factors*, 35, 115-139.

Fleishman, E.A., and Quaintance, M.K. (1984). *Taxonomies of human performance: The description of human tasks.* New York: Academic Press.

Fozard, J., and Gordon-Salant, S. (2001). Changes in vision and hearing with aging. In J.E. Birren and K.W. Schaie (eds.), *Handbook of the psychology of aging* (5th ed., pp. 241-266). San Diego: Academic Press.

Fransen, M., McConnell, S., and Bell, M. (2002). Therapeutic exercise for people with osteoarthritis of the hip or knee. A systematic review. *Journal of Rheumatology*, 29(8), 1737-1745.

French, M.T., Zarkin, G.A., Bray, J.W., and Hartwell, T.D. (1999). Cost of employee assistance programs: Comparison of national estimates from 1993 and 1995. *Journal of Behavioral Health Services & Research*, 26(1), 95-103.

Gallo, W.T., Bradley, E.H., Siegel, M. and Kasl, S.V. (2000). Health effects of involuntary job loss among older workers: Findings from the health and retirement survey. *Journal of Gerontology: Social Sciences*, 55, S131-S140.

Gaton, G.H. (1986). The relationship of employee assistance programs (EAPs) to employee absenteeism: A hospital management study. Dissertation, Adelphi University.

Goldmeier, J. (1994). Interventions with elderly substance abusers in the workplace. *Families in Society*, 75(10), 624-629.

Googins, B., and Davidson, B.N. (1993). The organization as client: Broadening the concept of employee assistance programs. *Social Work*, 38(4), 477-488.

Hale, S., and Myerson, J. (1995). Fifty years older, fifty percent slower? Meta-analytic regression models and semantic context effects. *Aging and Cognition*, 2, 132-145.

Hancock, H.E., Rogers, W.A., and Fisk, A.D. (2001). An evaluation of warning habits and beliefs across the adult life span. *Human Factors*, 43, 343-354.

Hauer, K., Rost, B., Rutschle, K., Opitz, H., Sprecht, N., Bartsch, P., Oster, P., and Schlierf, G. (2001). Exercise training for rehabilitation and secondary prevention of falls in geriatric patients with a history of injurious falls. *Journal of the American Geriatrics Society*, 49, 10-20.

Hayashi, L.C., Hayashi, S., Yamaoka, K., Tamiya, N., Chikuda, M., and Yano, E. (2003). Ultraviolet B exposure and type of lens opacity in ophthalmic patients in Japan. *The Science of The Total Environment*, 302, 53-62.

Heathcote, A., Brown, S., and Mewhort, D.J.K. (2000). The power law repealed: The case for an exponential law of practice. *Psychonomic Bulletin and Review, 7*, 185-207.

Hechanova-Alampay, R., and Beehr, T.A. (2001). Empowerment, span of control, and safety performance in work teams after workforce reduction. *Journal of Occupational Health Psychology, 6*, 275-282.

Herbert, R., Plattus, B., Kellogg, L., Luo, J., Marcus, M., Mascolo, A., and Landrigan, P.J. (1997). The union health center: A working model of clinical care linked to preventive occupational health services. *American Journal of Industrial Medicine, 31*, 263-273.

Herlihy, P.A. (1996). Examination of integration and differentiation of employee assistance programs and work/family programs. Dissertation, Brandeis University, May 1996.

Herzog, A.R., House, J.S., and Morgan, J.N. (1991). Relation of work and retirement to health and well-being in older age. *Psychology and Aging, 6*, 202-211.

Hewitt Associates. (1997). *Work and family benefits provided by major U.S. employers in 1996, based on practices of 1,050 employers.* Lincolnshire IL: Hewitt Associates.

Hunt, E. (1995). *Will We Be Smart Enough? A Cognitive Analysis of the Coming Workforce.* New York: Russell Sage Foundation. 332 pp.

Hutchens, R.M. (1986). Delayed payment contracts and a firm's propensity to hire older workers. *Journal of Labor Economics, 4*(4), 439-457.

Ilmarinen, J. (1994). Aging, work and health. In J. Snel and R. Cremer (eds.), *Work and aging: A European perspective* (pp. 47-63). London: Taylor and Francis.

Ilmarinen, J., and Louhevaara, V. (1999). *Finnage—Respect for the ageing: Action programme to promote health, work ability and well-being of ageing workers 1990-1996.* People and Work. Research Reports 26. Helsinki, Finland: Finnish Institute of Occupational Health.

Infante-Rivard, C., and Lortie, M. (1996). Prognostic factors for return to work after a first compensated episode of back pain. *Occupational Environmental Medicine, 53*(7), 488-494.

Institute of Medicine. (1991). *Disability in America: Toward a national agenda for prevention.* In A.M. Pope and A.R. Tarlov (eds.), Committee on a National Agenda for the Prevention of Disabilities, Division of Health Promotion and Disease Promotion. Washington, DC: National Academy Press.

Institute of Medicine. (1997). *Enabling America: Assessing the role of rehabilitation science and engineering.* In E.N. Brandt, Jr. and A.M. Pope (eds.), Committee on Assessing Rehabilitation Science and Engineering, Division of Health Sciences Policy of Medicine. Washington, DC: National Academy Press.

International Labour Office. (1992). *Conditions of Work Digest: Preventing Stress at Work.* Geneva: International Labour Office.

Israel, B.A., Schurman, S.J., and House, J.S. (1989). Action research on occupational stress: involving workers as researchers. *International Journal of Health Services, 19*, 135-155.

Johnson, L. (1981). Union responses to alcoholism. *Journal of Drug Issues, 11*(3), 263-277.

Kaminski, M. (2001). Unintended consequences: Organizational practices and their impact on workplace safety and productivity. *Journal of Occupational Health Psychology, 6*, 127-138.

Karasek, R.A., Gordon, G., Pietrokovsky, C., Frese, M., Pieper, C., Schwartz, J., Fry, L., and Schirer, D. (1985). *Job content instrument: Questionnaire and user's guide.* Los Angeles/ Lowell, MA: University of Southern California/University of Massachusetts, Lowell.

Karoff, M., Roseler, S., Lorenz, C., and Kittel, J. (2000). Intensified after-care: A method for improving occupational reintegration after myocardial infarct and/or bypass operation. *Zeitschrift fur Kardiologie, 89*(5), 423-433.

Ketola, R., Toivonen, R., Hakkanen, M., Luukkonen, R., Takala, E.P., and Viikari-Juntura, E. (2002). Effects of ergonomic intervention in work with video display units. *Scandinavian Journal of Work Environment and Health*, *28*, 18-24.

Kite, M.E., and Johnson, B.T. (1988). Attitudes toward younger and older adults: A meta-analysis. *Psychology and Aging*, *3*, 233-244.

Klein, R., Klein, B.E.K., Jensen, S.C., and Moss, S.E. (2001). The relation of socioeconomic factors to the incidence of early age-related maculopathy: The Beaver Dam eye study. *American Journal of Ophthalmology*, *132*, 128-131.

Kline, D.W., and Fuchs, P. (1993). The visibility of symbolic highway signs can be increased among drivers of all ages. *Human Factors*, *35*, 25-34.

Kline, T.J., Ghali, L.M., and Kline, D.W. (1990). Visibility distance of highway signs among young, middle-aged, and older observers: Icons are better than text. *Human Factors*, *32*, 609-619.

Kola, L., and Dunkle, R. (1988). Eldercare in the workplace. *Social Casework, 69*, 569-574.

Kozma, A., Stones, M.J., and Hannah, T.E. (1991). Age, activity, and physical performance: An evaluation of performance models. *Psychology and Aging, 6*, 43-49.

Kramer, A.F., Hahn, S., McAuley, E., Cohen, N.J., Banich, M.T., Harrison, C., Chason, J., Boileau, R.A., Bardell, L., Colcombe, A., and Vakil, E. (2001). Exercise, aging, and cognition: Health body, healthy mind? In W.A. Rogers and A.D. Fisk (eds.), *Human factors interventions for the health care of older adults* (pp. 91-120). Mahwah, NJ: Erlbaum.

Krause, N., Ragland, D.R., Fisher, J.M., and Syme, S.L. (1998). Psychosocial job factors, physical workload, and incidence of work-related spinal injury: A 5-year prospective study of urban transit operators. *Spine, 23*(23), 2507-2516.

Krause, N., Dasinger, L.K., Deegan, L.J., Rudolph, L., and Brand, R.J. (2001a). Psychosocial job factors Sand return to work after low back injury: a disability phase-specific analysis. *American Journal of Industrial Medicine, 40*, 374-392.

Krause, N., Frank, J.W., Dasinger, L.K., Sullivan, T.J., and Sinclair, S.J. (2001b). Determinants of duration of disability and return-to-work after work-related injury and illness: challenges for future research. *American Journal of Industrial Medicine, 40*, 464-484.

Kroemer, K.H.E. (1997). Anthropometry and biomechanics. In A.D. Fisk and W. Rogers (eds.), *Handbook of human factors and the older adult* (pp. 87-124). San Diego: Academic Press.

Kubeck, J.E., Delp, N.D., Haslett, T.K., and McDaniel, M.A. (1996). Does job-related training performance decline with age? *Psychology and Aging, 11*, 92-107.

Kurtz, J., Robins, T., and Schork, M. (1997). An evaluation of peer and professional trainers in a union-based occupational health and safety program. *Journal of Occupational and Environmental Medicine, 39*(7), 661-671.

Lando, M.E., Cutler, R.R., and Gamber, E. (1982). Data book: 1978 survey of disability and work. Washington, DC: U.S. Department of Health and Social Services, Social Security Administration, SSA publication no. 13-11745.

Landsbergis, P.A. (2000). Collective bargaining to reduce CVD risk factors in the work environment. *Occupational Medicine: State-of-the-Art Reviews, 15*(1), 287-292.

Landsbergis, P.A. (2003). The changing organization of work and the health and safety of working people: A commentary. *Journal of Occupational and Environmental Medicine, 45*(1), 61-72.

Landsbergis, P.A., Schurman, S.J., Israel, B.A., Schnall, P.L., Hugentobler, M.K., Cahill, J., and Baker, D. (1997). Job stress and heart disease: Evidence and strategies for prevention. In C. Levenstein and J. Wooding (eds.), *Work, Health and Environment: Old Problems, New Solutions*. New York: Guilford Press.

Landsbergis, P.A., Cahill, J., and Schnall, P. (1999). The impact of lean production and related new systems of work organization on worker health. *Journal of Occupational Health Psychology*, 4, 108-130.

Landsbergis, P.A., Schnall, P., Belkic, K., Baker, D., Schwartz, J., and Pickering, T. (2002). Job stress and cardiovascular disease. In J. Quick and L. Tetrick (eds.), *Handbook of Occupational Health Psychology*. Washington, DC: American Psychological Association.

LaRock, S. (1998). How five different employers provide retirement planning to their employees. *Employee Benefit Plan Review*, 3, 14.

Layne, L.A., and Landen, D.D. (1997). A descriptive analysis of nonfatal occupational injuries to older workers, using a national probability sample of hospital emergency departments. *Journal of Occupational and Environmental Medicine/American College of Occupational and Environmental Medicine*, 39, 855-865.

Lefkovich, J.L. (1992). Business responds to elder-care needs. *Human Resource Magazine*, 37(6), 103-104.

Leigh, J.P., Markowitz, S.B., Fahs, M., Shin, C., and Landrigan, P.J. (1997). Occupational injury and illness in the United States. Estimates of cost, morbidity, and mortality. *Archives of Internal Medicine*, 157(14), 1557-1568.

Levi, L. (2000). Legislation to protect worker CV health in Europe. *Occupational Medicine: State-of-the-Art Reviews*, 15(1), 269-273.

Li, G., Braver, E.R., and Chen, L-H. (2003). Fragility versus excessive crash involvement as determinants of high death rates per vehicle-mile of travel among older drivers. *Accident Analysis and Prevention*, 35, 227-235.

Lieber, C.S. (2000). Alcohol and the liver: metabolism of alcohol and its role in hepatic and extrahepatic diseases. *Mount Sinai Journal of Medicine*, 67(1), 84-94.

Lincoln, A.E., Vernick, J.S., Ogaitis, S., Smith, G.S., Mitchell, C.S., and Agnew, J. (2000). Interventions for the primary prevention of work-related carpal tunnel syndrome. *American Journal of Preventive Medicine*, 18, 37-50.

Lipsy, R.J. (2003). Effective management of patients with dyslipidemia. *American Journal of Managed Care*, 9(2 Suppl), S39-S58.

Loisel, P., Abenhaim, L., Durand, P., Esdaile, J., Suissa, S., Gosselin, L., Simard, R., Turcotte, J., and Lemaire, J.A. (1997). Population-based, randomized clinical trial on back pain management. *Spine*, 22, 2911-2918.

Lötters, F., and Burdof, A. (2002). Are changes in mechanical exposure and musculoskeletal health good performance indicators for primary interventions? *International Archives of Occupational and Environmental Health*, 75(8), 549-561.

Lubin, B., Shanklin, H.D., and Polk, A.M. (1996). The EAP literature: 1991 to 1995. *Employee Assistance Quarterly*, 11(4), 59-81.

Macdonald, S., and Wells, S. (1994). The prevalence and characteristics of employee assistance, health promotion and drug testing programs in Ontario. *Employee Assistance Quarterly*, 10(1), 25-60.

Macdonald, S., Wells, S., Lothian, S., and Shain, M. (2000). Absenteeism and other workplace indicators of Employee Assistance Program clients and matched controls. *Employee Assistance Quarterly*, 15(3), 41-57.

MacKenzie, E.J.A., Morriss, J., Jurkovich, G., Yasui, Y., Cushing, B., Burgess, A., DeLateur, B., McAndrew, M., and Swiontkowski, M. (1998). Return to work following injury: The role of economic, social, and job-related factors. *American Journal of Public Health*, 88(11), 1630-1637.

Marbach, G. (1968). *Job redesign for older workers*. Paris: Organisation for Economic Co-operation and Development Employment of Older Workers.

Marosy, J.P. (1998). Working caregivers: A growing market. *Caring, 17*(9), 12-14.

Marras, W.S., Allread, W.G., Burr, D.L., and Fathallah, F.A. (2000). Prospective validation of a low-back disorder risk model and assessment of ergonomic interventions associated with manual materials handling tasks. *Ergonomics, 43*, 1866-1886.

Marshall, V.W., and Mueller, M.M. (2002). CPRN Discussion Paper No W/18. Rethinking Social Policy for an Aging Workforce and Society: Insights from the Life Course Perspective. Ottawa: Canadian Policy Research Networks.

Martocchio, J.J. (1989). Age-related differences in employee absenteeism: A meta-analysis. *Psychology and Aging, 4*, 409-414.

McEvoy, G.M., and Cascio, W.F. (1989). Cumulative evidence of the relationship between employee age and job performance. *Journal of Applied Psychology, 74*, 1117.

McIntosh, G., Frank, J., Hogg-Johnson, S., Bomdardier, C., and Hall, H. (2000). Prognositc factors for time on workers' compensation benefits in a cohort of low back pain patients. *Spine, 25*(2), 147-157.

McKibbon, D.J. (1993). Staffing characteristics of Canadian EAP professionals. *Employee Assistance Quarterly, 9*(1), 31-66.

McNaught, W., and Barth, M. (1992). Are older workers "good buys"—A case study of Days Inns of America. *Sloan Management Review, Spring*, 53-63.

McQuiston, T. (2000). Empowerment evaluation of worker safety and health education programs. *American Journal of Industrial Medicine, 38*, 584-597.

McQuiston, T., Coleman, P., Wallerstein, N., Marcus, A., Morawetz, J., and Ortleib, D. (1994). Hazardous waste worker education. *Journal of Occupational Medicine, 36*(12), 1310-1323.

Mead, S.E., and Fisk, A.D. (1998). Measuring skill acquisition and retention with an ATM simulator: The need for age-specific training. *Human Factors, 40*, 516-523.

Mead, S.E., Spaulding, V.A., Sit, R.A., Meyer, B., and Walker, N. (1997). Effects of age and training on World Wide Web navigation strategies. *Proceedings of the Human Factors and Ergonomics Society 41st Annual Meeting*, 152-156. Santa Monica, CA: Human Factors and Ergonomics Society.

Melin, B., Lundberg, U., Soderlund, J., and Granqvist, M. (1999). Psychophysiological stress reactions of male and female assembly workers: A comparison between two different forms of work organization. *Journal of Organizational Behavior, 20*, 47-61.

Merrill, M. (1995). The small group activity method. *New Solutions, 5*(2), 42-46.

Miller, P.S. (2000). The evolving ADA. In P.D. Blank, (ed.), *Employment, disability and the Americans with Disabilities Act* (pp. 3-15). Evanston, IL: Northwestern University Press.

Mitchell, O.S., Levine, P.B., and Phillips, J.W. (1999). Impact of pay inequality, occupational segregation, and lifetime work experience on the retirement income of women and minorities. Washington DC: Public Policy Institute, AARP.

Moen, P. (1996). Life course perspective on retirement, gender, and well-being. *Journal of Occupational Health Psychology, 1*(2), 131-144.

Moen, P. (1998). Recasting careers: Changing reference groups, risks, and realities. *Generations, 22*(1), 40-45.

Murphy, L., Hurrell, J., Sauter, S., and Keita, G.E. (1995). *Job Stress Interventions*. Washington, DC: American Psychological Association.

National Institute for Occupational Safety and Health. (1997). *Effective Workplace Practices and Programs*. Chicago, IL: NIOSH.

National Institute for Occupational Safety and Health. (2002a). *Worker health chartbook 2000: Fatal injury*. Department of Health and Human Services and NIOSH. Publication Number 2002-117. Available: http://www.cdc.gov/niosh/pdfs/2002-117.pdf [accessed February 2004].

National Institute for Occupational Safety and Health. (2002b). *The changing organization of work and the safety and health of working people: Knowledge gaps and research directions.* (2002-116). Cincinnati, OH: NIOSH.

National Research Council and the Institute of Medicine. (2001). *Musculoskeletal Disorders and the Workplace: Low Back and Upper Extremities.* Panel on Musculoskeletal Disorders and the Workplace, Commission on Behavioral and Social Sciences and Education. Washington, DC: National Academy Press.

Nelson, N., and Silverstein, B. (1998). Workplace changes associated with a reduction in musculoskeletal symptoms in office workers. *Human Factors, 40,* 337-350.

Newell, A., and Rosenbloom, P.S. (1981). Mechanisms of skill acquisition and the power law of practice. In J.R. Anderson (ed.), *Cognitive skills and their acquisition* (pp. 1-55). Hillsdale, NJ: Lawrence Erlbaum Associates.

Noe, R.A., and Wilk, S.L. (1993). Investigation of the factors that influence employees' participation in developmental activities. *Journal of Applied Psychology, 78,* 291-302.

Nordin, B.E., Need, A.G., Steurer, T., Morris, H.A., Chatterton, B.E., Horowitz, M. (1998). Nutrition, osteoporosis, and aging. *Annals of the New York Academy of Sciences, 854,* 336-351.

Occupational Safety and Health Act. (2002). BSR/HFES100 Draft Standard for Trial Use: Human Factors Engineering of Computer Workstations. Ergonomic Solutions: Computer Workstations. Available: http://www.osha.gov/pls/oshaweb/owadisp.show_document?p_table=NEWS_RELEASES&p_id=1245 [accessed April 22, 2004].

O'Rand, A.M., and Henretta, J.C. (1999). *Age and inequality: Diverse pathways through later life.* Boulder, CO: Westview Press.

Orth-Gomer, K., Eriksson, I., Moser, V., Theorell, T., and Fredlund, P. (1994). Lipid lowering through work stress reduction. *International Journal of Behavioral Medicine, 1*(3), 204-214.

Owsley, C., Ball, K., Sloane, M.E., Roenker, D.L., and Bruni, J.R. (1991). Visual/cognitive correlates of vehicle accidents in older drivers. *Psychology and Aging, 6,* 403-415.

Park, D.C., Hertzog, C., Leventhal, H., Morrell, R.W., Leventhal, E., Birchmore, D., Martin, M., and Bennett, J. (1999) Medication adherence in rheumatoid arthritis patients: Older is wiser. *Journal of the American Geriatrics Society, 47*(2), 172-183.

Parker, S.K., and Wall, T.D. (1998). *Job and work design: Organizing work for well-being and performance.* Newbury Park, CA: Sage.

Parkes, K.R., and Sparkes, T.J. (1998). *Organizational interventions to reduce work stress. Are they effective? A review of the literature.* Sudbury, Suffolk, England: HSE Books.

Peebles, L., and Norris, B. (2003). Filling "gaps" in strength data for design. *Applied Ergonomics, 34,* 73-88.

Perkins, K. (1994). Older women in the workplace and implications for retirement: EAP can make a difference. *Employment Assistance Quarterly, 9* (3/4), 81-97.

Perkins, K. (2000). EAP services to older adults in the workplace: A strengths perspective. *Employee Assistant Quarterly, 16* (1/2), 53-75.

Pessina, D., and Guerretti, M. (2000). Effectiveness of hearing protection devices in the hazard reduction of noise from used tractors. *Journal of Agricultural Engineering Research, 75,* 73-80.

The President's Committee on Employment of People with Disabilities Report. (1995). Available: http://www.jfanow.org/cgi/getli.pl?105 [accessed April 2004].

Probst, T.M., and Brubaker, T.L. (2001). The effects of job insecurity on employee safety outcomes: Cross-sectional and longitudinal explorations. *Journal of Occupational Health Psychology, 6,* 139-159.

Punnett L., and Herbert, R. (2000). Work-related musculoskeletal disorders: Is there a gender differential, and if so, what does it mean? In M.B. Goldman and M.C. Hatch (eds.), *Women and health* (pp. 474-492). New York: Academic Press.

Rogers, W.A., and Fisk, A.D. (2000). Human factors, applied cognition, and aging. In F.I.M. Craik and T.A. Salthouse (eds.), *Handbook of Aging and Cognition* (2nd ed., pp. 559-591). Mahwah, NJ: Erlbaum.

Rogers, W.A., Lamson, N., and Rousseau, G.K. (2000). Warning Research: An integrative perspective. *Human Factors, 42*(1), 102-139.

Ronald, L.A., Yassi, A., Spiegel, J., Tate, R.B., Tait, D., and Mozel, M.R. (2002). Effectiveness of installing overhead ceiling lifts. *American Association of Occupational Health Nurses Journal, 50*, 120-127.

Root, N. (1981). Injuries at work are fewer among older employees. *Monthly Labor Review, 104*, 30-34.

Ruhm, C.J. (1994). Bridge employment and job stopping: Evidence from the Harris/Commonwealth Fund survey. *Journal of Aging & Social Policy, 66*(4), 73-99.

Rydstedt, L.W., Johansson, G., and Evans, G.W. (1998). The human side of the road: Improving the working conditions of urban bus drivers. *Journal of Occupational Health Psychology, 3*, 161-171.

Salas, E., and Cannon-Bowers, J.A. (2001). The science of training: A decade of progress. *Annual Review of Psychology, 52*, 471-499.

Salthouse, T.A. (1996). The processing-speed theory of adult age differences in cognition. *Psychological Review, 103*, 403-428.

Salthouse, T.A., and Maurer, J.J. (1996). Aging, job performance, and career development. In J.E. Birren and K.W. Schaie (eds.), *Handbook of the psychology of aging* (4th ed., pp. 353-364). New York: Academic Press.

Sauter, S., and Hurrell, J. (1999). Occupational health psychology: Origins, content and direction. *Professional Psychology: Research and Practice, 30*(2), 17-22.

Scharlach, A.E., and Boyd, S.L. (1989). Caregiving and employment: Results of an employment survey. *The Gerontologist, 29*(3), 383-387.

Schechter, E.S. (1981). *Employment and work adjustments of the disabled.* Disability Survey 72: Disabled and non-disabled adults. Washington, DC: U.S. Department of Health and Human Services, Social Security Administration, Office of Research and Statistics. Research report no. 56.

Schibye, B., Hansen, A.F., Søgaard, K., and Christensen, H. (2001). Aerobic power and muscle strength among young and elderly workers with and without physically demanding work tasks. *Applied Ergonomics, 5*, 425-431.

Schmidt, F.L. (1996). Statistical significance testing and cumulative knowledge in psychology: Implications for training of researchers. *Psychological Methods, 1*, 115-129.

Schnall, P., and Belkic, K. (2000). Point estimates of blood pressure at the worksite. *Occupational Medicine: State-of-the-Art Reviews, 15*(1), 203-208.

Schooler, C., Mulatu, M.S., and Oates, G. (1999). The continuing effects of substantively complex work on the intellectual functioning of older workers. *Psychology and Aging, 14*, 483-506.

Sciegaj, M., Garnick, D.W., Horgan, C.M., Merrick, E.L., Goldin, D., Urato, M., and Hodgkin, D. (2001). Employee assistance programs among Fortune 500 firms. *Employee Assistance Quarterly, 16*(3), 25-35.

Seccombe, K. (1992). Employment, the family, and employer-based policies. In J.W. Dwyer and R.T. Coward (eds.), *Gender, families, and elder care* (vol. 138, pp. 165-180). Thousand Oaks, CA: Sage Focus Editions.

Shephard, R.J. (1995). A personal perspective on aging and productivity, with particular reference to physically demanding work. *Ergonomics, 38*, 617-636.

Sherman, R.H. (1997). Sources of help in financial preparation for retirement: AAAs to Web sites. *Generations, 21*(2), 55-60.

Shimomitsu, T., and Odagiri, Y. (2000). Working life in Japan. *Occupational Medicine: State of the Art Reviews, 15*(1), 280-281.

Siegrist, J., and Peter, R. (1996). *Measuring effort-reward imbalance at work: Guidelines.* Dusseldorf: University of Dusseldorf.

Sijuwade, P.O. (1996). Older workers: Their employment and occupational problems in the labor market. *Social Behavior and Personality, 24*(3), 235-238.

Silverman, K., Svikis, D., Robles, E., Stitzer, M.L., and Bigelow, G.E. (2001). A reinforcement-based therapeutic workplace for the treatment of drug abuse: Six-month abstinence outcomes. *Experimental and Clinical Psychopharmacology, 9*, 14-23.

Simon, H.A. (1969). *The sciences of the artificial.* Cambridge, MA: MIT Press.

Singley, M.K., and Anderson, J.R. (1989). *The transfer of cognitive skill.* Cambridge, MA: Harvard University Press.

Smith, M., and Zehel, D. (1992). A stress reduction intervention programme for meat processors emphasizing job design and work organization. *Conditions of Work Digest, 11*(2), 204-213.

Smith, W., Assink, J., Klein, R., Mitchell, P., Klaver, C.C.W., Klein, B.E.K., Hofman, A., Jensen, S., Wang, J.J., and de Jong, P.T.V.M. (2001). Risk factors for age-related macular degeneration: Pooled findings from three continents. *Ophthalmology, 108*, 697-704.

Sorenson, G. (2001). Worksite tobacco control programs: The role of occupational health. *Respiration Physiology, 128*, 89-102.

Sparrow, P.R., and Davies, D.R. (1988). Effects of age, tenure, training, and job complexity on technical performance. *Psychology and Aging, 3*, 307-314.

Sprince, N., Park, H., Zwerling, C., Lynch, C., Whitten, P., Thu, K., Gillette, P., Burmeister, L., and Alavanja, N. (2003). Risk factors for animal-related injury among Iowa large livestock farmers: A case-control study nested in the Agricultural Health Study. *Journal of Rural Health, 19*, 165-173.

Starkman, P.E. (2000). Answering the tough questions about alcoholism and substance abuse under the ADA and FMLA. *Employee Relations Law Journal, 25*(4), 43-77.

Steenbekkers, L.P.A., and van Beijsterveldt, C.E.M. (1998). *Design-relevant characteristics of ageing users.* Delft, The Netherlands: Delft University Press.

Sterns, H.L., Barrett, G.V., and Alexander, R.A. (1985). Accidents and the aging individual. In J.E. Birren and K.W. Schaie (eds.), *Handbook of the psychology of aging* (2nd ed., pp. 703-724). New York: Van Nostrand Reinhold.

Stine, E.L., Wingfield, A., and Poon, L.W. (1986). How much and how fast: Rapid processing of spoken language in later adulthood. *Psychology and Aging, 1*, 303-311.

Straussner, S.L.A. (1988). Comparison of in-house and contracted-out employee assistance programs. *Social Work, 33*(1), 53-55.

Strayer, D.L., and Kramer, A.F. (1994). Aging and skill acquisition: Learning-performance distinctions. *Psychology and Aging, 9*(4), 589-605.

Stutts, J.C. (in press). The safety of older drivers—the U.S. perspective. In K.W. Schaie, H.-W. Wahl, H. Mollenkopf, and F. Oswald (eds.), *Aging in the Community: Living Arrangements and Mobility.* New York: Springer.

Sverke, M., Hellgren, J., and Naswall, K. (2002). No security: A metaanalysis and review of job insecurity and its consequences. *Journal of Occupational Health Psychology, 7*(3), 242-264.

Swaen, G.M., Kant, I.J., van Amelsvoort, L.G., and Beurskens, A.J. (2002). Job mobility, its determinants, and its effects: Longitudinal data from the Maastricht Cohort Study. *Journal of Occupational Health Psychology, 7*(2), 121-129.

Swagerty, D.L. Jr., Walling, A.D., and Klein, R.M. (2002). Lactose intolerance. *American Family Physician*, 65(9), 1855-1856.

Theorell, T., Perski, A., Orth-Gomer, K., Hamsten, A., and de Faire, U. (1991). The effects of the strain of returning to work on the risk of cardiac death after a first myocardial infarction before age 45. *International Journal of Cardiology, 30*, 61-67.

Thorndike, E.L. (1924). Mental discipline in high school studies. *Journal of Educational Psychology, 15*, 1-22, 83-98.

Tober, P.A. (1987). Eldercare: An issue of emerging importance. *Credit, 13*(6), 22-23.

The Tokyo Declaration. (1998). *Journal of the Tokyo Medical University, 56*(6), 760-767.

Touron, D.R., Hoyer, W.J., and Cerella, J. (2001). Cognitive skill acquisition and transfer in younger and older adults. *Psychology & Aging, 16*, 555-563.

Trice, H.M., and Schonbrunn, M. (1981). A history of job-based alcoholism programs: 1900-1955. *Journal of Drug Issues, 11*(2), 171-198.

U.S. Bureau of the Census. (2002). *Income 2001*. Available: http://www.census.gov/hhes/income/income01/inctab7.html [accessed February 2004]

U.S. Department of Labor, (1996). *Older workers' injuries entail lengthy absences from work*. Bureau of Labor Statistics. Washington, DC: U.S. Government Printing Office. Summary 96-6.

U.S. General Accounting Office. (2004). *Older workers: Employment assistance focuses on subsidized jobs and job search, but revised performance measures could improve access to other services*. Report No.GAO-03-350. Available: http://www.gao.gov/review/d03478sp.pdf. [accessed Feburary 2004].

U.S. Preventive Services Task Force. (1996). *Guide to Clinical Preventive Services*. 2nd ed. A Report of the U.S. Preventive Services Task Force. Baltimore, MD: Lippincott Williams and Wilkins.

Vanderheiden, G.C. (1997). Design for people with functional limitations resulting from disability, aging, or circumstance. In G. Salvendy (ed.), *Handbook of human factors and ergonomics* (pp. 2010-2052). New York: John Wiley and Sons.

Verbrugge, L.M., Lepkowski, J.M., and Konkol, L.L. (1991). Levels of disability among U.S. adults with arthritis. *Journal of Gerontology, 46*, S71–S83.

Vinokur, A.D., and Schul, Y. (2002). The web of coping resources and pathways to reemployment following a job loss. *Journal of Occupational Health Psychology, 7*, 68-83.

Volkoff, S., Touranchet, A., and Derriennic, F. (1998). The statistical study of the links between age, work and health and the ESTEV survey sample. In J.C. Marquié, D.P. Cau-Bareille, and S. Volkoff (eds.), *Working with age* (pp. 91-97). London: Taylor and Francis.

Wagner, D.L. (1990). Eldercare: A workplace issue. In E.W. Markson and B.B. Hess (eds.), *Growing Old in America* (pp. 377-388). New Brunswick, NJ: Transaction Publishers.

Wagner, D.L. (1997). *Comparative Analysis of Caregiver Data for Caregivers to the Elderly 1987 to 1997*. Bethesda, MD: National Alliance for Caregivers.

Waldman, D.A., and Avolio, B.J. (1986). A meta-analysis of age differences in job performance. *Journal of Applied Psychology, 71*, 33-38.

Wallerstein, N., and Weinger, M. (1992). Health and safety education for worker empowerment. *American Journal of Industrial Medicine, 22*, 619-635.

Walsh, D.C. (1982). Employee assistance programs. *Milbank Memorial Fund Quarterly, Health and Society, 60*(3), 492-517.

Warr, P.B. (1992). Age and occupational well-being. *Psychology and Aging, 7*, 37-45.

Warr, P.B. (1998). Age, work, and mental health. In K.W. Schaie and C. Schooler (eds.), *Impact of work on older adults* (pp. 252-296). New York: Springer.

Warr, P.B. (2001). Age and work behaviour: Physical attributes, cognitive abilities, knowledge, personality traits and motives. In C.L. Cooper and I.T. Robinson (eds.), *International Review of Industrial and Organizational Psychology*, *16*, 1-36.

Warren, N. (2000). U.S. regulations for work organization. *Occupational Medicine: State-of-the-Art Reviews*, *15*(1), 275-280.

Weckerle, J.R., and Shultz, K.S. (1999). Influences on the bridge employment decision among older USA workers. *Journal of Occupational and Organizational Psychology*, *72*, 317-329.

Weisberg, M. (1993). Ergonomic guidelines for designing effective and healthy learning environments for interactive technologies. Interpersonal Computing and Technology: An Electronic Journal for the 21st Century. ISSN 1064-4326. Vol 1, No. 2. Available: http://tlc.nlm.nih.gov/resources/publications/ergo/ergonomics.html [accessed June 21, 2002].

Welford, A.T. (1958). *Aging and human skills*. London: Oxford University Press.

Westgaard, R.H., and Winkel, J. (1997). Ergonomic intervention research for improved musculoskeletal health: A critical review. *International Journal of Industrial Ergonomics*, *20*, 463-500.

Williams, C.M. (2002). Using medications appropriately in older adults. *American Family Physician*, *66*(10), 1917-1924.

Williams, R.A., and Strasser, P.B. (1999). Depression in the workplace. Impact on employees. *American Association of Occupational Health Nurses Journal*, *47*(11), 526-537.

Willis, S.L., and Schaie, K.W. (1986). Training the elderly on the ability factors of spatial orientation and inductive reasoning. *Psychology and Aging*, *1*, 239-247.

Winfield, F.E. (1987). Workplace solutions for women under eldercare pressure. *Personnel*, *64*(7), 31-39.

Yassi, A., Cooper, J.E., Tate, R.B., Gerlach, S., Muir, M., Trottier, J., and Massey, K. (2001). A randomized controlled trial to prevent patient lift and transfer injuries of health care workers. *Spine*, *26*, 1739-1746.

Zwerling, C., Sprince, N.L., Wallace, R.B., Davis, C.S., and Whitten, P.S. (1996). Alcohol and occupational injuries among older workers. *Accident Analysis and Prevention*, *28*(3), 371-376.

Zwerling, C., Sprince, N.L., Davis, C.S., Whitten, P.S., Wallace, R.R., and Heeringa, S.G. (1998a). Occupational injuries among older workers with disabilities: A prospective cohort study of the Health and Retirement Survey, 1992-1994. *American Journal of Public Health*, *88*(11), 1691-1695.

Zwerling, C., Whitten, P.S., Davis, C.S., and Sprince, N.L. (1998b). Occupational injuries among older workers with visual, auditory, and other impairments: A validation study. *Journal of Occupational and Environmental Medicine*, *40*(8), 720-723.

CHAPTER 9

National Research Council. (2001). Preparing for an Aging World: The case for Cross-National Research. Panel on a Research Agenda and New Data for an Aging World, Committee on Population, and Committee on National Statistics. Washington, DC: National Academy Press.

Appendix A

Epidemiological and Demographic Tables

Appendix A is not printed in this volume but is available online. Go to http://www.nap.edu and search for *Health and Safety Needs of Older Workers*.

TABLE A-1 U.S. Labor Force Participation Rates of Men by Age, 1940–2001.
SOURCE: Labor force participation figures for 1970–2001 are authors' calculations using March CPS Annual Demographic files.

TABLE A-2 Poverty Rate (percent) of Older Americans, by Age Group and Work Status, 1970–2000.
SOURCE: Authors' tabulations of March CPS files, various years.

TABLE A-3 U.S. Labor Force Participation Rates of Women by Age, 1970–2001.
SOURCE: Labor force participation figures for 1970–2001 are author's calculations using March CPS Annual Demographic files.

TABLE A-4 Distribution of Older Workers Across Major Industrial Categories.
SOURCE: Current Population Survey, March 2001.

TABLE A-5 Distribution of Older Workers Across Major Occupational Categories.
SOURCE: Current Population Survey, March 2001.

TABLE A-6 Current Employment Situation.
SOURCE: Current Population Survey, March 2001.

TABLE A-7 Work Characteristics.
SOURCE: Current Population Survey, March 2001.

TABLE A-8 Job Characteristics.
SOURCE: Current Population Survey, March 2001.

TABLE A-9 Physical Functioning Among Workers.
SOURCE: Current Population Survey, March 2001.

TABLE A-10 Health Characteristics.
SOURCE: Current Population Survey, March 2001.

TABLE A-11 Incidence Rates (1) of Occupational Injuries and Illnesses for Private Industry by Selected Case Types, 1973–2001.
SOURCE: Bureau of Labor Statistics, U.S. Department of Labor.

TABLE A-12 Number of Nonfatal Occupational Illnesses by Industry Division and Selected Case Types, 2001 (thousands).
SOURCE: Bureau of Labor Statistics, U.S. Department of Labor.

TABLE A-13 Number of Nonfatal Occupational Injuries and Illnesses Involving Days Away from Work (1) by Selected Occupation and Industry Division, 2000 (thousands).
SOURCE: Bureau of Labor Statistics, U.S. Department of Labor.

TABLE A-14 Number of Nonfatal Occupational Injuries and Illnesses Involving Days Away from Work (1) by Selected Injury or Illness Characteristics and Industry Division, 2000 (thousands).
SOURCE: Bureau of Labor Statistics, U.S. Department of Labor.

TABLE A-15 Incidence Rates (1) for Nonfatal Occupational Injuries and Illnesses Involving Days Away from Work (2) per 10,000 Full-Time Workers for Selected Characteristics and Industry Division, 2000.
SOURCE: Bureau of Labor Statistics, U.S. Department of Labor.

TABLE A-16 Number of Nonfatal Occupational Injuries and Illnesses Involving Days Away from Work (1) by Selected Worker Characteristics and Industry Division, 2000 (thousands).
SOURCE: Bureau of Labor Statistics, U.S. Department of Labor.

TABLE A-17 Worker Compensation Claims for Work-Related Musculoskeletal Disorders, Washington State, 1992–2000.

TABLE A-18 Fatal Occupational Injuries and Employment by Selected Worker Characteristics, 2001.
SOURCE: Bureau of Labor Statistics, U.S. Department of Labor, in cooperation with state, New York City, District of Columbia, and federal agencies, Census of Fatal Occupational Injuries, 2001. Claims include all those from approximately 160,000 employers covered by the Washington State Insurance Fund.

TABLE A-19 Number and Percent Distribution of Currently Employed Adults 18 Years of Age and Over, by Sex and Length of Time Spent Daily at Specified Types of Work Activity, According to Selected Socioeconomic Characteristics: United States, 1988.
SOURCE: Wegener, D.K., Walstedt, J., Jenkins, L. et al. (1997). Women: Work and health. *Vital Health Statistics* 3(31).

TABLE A-20 Number and Percent Distribution of Currently Employed Adults 18 Years of Age and Over, by Sex and Reported Exposure to Substances or Radiation at Work and Concern Regarding Exposure, According to Selected Socioeconomic Characteristics: United States, 1992.
SOURCE: Wegener, D.K., Walstedt, J., Jenkins, L. et al. (1997). Women: Work and health. *Vital Health Statistics* 3(31).

TABLE A-21 Health Insurance Coverage Status and Type of Coverage by Selected Characteristics, Calendar Year 2001.
SOURCE: Mills, R.J. (2002). *Health Insurance Coverage: 2001*. Washington, DC: U.S. Bureau of the Census. Pp. 60-220.

Appendix B

Estimated Survival Functions
for Men and Women

Appendix B is not printed in this volume but is available online. Go to http://www.nap.edu and search for *Health and Safety Needs of Older Workers.*

TABLE B-1 Estimated Survival Functions for Men and Women Employed at Age 50, by Industry.
SOURCE: Current Population Surveys 1981–2001.

TABLE B-2 Estimated Survival Functions for Men and Women Employed at Age 50, by Occupation.
SOURCE: Current Population Surveys 1981–2000.

TABLE B-3 Estimated Survival Functions and Employment Rates by Race for Men and Women Employed at Age 50.
SOURCE: Current Population Surveys 1981–2001.

TABLE B-4 Estimated Survival Function and Employment Rates by Education for Men and Women Employed at Age 50.
SOURCE: Current Population Surveys 1981–2001.

Appendix C

Biographical Sketches of Committee Members and Staff

David H. Wegman (*Chair*) is the dean of the School of Health and Environment and founding chair of the Department of Work Environment in the Engineering College at the University of Massachusetts, Lowell. He is board certified in preventive medicine (occupational medicine). His research has focused on epidemiological studies of occupational disease, musculoskeletal disorders, and cancer; developing methods to study subjective outcomes, such as musculoskeletal and respiratory or irritant symptoms reports; and health and safety needs of older workers. At the National Research Council, he chaired the Committee on Health and Safety Implications of Child Labor and was a member of the Panel on Musculoskeletal Disorders and the Workplace; the Committee on Gender Differences in Susceptibility to Environmental Factors: A Priority Assessment; the Committee to Review the Health Consequences of Service During the Persian Gulf War; and the Committee on the Role of the Primary Care Physician in Occupational/Environmental Medicine. He has M.Sc. and M.D. degrees from Harvard University.

Richard V. Burkhauser is chair of the Department of Policy Analysis and Management and Sarah Gibson Blanding Professor of Policy Analysis in the College of Human Ecology at Cornell University. His current research interests focus on the importance of social environment on the work outcomes of people with disabilities; how disability influences economic well-being; how Social Security reforms will affect the work and economic well-being of older persons; and on cross-national comparisons of the economic

285

well-being and work of older persons. He is a member of the Panel Study on Income Dynamics board of overseers and the editorial boards of *The Gerontologist*, *The Journal of Disability Policy Studies*, *The Review of Income and Wealth*, *Labor Economics*, *Research on Aging*, and *The Journal of Applied Social Science Studies*. He was a member of the technical panel of the 1994–1996 Advisory Council on Social Security and the 1994–1996 National Academy of Social Insurance Panel on Disability Policy Reform. At the National Research Council, he served on the Committee on Disability Determination for Individuals with Visual Impairments and is currently a member of the Panel on a Research Agenda and New Data for an Aging World. He has a Ph.D. in economics from the University of Chicago.

Gary Burtless is a senior fellow and holds the John C. and Nancy D. Whitehead Chair in Economic Studies at the Brookings Institution. Previously, he served as an economist in the policy and evaluation offices of the secretary of labor and the secretary of health, education, and welfare. His recent research has focused on sources of growing wage and income inequality in the United States, the influence of international trade on income inequality, the job market prospects of public aid recipients, reform of social insurance in developing countries and formerly socialist economies, and the implications of privatizing the American social security system. He is coauthor or editor of numerous books, including *Can America Afford to Grow Old? Paying for Social Security* (1989), and editor of and contributor to *Aging Societies: The Global Dimension* (1998); *Work Health and Income Among the Elderly* (1987); and *Retirement and Economic Behavior* (1984). He has a Ph.D. from the Massachusetts Institute of Technology.

Neil Charness is professor of psychology at the Florida State University and a research associate at the Pepper Institute on Aging and Public Policy. His current research interests focus on the topics of human factors in computer use by older adults and on age and expert performance. He has published numerous journal articles and book chapters, and was editor of *Aging and Human Performance* (1985) and coeditor of *Gerontechnology: A Sustainable Investment in the Future* (1998) and *Communication, Technology and Aging: Opportunities and Challenges for the Future* (2001). He is a fellow of the Canadian Psychological Association, the American Psychological Association (Division 20), the American Psychological Society, and the Gerontological Society of America. He has M.S. and Ph.D. degrees from Carnegie Mellon University.

Paul A. Landsbergis is an epidemiologist and associate professor in the Department of Community and Preventive Medicine (Center for Occupational and Environmental Medicine) and in the Department of Medicine (cardiology) at the Mount Sinai School of Medicine in New York City. His areas of research interest include occupational health and safety, occupational stress, ergonomics, psychosocial factors, new systems of work organization, and socioeconomic status and cardiovascular disease. He is a coeditor of the first textbook on work-related cardiovascular disease and a coinvestigator of the Work Site Blood Pressure Study in New York City. He is currently principal investigator of a study of work organization, work stress, hypertension, and cardiovascular disease among auto workers funded by the DaimlerChrysler–United Auto Workers Health and Safety Fund, and a study of the impact of extended work schedules on risk of work-related musculoskeletal disorders, hypertension, and cardiovascular disease funded by the National Institute for Occupational Safety and Health (NIOSH). He has a Ph.D. from Columbia University School of Public Health.

Charles Levenstein is professor of work environment policy at University of Massachusetts, Lowell. He is the author or coauthor of a number of books and has published many articles in refereed journals concerning occupational and environmental policy in the United States and abroad. He is editor of *New Solutions: Journal of Occupational and Environmental Health Policy*. He is a codirector of the Dana-Farber Cancer Institute– University of Massachussetts Lowell Consortium on organized labor and tobacco control, recently funded by the American Legacy Foundation, and is also codirector of the WHO/PAHO collaborating center in occupational health at the University of Massachussetts, Lowell. He has a Ph.D. in economics from the Massachusetts Institute of Technology.

Michael Marmot is professor of epidemiology and public health and director of the International Centre for Health and Society at University College London. He is also adjunct professor of health and social behavior at the Harvard School of Public Health. He has coordinated two European research networks and is now co-coordinator of the European Science Foundation Network on Inequalities in Healthy Life Expectancy. He has been a member of two research networks of the Chicago-based MacArthur Foundation, and a member of the Canadian Institute of Advanced Research Population Research program. He also chaired the Ontario Institute for Work and Health Research Advisory Committee and is a member of the Royal Commission on Environmental Pollution. At the National Research Council, he is a member of the Panel on a Research Agenda and New Data for an Aging World. He has an M.D. from the University of Sydney and a Ph.D. in epidemiology from the University of California, Berkeley.

James P. McGee (*Study Director*) has been a senior project officer at the National Research Council since 1994, supporting projects in the areas of applied psychology, engineering, and education. In addition to directing the Committee on the Health and Safety Needs of Older Workers, he directs the Board on Assessment of NIST Programs, for the Division on Engineering and Physical Sciences, and the Panels on Operational Testing and Evaluation of the Stryker Vehicle and on Assessing the Scientists and Engineers Statistical Data System, for the Committee on National Statistics. He has also served as staff officer for projects on musculoskeletal disorders and the workplace, the changing nature of work, the susceptibility of older persons to environmental hazards, and educational needs of people with autism, all for the Board on Behavioral, Cognitive, and Sensory Sciences. He also directs the Army Research Laboratory Technical Assessment Board. Prior to joining the NRC, he held technical and management positions as an applied psychologist at IBM, General Electric, RCA, General Dynamics, and Sikorsky Aircraft corporations. He has B.A. from Princeton University and a Ph.D. from Fordham University, both in psychology.

Carolyn Emerson Needleman is a professor in the Graduate School of Social Work and Social Research at Bryn Mawr College, where she teaches courses in social policy and research. She has served as the director of Bryn Mawr's social work doctoral program and heads the school's doctoral concentration in occupational and environmental health. She has written widely in the areas of public health, risk communication, occupational safety and health, environmental health, and community development. She has headed a number of community-based research projects dealing with occupational and environmental health and has more than 20 years of experience with program development and evaluation in a wide variety of health and human service programs serving low-income and minority populations. She has a Ph.D. from Washington University in St. Louis.

Timothy A. Salthouse is Brown-Forman Professor of Psychology in the Department of Psychology at the University of Virginia. Previously he was professor of psychology at the University of Missouri, Columbia, and regents professor of psychology at the Georgia Institute of Technology. He is a fellow of the American Association for the Advancement of Science, the American Psychological Association, the American Psychological Society, and the Gerontological Society of America and a member of the Psychonomic Society. He was a recipient of the APA Division 20 Distinguished Contribution Award in 1995, and was named an APS William James Fellow in 1998. At the National Research Council, he was a member of the Panel on Human Factors Research Needs for an Aging Population and on the Panel on Future Directions for Cognitive Research on Aging. He has a Ph.D. in experimental psychology from the University of Michigan.

Michael Silverstein is assistant director for industrial safety and health with the Washington State Department of Labor and Industries, a job that includes responsibility for the state's occupational safety and health program. In the early 1990s he spent two years in Washington, DC, as director of policy for the Occupational Safety and Health Administration and returned to Washington state in 1995. Prior to these government positions, he was assistant director for the Occupational Health and Safety Department of the United Auto Workers Union in Detroit, Michigan. Board-certified as a specialist in occupational medicine, he has also practiced family medicine and occupational medicine in Michigan and California. At the National Research Council, he was a member of the Committee on Health and Safety Implications of Child Labor. He has an M.D. from Stanford Medical School and an M.P.H. from the University of Michigan.

Glorian Sorensen is director of the Dana-Farber Center for Community-Based Research and professor of health and social behavior at the Harvard School of Public Health. Her research has focused on identifying effective means to address disparities in cancer prevention and control by socioeconomic status, social class, and race/ethnicity, with the aim of developing innovative intervention methodologies that are relevant to the needs of these diverse populations. She has conducted a broad spectrum of worksite intervention studies testing the efficacy of cancer prevention methods for low-income and blue-collar workers. She has also studied the role of labor unions in tobacco control efforts. In addition, she has provided a voice for the role of community and worksite-based research in understanding the influence of social and environmental influences on cancer risk. At the Institute of Medicine, she was a member of the Committee on Capitalizing on Social Science and Behavioral Research to Improve the Public's Health and is currently a member of the Committee for Behavior Change in the 21st Century. She has a Ph.D. from the University of Minnesota.

Emily A. Spieler is dean and Edwin Hadley Professor of Law at the Northeastern University School of Law. She has written and spoken extensively on issues related to occupational safety and health, employment and disability law, and workers' compensation. She currently also serves as a member of the Workers' Compensation Steering Committee for the National Academy of Social Insurance and as a member of the Social and Economic Consequences of Workplace Illness and Injury Implementation Team for the National Occupational Research Agenda of the National Institute for Occupational Safety and Health. She has a J.D. from Yale Law School.

Robert B. Wallace is professor of epidemiology and internal medicine at the University of Iowa Colleges of Public Health and Medicine, as well as interim director of the University's Center on Aging. His research interests concern the causes and prevention of disabling conditions of older persons. He has had substantial experience in the conduct of both observational cohort studies of older persons and clinical trials, including preventive interventions related to osteoporotic fracture and coronary disease prevention. He is the principal site investigator for the Women's Health Initiative (WHI), a national intervention trial exploring the prevention of breast and colon cancer and coronary disease. A member of the Institute of Medicine, he has served on many study committees and is currently chair of its health promotion and disease prevention board. He is a senior advisor to the U.S. Preventive Services Task Force and has served on the executive committee of the Association of Teachers of Preventive Medicine and chaired the epidemiology section of the American Public Health Association. He has an M.D. from Northwestern University.

Craig Zwerling is a professor in the departments of Occupational and Environmental Health, Epidemiology, and Internal Medicine at the University of Iowa. He is head of the Department of Occupational and Environmental Health in the University of Iowa College of Public Health and directs the University's Injury Prevention Research Center. His research has included studies of occupational injuries among workers with disabilities. He is currently studying workplace accommodations for workers with disabilities and their effect in reducing occupational injury rates. At the Institute of Medicine, he served on the Committee on Injury Prevention and Control. He has an M.D. from Case Western Reserve University and M.P.H. and Ph.D. degrees from Harvard University.

Index

A

Absenteeism, 188–189. *See also* Lost workdays
Accommodation, workplace, 9, 16, 176–177
  concept of disability and, 16, 214–215
  cost, 216
  current implementation, 216, 226
  effectiveness, 216–217, 226
  goals, 175, 216
  hierarchy of controls concept, 175–176
  legal basis, 159–163, 215
  public policy conceptualization, 215
  reasonable, 215
  relief of obligation to provide, 161–163, 164–165
  research needs, 225, 226
  See also Job design/redesign
Administrative support occupations, 50, 147
Age Discrimination in Employment Act, 156, 157, 158, 224, 225
Age-related changes, 2–3, 95
  acute stress response and, 101
  assessment considerations, 100–101
  bone anatomy and function, 104–105
  cognitive functioning, 113–115
  conceptual models, 97–100
  future trends, 99–100
  hearing loss, 103, 179–180
  homeostasis concept of, 98
  immune function, 106
  implications for work performance, 2, 116–118
  individual differences, 99
  life course perspective, 18–19, 96
  metabolic functions, 105–106
  mitigation of cognitive decrements, 118–120, 187
  musculoskeletal system, 102
  positive changes, 95, 118
  productivity, 187–188
  psychological, 112–113, 116
  pulmonary function, 103–104
  respiratory capacity, 181
  scope of workplace interventions for, 8–9
  skin conditions, 105
  stress response, 108
  thermoregulation, 106–107
  visual function, 102–103, 177–178
Agriculture, 17, 180
  injury and illness patterns, 146
  older worker employment, 49, 51, 52
Alcohol use, 3–4
  assessment, 213
  controlled drinking, 112
  extent of problems related to, 111–112
  See also Substance abuse